CHILTON'S REPAIR & TUNE-UP GUIDE
CORVETTE 1963 to 1979

327 • 350 • 396 • 427 • 454

Managing Editor KERRY A. FREEMAN, S.A.E.
Senior Editor RICHARD J. RIVELE, S.A.E.
Editor MARTIN GUNTHER

President WILLIAM A. BARBOUR
Executive Vice President JAMES A. MIADES
Vice President and General Manager JOHN P. KUSHNERICK

CHILTON BOOK COMPANY
Radnor, Pennsylvania
19089

SAFETY NOTICE

Proper service and repair procedures are vital to the safe, reliable operation of all motor vehicles, as well as the personal safety of those performing repairs. This book outlines procedures for servicing and repairing vehicles using safe, effective methods. The procedures contain many NOTES, CAUTIONS and WARNINGS which should be followed along with standard safety procedures to eliminate the possibility of personal injury or improper service which could damage the vehicle or compromise its safety.

It is important to note that repair procedures and techniques, tools and parts for servicing motor vehicles, as well as the skill and experience of the individual performing the work vary widely. It is not possible to anticipate all of the conceivable ways or conditions under which vehicles may be serviced, or to provide cautions as to all of the possible hazards that may result. Standard and accepted safety precautions and equipment should be used when handling toxic or flammable fluids, and safety goggles or other protection should be used during cutting, grinding, chiseling, prying, or any other process that can cause material removal or projectiles.

Some procedures require the use of tools specially designed for a specific purpose. Before substituting another tool or procedure, you must be completely satisfied that neither your personal safety, nor the performance of the vehicle will be endangered.

Although information in this guide is based on industry sources and is as complete as possible at the time of publication, the possibility exists that the manufacturer made later changes which could not be included here. While striving for total accuracy, Chilton Book Company cannot assume responsibility for any errors, changes, or omissions that may occur in the compilation of this data.

PART NUMBERS

Part numbers listed in this reference are not recommendations by Chilton for any product by brand name. They are references that can be used with interchange manuals and aftermarket supplier catalogs to locate each brand supplier's discrete part number.

ACKNOWLEDGMENTS

The Chilton Book Company expresses its appreciation to the Chevrolet Motor Division, General Motors Corporation for their generous assistance.

Information has been selected from Chevrolet shop manuals, owners manuals, service bulletins, and technical training manuals.

Copyright © 1979 by Chilton Book Company
All Rights Reserved
Published in Radnor, Pa. by Chilton Book Company
and simultaneously in Ontario, Canada
by Nelson Canada, Limited

Manufactured in the United States of America
567890   8765432

Chilton's Repair & Tune-Up Guide: Corvette 1963–79
ISBN 0-8019-6843-7 pbk.
Library of Congress Cataloging Card No. 78-20255

CONTENTS

Quick Reference Specifications For Your Vehicle

Fill in this chart with the most commonly used specifications for your vehicle. Specifications can be found in Chapters 1 through 3 or on the tune-up decal under the hood of the vehicle.

 ## Tune-Up

Firing Order_____

Spark Plugs:

    Type_____

    Gap (in.)_____

Point Gap (in.)_____

Dwell Angle (°)_____

Ignition Timing (°)_____

    Vacuum (Connected/Disconnected)_____

Valve Clearance (in.)

    Intake_____   Exhaust_____

Capacities

Engine Oil (qts)

    With Filter Change_____

    Without Filter Change_____

Cooling System (qts)_____

Manual Transmission (pts)_____

    Type_____

Automatic Transmission (pts)_____

    Type_____

Front Differential (pts)_____

    Type_____

Rear Differential (pts)_____

    Type_____

Transfer Case (pts)_____

    Type_____

FREQUENTLY REPLACED PARTS

Use these spaces to record the part numbers of frequently replaced parts.

PCV VALVE

Manufacturer_____

Part No._____

OIL FILTER

Manufacturer_____

Part No._____

AIR FILTER

Manufacturer_____

Part No._____

General Information and Maintenance

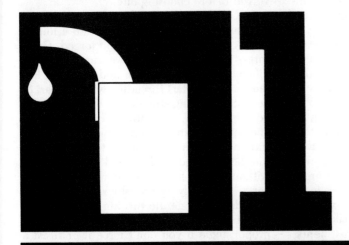

HOW TO USE THIS BOOK

Chilton's Repair & Tune-Up Guide for the Corvette is intended to help you learn more about the inner workings of your vehicle and save you money on its upkeep and operation.

The first two chapters will be the most used, since they contain maintenance and tune-up information and procedures. Studies have shown that a properly tuned and maintained car can get at least 10% better gas mileage than an out-of-tune car. The other chapters deal with the more complex systems of your car. Operating systems from engine through brakes are covered to the extent that the average do-it-yourselfer becomes mechanically involved. This book will not explain such things as rebuilding the differential for the simple reason that the expertise required and the investment in special tools make this task uneconomical. It will give you detailed instructions to help you change your own brake pads and shoes, replace points and plugs, and do many more jobs that will save you money, give you personal satisfaction, and help you avoid expensive problems.

A secondary purpose of this book is a reference for owners who want to understand their car and/or their mechanics better. In this case, no tools at all are required.

Before removing any bolts, read through the entire procedure. This will give you the overall view of what tools and supplies will be required. There is nothing more frustrating than having to walk to the bus stop on Monday morning because you were short one bolt on Sunday afternoon. So read ahead and plan ahead. Each operation should be approached logically and all procedures thoroughly understood before attempting any work.

All chapters contain adjustments, maintenance, removal and installation procedures, and repair or overhaul procedures. When repair is not considered practical, we tell you how to remove the part and then how to install the new or rebuilt replacement. In this way, you at least save the labor costs. Backyard repair of such components as the alternator is just not practical.

Two basic mechanic's rules should be mentioned here. One, whenever the left side of the car or engine is referred to, it is meant to specify the driver's side of the car. Conversely, the right side of the car means the passenger's side. Secondly, most screws and bolts are removed by turning counterclockwise, and tightened by turning clockwise.

Safety is always the most important rule. Constantly be aware of the dangers involved in working on an automobile and take the proper precautions. (See the section in this chapter "Servicing Your Vehicle Safely" and the SAFETY NOTICE on the acknowledgement page.)

Pay attention to the instructions provided. There are 3 common mistakes in mechanical work:

1. Incorrect order of assembly, disassembly or adjustment. When taking something apart or putting it together, doing things in the wrong order usually just costs you extra time; however, it CAN break something. Read the entire procedure before beginning disassembly. Do everything in the order in which the instructions say you should do it, even if you can't immediately see a reason for it. When you're taking apart something that is very intricate (for example, a carburetor), you might want to draw a picture of how it looks when assembled at one point in order to make sure you get everything back in its proper position. (We will supply exploded view whenever possible). When making adjustments, especially tune-up adjustments, do them in order; often, one adjustment affects another, and you cannot expect even satisfactory results unless each adjustment is made only when it cannot be changed by any other.

2. Overtorquing (or undertorquing). While it is more common for overtorquing to cause damage, undertorquing can cause a fastener to vibrate loose causing serious damage. Especially when dealing with aluminum parts, pay attention to torque specifications and utilize a torque wrench in assembly. If a torque figure is not available, remember that if you are using the right tool to do the job, you will probably not have to strain yourself to get a fastener tight enough. The pitch of most threads is so slight that the tension you put on the wrench will be multiplied many, many times in actual force on what you are tightening. A good example of how critical torque is can be seen in the case of spark plug installation, especially where you are putting the plug into an aluminum cylinder head. Too little torque can fail to crush the gasket, causing leakage of combustion gases and consequent overheating of the plug and engine parts. Too much torque can damage the threads, or distort the plug, which changes the spark gap.

There are many commercial products available for ensuring that fasteners won't come loose, even if they are not torqued just right (a very common brand is "Loctite®"). If you're worried about getting something together tight enough to hold, but loose enough to avoid mechanical damage during assembly, one of these products might offer substantial insurance. Read the label on the package and make sure the product is compatible with the materials, fluids, etc. involved before choosing one.

3. Crossthreading. This occurs when a part such as a bolt is screwed into a nut or casting at the wrong angle and forced. Cross threading is more likely to occur if access is difficult. It helps to clean and lubricate fasteners, and to start threading with the part to be installed going straight in. Then, start the bolt, spark plug, etc. with your fingers. If you encounter resistance, unscrew the part and start over again at a different angle until it can be inserted and turned several turns without much effort. Keep in mind that many parts, especially spark plugs, use tapered threads so that gentle turning will automatically bring the part you're threading to the proper angle if you don't force it or resist a change in angle. Don't put a wrench on the part until it's been turned a couple of turns by hand. If you suddenely encounter resistance, and the part has not seated fully, don't force it. Pull it back out and make sure it's clean and threading properly.

Always take your time and be patient; once you have some experience, working on your car will become an enjoyable hobby.

TOOLS AND EQUIPMENT

Naturally, without the proper tools and equipment it is impossible to properly service your vehicle. It would be impossible to catalog each tool that you would need to perform each or any operation in this book. It would also be unwise for the amateur to rush out and buy an expensive set of tools on the theory that he may need one or more of them at sometime.

The best approach is to proceed slowly, gathering together a good quality set of those tools that are used most frequently. Don't be misled by the low cost of bargain tools. It is far better to spend a little more for better quality. Forged wrenches, 10 or 12 point sockets and fine tooth ratchets are by far preferable to their less expensive counterparts. As any good mechanic can tell you, there are few worse experiences than trying to work on a car or truck with bad tools. Your monetary savings will be far outweighed by frustration and mangled knuckles.

Begin accumulating those tools that are used most frequently; those associated with routine maintenance and tune-up.

In addition to the normal assortment of screwdrivers and pliers you should have the following tools for routine maintenance jobs:

1. SAE (or Metric) or SAE/Metric wrenches—sockets and combination open end/box end wrenches in sizes from ⅛ in. (3 mm) to ¾ in. (19 mm) and a spark plug socket (¹³/₁₆ or ⅝ in. depending on plug type).

If possible, buy various length socket drive extensions. One break in this department is that the metric sockets available in the U.S. will all fit the ratchet handles and extensions you may already have (¼, ⅜, and ½ in. drive.)

2. Jackstands—for support.
3. Oil filter wrench.
4. Oil filler spout—for pouring oil.
5. Grease gun—for chassis lubrication.
6. Hydrometer—for checking the battery.
7. A container for draining oil.
8. Many rags for wiping up the inevitable mess.

In addition to the above items there are several others that are not absolutely necessary, but handy to have around. These include oil dry, a transmission funnel and the usual supply of lubricants, antifreeze and fluids, although these can be purchased as needed. This is a basic list for routine maintenance, but only your personal needs and desire can accurately determine your list of tools.

The second list of tools is for tune-ups. While the tools involved here are slightly more sophisticated, they need not be outrageously expensive. There are several inexpensive tach/dwell meters on the market that are every bit as good for the average mechanic as a $100.000 professional model. Just be sure that it goes to a least 1,200–1,500 rpm on the tach scale and that it works on 4, 6 or 8 cylinder engines. A basic list of tune-up equipment could include:

1. Tach-dwell meter.
2. Spark plug wrench.
3. Timing light (a DC light that works from the car's battery is best, although an AC light that plugs into 110V house current will suffice at some sacrifice in brightness).
4. Wire spark plug gauge/adjusting tools.
5. Set of feeler blades.

Here again, be guided by your own needs.

A feeler blade will set the points as easily as a dwell meter will read dwell, but slightly less accurately. And since you will need a tachometer anyway . . . well, make your own decision.

In addition to these basic tools, there are several other tools and gauges you may find useful. These include:

1. A compression gauge. The screw-in type is slower to use, but eliminates the possibility of a faulty reading due to escaping pressure.
2. A manifold vacuum gauge.
3. A test light.
4. An induction meter. This is used for determining whether or not there is current in a wire. These are handy for use if a wire is broken somewhere in a wiring harness.

As a final note, you will probably find a torque wrench necessary for all but the most basic work. The beam type models are perfectly adequate, although the newer click type are more precise.

Special Tools

Normally, the use of special factory tools is avoided for repair procedures, since these are not readily available for the do-it-yourself mechanic. When it is possible to perform the job with more commonly available tools, it will be pointed out, but occassionally, a special tool was designed to perform a specific function and should be used. Before substituting another tool, you should be convinced that neither your safety nor the performance of the vehicle will be compromised.

Some special tools are available commercially from major tool manufacturers. Others can be purchased from your car dealer or from:

Service Tool Division
Kent-Moore Corporation
1501 South Jackson Street
Jackson, Michigan 49203

SERVICING YOUR VEHICLE SAFELY

It is virtually impossible to anticipate all of the hazards involved with automotive maintenance and service but care and common sense will prevent most accidents.

The rules of safety for mechanics range from "don't smoke around gasoline," to "use the proper tool for the job." The trick to avoiding injuries is to develop safe work habits and take every possible precaution.

Do's

• Do keep a fire extinguisher and first aid kit within easy reach.

• Do wear safety glasses or goggles when cutting, drilling, grinding or prying, even if you have 20-20 vision. If you wear glasses for the sake of vision, then they should be made of hardened glass that can serve also as safety glasses, or wear safety goggles over your regular glasses.

• Do shield your eyes whenever you work around the battery. Batteries contain sulphuric acid; in case of contact with the eyes or skin, flush the area with water or a mixture of water and baking soda and get medical attention immediately.

• Do use safety stands for any undercar service. Jacks are for raising vehicles; safety stands are for making sure the vehicle stays raised until you want it to come down. Whenever the vehicle is raised, block the wheels remaining on the ground and set the parking brake.

• Do use adequate ventilation when working with any chemicals. Like carbon monoxide, the asbestos dust resulting from brake lining wear can be poisonous in sufficient quantities.

• Do disconnect the negative battery cable when working on the electrical system. The primary ignition system can contain up to 40,000 volts.

• Do follow manufacturer's directions whenever working with potentially hazardous materials. Both brake fluid and antifreeze are poisonous if taken internally.

• Do properly maintain your tools. Loose hammerheads, mushroomed punches and chisels, frayed or poorly grounded electrical cords, excessively worn screwdrivers, spread wrenches (open end), cracked sockets, slipping ratchets, or faulty droplight sockets can cause accidents.

• Do use the proper size and type of tool for the job being done.

• Do when possible, pull on a wrench handle rather than push on it, and adjust your stance to prevent a fall.

• Do be sure that adjustable wrenches are tightly adjusted on the nut or bolt and pulled so that the face is on the side of the fixed jaw.

• Do select a wrench or socket that fits the nut or bolt. The wrench or socket should sit straight, not cocked.

• Do strike squarely with a hammer—avoid glancing blows.

• Do set the parking brake and block the drive wheels if the work requires that the engine be running.

Dont's

• Don't run an engine in a garage or anywhere else without proper ventilation—EVER! Carbon monoxide is poisonous; it takes a long time to leave the human body and you can build up a deadly supply of it in your system by simply breathing in a little every day. You may not realize you are slowly poisoning yourself. Always use power vents, windows, fans or open the garage doors.

• Don't work around moving parts while wearing a necktie or other loose clothing. Short sleeves are much safer than long, loose sleeves and hard-toed shoes with neoprene soles protect your toes and give a better grip on slippery surfaces. Jewelry such as watches, fancy belt buckles, beads or body adornment or any kind is not safe working around a car. Long hair should be hidden under a hat or cap.

• Don't use pockets for toolboxes. A fall or bump can drive a screwdriver deep into your body. Even a wiping cloth hanging from the back pocket can wrap around a spinning shaft or fan.

• Don't smoke when working around gasoline, cleaning solvent or other flammable material.

• Don't smoke when working around the battery. When the battery is being charged, it gives off explosive hydrogen gas.

• Don't use gasoline to wash your hands; there are excellent soaps available. Gasoline may contain lead, and lead can enter the body through a cut, accummulating in the body until you are very ill. Gasoline also removes all the natural oils from the skin so that bone dry hands will suck up oil and grease.

• Don't service the air conditioning system unless you are equipped with the necessary tools and training. The refrigerant, R-12, is extremely cold and when exposed to the air, will instantly freeze any surface it comes in contact with, including your eyes. Although the refrigerant is normally non-toxic,

R-12 becomes a deadly poisonous gas in the presence of an open flame. One good whiff of the vapors from burning refrigerant can be fatal.

HISTORY

The 1963 Corvette Stingray is a complete departure from the Corvettes which preceded it. The body, frame, and front and rear suspensions are all of new design. Engines and transmissions are the only components that were shared with the older models. Stingray body styling evolved from the original William Mitchell Stingray sports/racing car which competed in 1959–60. Fiberglass bodywork was retained, but included a steel, reinforcing framework around the passenger compartment. The convertible model, with or without hardtop, was retained and a new body style added, the fastback coupe. Retractable headlights, rotated by two electric motors, were also a new feature for the Corvette.

The frame is a ladder type with five cross-members. The wheelbase has been reduced from the 102 in. of previous models to a more compact 98 in., and the rear track shortened by 2 in. This, coupled with component relocation, resulted in a 48/52 percent front/rear weight distribution; a marked improvement over the 53 percent front weight bias of earlier model Corvettes. Overall body height was reduced by 2 in. Front and rear suspensions are both independent and newly designed for the Stingray. The short/long arm front suspension has the upper arm tilted at an angle of 9° for an anti-dive effect under braking. Steering knuckles pivot in ball joints, instead of the king pins and bushings of the early Corvettes. The fully independent rear suspension is sprung with a nine-leaf transverse spring. Universal-jointed axle driveshafts transmit power to the wheels. Steering gear is recirculating ball type and the linkage includes a hydraulic damper. Power steering and brakes both became optionally available for the first time on a Corvette. Brake drums were enlarged and the brakes were made self-adjusting. Air conditioning became optionally available in late 1963.

1964 saw detail body changes: functional passenger-compartment exhaust vents and elimination of the split rear window on the coupe, removal of the non-functional vents on the hood, and new wheel covers. The Muncie four-speed transmission, introduced in mid-year 1963 to replace the Borg-Warner T-10, became the optional four-speed. The solid lifter engines received larger intake and exhaust valves, and horsepower increased from 340 to 365 and from 360 to 375 for the carburetted and fuel-injected engines respectively. Transsistorized, breakerless ignition became optionally available on high performance engines in 1964.

In 1965, the big change was the introduction of four-wheel disc brakes. Braking power and fade resistance were greatly increased over the drum brakes. A flat hood replaced the 1964 hood which had twin indentations and other body changes included restyled wheel covers and functional exhaust vents behind the front wheels. A new version of the 327 cubic inch engine was introduced, the 350 horsepower, hydraulic-cam option. In midyear, a 396 cubic inch 425 horsepower engine was made available in the Corvette. 396 Corvettes were distinguished by the domed hood required for carburetor clearance. Cars equipped with the 396 received a larger front stabilizer bar and the addition of a rear stabilizer bar. Side-mounted exhausts with chambered mufflers joined the option list in 1965.

The 250, 365, and 375 horsepower engines were dropped in 1966. The 300 horsepower, 327 cubic inch engine became the standard power plant and the standard three-speed transmission was synchronized in all forward gears. The 396 was bored out to 427 cubic inches and offered in two versions, a 425 horsepower and a milder 390 horsepower model. A heavy-duty, four-speed transmission was introduced for use with the high performance 427. Body changes included a new, egg-crate grille, restyled wheel covers, and the addition of backup lights.

1967 body styling changes included a hood scoop on 427 Stingrays, more subdued exhaust vents on the front fenders, and a center back-up light. Wheels were widened ½ inch to 6 inches and were slotted. The full wheel covers of former models were discarded for trim rings and center caps. The handbrake was changed to the pull-up type, and relocated to the center console. The 300, 350, and 390 horsepower engines remained the same for 1967. Three, two-barrel carburetors were added to the 390 horsepower engine to produce an additional engine rated at 400 horsepower. The same manifold and carburetors, plus aluminum cylinder heads, installed on the former 425 horsepower block gave a 435 horsepower rating.

For the 1968 Corvette, a completely redesigned body and interior were installed on a basically unchanged chassis. Many of the styling features of the new body had been previewed on the Mako Shark show car. Overall body width and height were reduced, while front and rear tread increased with the use of one inch wider wheels. The convertible model was retained and the fastback coupe was replaced with a hardtop model featuring removable roof panels and rear window. Headlights on 1968 and later cars are raised automatically, with vacuum power when the lights are switched on. Wide oval F70-15 tires replaced the 7.75-15 tires of previous years. The two-speed, Powerglide automatic transmission was superseded by the three-speed Turbo Hydra-Matic, a significant improvement for general driving and performance usage. Engines remained the same, except for the addition of the air-injection reactor pump to control exhaust emissions. Corvettes sold in California have been equipped with the A.I.R. system since 1966.

Body styling remained the same for 1969 except for the addition of a Stingray script above the engine exhaust vent. The doors were slightly reshaped, widening the cockpit by one inch at shoulder height. Wheel width was increased to 8 inches, which also increased front and fear tread. The anti-theft ignition, steering, and transmission lock were introduced in 1969, with the ignition switch mounted on the steering column. Side exhausts were offered for the first time on the new body in 1969. Headlight washers were now included in the standard equipment. The small block stroke was increased to give a displacement of 350 cubic inches; however, horsepower ratings remained the same. 427 engine options were the same as in 1968, except that the L88 430 horsepower model was available with a Turbo Hydra-Matic.

A new grille, larger parabolic reflector turn signals, and wheel well flares were added to the Stingray body for 1970. Cast metal grilles were added over the engine compartment exhaust vents and the tailpipe exits were made retangular. The seats were redesigned, lowering them one inch for more headroom and making the headrests integral. The 427 stroke was increased for 1970 to give a dis-

placement of 454 cubic inches. Triple, two-barrel carburetion was dropped from the big blocks in 1970. A 370 horsepower 350 cubic inch engine, the LT-1, was introduced to answer the need for a solid lifter, small block engine. The three-speed, manual transmission was discontinued in 1970, and the four-speed transmission and Positraction rear axle were made standard equipment.

Horsepower was decreased in 1971 through an across-the-board compression reduction. The 350 horsepower, hydraulic-cam version of the small block was deleted from the option list and a big block, mechanical-lifter engine was introduced. This engine, the LS6, produced 425 horsepower on regular gasoline.

1972 saw very few changes made to the Corvette. Rated horsepower was again down, due mostly to a new rating system which utilizes net instead of gross power outputs. The audio alarm antitheft system is not a standard item, and the fiber optic light monitors have been discontinued. Only three engines are offered for 1972, two 350 cubic inch engines and one 454 cubic inch engine. There were no body changes, except for the addition of four new colors.

1973 saw the Corvette receive a new front end with a resilient body color bumper. The cool air induction hood covers the windshield wipers, allowing the wiper door and mechanism to be eliminated. New body mounts and extra soundproofing were also added for 1973. GR70-15 steel-belted radial tires are standard equipment. Two 350 cu in. engines were offered, but the optional L82 engine now had hydraulic lifters, replacing the solids available in 1972. The 454 Turbo-Jet was also available with a rating of 275 horsepower.

1974 was a year of very little change for the Corvette. A resilient rear section was added similar to the front system introduced in 1973. Three engines continued to be available, except in California where only the two 350s were available.

Changes to the 1975 Corvette include a catalytic reactor to reduce emissions, a fuel cell-type fuel tank, and the dropping of the 454 engine.

Only one Corvette body style was available for 1976, the convertible was dropped. The Turbo Hydra-Matic 350 replaced the 400 on the base engine. A partial steel underbody replaced the traditional fiberglass, which both improved body strength and head protection from the exhaust system.

1977 was a year of refinements and a slight appearance change from the 1976 model.

The 1978 Corvette received its most extensive change since its introduction of the current series in 1968 with a new fastback roof line resulting in a new cockpit design and a larger cargo area. A larger 24 gallon fuel cell type fuel tank is used for greater fuel capacity. Increased horsepower and torque ratings are achieved for the special performance engine over the base engine as a result of improvements of the induction and exhaust systems. The base engine uses a Muncie 4-speed manual transmission while the special performance engine uses a Borg-Warner. Both engines use the same Turbo Hydra-Matic transmission.

1979 was a year of very little change with slight refinements of performance and appearance.

Corvettes have proven themselves in all types of automotive competition, and the Stringray has continued to bear the Corvette standard in many forms of racing. A Stingray coupe won the first race entered in October 1962 at Riverside Raceway. Since then, Corvettes have continued their winning ways in road racing in the SCCA A and B-Production classes. Corvettes have also taken numerous trophies in drag racing, in both the stock and modified classes. Sebring, Daytona, and Le Mans have witnessed many Corvette entries; Corvettes have placed well overall and succeeded in winning the GT class several times at these endurance races. The aerodynamic Stingray has also been utilized several times in setting Grand Touring class records during the Bonneville Speed Weeks. That racing improves the breed has certainly proved to be true in the case of the Corvette, with many race-proven pieces having become standard equipment or options on production Corvettes.

SERIAL NUMBER IDENTIFICATION

Vehicle

The 1963 through 1967 Corvette vehicle serial number, body style, body trim number, and paint combination is loated on the instrument panel reinforcing member directly under the glove compartment. The vehicle serial number plate is located on the top left of the instrument panel (1968–76)

1963–67 vehicle serial number location

and on the inside left windshield pillar (1977–79). The body number, trim, and paint number plate is located on the upper left-hand door hinge pillar (1968–78) and on the upper horizontal surface of the shroud (1979). The vehicle serial number identifies the body style, model year, assembly plant (always S, for St. Louis), and production number.

Engine

All Corvette engine serial numbers are located on a pad between the water pump and the front of the right cylinder head. The first letter identifies the plant the engine was manufactured in and the numbers identify the date of production. The two or three-letter suffix identifies the engine type and equipment.

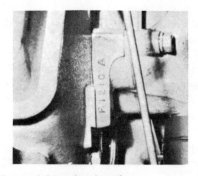

Engine serial number location

INTERPRETING THE SERIAL NUMBER

A typical vehicle serial number tag yields manufacturer's identity, vehicle type, model year, assembly plant and production unit number when broken down as shown in the following charts.

1963–71

Mfr Identity [1]	Body Style [2]	Model Year [3]	Assy Plant [4]	Unit No. [5]
1	5645	8	F	100025

[1] Manufacturer's identity number assigned to all Chevrolet built vehicles
[2] Model identification
[3] Last number of model year (1968)
[4] F-Flint
[5] Unit numbering will start at 100,001 at all plants

1972–79

Mfr Identity [1]	Series Code Letter [2]	Body Style [3]	Engine Model [4]	Model Year [5]	Assembly Plant [6]	Unit Number [7]
1	N	47	R	4	F	100025

[1] Manufacturer's identity number assigned to all Chevrolet built vehicles
[2] Model identification
[3] Model identification
[4] Engine code
[5] Last number of model year (1974)
[6] F-Flint
[7] Unit numbering will start at 000001 or 100,001 depending on the model

Engine Identification

1963–64
327 cubic inch engine

Manual transmission	RC
Manual transmission and high performance	RD
Special high performance	RE
Manual transmission and fuel injection	RF
Powerglide	SC
Powerglide and high performance	SD

1964
327 cubic inch engine

Manual transmission and A/C	RP
Manual transmission, high performance, A/C	RQ
Manual transmission, special high performance, A/C	RR
Manual transmission and transistor ignition	RT
Fuel injection and transistor ignition	RX
Manual transmission, transistor ignition, A/C	RU
Powerglide and A/C	SK
Powerglide, high performance, A/C	SL

Engine Identification (cont.)

1965
327 cubic inch engine

Manual transmission	HE
High performance	HF
Fuel injection	HG
Special high performance	HH
A/C	HI
High performance and A/C	HJ
Special high performance and A/C	HK
Transistor ignition	HL
Transistor ignition and A/C	HM
Fuel injection and transistor ignition	HN
Powerglide	HO
Powerglide and high performance	HP
Powerglide and A/C	HQ
Powerglide, high performance, A/C	HR
Special high performance and hydraulic lifters	HT
Special high performance, hydraulic lifters, A/C	HU
Special high performance, hydraulic lifters, transistor ignition	HV
Special high performance, hydraulic lifters, transistor ignition, A/C	HW

396 cubic inch engine

Special high performance	IF

1966
327 cubic inch engine

Manual transmission	HE
A.I.R.	HH
A.I.R. and Powerglide	HR
Special high performance and A.I.R.	HD
Powerglide	HO
Special high performance	HT
Power steering, special high performance, A.I.R.	HP
Special high performance, A/C, A.I.R.	KH

427 cubic inch engine

Special high performance and hydraulic lifters	IK
High performance	IL
A.I.R.	IM
Special high performance	IP
Powerglide	IQ
Powerglide and A.I.R.	IR

1967
327 cubic inch engine

Manual transmission	HE
A.I.R.	HH
A.I.R. and Powerglide	HR
Special high performance and A.I.R.	HD
Powerglide	HO

Engine Identification (cont.)

1967
327 cubic inch engine

Special high performance	HT
Power steering, special high performance, A/C	HP
Special high performance, A/C, A.I.R.	KH

427 cubic inch engine

4-speed or Powerglide	IL
Triple carburetion	JC
A.I.R., special high performance, triple carburetion	JE
Heavy duty	IT
Aluminum heads	IU
A.I.R.	IM
A.I.R. and triple carburetion	JF
A.I.R. and aluminum heads	JH
Powerglide	IQ
Powerglide and triple carburetion	JD
A.I.R. and Powerglide	IR
A.I.R., triple carburetion, Powerglide	JG
A.I.R., special high performance, triple carburetion	JA

1968
327 cubic inch engine

Manual transmission	HE
Turbo Hydra-Matic	HO
Power steering and A/C	HP
Special high performance	HT

427 cubic inch engine

High performance	IL
High performance and triple carburetion	IM
High performance, triple carburetion, Turbo Hydra-Matic	IO
Turbo Hydra-Matic	IQ
Special high performance and triple carburetion	IR
High performance	IT
Special high performance, triple carburetion, aluminum heads	IU

1969
350 cubic inch engine

High performance	HW
High performance and A/C	HX
Manual transmission	HY
Turbo Hydra-Matic	HZ

427 cubic inch engine

High performance, Turbo Hydra-Matic	LL
High performance	LM
Triple carburetion, high performance, Turbo Hydra-Matic	LN

Engine Identification (cont.)

1969
427 cubic inch engine

Heavy duty	LO
Aluminum heads	LP
Triple carburetion and high performance	LQ
Triple carburetion and special high performance	LR
Triple carburetion, special high performance, heavy duty clutch	LU
Heavy duty and Turbo Hydra-Matic	LV
Triple carburetion, special high performance, Turbo Hydra-Matic	LX

1970
350 cubic inch engine

Manual transmission	CTL
Turbo Hydra-Matic	CTM
High performance	CTN
High performance and A/C	CTO
High performance and transistor ignition	CTP
High performance, transistor ignition, A/C	CTQ
Special high performance	CTR
Special high performance and transistor ignition	CTU
Special high performance, transistor ignition, 4-speed	CTV
High performance, 4-bbl carburetor, Turbo Hydra-Matic	CZN
High performance, 4-bbl carburetor, transistor ignition	CRI

454 cubic inch engine

High performance, 4-bbl carburetor, Turbo Hydra-Matic	CGW
High performance and 4-bbl	CZU
Heavy duty with 4-bbl	CZL
Heavy duty with 4-bbl and Turbo Hydra-Matic	CZN
High performance, 4-bbl, transistor ignition	CRI

1971
350 cubic inch engine

270 hp, 4-speed	CJL
270 hp, THM	CGT
330 hp, 4-speed	CGZ
330 hp, THM	CJK
330 hp, 4-speed (HD)	CGY

454 cubic inch engine

365 hp, THM	CPJ
365 hp, 4-speed	CPH
425 hp, 4-speed	CPW
425 hp, THM	CPX

Engine Identification (cont.)

1972
350 cubic inch engine

200 hp with 4-speed	CKW
200 hp with 4-speed and NOX control (Calif.)	CDH
200 hp with Turbo Hydra-Matic	CKX
200 hp with Turbo Hydra-Matic and NOX control (Calif.)	CDJ
255 hp with 4-speed	CKY
255 hp with Turbo Hydra-Matic	CKZ
255 hp with 4-speed and A.I.R.	CRT
255 hp with Turbo Hydra-Matic and A.I.R.	CRS

454 cubic inch engine

270 hp with 4-speed	CPH
270 hp with Turbo Hydra-Matic	CPJ
270 hp	CSR, CSS

1973
350 cubic inch engine

190 hp with 4-speed	CKZ
190 hp with 4-speed (Calif.)	CLB
190 hp with Turbo Hydra-Matic	CLA
190 hp with Turbo Hydra-Matic (Calif.)	CLC
250 hp with 4-speed	CLR
250 hp with 4-speed (Calif.)	CLS
250 hp with Turbo Hydra-Matic	CLD
250 hp with Turbo Hydra-Matic (Calif.)	CLH

454 cubic inch engine

275 hp with 4-speed	CWM
275 hp with 4-speed (Calif.)	CWT
275 hp with Turbo Hydra-Matic	CWR
275 hp with Turbo Hydra-Matic (Calif.)	CWS

1974
350 cubic inch engine

195 hp with 4-speed	CKZ
195 hp with 4-speed (Calif.)	CLB
195 hp with Turbo Hydra-Matic	CLA
195 hp with Turbo Hydra-Matic (Calif.)	CLC
250 hp with 4-speed	CLR
250 hp with 4-speed (Calif.)	CLS
250 hp with Turbo Hydra-Matic	CLD
250 hp with Turbo Hydra-Matic (Calif.)	CLH

454 cubic inch engine

270 hp with 4-speed	CWM
270 hp with 4-speed (Calif.)	CWT
270 hp with Turbo Hydra-Matic	CWR
270 hp with Turbo Hydra-Matic (Calif.)	CWS

Engine Identification (cont.)

1975
350 cubic inch engine

195 hp with 4-speed	CRJ, CUA, CUB
195 hp with Turbo Hydra-Matic	CRK
250 hp with 4-speed	CRL, CUT, CUD
250 hp with Turbo Hydra-Matic	CRM

1976
350 cubic inch engine

180 hp, 210 hp	CLM, CLR, CLS, CKW, CKX, CLS, CHC, CHR, CKC

1977
350 cubic inch engine

180 hp, 210 hp	CKZ, CLA, CLB, CLC, CHD, CKD, CLD, CLF

1978
350 cubic inch engine

185 hp (Calif.)	CLR
185 hp (high altitude)	CLS
185 hp A.T. (Fed.)	CUT
185 hp M.T.	CLM
225 hp M.T.	CMR
225 hp A.T.	CMS

1979

195 hp (Calif.)	ZAC
195 hp with 4 speed	ZAA
195 hp with Turbo Hydra-Matic	ZAB
195 hp (High altitude)	ZAD
225 hp 4-speed	ZBA
225 hp Turbo Hydra-Matic	ZBB

Transmission

The Borg-Warner T-10, 4-speed serial number is located on the rear face of the transmission case in the upper right corner. The Muncie 3-speed serial number is located on a boss above the filler plug. Powerglide codes are stamped on the bottom of the oil pan. Serial numbers of 4-speed Muncie transmissions are located on the left-side cover flange of the case. Turbo Hydra-Matic 400 serial numbers are found on the light blue plate on the right side of the transmission. Turbo Hydra-Matic 350 serial numbers are found on the right vertical surface of the oil pan. The Borg-Warner T-16, 3-speed serial number is located on a boss at the right rear cover of the transmission extension. Transmission serial numbers give the plate and date of manufacture.

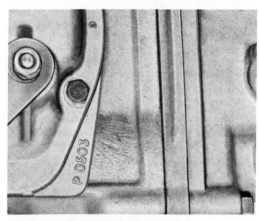

Muncie 4-speed serial number location

Rear Axle

All Corvette Stingrays have the rear axle serial number located on the bottom surface of the carrier at the cover mounting flange. The two or three-letter prefix in the serial number identifies the rear-axle gear ratio.

Rear axle serial number

Rear Axle Ratio Identification

Year	Prefix	Axle Ratio and Type
1963–64	CA	3.36 with 3-speed
	CJ	3.08 Positraction
	CB	3.36 Positraction
	CC	3.55 Positraction
	CD	3.70 Positraction
	CE	4.11 Positraction
	CF	4.56 Positraction
	CZ	3.08 with 4-speed
	CX	3.70 with 4-speed
1965	AK	3.36
	AL	3.08 Positraction
	AM	3.36 Positraction
	AN	3.55 Positraction

Rear Axle Ratio Identification (cont.)

Year	Prefix	Axle Ratio and Type
1965	AO	3.70 Positraction
	AP	4.11 Positraction
	AQ	4.56 Positraction
	AR	3.08
	AS	3.70 with 4-speed
	AT	3.08 Positraction with 396 engine
	AU	3.36 Positraction with 396 engine
	AZ	3.55 Positraction with 396 engine
	FA	3.70 Positraction with 396 engine
	FB	4.11 Positraction with 396 engine
	FC	4.56 Positraction with 396 engine
1966	AK	3.36
	AL	3.08 Positraction
	AM	3.36 Positraction
	AN	3.55 Positraction
	AO	3.70 Positraction
	AP	4.11 Positraction
	AR	3.08 Positraction
	AS	3.70 with 4-speed
	AT	3.08 Positraction with 427 engine
	AU	3.36 Positraction with 427 engine
	AZ	3.55 Positraction with 427 engine
	FA	3.70 Positraction with 427 engine
	FB	4.11 Positraction with 427 engine
	FC	4.56 Positraction with 427 engine
1967	AK	3.36
	AL	3.08 Positraction
	AM	3.36 Positraction
	AN	3.55 Positraction
	AO	3.70 Positraction
	AP	4.11 Positraction
	AS	3.70 with 4-speed
	AT	3.08 Positraction with 427 engine
	AU	3.36 Positraction with 427 engine

Rear Axle Ratio
Identification (cont.)

Year	Prefix	Axle Ratio and Type
1967	AZ	3.55 Positraction with 427 engine
	FA	3.70 Positraction with 427 engine
	FB	4.11 Positraction with 427 engine
	FC	4.56 Positraction with 427 engine
1968	AK	3.36
	AL	3.08 Positraction
	AM	3.36 Positraction
	AN	3.55 Positraction
	AO	3.70 Positraction
	AP	4.11 Positraction
	AS	3.70
	AT	3.08 Heavy duty Positraction
	AU	3.36 Heavy duty Positraction
	AV	3.08 Positraction
	AW	3.08 Heavy duty Positraction
1969	AK	3.36
	AL	3.08 Positraction
	AM	3.36 Positraction
	AN	3.55 Positraction
	AO	3.70 Positraction
	AP	4.11 Positraction
	AS	3.70
	AT	3.08 Heavy duty Positraction
	AU	3.36 Heavy duty Positraction
	AV	3.08
	AW	3.08 Heavy duty Positraction
	AY	2.73 Heavy duty Positraction
	AZ	3.55 Heavy duty Positraction
	FA	3.70 Heavy duty Positraction
	FB	4.11 Heavy duty Positraction
	FC	4.56 Positraction
1970	CAK	3.36
	CAL	3.08 Positraction

Rear Axle Ratio
Identification (cont.)

Year	Prefix	Axle Ratio and Type
1970	CAM	3.36 Positraction
	CAN	3.55 Positraction
	CAO, CAS	3.70 Positraction with high performance 350 and close-ratio 4-speed
	CAP	4.11 Positraction
	CAT	3.08 Positraction
	CAU	3.36 Positraction
	CAV	3.08 Positraction
	CAW	3.08 Positraction with Turbo Hydra-Matic
	CAY	2.73 Positraction
	CAX	3.36 Positraction with Turbo Hydra-Matic
	CAZ	3.55 Positraction
	CFA	3.70 Positraction
	CFB	4.11 Positraction
	CFC	4.56 Positraction
	CLR	3.36 Positraction
1971	AA	3.55 Positraction
	AB	3.70 Positraction
	AC	4.11 Positraction
	AD	4.56 Positraction
	AW	3.08 Positraction
	AX, LR	3.36 Positraction
1972–75	AX, LR	3.36 Positraction
	AC	4.11 Positraction
	AB	3.70 Positraction
	AA	3.55 Positraction
	AW	3.08 Positraction
	AV	2.73 Positraction
1976–77	OA	3.08 Positraction
	LR, OD	3.36 Positraction
	OB	3.55 Positraction
	OC	3.70 Positraction
1978	OK	3.08 Positraction
	OM	3.36 Positraction
	OH	3.55 Positraction
	OJ	3.70 Positraction
1979	OM	3.36 Positraction
	OH	3.55 Positraction
	OJ	3.70 Positraction

ROUTINE MAINTENANCE

Air Cleaner

The air cleaner consists of a metal housing for a replaceable paper filter or permanent polyurethane element and the necessary hoses connecting it to the crankcase ventilation system. The air cleaner cover is held by a wing nut on all models. If your Corvette is equipped with a paper element, the factory recommends it should be replaced once every 12,000 miles (1963–72), every 24,000 miles (1973–74), every 30,000 miles (1975–79). Inspection and replacement should come more often when the car is operated under dusty conditions. To check the effectiveness of your paper element, remove the air cleaner assembly and, if the idle speed increases noticeably, the element is restricting airflow and should be replaced. Some high-performance models or cars equipped with optional air cleaners use a polyurethane element that must be re-

Check the small crankcase breather

Using a clean rag or a paper towel, wipe out the inside of the air cleaner

moved, cleaned, and reoiled at 12,000 mile or 12 month intervals. Remove the filter and clean it in kerosene. Do not use paint thinner or a similar solvent and then squeeze it dry. Allow it to soak in SAE 30 oil and again squeeze it dry using a clean cloth to remove excess oil. Clean the inside of the air cleaner housing before reinstalling either type of filter.

Unscrew the wing nut and remove the cover

Remove and discard the old filter

Positive Crankcase Ventilation (PCV)

The PCV valve is screwed into the carburetor or located in the ventilation hose on 1963 models. 1964 and 1965 models are not equipped with a PCV valve, but use a metered orifice fitting instead. This is not replaced, as it is a permanent part of the system, but it should be cleaned with solvent as a part of regular maintenance. The PCV valve is located in the hose or in the rocker cover on later models. Replace the PCV valve and if so equipped the PCV filter, located in the air cleaner, every 12,000 miles (1963–71), every 24,000 miles (1972–74), every 30,000 miles (1975–79).

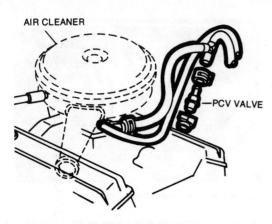

AIR CLEANER

—PCV VALVE

The PCV valve is located in the rocker arm cover on later models

Evaporative Emissions Control System

This system, standard since 1970, eliminates the release of unburned fuel vapors into the atmosphere. The only periodic maintenance required is an occasional check of the connecting lines of the system for kinks or other damage and deterioration. Lines should only be replaced with quality fuel line or special hose marked "evap." Every 12,000 miles or 12 months (1970–71), every 24,000 miles or 24 months (1972–74), every 30,000, miles or 24 months (1975–79), the filter in the bottom of the carbon canister which is located in the engine compartment should be removed and replaced.

Battery

Loose, dirty, or corroded battery terminals are a major cause of "no-start". Every 3 months or so, remove the battery terminals and clean them, giving them a light coating of petroleum jelly when you are finished. This will help to retard corrosion.

Check the battery cables for signs of wear or chafing and replace any cable or terminal that looks marginal. Battery terminals can be easily cleaned and inexpensive terminal cleaning tools are an excellent investment that will pay for themselves many times over. They can usually be purchased from any well-equipped auto store or parts department. Side terminal batteries require a different tool to clean the threads in the battery case. The accumulated white powder and corrosion can be cleaned from the top of the battery with an old toothbrush and a solution of baking soda and water.

Unless you have a "maintenance-free' battery, check the electrolyte level (see Battery under Fluid Level Checks in this chapter) and check the specific gravity of each cell. Be sure that the vent holes in each cell cap are not blocked by grease or dirt. The vent holes allow hydrogen gas, formed by the chemical reaction in the battery, to escape safely.

REPLACEMENT BATTERIES

The cold power rating of a battery measures battery starting performance and provides an approximate relationship between battery size and engine size. The cold power rating of a replacement battery should match or exceed your engine size in cubic inches.

Heat Riser

The heat riser is a thermostatically or vacuum operated valve in the exhaust manifold. Not all engines have one. It closes when the engine is warming up, to direct hot exhaust gases to the intake manifold, in order to preheat the incoming fuel/air mixture. If it sticks shut, the result will be frequent stalling during warmup, especially in cold and damp weather. If it sticks open, the result will be a rough idle after the engine is warm. There is only one heat riser on a V8. The heat riser should move freely. If it sticks, apply GM Manifold Heat Control Solvent or something similar (engine cool) to the ends of the shaft. Sometimes rapping the end of the shaft sharply with a hammer (engine hot) will break it loose. If this fails, components must be removed for further repairs.

Drive Belts

CHECKING AND ADJUSTING TENSION

Check the drive belts every 6,000 miles for evidence of wear such as cracking, fraying, and incorrect tension. Determine the belt tension at a point halfway between the pulleys by pressing on the belt with moderate thumb pressure. The belt should deflect about ¼ inch at this point. If the deflection is found to be too much or too little, loosen the mounting bolts and make the adjustments.

Cooling System

At least once every 2 years, the engine cooling system should be inspected, flushed, and refilled with fresh coolant. If the coolant is

HOW TO SPOT WORN V-BELTS

V-Belts are vital to efficient engine operation—they drive the fan, water pump and other accessories. They require little maintenance (occasional tightening) but they will not last forever. Slipping or failure of the V-belt will lead to overheating. If your V-belt looks like any of these, it should be replaced.

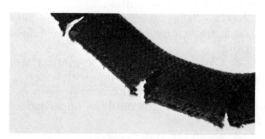

This belt has deep cracks, which cause it to flex. Too much flexing leads to heat build-up and premature failure. These cracks can be caused by using the belt on a pulley that is too small. Notched belts are available for small diameter pulleys.

Cracking or weathering

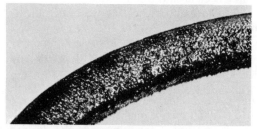

Oil and grease on a belt can cause the belt's rubber compounds to soften and separate from the reinforcing cords that hold the belt together. The belt will first slip, then finally fail altogether.

Softening (grease and oil)

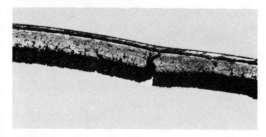

Glazing is caused by a belt that is slipping. A slipping belt can cause a run-down battery, erratic power steering, overheating or poor accessory performance. The more the belt slips, the more glazing will be built up on the surface of the belt. The more the belt is glazed, the more it will slip. If the glazing is light, tighten the belt.

Glazing

The cover of this belt is worn off and is peeling away. The reinforcing cords will begin to wear and the belt will shortly break. When the belt cover wears in spots or has a rough jagged appearance, check the pulley grooves for roughness.

Worn cover

This belt is on the verge of breaking and leaving you stranded. The layers of the belt are separating and the reinforcing cords are exposed. It's just a matter of time before it breaks completely.

Separation

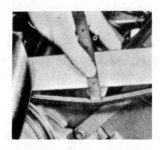

Measuring fan belt tension (© Chevrolet Motor Division)

left in the system too long, it loses its ability to prevent rust and corrosion. If the coolant has too much water, it won't protect against freezing.

The pressure cap should be looked at for signs of age or deterioration. Fan belt and other drive belts should be inspected and adjusted to the proper tension. (See checking belt tension).

Hose clamps should be tightened, and soft or cracked hoses replaced. Damp spots, or accumulations of rust or dye near hoses, water pump or other areas, indicate possible leakage, which must be corrected before filling the system with fresh coolant.

CHECK THE RADIATOR CAP

While you are checking the coolant level, check the radiator cap for a worn or cracked gasket. If the cap doesn't seal properly, fluid will be lost and the engine will overheat.

Worn caps should be replaced with a new one.

CLEAN RADIATOR OF DEBRIS

Periodically clean any debris—leaves, paper, insects, etc.—from the radiator fins. Pick the large pieces off by hand. The smaller pieces can be washed away with water pressure from a hose.

Carefully straighten any bent radiator fins with a pair of needle nose pliers. Be careful— the fins are very soft. Don't wiggle the fins back and forth too much. Straighten them once and try not to move them again.

DRAIN AND REFILL THE COOLING SYSTEM

Completely draining and refilling the cooling system every two years at least will remove accumulated rust, scale and other deposits. Coolant in late model cars is a 50-50 mixture of ethylene glycol and water for year round use. Use a good quality antifreeze with water

pump lubricants, rust inhibitors and other corrosion inhibitors along with acid neutralizers.

1. Drain the existing antifreeze and coolant. Open the radiator and engine drain petcocks, or disconnect the bottom radiator hose, at the radiator outlet.

NOTE: *Before opening the radiator petcock, spray it with some penetrating lubricant.*

2. Close the petcock or re-connect the lower hose and fill the system with water.

3. Add a can of quality radiator flush.

4. Idle the engine until the upper radiator hose gets hot.

5. Drain the system again.

6. Repeat this process until the drained water is clear and free of scale.

7. Close all petcocks and connect all the hoses.

8. If equipped with a coolant recovery system, flush the reservoir with water and leave empty.

9. Determine the capacity of your cooling system (see capacities specifications). Add a 50/50 mix of quality antifreeze (ethylene glycol) and water to provide the desired protection.

10. Run the engine to operating temperature.

11. Stop the engine and check the coolant level.

12. Check the level of protection with an anti-freeze tester, replace the cap and check for leaks.

Air Conditioning
SAFETY PRECAUTIONS

There are two particular hazards associated with air conditioning systems and they both relate to the refrigerant gas.

First, the refrigerant gas is an extremely cold substance. When exposed to air, it will instantly freeze any surface it comes in contact with, including your eyes. The other hazard relates to fire. Although normally non-toxic, refrigerant gas becomes highly poisonous in the presence of an open flame. One good whiff of the vapor formed by burning refrigerant can be fatal. Keep all forms of fire (including cigarettes) well clear of the air-conditioning system.

Any repair work to an air conditioning system should be left to a professional. Do not, under any circumstances, attempt to loosen

HOW TO SPOT BAD HOSES

Both the upper and lower radiator hoses are called upon to perform difficult jobs in an inhospitable environment. They are subject to nearly 18 psi at under hood temperatures often over 280°F., and must circulate nearly 7500 gallons of coolant an hour—3 good reasons to have good hoses.

Swollen hose

A good test for any hose is to feel it for soft or spongy spots. Frequently these will appear as swollen areas of the hose. The most likely cause is oil soaking. This hose could burst at any time, when hot or under pressure.

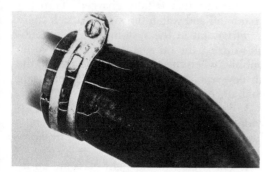

Cracked hose

Cracked hoses can usually be seen but feel the hoses to be sure they have not hardened; a prime cause of cracking. This hose has cracked down to the reinforcing cords and could split at any of the cracks.

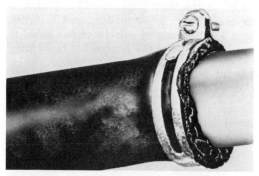

Frayed hose end (due to weak clamp)

Weakened clamps frequently are the cause of hose and cooling system failure. The connection between the pipe and hose has deteriorated enough to allow coolant to escape when the engine is hot.

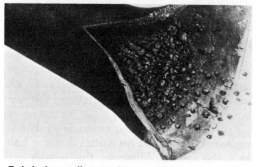

Debris in cooling system

Debris, rust and scale in the cooling system can cuase the inside of a hose to weaken. This can usually be felt on the outside of the hose as soft or thinner areas.

or tighten any fittings or perform any work other than that outlined here.

CHECKING FOR OIL LEAKS

Refrigerant leaks show up as oily areas on the various components because the compressor oil is transported around the entire system along with the refrigerant. Look for oily spots on all the hoses and lines, and especially on the hose and tubing connections. If there are oily deposits, the system may have a leak, and you should have it checked by a qualified repairman.

NOTE: *A small area of oil on the front of the compressor is normal and no cause for alarm.*

CHECK THE COMPRESSOR BELT

Refer to the section in this chapter on "Drive Belts."

KEEP THE CONDENSER CLEAR

Periodically inspect the front of the condenser for bent fins or foreign material (dirt, bugs, leaves, etc.) If any cooling fins are bent, straighten them carefully with needle-nosed pliers. You can remove any debris with a stiff bristle brush or hose.

OPERATE THE A/C SYSTEM PERIODICALLY

A lot of A/C problems can be avoided by simply running the air conditioner at least once a week, regardless of the season. Simply let the system run for at least 5 minutes a week (even in the winter), and you'll keep the internal parts lubricated as well as preventing the hoses from hardening.

REFRIGERANT LEVEL CHECK

There are two ways to check refrigerant level, depending on how your model is equipped.

With Sight Glass

The first order of business when checking the sight glass is to find the sight glass. It will either be in the head of the receiver/drier, or in one of the metal lines leading from the top of the receiver/drier. Once you've found it, wipe it clean and proceed as follows:

1. With the engine and the air conditioning system running, look for the flow of refrigerant through the sight glass. If the air conditioner is working properly, you'll be able to see a continuous flow of clear refrigerant through the sight glass, with perhaps an

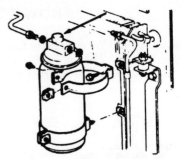

Air conditioning sight glass (© Chevrolet Motor Division)

occasional bubble at very high temperatures.

2. Cycle the air conditioner on and off to make sure what you are seeing is clear refrigerant. Since the refrigerant is clear, it is possible to mistake a completely discharged system for one that is fully charged. Turn the system off and watch the sight glass. If there is refrigerant in the system, you'll see bubbles during the off cycle. If you observe no bubbles when the system is running, and the air flow from the unit in the car is delivering cold air, everything is OK.

3. If you observe bubbles in the sight glass while the system is operating, the system is low on refrigerant. Have it checked by a professional.

4. Oil streaks in the sight glass are an indication of trouble. Most of the time, if you see oil in the sight glass, it will appear as a series of streaks, although occasionally it may be a solid stream of oil. In either case, it means that part of the charge has been lost.

Without Sight Glass

On vehicles that are not equipped with sight glasses, it is necessary to feel the temperature difference in the inlet and outlet lines at the receiver/drier to gauge the refrigerant level. Use the following procedure:

1. Locate the receiver/drier. It will generally be up front near the condenser. It is shaped like a small fire extinguisher and will always have two lines connected to it. One line goes to the expansion valve and the other goes to the condenser.

2. With the engine and the air conditioner running, hold a line in each hand and gauge their relative temperatures. If they are both the same approximate temperature, the system is correctly charged.

3. If the line from the expansion valve to the receiver/drier is a lot colder than the line from the receiver/drier to the condenser, then the system is overcharged. It should be

noted that this is an extremely rare condition.

4. If the line that leads from the receiver/drier to the condenser is a lot colder than the other line, the system is undercharged.

5. If the system if undercharged or overcharged, have it checked by a professional air conditioning mechanic.

Windshield Wipers

Intense heat from the sun, snow and ice, road oils and the chemicals used in windshield washer solvents combine to deteriorate the rubber wiper refills. The refills should be replaced about twice a year or whenever the blades begin to streak or chatter.

WIPER REFILL REPLACEMENT

Normally, if the wipers are not cleaning the windshield properly, only the refill has to be replaced. The blade and arm usually require replacement only in the event of damage. It is not necessary (except on new Tridon refills) to remove the arm or the blade to replace the refill (rubber part), though you may have to position the arm higher on the glass. You can do this turning the ignition switch on and operating the wipers. When they are positioned where they are accessible, turn the ignition switch off.

There are several types of refills and your vehicle could have any kind, since aftermarket blades and arms may not use exactly the same type refill as the original equipment.

Most Trico styles use a release button that is pushed down to allow the refill to slide out of the yoke jaws. The new refill slides in and locks in place. Some Trico refills are removed by locating where the metal backing strip or the refill is wider. Insert a small screwdriver blade between the frame and metal backing strip. Press down to release the refill from the retaining tab.

The Anco style is unlocked at one end by squeezing 2 metal tabs, and the refill is slid out of the frame jaws. When the new refill is installed, the tabs will click into place, locking the refill.

The polycarbonate type is held in place by a locking lever that is pushed downward out of the groove in the arm to free the refill. When the new refill is installed, it will lock in place automatically.

The Tridon refill has a plastic backing strip with a notch about an inch from the end. Hold the blade (frame) on a hard surface so that the frame is tightly bowed. Grip the tip of the backing strip and pull up while twisting counterclockwise. The backing strip will snap out of the retaining tab. Do this for the remaining tabs until the refill is free of the arm. The length of these refills is molded into the end and they should be replaced with identical types.

No matter which type of refill you use, be sure that all of the frame claws engage the refill. Before operating the wipers, be sure that no part of the metal frame is contacting the windshield.

Fluid Level Checks
ENGINE OIL

The engine oil level is checked with the dipstick, which is located at the left side of the engine block.

NOTE: *The oil should be checked before the engine is started or five minutes after the engine has been shut off. This gives the oil time to drain back to the oil pan and prevents an inaccurate oil level reading.*

Remove the dipstick from its tube, wipe it clean, and insert it back into the tube. Remove it again and observe the oil level. It should be maintained between the "full" and "add" marks without going above "full" or below "add."

CAUTION: *Do not overfill the crankcase. It may result in oil-fouled spark plugs or oil leaks caused by oil seal failure.*

TRANSMISSION FLUID
Manual Transmission

Remove the filler plug from the side of the transmission. The oil should be level with the bottom edge of the filler hole. This should be checked at least once every 6,000 miles and more often if any leakage or seepage is observed. Fill with SAE 80 or 90 multipurpose gear lubricant.

Automatic Transmission

Run the engine until it reaches normal operating temperature. Park the car on a level surface. With the transmission in Park and the engine idling, the fluid level on the dipstick should be between the "full" mark and ¼ inch below "full" mark. Replace the

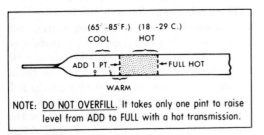

NOTE: DO NOT OVERFILL. It takes only one pint to raise level from ADD to FULL with a hot transmission.

Automatic transmission dipstick (© Chevrolet Motor Division)

dipstick making sure that it is pushed fully into the filler tube.

CAUTION: *Do not overfill the automatic transmission. Use Dexron® or Type A automatic transmission fluid or any other equivalent fluid. One pint raises the level from "add" to "full."*

BRAKE MASTER CYLINDER

Once every 6,000 miles or four months, check the brake fluid level in the master cylinder. The master cylinder is mounted on the firewall and is divided into two reservoirs and the fluid level in each reservoir must be maintained at ¼ inch below the top edge. Use only heavy-duty brake fluid (DOT 3 or 4), which is recommended for disc brake applications.

COOLANT

Check the coolant level when the engine is cold. The level of coolant should be maintained 2 in. below the bottom of the filler neck, or the line on expansion tank-equipped models.

CAUTION: *Allow the engine to cool considerably and then add water while the engine is running.*

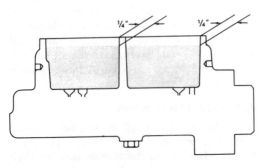

Checking the master cylinder fluid level (© Chevrolet Motor Division)

REAR AXLE

Standard Differential

The rear axle oil level should be checked when the chassis is lubricated. Remove the plug from the side of the housing. The lubricant level should be maintained at the bottom of the filler plug hole. When replacing oil, use SAE 80 or 90 multipurpose hypoid gear lubricant.

Positraction Differential

Lubricant level should be checked at each chassis lubrication and maintained at the bottom of the filler plug hole. Special Positraction oil must be used in this differential.

CAUTION: *Never use standard differential lubricant in a Positraction differential.*

STEERING GEAR

Check the lubricant by removing the center bolt on the side cover of the steering gear. Grease must be up to the level of this bolt hole.

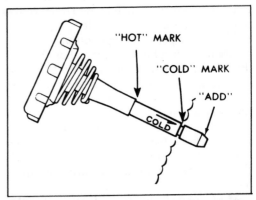

Power steering dipstick (© Chevrolet Motor Division)

POWER STEERING RESERVOIR

Maintain the proper fluid level as indicated on the cap of the reservoir. Check this level with the engine off and warm. Use GM power steering fluid or Dexron® automatic transmission fluid.

BATTERY

The battery in 1963 through 1967 Corvettes is located on the right-side of the engine compartment behind the wheel well and under the radiator expansion tank. 1968 and later Corvettes have the battery located in the left-side well of the stowage compartment behind the seats. All are equipped with

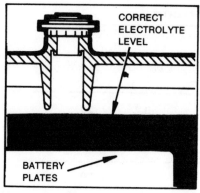

Correct battery electrolyte level—1963–75 (© Chevrolet Motor Division)

a negative ground, twelve-volt battery. The electrolyte level in the battery should be checked about once every month and more often during hot weather or long trips. If the level is below the bottom of the split ring, distilled water should be added until the level reaches the ring.

1976 and later models use the Freedom® battery which is sealed at the factory and never needs any water added to it. The sealed battery has a built-in temperature compensated hydrometer in the top of the battery. Make sure the top of the battery is clean and check the color of the indicator.

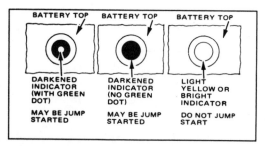

Built-in hydrometer—Freedom®-battery (© Chevrolet Motor Division)

Tires

INFLATION PRESSURE

Tire inflation is the most ignored item of auto maintenance. Gasoline mileage can drop as much as .8% for every 1 pound per square inch (psi) of under inflation.

Two items should be a permanent fixture in every glove compartment; a tire pressure gauge and a tread depth gauge. Check the tire air pressure (including the spare) regularly with a pocket type gauge. Kicking the tires won't tell you a thing, and the gauge on

the service station air hose is notoriously inaccurate.

The tire pressures recommended for your car are usually found on the glove-box door or in the owner's manual. Ideally, inflation pressure should be checked when the tires are cool. When the air becomes heated it expands and the pressure increases. Every 10° rise (or drop) in temperature means a difference of 1 psi, which also explains why the tire appears to lose air on a very cold night. When it is impossible to check the tires "cold," allow for pressure build-up due to heat. If the "hot" pressure exceeds the "cold" pressure by more than 15 psi, reduce your speed, load or both. Otherwise internal heat is created in the tire. When the heat approaches the temperature at which the tire was cured, during manufacture, the tread can separate from the body.

CAUTION: *Never counteract excessive pressure build-up by bleeding off air pressure (letting some air out). This will only further raise the tire operating temperature.*

Before starting a long trip with lots of luggage, you can add about 2–4 psi to the tires to make them run cooler, but never exceed the maximum inflation pressure on the side of the tire.

TREAD DEPTH

All tires made since 1968, have 8 built-in tread wear indicator bars that show up as ½" wide smooth bands across the tire when 1/16" of tread remains. The appearance of tread wear indicators means that the tires should be replaced. In fact, many states have laws prohibiting the use of tires with less than 1/16" tread.

You can check your own tread depth with an inexpensive gauge or by using a Lincoln head penny. Slip the Lincoln penny into several tread grooves. If you can see the top of Lincoln's head in 2 adjacent grooves, the tires have less than 1/16" tread left and should be replaced. You can measure snow tires in the same manner by using the "tails" side of the Lincoln penny. If you can see the top of the Lincoln memorial, it's time to replace the snow tires.

TIRE ROTATION

Tire wear can be equalized by switching the position of the tires about every 6000 miles. Including a conventional spare in the rotation pattern can give up to 20% more tire life.

Capacities & Pressures

Year	Model (cu in.)	Engine Crankcase Add 1 Qt for New Filter	Transmission Pts to Refill after Draining Manual 3-spd	4-spd	Automatic	Differential (pts)	Fuel Tank (gal)	Cooling System (qts)	Max Coolant Pressure (psi)
1963	327	4	2	2.5	18	3.7	20	17	13
	327 HP	5	—	2.5	—	3.7	20	17	13
1964	327	4	2	2.5	18	3.7	20	17	13
	327 HP	5	—	2.5	—	3.7	20	17	13
1965	327	4	2	2.5	18	3.7	20	17	13
	327 HP	4	2	2.5	18	3.7	20	17	13
1966	327	4	3	3.0	18	3.7	20	19	15
	327 HP	5	—	3.0	—	3.7	20	19	15
	427	5	—	3.0	—	3.7	20	22	15
1967	327	4	3	3.0	19	3.7	20	19	15
	327 HP	5	—	3.0	—	3.7	20	19	15
	427	5	—	3.0	19	3.7	20	22	15
	427 HP	5	—	3.0	—	3.7	20	22	15
1968	327	4	3	3.0	22	3.7	20	15	15
	327 HP	4	—	3.0	—	3.7	20	15	15
	427	5	—	3.0	22	3.7	20	22	15
	427 HP	5	—	3.0	—	3.7	20	22	15
1969	350 HP	4	—	3.0	—	4.0	20	—	15
	427	5	—	3.0	—	4.0	20	—	15
	427 HP	5	—	3.0	—	4.0	20	—	15
1970	350	4	—	3.0	22	4.0	20	15	15
	350 HP	4	—	3.0	—	4.0	20	18	15

Capacities & Pressures (cont.)

1970	454	5	—	3.0	22	4.0	20	22	15
	454 HP	5	—	3.0	22	4.0	20	22	15
1971	350	4	—	3.0	22	4.0	18	15	15
	350 HP	4	—	3.0	—	4.0	18	18	15
	454	5	—	3.0	22	4.0	18	22	15
	454 HP	5	—	3.0	22	4.0	18	20	15
1972	350	4	—	3.0	22	4.0	18	15	15
	350 HP	4	—	3.0	—	4.0	18	18	15
	454	5	—	3.0	22	4.0	18	22	15
1973	350	4	—	3.0	7½*	4.0	18	18	15
	454	5	—	3.0	7½*	4.0	18	24	15
1974	350	4	—	3.0	9*	4.0	18	17	17
	454	5	—	3.0	9*	4.0	18	22	23
1975–76	350	4	—	3.0	8*	4.0	18	17	17
1977	350	4	—	3.0	8*②	3.75	17	21	15
1978	350	4	—	3.0	6*	3.75	24	21.6	15
1979	350	4	—	3.4①	6*	3.75	24	21.6	15

① 2.75—Optional close ratio 4-speed   * Normal change does not include torque converter
② T.H. 400—5 pt.   — Not applicable
HP High performance engine

CAUTION: *Do not include the new "Space-Saver®" or temporary spare tires in the rotation pattern.*

There are certain exceptions to tire rotation, however. Studded snow tires should not be rotated, and radials should be kept on the same side of the car (maintain the same direction of rotation). The belts on radial tires get set in a pattern. If the direction of rotation is reversed, it can cause rough ride and vibration.

NOTE: *When radials or studded snows are taken off the car, mark them, so you can maintain the same direction of rotation.*

TIRE STORAGE

Store the tires at proper inflation pressures if they are mounted on wheels. All tires should be kept in a cool, dry place. If they are stored in the garage or basement, do not let them stand on a concrete floor; set them on strips of wood.

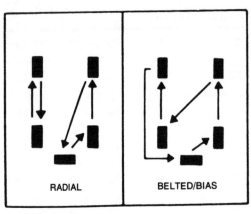

Tire rotation patterns

Wheel and Tire Size Chart

Year	Wheel Size	Tire Size
1963–64	15 x 5.5K①	6.70 x 15
1965–66	15 x 5.5K①	7.75 x 15
1967	15 x 6JK②	7.75 x 15
1968	15 x 7JK	F70 x 15
1969–72	15 x 8JJ	F70 x 15
1973–77	15 x 8JJ	GR70 x 15
1978–79	15 x 8	P225/70R15

① 15 x 6L aluminum knock-off wheel optionally available

② 15 x 6L aluminum bolt on wheel optionally available

Knock-off wheel adapter

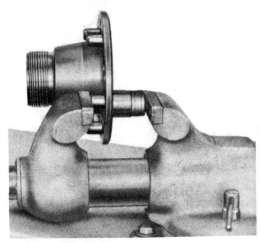

Removing adapter pin

ALUMINUM WHEELS

An optional knock-off wheel was introduced with the 1963 Stingray. This wheel option consisted of 15 x 6L cast aluminum wheels, knock-off locking nuts, and wheel adapters. The latter bolt to the hub, using the existing wheel hub bolts. The flange of the adapter had five pins that fitted into corresponding holes in the optional wheels and located the wheel to the hub. The securing device was the single, center, knock-off nut.

Each Corvette delivered with the optional, knock-off aluminum wheels, was equipped with a special knock-off hammer. Owners of these cars were urged to tighten the knock-off nut every 100 miles for the first 500 miles. The suggested method was to strike the ears of the nut eight hard blows.

For owners of these cars, the following maintenance suggestions are offered: exercise caution when using commercially available cleaners and use only those that will not react unfavorably with aluminum.

Should adapter pin replacement become necessary, remove the wheel and tire assembly and remove the adapter from the wheel hub. Select a socket of suitable size that will slip over the adapter pin. Position the socket over the back of the pin and clamp the entire assembly in a vise so that the socket acts as a spacer to receive the damaged pin. Tighten the vise and press the pin from the adapter. Position the replacement pin and start it into the hole by tapping lightly. Position the spacer socket on the opposite side and again clamp the assembly in the vise. Press the replacement pin into the adapter. Check to see that it seats firmly against its bore. Install the adapter and wheel.

Fuel Filter

The filter in Carter WCFB, Rochester Quadrajet, Holley 2300, and Holley 4150 carbu-

Inline fuel filter

retors is located in the fuel inlet connection and should be replaced every 12,000 miles or sooner if engine flooding occurs. The Carter AFB uses an in-line filter, which should be replaced every 24,000 miles. The Rochester fuel injection unit also uses an in-line filter, which should be replaced every 15,000 miles.

To replace an in-line filter, disconnect the fitting at each end of the filter canister, discard the old filter, and install the replacement in the reverse order of removal.

To replace a fuel inlet filter:

1. Using an open-end wrench (preferably a line wrench), disconnect the fuel line connection from the larger fuel filter nut.

2. Remove the larger nut from the carburetor.

3. Remove the filter element and spring from the carburetor.

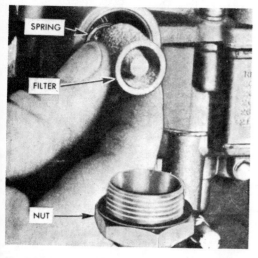

Most late models have this bronze fuel filter located behind the fuel fitting

4. Check the bronze element for dirt blockage by blowing on the cone end. If the element is good, air should pass through easily.

5. If the car has a paper element instead of a bronze element, check by blowing into the fuel inlet end. If air does not pass through easily replace the element. Do not attempt to clean these elements.

6. Install the spring and then the element into the carburetor, making sure that the small end of the bronze cone is facing outward.

7. Install a new gasket on the large nut and tighten securely.

8. Insert the fuel line and tighten the nut with a line wrench.

LUBRICATION

Oil and Fuel Recommendations

Chevrolet recommends the use of a high quality, heavy-duty detergent oil having the proper viscosity for prevailing temperatures and an SE service rating. The SE rating will be printed on the top of the can. Under the classification system adopted by the American Petroleum Institute (API) in May, 1970, SE is the highest designation given for normal passenger car use. The S stands for passenger car and the second letter denotes a more specific application. SA oil, for instance, contains no additives and is suitable only for very light-duty. Oil designated MS may also be used, since this was the highest classification under the old API rating system. Pick your oil viscosity with regard to the anticipated temperatures during the period before your next oil change. Using the chart below, choose the oil viscosity for the lowest expected temperature. You will be assured of easy cold starting and sufficient engine protection.

Fuel should be selected for the brand and octane which performs without pinging. Find your exact engine model in the "General Engine Specifications" chart in Chapter 3. If the compression ratio is higher than 9.0:1, you will have to use a premium gasoline. If your compression ratio is lower than 9.0:1, you can safely go with regular octane. Most 1971 and later models will operate successfully on regular if the car is properly tuned, especially as to correct ignition timing.

CAUTION: *It is absolutely imperative that*

Maintenance Intervals

Maintenance	1963–67	1968–71	1972–74	1975–79
Air Cleaner (Check and Clean)				
Oil bath	12,000 mi			
Paper element①	12,000 mi (replace)	12,000 mi (replace)	24,000 mi (replace)	30,000 mi (replace)
PCV Valve (Replace)	12 mo/12,000 mi	12 mo/12,000 mi	12 mo/12,000 mi	15,000 mi
Evaporative Canister				
Replace filter	—	12 mo/12,000 mi (1970–71)	12 mo/12,000 mi	24 mo/30,000 mi
Engine Oil				
Check	Each fuel stop	each fuel stop	each fuel stop	each fuel stop
Replace	4 mo/6,000 mi	4 mo/6,000 mi	4 mo/6,000 mi	6 mo/7,500 mi
Engine Oil Filter (Replace)	every oil change	every oil change	every oil change	every oil change
Fuel Filter				
Replace	12,000 mi	12,000 mi	12,000 mi	15,000 mi
Powerglide Transmission Fluid				
Check	6,000 mi	6,000 mi	—	—
Replace	24,000 mi	24,000 mi		
Turbo Hydra-Matic Fluid & Filter				
Check fluid	—	6,000 mi	6,000 mi	6,000 mi
Change fluid		24,000 mi	24,000 mi	30,000 mi
Replace filter		24,000 mi	24,000 mi	30,000 mi

Manual Transmissions (All)				
Check lubricant	6,000 mi	6,000 mi	6,000 mi	7,500 mi
Add lubricant	as necessary	as necessary	as necessary	as necessary
Battery				
Lubricate terminal felt washer	6,000 mi②	6,000 mi②	—	—
Clean terminals	6,000 mi	6,000 mi	as necessary	as necessary
Check electrolyte level	Twice monthly	twice monthly	twice monthly	twice monthly
Coolant Level	Each fuel stop	each fuel stop	each fuel stop	each fuel stop
Front Wheel Bearings				
Lubricate	24,000 mi	24,000 mi	24,000 mi	30,000 mi
Rear Axle Lube				
Check	6,000 mi	6,000 mi	6,000 mi	7,500 mi
Replace	as necessary	as necessary	as necessary	1st 15,000 mi
Brake Fluid (Master Cylinder)				
Check fluid level	6,000 mi	6,000 mi	6,000 mi	7,500 mi
Add fluid	as necessary	as necessary	as necessary	as necessary
Manual Steering Gear Lubricant				
Check level	30,000 mi	30,000 mi	30,000 mi	30,000 mi
Add lubricant	as necessary	as necessary	as necessary	as necessary
Power Steering Reservoir				
Check fluid level	6 mo/6,000 mi	6 mo/6,000 mi	6 mo/6,000 mi	7,500 mi
Add fluid	as necessary	as necessary	as necessary	as necessary
Rotate Tires	4,000 mi	4,000 mi	6,000 mi	1st 7,500 mi Then every 15,000 mi (Radials) Bias belted every 7,500 mi

Maintenance Intervals (cont.)

Maintenance	1963–67	1968–71	1972–74	1975–79
Chassis Lubrication	6 mo/6,000 mi	6 mo/6,000 mi	6 mo/6,000 mi	6 mo/7,500 mi
Drive Belts Check and adjust (as necessary)	6,000 mi	6,000 mi	6,000 mi	7,500 mi
Rear Wheel Bearings Lubricate	—	—	24,000 mi (1973–74)	—
Manifold Heat Valve Lubricate	6,000 mi	6,000 mi	6,000 mi	7,500 mi

① Paper element air cleaners should be rotated 180° each time they are checked
② May be equipped with a felt terminal washer
NOTE: Heavy-duty operation (trailer towing, prolonged idling, severe stop-and-start driving) should be accompanied by a 50% increase in maintenance. Cut the interval in half for these conditions. Figures given are maintenance intervals when service should be performed.

only lead-free gasoline be used in 1975–76 models. Leaded fuel will render the catalytic converter ineffective.

Fluid Changes

ENGINE OIL AND FILTER

The mileage figures given in your owner's manual are the Chevrolet recommended intervals for oil and filter changes assuming average driving. If your Corvette is being used under dusty, polluted, or off-road conditions, change the oil and filter sooner than specified. The same thing goes for cars driven in stop-and-go traffic or only for short distances.

Always drain the oil after the engine has been running long enough to bring it to operating temperature. Hot oil will flow easier and more contaminants will be removed along with the oil than if it were drained cold. You will need a large capacity drain pan, which you can purchase at any store which sells automotive parts. Another necessity is containers for the used oil. You will find that plastic bottles, such as those used for bleach or fabric softener, make excellent storage jugs. One ecologiclly desirable solution to the used oil disposal problem is to find a co-operative gas station owner who will allow you to dump your used oil into his tank.

Oil Viscosity Selection Chart

	Anticipated Temperature Range	SAE Viscosity
Multi-grade	Above 32° F	10W—40
		10W—50
		20W—40
		20W—50
		10W—30
	May be used as low as — 10° F	10W—30
		10W—40
	Consistently below 10° F	5W—20
		5W—30
Single-grade	Above 32° F	30
	Temperature between + 32° F and — 10° F	10W

Another is to keep the oil for use around the house as a preservative on fences, railroad tie borders, etc.

Chevrolet recommends changing both the oil and filter during the first oil change and the filter every other oil change thereafter. For the small price of an oil filter, it's cheap insurance to replace the filter at every oil change. One of the larger filter manufacturers points out in its advertisements that not changing the filter leaves one quart of dirty oil in the engine. This claim is true and should be kept in mind when changing your oil.

CHANGING YOUR OIL

1. Run the engine until it reaches normal operating temperature.

2. Jack up the front of the car and support it on safety stands.

3. Slide a drain pan of at least 6 quarts capacity under the oil pan.

4. Loosen the drain plug. Turn the plug out by hand. By keeping an inward pressure on the plug as you unscrew it, oil won't escape past the threads and you can remove it without being burned by hot oil.

5. Allow the oil to drain completely and then install the drain plug. Don't overtighten the plug, or you'll be buying a new pan or a trick replacement plug for buggered threads.

6. Using a strap wrench, remove the oil filter. Keep in mind that it's holding about one quart of dirty, hot oil.

1963 through 1967 Corvettes use a cartridge type oil filter, and 1968 and later cars use the spin-off type. Adapters are available on the aftermarket to adapt the spin-off type to the 1963–67 cars.

7. Empty the old filter into the drain pan and dispose of the filter.

8. Using a clean rag, wipe off the filter adapter on the engine block. Be sure that the rag doesn't leavy any lint which could clog an oil passage.

9. Coat the rubber gasket on the filter with fresh oil. Spin it onto the engine *by hand;* when the gasket touches the adapter surface give it another ½–¾ turn. No more, or you'll squash the gasket and it will leak.

10. Refill the engine with the correct amount of fresh oil. See the "Capacities" chart.

11. Crank the engine over several times and then start it. If the oil pressure gauge shows zero, shut the engine down and find out what's wrong.

12. If the oil pressure is OK and there are no leaks, shut the engine off and lower the car.

13. Wait a few minutes and check the oil level. Add oil, as necessary, to bring the level up to Full.

MANUAL TRANSMISSION

No intervals are specified for changing the transmission lubricant, but after extended heavy duty operation it may be a good idea. The vehicle should be on a level surface and the lubricant should be at operating temperature.

1. Position the vehicle on a level surface.
2. Place a pan of sufficient capacity under the transmission drain plug.
3. Remove the upper (fill) plug to provide a vent opening.
4. Remove the lower (drain) plug and let the lubricant drain out.
5. Replace the drain plug.
6. Add lubricant with a suction gun or squeeze bulb. The correct lubricant is SAE 80W-90 GL-5 Gear Lubricant, or SAE 80W GL-5 for cold climates. Refer to the Capacities and Pressures Chart for the correct quantity.

AUTOMATIC TRANSMISSION

The fluid should be drained with the transmission warm. It is easier to change the fluid if the vehicle is raised somewhat from the ground, but this is not always easy without a lift. The transmission must be level for it to drain properly.

1. Place a shallow pan underneath to catch the transmission fluid. On earlier models, the transmission pan has a drain plug. Remove this and drain the fluid. For later models, loosen all the pan bolts, then pull one corner down to drain most of the fluid. If it sticks, VERY CAREFULLY pry the pan loose with a screwdriver. You can buy aftermarket drain plug kits that make this operation a bit less messy, once installed.

NOTE: *If the fluid removed smells burnt, serious transmission troubles, probably due to overheating, should be suspected.*

2. Remove the pan screws and empty out the pan.
3. Clean the pan with solvent and allow it to air dry. If you use a rag to wipe it out, you risk leaving bits of lint and threads in the transmission.
4. Remove the filter or strainer retaining bolts. On the Turbo Hydra-Matic 400, there are two screws securing the filter or screen to the valve body. A reusable strainer may be found on some models. The strainer may be cleaned in solvent and air dried thoroughly. The filter and gasket must be replaced.

5. Install a new gasket and filter.
6. Install a new gasket on the pan and tighten the bolts evenly to 12 foot pounds in a criss-cross pattern.
7. Add DEXRON® or DEXRON II® transmission fluid through the dipstick tube. The correct amount is in the Capacities Chart. Do not overfill.
8. With the gearshift level in PARK, start the engine and let it idle. Do not race the engine.
9. Move the gearshift lever through each position, holding the brakes. Return the lever to PARK, and check the fluid level with the engine idling. The level should be between the two dimples on the dipstick, about ¼ in. below the ADD mark. Add fluid, if necessary.
10. Check the fluid level after the vehicle has been driven enough to thoroughly warm up the transmission. Details are given under Fluid Level Checks earlier in the Chapter. If the transmission is overfilled, the excess must be drained off. Overfilling causes aerated fluid, resulting in transmission slippage and probable damage.

REAR AXLE

The factory recommends that the rear axle lubricant be changed at the 1st 7,500 mi. and a 4 oz. lubricant additive (GM part no. 1052358) added. If the vehicle is used to pull a trailer the lubricant should be changed every 15,000 mi.

1. Run the vehicle so the lubricant reaches operating temperature.
2. Position a drain pan under the rear axle.
3. Remove the axle housing cover and gasket and drain the lubricant.
4. Clean the gasket sealing surfaces and install the cover with a new gasket.
5. Torque the cover bolts in a crosswise pattern to 20 ft lbs.
6. Add 4 oz. of rear axle lubricant additive (GM 1052358).
7. Use a suction gun or a squeeze bulb and refill the differential housing to a level within ⅜' of the filler plug with rear axle lubricant (GM 1052271) or equivalent. (See the Capacities Chart).
8. Install the filler plug.

COOLANT

Refer to the Cooling System Section under Routine Maintenance.

Chassis Greasing

Chassis greasing can be performed with a pressurized grease gun or it can be performed at home by using a hand-operated grease gun. Wipe the grease fittings clean before greasing in order to prevent the possibility of forcing any dirt into the component.

WHEEL BEARINGS

Once every 24,000 miles, clean and repack wheel bearings with a wheel bearing grease. Use only enough grease to completely coat the rollers. Remove any excess grease from the exposed surface of the hub and seal.

It is important that wheel bearings be properly adjusted after installation. Improperly adjusted wheel bearings can cause steering instability, front-end shimmy and wander, and increased tire wear. For complete adjustment procedures, see the "Wheel Bearing" section in Chapter 8.

PUSHING AND TOWING

Corvettes equipped with either the Powerglide or Turbo Hydra-Matic automatic transmissions cannot be push-started. To push-start a Corvette that has either a three-speed or four-speed manual transmission, switch on the ignition, select the highest forward gear and keep the clutch pedal depressed until suitable speed has been provided by the pushing vehicle. When this speed, approximately 15 mph, is reached, slowly release the clutch to start the engine.

Corvettes may be towed at speeds up to 35 mph and distances not over 50 miles with the

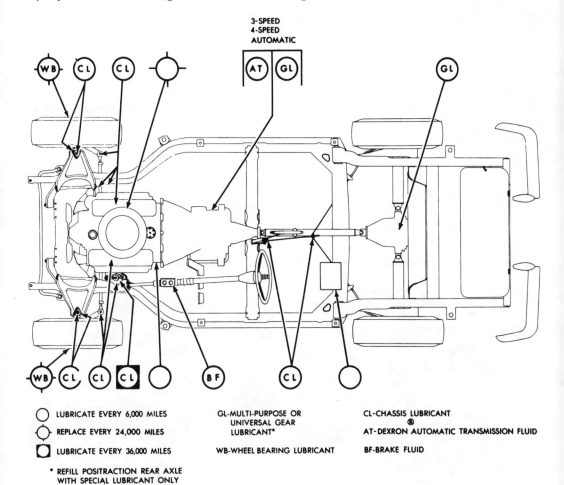

LUBRICATE EVERY 6,000 MILES
REPLACE EVERY 24,000 MILES
LUBRICATE EVERY 36,000 MILES
* REFILL POSITRACTION REAR AXLE WITH SPECIAL LUBRICANT ONLY

GL-MULTI-PURPOSE OR UNIVERSAL GEAR LUBRICANT*
WB-WHEEL BEARING LUBRICANT

CL-CHASSIS LUBRICANT
AT-DEXRON AUTOMATIC TRANSMISSION FLUID
BF-BRAKE FLUID

Lubrication points—1963–74 (© Chevrolet Motor Division)

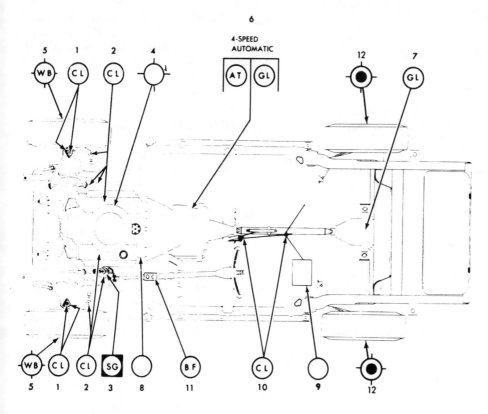

LUBRICATE EVERY 7,500 MILES

LUBRICATE FIRST 12,000 MILES

REPLACE EVERY 30,000 MILES

CHECK FOR GREASE LEAKAGE
EVERY 30,000 MILES

* REFILL POSITRACTION REAR AXLE
WITH SPECIAL LUBRICANT ONLY

GL-MULTI-PURPOSE OR
UNIVERSAL GEAR
LUBRICANT*

WB-WHEEL BEARING LUBRICANT

CL-CHASSIS LUBRICANT

AT-DEXRON-II® AUTOMATIC TRANSMISSION FLUID

BF-BRAKE FLUID
SG-STEERING GEAR LUBRICANT

1. Front suspension	7. Rear axle
2. Steering linkage	8. Oil filter
3. Steering gear	9. Battery
4. Air cleaner	10. Parking brake
5. Front wheel bearings	11. Brake master cylinder
6. Transmission	12. Rear wheel inner bearing

Lubrication points—1975–79 (© Chevrolet Motor Division)

Front towing point

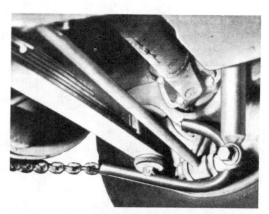

Rear towing point

driveshaft in place, if no engine/drive-line damage is present. If engine/drive-line damage is known or suspected, the driveshaft should be disconnected before towing. Towing connections should not be made on bumpers, only on the spindle struts at the rear and the frame crossmember or lower control arm at the front.

JUMP STARTING

The following procedure is recommended by the manufacturer. Be sure that the booster battery is 12 volt with negative ground.

CAUTION: *Do not attempt this procedure on a frozen battery; it will probably explode. Do not attempt it on a sealed Delco Freedom battery showing a light color in the charge indicator. Be certain to observe correct polarity connections. Failure to do so will result in almost immediate alternator and regulator destruction. Never allow the jumper cable ends to touch each other.*

1. Position the 2 vehicles so that they are not touching. Set the parking brake and place automatic transmissions in Park and manual transmissions in Neutral. Turn off the lights, heater and other electrical loads.

2. Remove the vent caps from both the booster and discharged battery. Lay a cloth over the open vent cells of each battery. This isn't necessary on batteries equipped with sponge type flame arrestor caps, and it isn't possible on sealed Freedom batteries.

3. Attach one cable to the positive (+) terminal of the booster battery and the other end to the positive terminal of the discharged battery.

4. Attach one end of the remaining cable to the negative (−) terminal of the booster battery and the other end to the alternator bracket. Do not attach to the negative terminal of discharged batteries.

5. Start the engine of the vehicle with the booster battery. Start the engine of the vehicle with the discharged battery. If the engine will not start, disconnect the batteries as soon as possible. If this is not done, the two batteries will soon reach a state of equilibrium, with both too weak to start an engine. This will not be a problem if the engine of the booster vehicle is kept running fast enough. Lengthy cranking can also overheat and damage the starter.

6. Reverse the above steps to disconnect the booster and discharged batteries. Be certain to remove negative connections first.

7. Reinstall the vent caps. Dispose of the cloths; they may have battery acid on them.

JACKING AND HOISTING

The jack supplied with the Corvette was meant for changing tires. It was not meant to support a vehicle while you crawl under it and work. Whenever it is necessary to get under a vehicle to perform service operations, always be sure that it is adequately

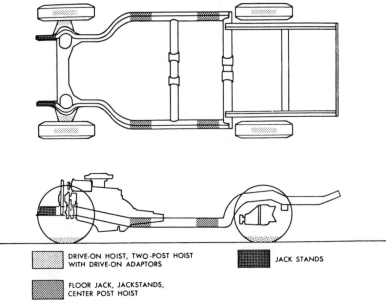

DRIVE-ON HOIST, TWO-POST HOIST WITH DRIVE-ON ADAPTORS

JACK STANDS

FLOOR JACK, JACKSTANDS, CENTER POST HOIST

Jacking and hoisting points

supported, preferably by jackstands at the proper points. Always block the wheels when changing tires.

Since the Corvette is equipped with a Positraction rear axle, do not run the engine for any reason with one rear wheel off the ground. Power will be transmitted through the rear wheel remaining on the ground, possibly causing the vehicle to drive itself off the jack.

Some of the service operations in this book require that one or both ends of the vehicle be raised and supported safely. The best arrangement for this, of course, is a grease pit or a vehicle lift, but these items are seldom found in the home garage. However, small hydraulic, screw, or scissors jacks are satisfactory for raising the vehicle.

Heavy wooden blocks or adjustable jackstands should be used to support the vehicle while it is being worked on. Drive-on trestles, or ramps, are also a handy and a safe way to raise the vehicle, assuming their capacity is adequate. These can be bought or constructed from suitable heavy timbers or steel.

In any case, it is always best to spend a little extra time to make sure that your Corvette is lifted and supported safely.

CAUTION: *Concrete blocks are not recommended. They may crumble if the load is not evenly distributed. Boxes and milk crates of any description must not be used.*

Tune-Up

T2

TUNE-UP PROCEDURES

This section gives specific procedures on how to tune-up your Corvette. It is intended to be as complete and as basic as possible. Those who are familiar with the steps involved in a tune-up may wish to skip the following procedures and use the generalized section in chapter 11. However, it is felt that nothing would be lost by first reading over this section. Perhaps the best procedure to follow would be to read both sections before starting your tune-up.

Spark Plugs

A typical spark plug consists of a metal shell surrounding a ceramic insulator. A metal electrode extends downward through the center of the insulator and protrudes a small distance. Located at the end of the plug and attached to the side of the outer metal shell is the side electrode. The side electrode bends in at a 90° angle so that its tip is even with, and parallel to, the tip of the center electrode. The distance between these two electrodes (measured in thousandths of an inch) is called the spark plug gap. The spark plug in no way produces a spark but merely provides a gap across which the current can arc. The coil produces anywhere from 20,000 to 40,000 volts which travels to the distributor where it is distributed through the spark plug wires to the spark plugs. The current passes along the center electrode and jumps the gap to the side electrode, and, in so doing, ignites the air/fuel mixture in the combustion chamber.

SPARK PLUG HEAT RANGE

Spark plug heat range is the ability of the plug to dissipate heat. The longer the insulator (or the farther it extends into the engine), the hotter the plug will operate; the shorter the insulator the cooler it will operate. A plug that absorbs little heat and remains too cool will quickly accumulate deposits of oil and carbon since it is not hot enough to burn them off. This leads to plug fouling and consequently to misfiring. A plug that absorbs too much heat will have no deposits, but, due to the excessive heat, the electrodes will burn away quickly and in some instances, preignition may result. Preignition takes place when plug tips get so hot that they glow sufficiently to ignite the fuel/air mixture before the actual spark occurs. This early ignition will usually cause a pinging during low speeds and heavy loads.

The general rule of thumb for choosing the correct heat range when picking a spark plug is: if most of your driving is long distance,

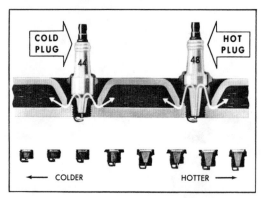

Spark plug heat range, the higher the number the hotter the plug (© Chevrolet Motor Division)

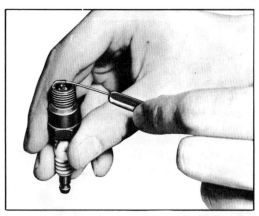

Check the gap with a round wire gauge (© Chevrolet Motor Division)

high speed travel, use a colder plug; if most of your driving is stop and go, use a hotter plug. Original equipment plugs are compromise plugs, but most people never have occasion to change their plugs from the factory-recommended heat range.

REPLACING SPARK PLUGS

A set of spark plugs usually requires replacement after about 10,000 miles on cars with conventional ignition systems and after about 20,000 to 30,000 miles on cars with electronic ignition, depending on your style of driving. In normal operation, plug gap increases about 0.001 in. for every 1,000–2,500 miles. As the gap increases, the plug's voltage requirement also increases. It requires a greater voltage to jump the wider gap and about two to three times as much voltage to fire a plug at high speeds than at idle.

When you're removing spark plugs, you should work on one at a time. Don't start by removing the plug wires all at once, because unless you number them, they may become mixed up. Take a minute before you begin and number the wires with tape. The best location for numbering is near where the wires come out of the cap.

1. Twist the spark plug boot and remove the boot and wire from the plug. Do not pull on the wire itself as this will ruin the wire.

2. If possible, use a brush or rag to clean the area around the spark plug. Make sure that all the dirt is removed so that none will enter the cylinder after the plug is removed.

3. Remove the spark plug using the proper size socket. ($^{13}/_{16}$ in. through 1971, ⅝ in. 1972 and later.) Turn the socket counterclockwise to remove the plug. Be sure to hold the socket straight on the plug to avoid

breaking the plug, or rounding off the hex on the plug.

4. Once the plug is out, check it against the plugs shown in chapter 11 to determine engine condition. This is crucial since plug readings are vital signs of engine condition.

5. Use a round wire feeler gauge to check the plug gap. The correct size gauge should pass through the electrode gap with a slight drag. If you're in doubt, try one size smaller and one larger. The smaller gauge should go through easily while the larger one shouldn't go through at all. If the gap is incorrect, use the electrode bending tool on the end of the gauge to adjust the gap. When adjusting the gap, always bend the side electrode. The center electrode is non-adjustable.

6. Squirt a drop of penetrating oil on the threads of the new plug and install it. Don't oil the threads too heavily. Turn the plug in clockwise by hand until it is snug.

7. When the plug is finger tight, tighten it with a wrench.

8. Install the plug boot firmly over the plug. Proceed to the next plug.

CHECKING AND REPLACING SPARK PLUG CABLES

Visually inspect the spark plug cables for burns, cuts, or breaks in the insulation. Check the spark plug boots and the nipples on the distributor cap and coil. Replace any damaged wiring. If no physical damage is obvious, the wires can be checked with an ohmmeter for excessive resistance. (See the tune-up and troubleshooting section.)

When installing a new set of spark plug cables, replace the cables one at a time so there will be no mixup. Start by replacing the longest cable first. Install the boot firmly

Tune-Up Specifications

| Year | Model | Spark Plugs | | Distributor | | Basic Ignition Timing (deg) | Valves Clearance (in.) | | Intake Opening (deg) | Idle Speed (rpm) | Normal Fuel Pressure (psi) |
		Type	Gap (in.)	Point Dwell (deg)	Point Gap (in.)		Intake	Exhaust			
1963	250 hp	44	0.035	28–32	0.019	4B	①	①	32½B	475②	5¼–6½
	300 hp	44	0.035	28–32	0.019	8B	①	①	32½B	475②	5¼–6½
	340 hp	44	0.035	28–32	0.019	10B	0.008	0.018	35B	750	5¼–6½
	360 hp	44	0.035	28–32	0.019	10B	0.008	0.018	35B	850	5¼–6½
1964	250 hp	44	0.035	28–32	0.019	4B	①	①	32½B	500②	5¼–6½
	300 hp	44	0.035	28–32	0.019	8B	①	①	32½B	500②	5¼–6½
	365 hp	44	0.035	28–32	0.019	10B	0.030	0.030	60½B	800	5¼–6½
	375 hp	44	0.035	28–32	0.019	10B	0.030	0.030	60½B	800	5¼–6½
1965	250 hp	44	0.035	28–32	0.019	4B	①	①	32½B	500②	5¼–6½
	300 hp	44	0.035	28–32	0.019	8B	①	①	32½B	500②	5¼–6½
	350 hp	44	0.035	28–32	0.019	8B	①	①	54B	750	5¼–6½
	365 hp	44	0.035	28–32	0.019	12B	0.030	0.030	60½B	850	6½–7½
	375 hp	44	0.035	28–32	0.019	12B	0.030	0.030	60B	850	6½–7½
	425 hp	43N	0.035	28–32	0.019	10B	0.020	0.024	54B	800	7½

Tune-Up Specifications (cont.)

Year	Model	Spark Plugs		Distributor		Basic Ignition Timing (deg)	Valves		Intake Opening (deg)	Idle Speed (rpm)	Normal Fuel Pressure (psi)
		Type	Gap (in.)	Point Dwell (deg)	Point Gap (in.)		Clearance (in.)				
							Intake	Exhaust			
1966	300 hp	44	0.035	28-32	0.019	8B③	①	①	32½B	500②	6
	350 hp	44	0.035	28-32	0.019	10B	①	①	54B	750	6
	390 hp	43N	0.035	28-32	0.019	4B	①	①	58B	600	6
	425 hp	43N	0.035	28-32	0.019	8B	0.020	0.024	54B	800	6
1967	300 hp	44	0.035	28-32	0.019	6B④	①	①	38B	500⑤	5-6½
	350 hp	44	0.035	28-32	0.019	10B	①	①	54B	700⑤	5-6½
	390 hp	43N	0.035	28-32	0.019	4B	①	①	56B	550⑤	5-6½
	400 hp	43N	0.035	28-32	0.019	4B	①	①	56B	550⑤	5-6½
	435 hp	43N	0.035	28-32	0.019	5B	0.024	0.028	44B	750⑥	5-6½
	430 hp	C42N	0.035	28-32	0.019	12B	0.022	0.024	54B	1000	5-6½
1968	300 hp	44	0.035	28-32	0.019	4B	①	①	28B	700⑦	5-6½
	350 hp	44	0.035	28-32	0.019	4B	①	①	54B	700⑦	5-6½
	390 hp	43N	0.035	28-32	0.019	4B	①	①	56B	700⑦	5-8½

Year	hp										
	400 hp	43N	0.035	28–32	0.019	4B	①	①	56B	750⑦	5–8½
	435 hp	43N	0.035	28–32	0.019	4B	0.024	0.028	44B	750	5–8½
	430 hp	C42N	0.035	28–32	0.019	12B	0.022	0.024	62B	1000	5–8½
1969	300 hp	R44	0.035	28–32	0.019	TDC⑧	①	①	28B	700⑦	5–6½
	350 hp	R44	0.035	28–32	0.019	4B	①	①	52B	750	5–6½
	390 hp	R43N	0.035	28–32	0.019	4B	①	①	56B	800⑦	5–8½
	400 hp	R43N	0.035	28–32	0.019	4B	①	①	56B	800⑦	5–8½
	435 hp	R43N	0.035	28–32	0.019	4B	0.024	0.024	44B	750	5–8½
	430 hp	C42N	0.035	28–32	0.019	12B	0.022	0.024	62B	1000	5–8½
1970	300 hp	R44	0.035	28–32	0.019	TDC⑧	①	①	28B	700⑦	5–6½
	350 hp	R44	0.035	28–32	0.019	4B	①	①	52B	750	5–6½
	370 hp	R43	0.035	Transistor Ignition		14B	0.024	0.030	43B	750	5–6½
	390 hp	R43T	0.035	28–32	0.019	6B	①	①	56B	700⑦	5–8½
	460 hp	R43T	0.035	Transistor Ignition		14B	0.024	0.028	62B	700	5–8½
1971	270 hp	R44TS	0.035	28–32	0.019	4B⑨	①	①	28B	600⑩	7½–9

Tune-Up Specifications (cont.)

Year	Model	Spark Plugs		Distributor		Basic Ignition Timing (deg)	Valves Clearance (in.)		Intake Opening (deg)	Idle Speed (rpm)	Normal Fuel Pressure (psi)
		Type	Gap (in.)	Point Dwell (deg)	Point Gap (in.)		Intake	Exhaust			
1971	330 hp	R43TS	0.035	Transistor Ignition		8B⑪	0.024	0.030	43B	700	7½–9
	365 hp	R43TS	0.035	28–32	0.019	8B	①	①	56B	600	7½–9
	425 hp	R44	0.035	Transistor Ignition		8B	0.024	0.028	44B	700	7½–9
1972	200 hp	R44T	0.035	29–31	0.019	8B	①	①	28B	800⑦	7½–9
	255 hp	R44T	0.035	29–31	0.019	4B	0.024	0.030	43B	900	7½–9
	270 hp	R44T	0.035	28–30	0.019	8B	①	①	56B	750⑦	7½–9
1973	190 hp	R44T	0.035	29–31	0.019	12B	①	①	28B⑫	900⑦⑭	7½–9
	250 hp	R44T	0.035	29–31	0.019	8B	①	①	52B	900⑤⑭	7½–9
	270 hp	R44T	0.035	29–31	0.019	10B	①	①	55B	900⑦⑭	7½–9
1974	195 hp	R44T	0.035	29–31	0.019	8B⑬	①	①	28B⑫	900⑦	7½–9
	250 hp	R44T	0.035	29–31	0.019	8B	①	①	52B	900⑤	7½–9
	270 hp	R44T	0.035	29–31	0.019	10B	①	①	55B	800⑦	7½–9

Year	hp	Spark Plug	Gap (in.)	Distributor									
1975–76	165 hp	R44TX	0.060	Electronic	6B	[1]	[1]	6B	[1]	[1]	28B	800[7]	7½-9
	205 hp	R44TX	0.060	Electronic	12B	[1]	[1]	12B	[1]	[1]	52B	900[5]	7½-9
1977	180 hp	R45TS	0.045	Electronic	8B	[15]	[15]	8B	[15]	[15]	28B	800[10]	7½-9
	210 hp	R45TS	0.045	Electronic	12B	[15]	[15]	12B	[15]	[15]	52B	900[16]	7½-9
1978	185 hp	R45TS	0.045	Electronic	6B[17]	Zero	Zero	6B[17]	Zero	Zero	28B	[18]	7½-9
	220 hp	R45TS	0.045	Electronic	12B	Zero	Zero	12B	Zero	Zero	52B	[18]	7½-9
1979	195 hp	R45TS	0.045	Electronic	6B[17]	Zero	Zero	6B[17]	Zero	Zero	28B	[18]	7½-9
	225 hp	R45TS	0.045	Electronic	12B	Zero	Zero	12B	Zero	Zero	52B	[18]	7½-9

[1] Hydraulic lifters—one turn down from zero lash
[2] 450 rpm auto trans
[3] 2°A with auto trans
[4] W/auto trans and A.I.R.—4°A
[5] W/Auto trans and A.I.R.—700 rpm
[6] W/auto trans and A.I.R.—750 rpm
[7] W/auto trans—600 rpm
[8] W/auto trans—4°B
[9] W/auto trans—8°B
[10] W/auto trans—550 rpm
[11] W/auto trans—12°B
[12] California—44°B
[13] California—4°B
[14] 450 rpm with idle solenoid disconnected
[15] Hydraulic lifters—¾ turn down from zero lash
[16] W/auto trans—750 rpm
[17] W/auto trans—Calif.—8°B
[18] Use the specification given on the tune-up sticker under the hood

NOTE: If specifications on the tune-up sticker under the hood differ from those given above, the sticker specifications take precedence.

NOTE: Part numbers listed in this reference are not recommendations by Chilton for any product by brand name.

over the spark plug. Route the wire exactly the same as the original. Insert the nipple firmly into the tower on the distributor cap. Repeat the process for each cable.

NOTE: *Always replace the points and condenser as a unit. Uniset® points are available which combine the point set and condenser, greatly simplifying installation.*

Breaker Points and Condenser
REMOVAL AND REPLACEMENT

Point alignment is preset at the factory and requires no adjustment. Point sets using the push-in type wiring terminal should be used on those distributors equipped with an R.F.I. (radio frequency interference) shield (1970–74). Points using a lockscrew type terminal may short out due to the shield contacting the screw.

NOTE: *The optional magnetic pulse distributor and the HEI (High Energy Ignition) system used on some 1974 and all 1975–79 models requires no maintenance other than checking the condition of the cap and wires. There are no points to wear out or adjust.*

1. Remove the distributor cap. Remove the ignition shield.
2. Remove the rotor.
3. If so equipped, remove the two-piece R.F.I. shield.
4. Loosen the two mounting screws and slide the contact point set from the breaker plate.
5. Remove the primary and condenser leads from the terminal.
6. Loosen the condenser bracket screw and slide the condenser from the bracket.
7. Install the new point set and condenser and then tighten the mounting screws.
8. Install the wires to the terminal so that they will not interfere with the cap, weight base, or breaker advance plate. Install the half of the R.F.I. shield which covers the points first.
9. Using a ⅛ in. allen wrench, make an initial point setting of 0.019 in.
10. The cam lubricator (if so equipped) must be replaced after 12 months or 12,000 miles. The end of the lubricator should be adjusted to just touch the cam lobes. Additional grease should not be applied to the lubricator.
11. Install the rotor. The two lugs on the bottom of the rotor are shaped differently, so

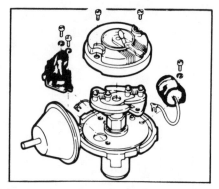

Point set and condenser mounting

that it can only be installed one way. Tighten the screws. Start the engine and check the point dwell and the ignition timing.

Dwell Angle

Dwell angle is the amount of time (measured in degrees of distributor cam rotation) that the contact points remain closed. Initial point gap (0.019 in.) determines dwell angle. If the points are too wide they open gradually and dwell angle (the time they remain closed) is small. This wide gap causes excessive arcing at the points and, because of this, point burning. This small dwell doesn't give the coil sufficient time to build up maximum energy and so coil output decreases. If the points are set too close, the dwell is increased but the points may bounce at higher speeds and the idle becomes rough and starting is made harder. The wider the point opening, the smaller the dwell and the smaller the gap, the larger the dwell. Adjusting the dwell by making the initial point gap setting with a feeler gauge is sufficient to get the car started but a finer adjustment should be made. A

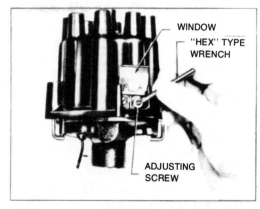

Adjusting point gap (dwell angle) with ⅛ in. allen wrench

dwell meter is needed to check the adjustment.

1. Run the engine to normal operating temperatures and then let it idle.

2. Raise the adjusting window on the distributor cap and insert a ⅛ in. allen wrench into the adjusting screw.

3. Turn the adjusting screw until the specified dwell angle is obtained on the dwell meter.

HEI SYSTEM TACHOMETER HOOKUP

Connect one tach lead to the "TACH" terminal on the side of the distributor and the other to ground. Some tachometers must be connected to the "TACH" terminal and the battery positive terminal. Not all tachometers will operate correctly with the HEI system. Check with the manufacturer if there is any doubt.

CAUTION: *The "TACH" terminal should never be connected to ground.*

When hooking up a remote starter switch, disconnect the "BATT" terminal.

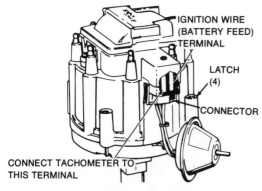

Hook up one tach lead to the tachometer terminal on the HEI system

Ignition Timing
ADJUSTMENT

1. Disconnect and plug the distributor vacuum advance hose.

2. Start the engine and run it at idle speed.

3. Connect the timing light and, with the engine running at an idle, aim it at the timing tab on the front engine cover.

NOTE: *It may be necessary to clean off the tab and slash mark on the crankshaft pulley before proceeding any further. To further improve visibility, take a piece of chalk and fill in the slash mark on the crankshaft pulley. The "0" marking on the*

Timing mark location

tab is TDC and all the BTDC (before top dead center) settings are on the "before" (advance) side of the "0" or the "A" (advance) side of the "0." Later models are marked to indicate Before and After.

4. Loosen the distributor clamp bolt and turn the distributor until the slash on the crankshaft pulley lines up with the specified timing mark on the tab. Once the timing is correct, tighten the distributor clamp bolt and recheck the timing.

5. Turn off the engine, remove the timing light, and connect the vacuum advance hose.

NOTE: *Since dwell is electronically controlled on HEI distributors, adjusting the ignition timing is no longer necessary as part of the normal tune-up procedure. However, if you suspect the timing is off, you can check and adjust the timing in the same manner as a conventioal distributor. Cars with HEI distributors require an inductive pickup style timing light, however.*

Valve Lash

Normalize the engine temperature by running it for approximately twenty minutes. Shut the engine off and remove the valve covers. Removal of the left valve cover on fuel-injection models requires that the air cleaner hose, air meter adapter, and pyrometer housing be removed first. Keep the screws and reinforcements together for ease of installation. After valve cover removal, torque the cylinder heads to specification. The use of oil stopper clips, readily available on the aftermarket, is highly recommended

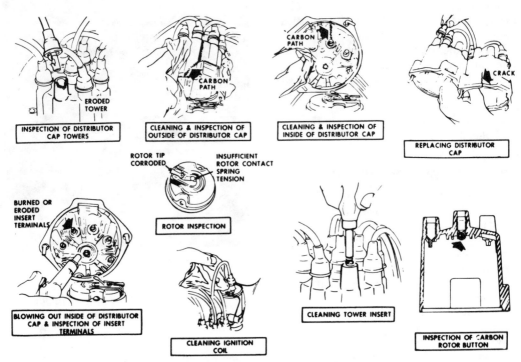

INSPECTION OF DISTRIBUTOR CAP TOWERS

CLEANING & INSPECTION OF OUTSIDE OF DISTRIBUTOR CAP

CLEANING & INSPECTION OF INSIDE OF DISTRIBUTOR CAP

REPLACING DISTRIBUTOR CAP

ROTOR TIP CORRODED   INSUFFICIENT ROTOR CONTACT SPRING TENSION

ROTOR INSPECTION

BURNED OR ERODED INSERT TERMINALS

BLOWING OUT INSIDE OF DISTRIBUTOR CAP & INSPECTION OF INSERT TERMINALS

CLEANING IGNITION COIL

CLEANING TOWER INSERT

INSPECTION OF CARBON ROTOR BUTTON

Distributor cap and rotor checkpoints

to prevent oil splatter. Restart the engine. Valve lash is set on both solid and hydraulic-lifter Corvettes with the engine warm and idling.

On solid-lifter Corvettes, use a feeler gauge of the thickness specified for the valve lash. Turn the rocker arm stud nut until the correct lash is achieved. On Corvettes with hydraulic lifters, turn the rocker arm nut counterclockwise until the rocker arm starts to clatter. Reverse the direction and turn the

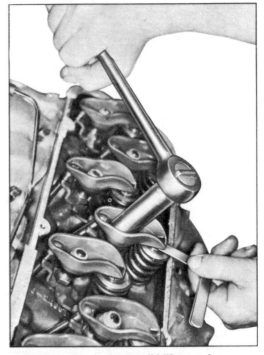

Adjusting valve lash on solid lifter engine

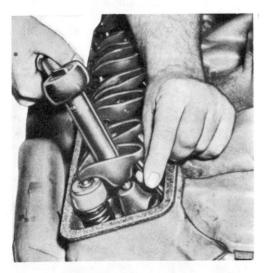

Adjusting valve lash on hydraulic lifter engine

rocker arm down slowly until the clatter just stops. This is the zero lash position. Turn the nut down ¼ additional turn and wait ten seconds until the engine runs smoothly. Continue with additional ¼ turns, waiting ten seconds each time, until the nut has been turned down one full turn from the zero lash position. This one turn, preload adjustment must be done slowly to allow the lifter to adjust itself and prevent possible interference between the intake valve head and the top of the piston. Such interference could cause internal engine damage and/or bent pushrods. Noisy lifters should be cleaned or replaced.

Idle Speed and Mixture Adjustment

Idle mixture and speed adjustments are critical aspects of exhaust emission control. It is important that all tune-up instructions be carefully followed to ensure satisfactory engine performance and minimum exhaust pollution. The different combinations of emission systems application on the different engine models have resulted in a great variety of tune-up specifications. See the "Tune-Up Specifications" chart at the beginning of this chapter. Beginning in 1968, all models have a decal conspicuously placed in the engine compartment giving tune-up specifications.

When adjusting a carburetor with two idle mixture screws, adjust them alternately and evenly, unless otherwise stated.

In the following adjustment procedures the term "lean roll" means turning the mixture adjusting screws in (clockwise) from optimum setting to obtain an obvious drop in engine speed (usually 20 rpm).

1963–67 WITHOUT A.I.R.

Adjust with air cleaner removed.

1. Connect a tachometer and vacuum gauge to the engine, then set the parking brake and shift the manual transmission into Neutral, automatic into Drive.

2. Turn the idle mixture screw(s) in until lightly seated, then back out 1½ turns.

3. With engine running, adjust the idle speed screw to obtain the specified rpm.

4. Adjust the idle mixture screw(s) to obtain the highest steady manifold vacuum at the specified speed. If necessary, reset the idle speed screw while adjusting mixture.

NOTE: *On air conditioned models, the air conditioner is turned on and the hot idle compensator valve is held closed while adjusting idle speed and mixture.*

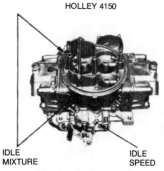

Holley 4150 idle mixture and speed adjustment screws

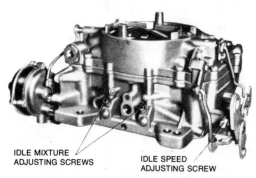

Carter WCFB idle mixture and speed adjustment screws

Carter AFB idle mixture and speed adjustment screws

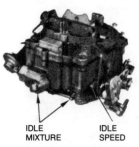

Rochester Quadrajet idle mixture and speed adjustment screws

5. Final adjustment should be made with the air cleaner installed.

6. Remove tachometer and vacuum gauge.

1966–67 WITH A.I.R.

Adjust with air cleaner removed.

1. Connect a tachometer to the engine, place manual transmission in Neutral, automatic in Drive.

2. Turn idle mixture screw(s) in until lightly seated, then back out 3 turns.

3. With engine running, adjust the idle speed screw to obtain the specified idle speed.

4. Adjust the idle mixture screw(s) in to "lean roll" position, then back them out (rich) ¼ turn. Readjust the idle speed screw to keep the engine at the specified idle speed while adjusting the mixture.

NOTE: *On air conditioned cars, turn the air conditioner off with 327 cu in. engines. Air conditioner must be on and hot idle compensator held closed with 427 cu in. engines.*

5. Final adjustment should be made with the air cleaner installed.

6. Remove the tachometer.

1968–69

Adjust with air cleaner installed.

1. Turn the idle mixture screw(s) in until lightly seated, then back out 3 turns.

2. With engine at operating temperature, adjust idle speed screw to obtain specified rpm, manual transmission in Neutral and automatic in Drive.

NOTE: *On all 1968 models except 350 H.P. 327 cu. in. with manual transmission, the air conditioner is turned off. On the above-mentioned vehicles the air condi-*

tioner is left on. On 1969 models, turn the air conditioner either on or off according to the instructions on the tune-up decal.

3. Adjust one idle mixture screw to obtain the highest steady idle speed.

4. Adjust the idle speed screw to the speed specified on the tune-up decal.

NOTE: *On models equipped with an idle solenoid, adjust the solenoid plunger hex to obtain 600 rpm. Disconnect the wire at the solenoid to deenergize it, allowing the throttle lever to contact the carburetor idle speed screw. Adjust the carburetor idle screw to obtain 400 rpm.*

5. Adjust the mixture screw in to "lean roll" position, then back out (rich) ¼ turn.

6. Repeat Steps 3, 4 and 5 for the other idle mixture screw.

7. Readjust the idle speed screw to obtain final specified rpm, if necessary.

1970

Adjust with air cleaner installed.

If the vehicle is equipped with Evaporative Emission, disconnect the fuel tank line from the vapor canister while making the idle speed and mixture adjustments. Warm up the engine and leave it running while adjusting. The choke valve and, if applicable, air cleaner damper door should remain open. Leave the air conditioning off.

350 (300, 350 and 370 H.P.) Engines

1. Adjust the idle mixture screws equally to obtain maximum idle speed.

2. On the 300 H.P. engine with manual transmission in Neutral adjust the idle speed screw to obtain 700 rpm. On the 300 H.P. engine with automatic transmission in Drive, adjust the idle speed screw to obtain 600 rpm.

3. On the 350 and 370 H.P. engines, adjust the idle speed screw to obtain 750 rpm with the manual transmission in Neutral.

454 (450 H.P.) Engine

1. Remove the air cleaner.

2. Disconnect the distributor vacuum hose at the distributor and plug the hose.

3. Adjust the mixture screws for maximum idle speed.

4. With manual transmission in Neutral, adjust the carburetor idle speed screw to obtain 750 rpm. With automatic transmission in Drive, adjust the carburetor idle speed screw to obtain 700 rpm.

5. Turn one idle mixture screw to obtain a

HOLLEY 2300C (PRIMARY)

IDLE
MIXTURE

IDLE
SPEED

Holley 2300 idle mixture and speed adjustment screws

20 rpm drop in idle speed, then back the screw out ¼ turn. Repeat for the second idle mixture screw.

6. Repeat Step 4 above.

7. Reconnect the distributor vacuum hose and install the air cleaner.

454 (345 H.P.) and 454 (390 H.P.) Engines

1. Disconnect the distributor vacuum hose at the distributor and plug the hose.

2. Turn the idle mixture screws in until they are lightly seated, then back them out 4 turns.

3. With automatic transmission in Drive, adjust the carburetor idle speed screw to obtain 630 rpm. Adjust the idle mixture screws in equally to obtain 600 rpm.

4. With manual transmission in Neutral, adjust the carburetor idle speed screw to obtain 700 rpm. Turn one of the mixture screws in until the engine speed drops to 400 rpm. Readjust the idle speed screw to obtain 700 rpm. Turn in the other mixture screw until the engine speed drops 40 rpm. Readjust the idle speed screw to obtain 700 rpm.

5. Reconnect the distributor vacuum hose.

1971

Adjust with air cleaner installed.

The following initial idle adjustments are part of the normal engine tune-up. There is a tune-up decal placed conspicuously in the engine compartment outlining the specific procedure and settings for each engine application. Follow all of the instructions when adjusting the idle. These tuning procedures are necessary to obtain the delicate balance of variables for the maintenance of both reliable engine performance and efficient exhaust emission control.

NOTE: *All engines except the 350 (330 H.P.) and 454 (425 H.P.) have limiter caps*

IDLE SPEED (SOLENOID) SCREW

Rochester Quadrajet (with idle solenoid) idle speed screw

on the mixture-adjusting screws. The idle mixture is preset and the limiter caps installed at the factory in order to meet emission control standards. Do not remove these limiter caps unless all other possible causes of poor idle condition have been thoroughly checked out.

The solenoid used on 1971 carburetors is different from the one used on earlier models. Combination Emission Control System (C.E.C. solenoid) valve regulates distributor vacuum as a function of transmission gear position.

CAUTION: *The C.E.C. solenoid is adjusted only after: 1) replacement of the solenoid, 2) major carburetor overhaul, or 3) after the throttle body is removed or replaced.*

All initial adjustments described below are made:

1. With the engine warmed up and running.

2. With the choke fully open.

3. With the fuel tank gas cap removed.

4. With the vacuum hose disconnected at the distributor and plugged.

IDLE MIXTURE

SOLENOID SCREW

CARBURETOR (IDLE SPEED) SCREW

Holley 4150 (with idle solenoid) idle mixture and speed adjustment locations

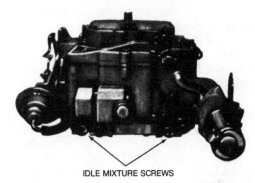

IDLE MIXTURE SCREWS

Rochester Quadrajet (with idle solenoid) idle mixture screws

Be sure to reconnect the distributor vacuum hose and to connect the fuel tank to evaporative emission canister line or install the gas cap when idle adjustments are complete.

350 (4-BBL Quadrajet) Engines

Adjust the carburetor idle speed screw (NOT the solenoid plunger) to obtain 600 rpm (manual transmission in Neutral with the air conditioner off) or 550 rpm (automatic transmission in Drive with the air conditioner on).

350 and 454 (4-BBL Holley) Engines

1. Adjust the carburetor idle speed screw (NOT the solenoid plunger) to obtain 700 rpm (manual transmission in Neutral or automatic transmission in Drive).

2. Adjust the idle mixture screws alternately to obtain the maximum smooth idle speed.

3. Adjust one of the idle mixture screws to obtain a 20 rpm drop ("lean roll"), then back it out ¼ turn.

4. Repeat Step 4 above for the other idle mixture screw.

5. Readjust the carburetor idle speed screw to obtain 700 rpm if necessary.

454 (4-BBL Quadrajet) Engines

Turn the air conditioner off. Adjust the carburetor idle speed screw (NOT the solenoid plunger) to obtain 600 rpm (manual transmission in Neutral or automatic transmission in Drive).

1972

NOTE: *All carburetors are equipped with idle limiter caps and idle mixture is preset at the factory and should not require adjustment.*

1. Remove the fuel filler cap but do not remove the vapor line.

2. Detach the distributor vacuum hose and plug the hose.

3. Set the parking brake and turn the air conditioner (if so equipped) off. On cars equipped with an automatic transmission, check the wheels.

4. Allow the engine to reach normal operating temperature. Be sure that the choke is open.

5. If the car has an automatic transmission, set the selector in Drive. If the car has a manual transmission keep the transmission in Neutral.

6. Adjust the anti-dieseling solenoid to the *higher* of the two rpm figures given in the specifications.

CAUTION: *Do not turn the solenoid more than one complete turn unless the electrical lead is disconnected (solenoid deenergized).*

7. Disconnect the solenoid lead and set the idle speed to the *lower* of the two figures given in the specifications. Use the normal idle speed adjusting screw.

NOTE: *If no lower figure is given, adjust the idle to 450 rpm.*

8. Reconnect all of the wires and hoses which were disconnected in order to perform these adjustments.

1973

All models are equipped with idle limiter caps and idle solenoids. Disconnect the fuel tank line from the evaporative canister. The engine must be running at operating temperature, choke off, parking brake on, and rear wheels blocked. Disconnect the distributor vacuum hose and plug it. After adjustment, reconnect the vacuum and evaporative hoses.

Four-barrel 350 and 454 cu in. V8s

1. Adjust the idle stop solenoid screw for 900 rpm on manual, 600 rpm on automatic.

2. Connect the distributor vacuum hose and position the fast idle cam follower on the top step of the fast idle cam (turn air conditioning off) and adjust the fast idle to 1300 rpm on manual transmission 350 engines; 1600 on manual 454 engines and all automatics (in Park).

Optional 350 cu in. (L82) V8

1. Adjust the idle stop solenoid screw (air conditioning off) for a speed of 900 rpm on manual transmission; 700 rpm on automatic (in Drive).

2. Connect the distributor vacuum hose and position the fast idle cam follower on the top step of the cam (turn air conditioning off) and adjust the fast idle to 1300 rpm on manual; 1600 rpm on automatic.

1974

The same preconditions as for 1973 apply.

Four-barrel 350 cu in. V8

1. Turn the air conditioning off. Adjust the idle stop solenoid screw for 900 rpm on man-

ual transmission models; 600 rpm on automatic (in Drive).

2. Connect the distributor vacuum hose. Position the fast idle cam follower on the top step of the fast idle cam and adjust the fast idle speed to 1300 rpm on manual; 1600 on automatic (in Park).

Optional 350 cu in. (L82) V8

1. Turn the air conditioning off. Adjust the idle stop solenoid for 900 rpm on manual; 700 rpm on automatic (in Drive).

2. Connect the distributor vacuum hose. Position the fast idle cam follower on the top step of the cam and adjust the fast idle to 1300 rpm on manual; 1600 rpm on automatic (in Park).

454 cu in. V8

1. Shut off the air conditioning. Adjust the idle stop solenoid screw for 800 rpm on manual; 600 rpm on automatic (in Drive).

2. Connect the distributor vaccuum hose and position the fast idle cam follower on the top step of the cam and adjust the fast idle to 1600 rpm on manual; 1500 rpm on automatic (in Park).

1975–76

The same preconditions as for 1973 apply.

1. Turn the air conditioning off.

2. Disconnect the idle speed solenoid. Turn the idle speed screw to adjust for the lower of the two idle speeds specified on the underhood tune-up decal. Adjust automatic transmission cars in Drive with wheels blocked; manual transmission cars in Neutral.

3. Connect the idle speed solenoid. Open the throttle to extend the solenoid plunger.

4. Use the solenoid plunger to adjust the idle speed to the higher of the two speeds on the underhood tune-up decal.

1977-IDLE SPEED

Run the engine to normal operating temperature, A/C off, vacuum advance line disconnected and plugged, FUEL TANK line at the canister disconnected. Place the manual transmission in neutral; automatic transmission in drive. Connect a tachometer to the engine.

NOTE: *Make sure the parking brake is on and the drive wheels are sufficiently blocked when placing the transmission in drive.*

Without A/C

1. Turn the idle speed screw to achieve the rpm specified on the underhood tune-up decal.

With A/C.

1. Turn the idle speed screw to the lower of the two idle speeds specified on the underhood tune-up decal.

2. Turn the A/C system on.

3. Disconnect the A/C compressor lead at the compressor.

4. Open the throttle slightly to allow the solenoid plunger to fully extend.

5. Turn the solenoid screw to higher of the two idle speeds specified on the underhood tune-up decal.

6. Reconnect the A/C compressor lead.

1977-IDLE MIXTURE

NOTE: *Idle mixture screws have been pre-set at the factory and capped and should not require adjustment, however if the need arises follow the procedure listed below.*

1. Set the parking brake and block the drive wheels.

2. Remove the air cleaner to gain access to the carburetor, but keep the vacuum hoses connected.

3. Run the engine to normal operating temperature with the choke open.

4. Turn the A/C off.

5. Disconnect and plug the vacuum advance hose at the distributor.

6. Check the ignition timing and adjust as necessary.

7. Using a sharp knife, carefully remove the plastic caps from the idle mixture screws. Use extreme caution to avoid bending the mixture screws.

8. Lightly seat the screws then back out equally just enough so the engine will run.

9. Place the automatic transmission in drive or the manual transmission in neutral.

10. Back out each screw (richen) ⅛ turn at a time until the maximum idle speed is obtained. Then set the idle speed screw to: Standard engine (180hp) M.T.-800 rpm, A.T.-550 rpm; Optional engine (210hp) M.T.-900 rpm, A.T. (low altitude) 750 rpm, A.T. (high altitude) 650 rpm.

11. Turn in each screw (lean) ⅛ turn at a time until the idle reaches the following rpm: Standard engine (180hp)-M.T.-700 rpm,

A.T.-500 rpm; Optional engine (210hp)-800 rpm, A.T. (low altitude)-700 rpm, A.T. (high altitude)-600 rpm.

12. Reset the idle speed to specification.

13. Reconnect the vacuum hoses and install the air cleaner.

1978–79 IDLE SPEED

Run the engine to normal operating temperature, A/C off, the purge hose at the vapor canister and the vacuum hose at the EGR valve disconnected and plugged. Place the manual transmission in neutral and the automatic transmission in drive.

NOTE: *Make sure the parking brake is on and the drive wheels are sufficiently blocked when placing the transmission in drive.*

Without A/C

1. Turn the idle speed screw to achieve the rpm specified on the underhood tune-up decal.

With A/C

1. Turn the idle speed screw to the lower of the two idle speeds specified on the underhood tune-up decal.

2. Turn the A/C system on.

3. Disconnect the A/C compressor lead at the compressor.

4. Open the throttle slightly to allow the solenoid plunger to fully extend.

5. Turn the solenoid screw to higher of the two idle speeds specified on the underhood tune-up decal.

6. Reconnect the A/C compressor lead.

1978–79 IDLE MIXTURE

Changes in the idle systems of these models make it impossible to adjust the mixture without the aid of a propane enrichment system, not available to the general public. Backing out of the mixture screw, of itself, will have little or no effect.

Throttle Linkage Adjustment
ALL MODELS EXCEPT THREE, TWO-BARREL CARBURETORS

Adjust the length of the throttle linkage to ensure full opening of the throttle plates. Turn the threaded swivel at the throttle so that with the accelerator pedal fully depressed and the carburetor throttle valve fully open, the threaded swivel will freely enter into the throttle lever. The lever should then be turned two full turns to lengthen the control rod. Corvettes with cable-controlled throttles are adjusted as follows: block the accelerator pedal fully depressed, block the throttle lever fully open, and torque the cable clamp to 45 in. lbs.

THREE, TWO-BARREL CARBURETORS

Loosen the cable clamp, then fully depress the accelerator pedal and fully open the throttle plate of the primary carburetor. Torque the cable clamp bolt to 45 in. lbs.

① PREPARE VEHICLE FOR ADJUSTMENTS

② TURN IDLE SPEED SCREW TO SET CURB IDLE SPEED TO SPECIFICATIONS – A/C OFF

IDLE SPEED ADJUSTMENT - WITHOUT SOLENOID

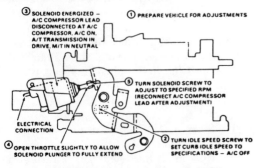

③ SOLENOID ENERGIZED – A/C COMPRESSOR LEAD DISCONNECTED AT A/C COMPRESSOR, A/C ON, A/T TRANSMISSION IN DRIVE, M/T IN NEUTRAL

① PREPARE VEHICLE FOR ADJUSTMENTS

⑤ TURN SOLENOID SCREW TO ADJUST TO SPECIFIED RPM (RECONNECT A/C COMPRESSOR LEAD AFTER ADJUSTMENT)

ELECTRICAL CONNECTION

④ OPEN THROTTLE SLIGHTLY TO ALLOW SOLENOID PLUNGER TO FULLY EXTEND

② TURN IDLE SPEED SCREW TO SET CURB IDLE SPEED TO SPECIFICATIONS – A/C OFF

A/C IDLE SPEED ADJUSTMENT - WITH SOLENOID

Idle speed adjustment (1977–79 M4MC) © Chevrolet Motor Division)

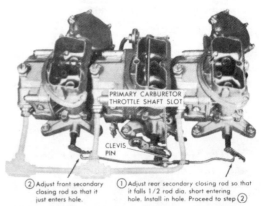

PRIMARY CARBURETOR THROTTLE SHAFT SLOT

CLEVIS PIN

② Adjust front secondary closing rod so that it just enters hole.

① Adjust rear secondary closing rod so that it falls 1/2 rod dia. short entering hole. Install in hole. Proceed to step ②

Three, two-barrel carburetor linkage adjustment

Bring the engine to operating temperature, set the idle to specifications, and turn it off. Bottom the clevis pin in the throttle slot of the primary carburetor and adjust the secondary closing rod of the rear carburetor so that it lacks ½ a rod diameter of being long enough to freely enter the rear secondary throttle hole. Connect the rod. Adjust the forward secondary rod so that it barely enters the throttle lever hole. Connect the rod and check the linkage operation to be sure the plates close completely.

Engine and Engine Rebuilding

ENGINE ELECTRICAL

Distributor

REMOVAL AND INSTALLATION

Remove the ignition shield covering the distributor and coil, and disconnect the tachometer drive cable and fuel injection drive from the distributor housing, if so equipped. Remove the primary coil wire or pick-up coil leads, and the distributor cap. Bring the engine to TDC, firing number one cylinder, and mark the rotor-to-distributor relationship. Remove the vacuum line and the hold-down clamp, and withdraw the distributor. As the distributor is removed, it will rotate the distributor shaft. Mark the new rotor-to-housing relation and set the rotor at that point when installing the distributor. When the distributor is seated, the rotation encountered during gear meshing should return the rotor to the original rotor-to-housing mark. Do not rotate the engine while the distributor is removed.

To install, position the rotor on the second reference mark that indicates the position of the rotor after its removal from the engine. Insert the distributor and replace the clamp; leaving it loose enough to turn the distributor for final timing. Connect the distributor cap, primary coil wires, vacuum lines, and ta-chometer drive. Also connect the fuel injection pump drive-cables when applicable. Time engine and replace the ignition shields.

DISASSEMBLY AND ASSEMBLY

Breaker Type

Two screws secure the rotor. Remove these and the rotor. Remove the primary coil and condenser leads, point set and condenser. Remove the gear cover plate, then tap out the roll pin and remove the distributor shaft drive-gear. Note the number of shims used on the gear. Disconnect the advance weight springs, remove the weights and slide the cam from the mainshaft. Loosen the breaker plate clamp, expand it, and slide the plate from the housing. Reverse the procedure to reassemble.

Breakerless Type

Remove the securing screws and withdraw the rotor. Remove the centrifugal weight springs and weights, and the tachometer drive gear. Tap out the roll pin and slide the distributor drive-gear from the distributor shaft. Remove the drive-shaft assembly, centrifugal weight support, and timer core. Remove the pick-up coil-leads connector and the magnetic-core support-plate retaining ring. Remove the magnetic pick-up assembly

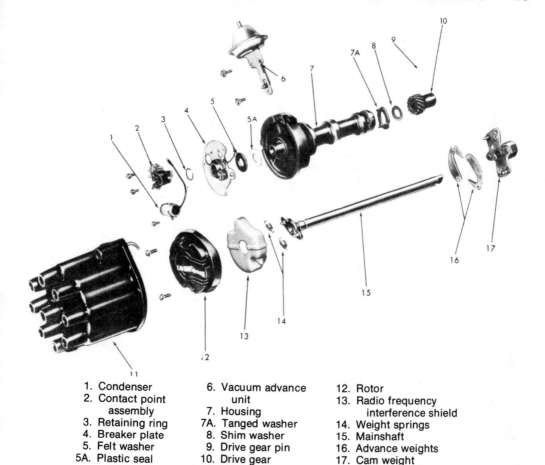

1. Condenser
2. Contact point
   assembly
3. Retaining ring
4. Breaker plate
5. Felt washer
5A. Plastic seal
6. Vacuum advance
   unit
7. Housing
7A. Tanged washer
8. Shim washer
9. Drive gear pin
10. Drive gear
11. Cap
12. Rotor
13. Radio frequency
   interference shield
14. Weight springs
15. Mainshaft
16. Advance weights
17. Cam weight
   base assembly

Exploded view of breaker point distributor

from the housing as one unit. Remove the brass washer and felt gasket, and the vacuum advance unit. Reverse the procedure to reassemble.

High Energy Ignition (HEI) System

The General Motors HEI system is a pulse-triggered, transistored-controlled, inductive discharge ignition system. The entire HEI system is contained within the distributor cap.

The distributor, in addition to housing the mechanical and vacuum advance mechanisms, contains the ignition coil, the electronic control module, and the magnetic triggering device. The magnetic pick-up assembly contains a permanent magnet, a pole piece with internal "teeth," and a pick-up coil (not to be confused with the ignition coil).

In the HEI system, as in other electronic ignition systems, the breaker points have been replaced with an electronic switch—a transistor—which is located *within* the control module. This switching transistor performs the same function the points did in a conventional ignition system; it simply turns coil primary current on and off at the correct time. Essentially then, electronic and conventional ignition systems operate on the same principle.

The module which houses the switching transistor is controlled (turned on and off) by a magnetically generated impulse induced in the pick-up coil. When the teeth of the rotating timer align with the teeth of the pole piece, the induced voltage in the pick-up coil signals the electronic module to open the coil primary circuit. The primary current then decreases, and a high voltage is induced in the ignition coil secondary windings which is then directed through the rotor and high

Distributor Specifications

NOTE: The following specifications are given in degrees advance at crankshaft speed. Half degrees for distributor machine testing.

Year	Model	Distributor Part Number	Centrifugal Advance			Vacuum Advance	
			Start Degrees @ rpm	Intermediate Degrees @ rpm	End Degrees @ rpm	Start Degrees @ in. Hg	End Degrees @ in. Hg
1963–64	All except fuel injection	1111024	0 @ 700	11 @ 1600	24 @ 4600	0 @ 8	15 @ 15.5
	Fuel injection	1111022	0 @ 700	11 @ 700	24 @ 4600	0 @ 8	15 @ 15.5
1965	Base engine	1111076	0 @ 750	15 @ 1500	26 @ 4100	0 @ 4	16.5 @ 8.2
	Special performance	1111069	0 @ 800	NA	24 @ 2350	0 @ 4	16.5 @ 8.2
	Fuel injection	1111070	0 @ 800	NA	24 @ 2350	0 @ 4	16.5 @ 8.2
	Base engine	1111087	0 @ 750	15 @ 1500	30 @ 5100	0 @ 4	16.5 @ 8.2
	Special performance w/transistor ign	1111060	0 @ 800	NA	26 @ 2500	0 @ 4	16.5 @ 8.2
	F.I. w/transistor ign	1111064	0 @ 800	NA	26 @ 2500	0 @ 4	16.5 @ 8.2
1966	300 hp	1111194	0 @ 900	15 @ 1500	30 @ 5100	0 @ 6	15 @ 12
	350 hp	1111438	0 @ 950	20 @ 1800	30 @ 4700	0 @ 8	15 @ 15.5

390 hp	1111293	0 @ 900	8 @ 1250	32 @ 5000	0 @ 7	12 @ 12
350 hp w/tran-sistor ign	1111441	0 @ 900	16.5 @ 1400	30 @ 4400	0 @ 8	15 @ 15.5
390 hp w/tran-sistor ign	1111294	0 @ 900	17 @ 2000	32 @ 5000	0 @ 7	12 @ 12
425 hp	1111170	0 @ 900	17 @ 2000	32 @ 5000	0 @ 7	12 @ 12
1967–68						
300 hp	1111194	0 @ 900	15 @ 1500	30 @ 5100	0 @ 6	15 @ 12
350 hp	1111438	0 @ 950	20 @ 1800	30 @ 4700	0 @ 8	15 @ 15.5
390 hp, 400 hp	1111293	0 @ 900	17 @ 2000	32 @ 5000	0 @ 7	12 @ 12
435 hp	1111296	0 @ 900	NA	30 @ 3800	0 @ 8	15 @ 15.5
430 hp L88	1111295	0 @ 1200	18 @ 1900	30 @ 5000	—	—
350 hp w/tran-sistor ign	1111441	0 @ 900	16.5 @ 1400	30 @ 4400	0 @ 8	15 @ 15.5
390 hp, 400 hp	1111294	0 @ 900	17 @ 2000	32 @ 5000	0 @ 7	12 @ 12
1969						
300 hp	1111490	0 @ 900	15 @ 1500	30 @ 5100	0 @ 8	19 @ 17
350 hp	1111493	0 @ 1000	10 @ 1700	26 @ 5000	0 @ 7	15 @ 12
390 hp, 400 hp	1111926	0 @ 900	17 @ 2000	26 @ 3800	0 @ 7	12 @ 12

Distributor Specifications (cont.)

NOTE: The following specifications are given in degrees advance at crankshaft speed. Half degrees for distributor machine testing.

Year	Model	Distributor Part Number	Centrifugal Advance			Vacuum Advance	
			Start Degrees @ rpm	Intermediate Degrees @ rpm	End Degrees @ rpm	Start Degrees @ in. Hg	End Degrees @ in. Hg
1969	435 hp	1111928	0 @ 900	2 @ 1100	30 @ 3800	0 @ 8	15 @ 15.5
	430 hp L88	1111927	0 @ 1200	16 @ 1900	29 @ 5000	—	—
1970	300 hp	1111490	0 @ 900	15 @ 1500	30 @ 5100	0 @ 8	19 @ 17
	350 hp	1111493	0 @ 1150	10 @ 1700	26 @ 5000	0 @ 8	19 @ 17
	370 hp	1111491	0 @ 1000	NA	26 @ 5000	0 @ 8	15 @ 15.5
	390 hp	1111464	0 @ 1085	17 @ 2100	22 @ 3200	0 @ 7	12 @ 12
	460 hp	1112026	0 @ 1000	NA	21 @ 2300	0 @ 7	12 @ 12
1971	270 hp	1112050	0 @ 1335	11 @ 2400	18 @ 4200	0 @ 8	15 @ 15.5
	330 hp	1112038	0 @ 1330	16 @ 2250	24 @ 5000	0 @ 8	15 @ 15.5
	365 hp	1112051	0 @ 1145	14 @ 2000	22 @ 3000	0 @ 8	20 @ 17
	425 hp w/manual trans	1112076	0 @ 1300	25 @ 2350	31 @ 6000	0 @ 7	12 @ 12

Year	Engine	Part No.					
	425 hp w/auto trans	1112053	0 @ 1310	21 @ 2350	28 @ 5000	0 @ 7	12 @ 12
1972	200 hp	1112050	0 @ 1335	11 @ 2400	18 @ 4200	0 @ 8	15 @ 15.5
	255 hp	1112101	0 @ 1200	14 @ 2000	28 @ 5000	0 @ 8	15 @ 15.5
	270 hp	1112051	0 @ 1145	14 @ 2000	22 @ 3000	0 @ 8	20 @ 17
1973	190 hp	1112098	0 @ 1100	—	14 @ 4200	0 @ 6	15 @ 14
	250 hp	1112150	0 @ 1200	—	20 @ 5000	0 @ 6	15 @ 12
	270 hp	1112114	0 @ 1500	—	18 @ 4200	0 @ 6	20 @ 15
1974	195 hp	1112850	0 @ 1000	—	22 @ 4200	0 @ 4	14 @ 7.5–8.5
	195 hp	1112851	0 @ 1100	—	18 @ 1200	0 @ 4	14 @ 7.5–8.5
	250 hp	1112247	0 @ 1100	—	18 @ 4200	0 @ 7	15 @ 13–14
	250 hp	1112853	0 @ 1000	—	20 @ 5000	0 @ 4	14 @ 7.5–8.5
	270 hp	1112114	0 @ 1100	—	18 @ 4200	0 @ 7	20 @ 14.2–15.7
1975–76	165 hp	1112880	0 @ 1200	12 @ 2000	22 @ 4200	0 @ 4	18 @ 12
	165 hp	1112888	0 @ 1100	12 @ 1600	16 @ 4200	0 @ 4	18 @ 12
	205 hp	1112883	0 @ 1100	12 @ 1600	22 @ 4600	0 @ 4	15 @ 10

Distributor Specifications (cont.)

NOTE: The following specifications are given in degrees advance at crankshaft speed. Half degrees for distributor machine testing.

Year	Model	Distributor Part Number	Centrifugal Advance			Vacuum Advance	
			Start Degrees @ rpm	Intermediate Degrees @ rpm	End Degrees @ rpm	Start Degrees @ in. Hg	End Degrees @ in. Hg
1977	180 hp (Fed.)	1103246	0 @ 1200	12 @ 2000	22 @ 4200	0 @ 4	18 @ 12
	(Calif.)	1103248	0 @ 1200	12 @ 2000	22 @ 4200	0 @ 4	10 @ 8
	210 hp	1103256	0 @ 1200	13 @ 1600	16 @ 2000	0 @ 4	10 @ 8
1978	185 hp w/M.T.	1103337	0 @ 1100	12 @ 1600	22 @ 4600	0 @ 4	24 @ 10
	w/A.T. (Fed.)	1103353	0 @ 1100	12 @ 1600	22 @ 4600	0 @ 4	20 @ 10
	w/A.T. (Calif.)	1103285	0 @ 1200	12 @ 2000	22 @ 4200	0 @ 4	10 @ 8
	220 hp	1103291	0 @ 1200	13 @ 1600	16 @ 2000	0 @ 4	10 @ 8
1979	195 hp (Fed.)	1103353	0 @ 1100	12 @ 1600	22 @ 4600	0 @ 4	20 @ 10
	(Calif.)	1103285	0 @ 1200	12 @ 2000	22 @ 4200	0 @ 4	10 @ 8
	225 hp	1103291	0 @ 1200	13 @ 1600	16 @ 2000	0 @ 4	10 @ 8

NA Not available
— Not applicable

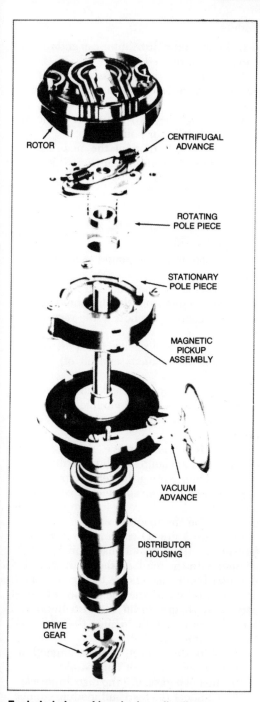

ROTOR

CENTRIFUGAL ADVANCE

ROTATING POLE PIECE

STATIONARY POLE PIECE

MAGNETIC PICKUP ASSEMBLY

VACUUM ADVANCE

DISTRIBUTOR HOUSING

DRIVE GEAR

Exploded view of breakerless distributor

voltage leads (spark plug wires) to fire the spark plugs.

In essence then, the pick-up coil module system simply replaces the conventional breaker points and condenser. The condenser found within the distributor is for radio suppression purposes only and has nothing to do with the ignition process. The module automatically controls the dwell period, increasing it with increasing engine speed. Since dwell is automatically controlled, it cannot be adjusted. The module itself is non-adjustable and non-repairable and must be replaced if found defective. See chapter 11 for detailed HEI system troubleshooting.

HEI SYSTEM PRECAUTIONS

Before going on to troubleshooting, it might be a good idea to take note of the following precautions:

Timing Light Use

Inductive pick-up timing lights are the best kind to use if your car is equipped with HEI. Timing lights which connect between the spark plug and the spark plug wire occasionally (not always) give false readings.

Spark Plug Wires

The plug wires used with HEI systems are of a different construction than conventional wires. When replacing them, make sure you get the correct wires, since conventional wires won't carry the voltage. Also, handle them carefully to avoid cracking or splitting them and *never* pierce them.

Tachometer Use

Not all tachometers will operate or indicate correctly when used on a HEI system. While some tachometers may give a reading, this does not necessarily mean the reading is correct. In addition, some tachometers hook up differently from others. If you can't figure out whether or not your tachometer will work on your car, check with the tachometer manufacturer. Dwell readings, of course, have no significance at all.

HEI System Testers

Instruments designed specifically for testing HEI systems are available from several tool manufacturers. Some of these will even test the module itself. However, the tests given in the following section will require only an ohmmeter and a voltmeter.

COMPONENT REPLACEMENT

Ignition Coil

1. Disconnect the feed and module wire terminal connectors from the distributor cap.
2. Remove the ignition set retainer.

3. Remove the 4 coil cover-to-distributor cap screws and the coil cover.

4. Remove the 4 coil-to-distributor cap screws.

5. Using a blunt drift, press the coil wire spade terminals up out of distributor cap.

6. Lift the coil up out of the distributor cap.

7. Remove and clean the coil spring, rubber seal washer and coil cavity of the distributor cap.

8. Coat the rubber seal with a dielectric lubricant furnished in the replacement ignition coil package.

9. Reverse the above procedures to install.

Distributor Cap

1. Remove the feed and module wire terminal connectors from the distributor cap.

2. Remove the retainer and spark plug wires from the cap.

3. Depress and release the 4 distributor cap-to-housing retainers and lift off the cap assembly.

4. Remove the 4 coil cover screws and cover.

5. Using a finger or a blunt drift, push the spade terminals up out of the distributor cap.

6. Remove all 4 coil screws and lift the coil, coil spring and rubber seal washer out of the cap coil cavity.

7. Using a new distributor cap, reverse the above procedures to assemble being sure to clean and lubricate the rubber seal washer with dielectric lubricant.

Rotor

1. Disconnect the feed and module wire connectors from the distributor.

2. Depress and release the 4 distributor cap to housing retainers and lift off the cap assembly.

3. Remove the two rotor attaching screws and rotor.

4. Reverse the above procedure to install.

Vacuum Advance

1. Remove the distributor cap and rotor as previously described.

2. Disconnect the vacuum hose from the vacuum advance unit.

3. Remove the two vacuum advance retaining screws, pull the advance unit outward, rotate and disengage the operating rod from its tang.

4. Reverse the above procedure to install.

Module

1. Remove the distributor cap and rotor as previously described.

2. Disconnect the harness connector and pick-up coil spade connectors from the module.

3. Remove the two screws and module from the distributor housing.

4. Coat the bottom of the new module with dielectric lubricant. Reverse the above procedure to install.

DISTRIBUTOR REMOVAL AND INSTALLATION

1. Disconnect the ground cable from the battery.

2. Disconnect the feed and module terminal connectors from the distributor cap.

3. Disconnect the hose at the vacuum advance.

4. Depress and release the 4 distributor cap-to-housing retainers and lift off the cap assembly.

5. Using crayon or chalk, make locating marks on the rotor and module and on the distributor housing and engine for installation purposes.

6. Loosen and remove the distributor clamp bolt and clamp, and lift distributor out of the engine. Noting the relative position of the rotor and module alignment marks, make a second mark on the rotor to align it with the one mark on the module.

7. With a new O-ring on the distributor housing and the second mark on the rotor aligned with the mark on the module, install the distributor, taking care to align the mark on the housing with the one on the engine. It may be necessary to lift the distributor and turn the rotor slightly to align the gears and the oil pump driveshaft.

8. With the respective marks aligned, install the clamp and bolt finger-tight.

9. Install and secure the distributor cap.

10. Connect the feed and module connectors to the distributor cap.

11. Connect a timing light to the engine and plug the vacuum hose.

12. Connect the ground cable to the battery.

13. Start the engine and set the timing.

14. Turn the engine off and tighten the distributor clamp bolt. Disconnect the timing light and unplug and connect the hose to the vacuum advance.

NOTE: *If the engine was accidentally cranked after the distributor was removed use the following procedure for installing:*

1. Remove the No. 1 spark plug.

2. Place a finger over the No. 1 spark hole and crank the engine slowly until compression is felt.

3. Align the timing mark on the pulley to "0" on the engine timing indicator.

4. Turn the rotor to point between the No. 1 and No. 8 spark plug towers on the distributor cap.

5. Install the distributor and connect the ignition feed wire.

6. Install the distributor cap and spark plug wires.

7. Check the ignition timing.

Firing Order

To avoid confusion, replace spark plug wires one at a time.

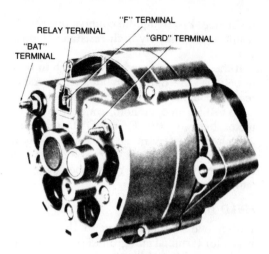

Alternator (with separate regulator) terminals

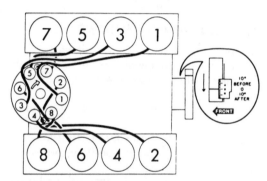

1963–74 except HEI

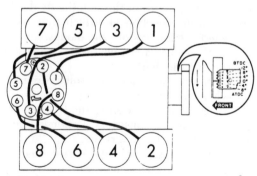

1974–79 HEI

Charging System
ISOLATION CHECKS

These are quick checks that will allow the tester to isolate the general source of charging circuit difficulty in either the alternator, regulator, or wiring harness. Once the defec-

tive component has been singled out, further checks and repairs may be made using the procedures given in the alternator or regulator sections. Make these checks after looking for obvious problems such as a weak battery or loose fan belt.

Start the engine and bring the idle to between 1500–2000 rpm. Turn off all accessories, lights, radio, etc., and then disconnect the battery ground cable. If the engine stops, it is safe to assume that the alternator is at fault. If, however, the engine continues to operate, the problem lies with either the regulator or wiring harness.

Having eliminated the alternator from suspicion, the next step is to isolate the regulator from the harness and the easiest way is to substitute a known component. Remove the push-on wiring connector from the regulator and insert a regulator that is known to be good into the circuit, remembering to ground the regulator to the car. Idle the engine, remove the battery cable, and check the ammeter. If it indicates a discharge condition, then the possible problem is an open resistor or a shorted, positive diode. If the ammeter continues to indicate a charge, then it is the regulator that is defective.

ALTERNATOR TESTS

Prepare the alternator for testing by disconnecting the battery ground terminal, the BAT, light relay, field, and GRD leads from the alternator terminals.

Check the positive diodes by connecting an ohmmeter between the R and BAT terminals, and noting the lowest range on the ohmmeter scale. It should indicate very low resistance. Reversing the connections should result in an infinitely high resistance indication.

If the ohmmeter reads low or high in both directions, the diodes are defective. A low reading could also indicate a grounded stator.

To test for an open field, connect the ohmmeter between the F and GRD terminals and check the low range scale for a reading between 7 and 20 ohms. A zero indication or one of excessively high resistance suggests a faulty alternator.

FIELD RELAY TESTS

Fasten one voltmeter lead to the no. two regulator terminal and ground the other lead to the regulator. Idle the engine between 1500 and 2000 rpm. If the GEN light still burns, and a volt reading of 3.5 to 6.5 is present, then the regulator field relay is faulty.

ACCESSORY CIRCUIT RESISTANCE TESTS

A resistor is connected to the ACC terminal ignition switch. To check for an open resistor, connect the voltmeter to the no. 4 connection of the wiring harness and ground the other voltmeter lead to the regulator. A zero reading, with the ignition switch turned to the ACC notch, indicates an open resistor.

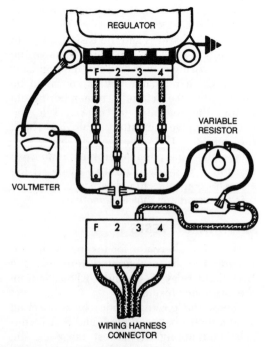

Field relay closing voltage check

The resistance wire is an integral part of the ignition harness and carries a rating minimum of 10 ohms, 6.25 watts. The wire is not solderable and must be crimp-connected.

Alternator

The alternator used on Corvettes is a continuous-output Delcotron unit. It is comprised of two major components; a stator and a rotor. The stator has a laminated core that is attached to the frame of the alternator. A large number of windings cover the inside diameter of the stator and it is within this circle that the rotor turns. Current passes from two brushes through two slip rings and finally to the field coils which are wound in a manner concentric to the rotor shaft. There are six rectifier diodes mounted in the slip ring end frame. These are joined to the stator windings at three points. The diodes are set in heat sinks to prevent overheating. The diodes convert the AC current to DC.

ALTERNATOR PRECAUTIONS

To prevent damage to the alternator and regulator, the following precautions should be taken when working with the electrical system.

1. Never reverse the battery connections.

2. Booster batteries for starting must be connected properly—positive-to-positive and negative-to-negative.

3. Disconnect the battery cables before using a fast charger; the charger has a tendency to force current through the diodes in the opposite direction for which they were designed. This burns out the diodes.

4. Never use a fast charger as a booster for starting the vehicle.

5. Never disconnect the voltage regulator while the engine is running.

6. Avoid long soldering times when replacing diodes or transistors. Prolonged heat is damaging to AC generators.

7. Do not use test lamps of more than 12 volts (V) for checking diode continuity.

8. Do not short across or ground any of the terminals on the AC generator.

9. The polarity of the battery, generator, and regulator must be matched and considered before making any electrical connections within the system.

10. Never operate the alternator on an open circuit. Make sure that all connections within the circuit are clean and tight.

11. Disconnect the battery terminals when performing any service on the electricial system. This will eliminate the possibility of accidental reversal of polarity.

12. Disconnect the battery ground cable if arc welding is to be done on any part of the car.

REMOVAL AND INSTALLATION

1. Disconnect the negative cable from the battery, this will prevent damaging the alternator diodes.

2. Disconnect the battery (BAT), light relay, and ground (GRD) leads from their terminals on the alternator.

3. Disconnect the harness connector from the field terminals at the brush holder.

4. Loosen the pivot bolt at the bottom of the alternator and remove the brace bolt at the top. Slip off the drive belt and support the alternator.

5. Remove the pivot bolt and remove the alternator.

6. To install the alternator, reverse removal procedure. Tighten the fan belt to the correct tension.

ALTERNATOR DISASSEMBLY

Remove the pulley by positioning a box-end wrench over the pulley retaining nut and inserting a $5/16$ in. allen wrench in the shaft to prevent it from turning. Unbolt the retaining nut and slide it off the pulley. Disconnect the battery ground strap to prevent diode damage and remove the generator. On the 6.2 in. perforated case generator, remove the blade-connector retaining nuts and remove the connectors. Slip the indicator light relay from the terminal post, then back out the retaining screws, and remove the brush holder. Leave the capacitor attached to the generator. Remove the four, long, case bolts and separate the end frame and rotor assembly from the stator assembly. Cover the slip ring and bearing with tape to prevent contamination.

Remove the rotor from the end frame. Extract the retainer plate screws and remove the retainer plate and the end frame bearing. Remove the three attaching screws and separate the stator from the end frame. Remove the heat sink.

Wash all metal parts with the exception of the stator and rotor assemblies. The rotor slip rings may be cleaned with 400 grain polishing cloth. It is a good idea to rotate the rotor while doing this to guard against rubbing flat spots on the slip rings. Maximum out-of-

round tolerance for slip rings is 0.001 in. Remove as little metal as possible when truing on a lathe. Polish with 400 grain cloth and blow dry.

TEST

Rotor

Attach one lead of a 110 volt test lamp or an ohmmeter to either slip ring, and the other lead to the rotor shaft or poles. A lighted test lamp or low ohmmeter reading indicates grounded field windings.

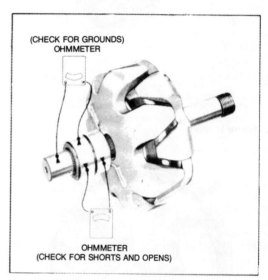

(CHECK FOR GROUNDS)
OHMMETER

OHMMETER
(CHECK FOR SHORTS AND OPENS)

Rotor testing

Attach the lamp or ohmmeter connections to each slip ring. The windings are open if the lamp fails to light or the ohmmeter reading is high.

Connect a 12 volt battery and an ammeter in series with the slip rings to check for shorts. The windings are shorted if the reading exceeds 1.5 amps. An ohmmeter may be substituted for the same check and will show a resistance reading of less than 6 ohms if the windings are shorted.

Stator

Attach the test lamp or ohmmeter to the stator frame and one of the stator leads. A lighted lamp or low resistance reading indicates grounded windings.

Successively connect the test equipment between each pair of stator leads. Open windings will produce a high resistance and prevent the test lamp from lighting.

Shorts require special test equipment. If

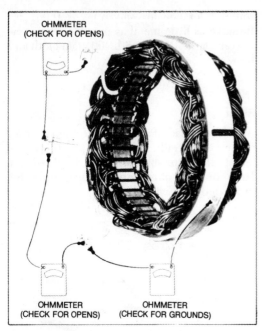

Stator testing

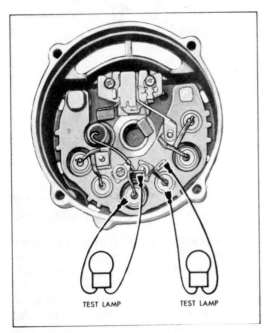

Diode check

all other tests fail to locate the problem, it is more than likely a short in the stator.

Diode

The diodes may be checked for shorts or opens by using an ohmmeter or a 12 volt test lamp.

CAUTION: *Under no circumstances use a 110 volt test lamp.*

Use a 1½ volt cell ohmmeter that has been adjusted to the lowest range scale. Attach one lead to the heat sink and the other to the diode lead. A good diode will show a high and a low reading depending on the connection switch. Two low or two high readings signal a faulty diode. Check the other diodes in the same manner.

Check the end-frame mounted diodes by connecting one test lead to the frame and the other to the diode lead. Reverse the connection and check the readings. The same diagnosis is true here as for the heat sink diodes.

If an ohmmeter is not available, substitute a 12 volt test lamp. Connect and switch connections in the same fashion as with the ohmmeter. The lamp will light in only one direction. If it lights or fails to light in both directions, the diode is bad.

REPAIRS

Diode Replacement

Despite rumors to the contrary, the diodes may be replaced. It is not necessary to replace the entire generator assembly as some unscrupulous garage owners convinced their unwary customers in the introductory days of the AC generator.

Two types of diodes, positive and negative, are used in the AC generator. The heat sink contains the positive diodes and these are marked with red. End frame diodes are the negative ones and they have black markings. Do not attempt to drive a diode from its bore or the other diodes may be damaged.

Support the end frame in an arbor press, select a suitable removal spacer, and press the diode from the frame. Use the same method to install a replacement diode.

To replace heat sink diodes, it is necessary to separate the heat sink from the end frame. Observe the stack-up closely to ensure correct reassembly of the BAT and GRD terminal bolts. Replace the diodes as described above, reassemble the bolt stack-ups and attach the heat sink to the end frame.

End Frame Replacement

Install the brush holder on the replacement end frame, being careful to build up the parts stack properly. A pin or wire will hold the brushes in position until the unit has been completely assembled. Install the heat sink as previously described. Remove the brush holding pin or wire after the unit is assembled and allow the brushes to drop into the slip rings.

Bearing Replacement

The drive end frame bearing is removed by detaching the retainer frame from the end plate and pressing the bearing out. Fill the bearing ¼ full with multipurpose grease; do not overfill. Press the bearing into the end frame. Install the retainer plate.

The slip ring end frame bearing of the 6 in. perforated-case generator is pressed off the rotor shaft. The replacement is pressed over the rotor shaft by using an arbor press.

The 5.5 in. aluminum Delcotron slip-ring end bearing is replaced by pressing it out from the inside of the case. To install the replacement, position a flat plate over the bearing and press it into the outside of the case. Press all bearings and diodes flush with their receptacles.

Slip Ring Replacement

Unsolder the field-to-slip ring connections and slide the rear bearing from the shaft. Attach a bearing puller and withdraw the slip ring from the shaft.

Start the replacement ring onto the shaft, with the slip ring and winding leads aligned. Align the slip ring lead that passes through the insulation with the winding lead that does not have a nylon insulator.

Press the aligned unit onto the shaft and position the slip ring $3^9/_{32}$ in. $\pm$ $^1/_{64}$ in., measured from the outside edge of the slip ring to the face of the stator nearest the pulley. Clip the excess lead material and solder the slip ring leads to the rotor winding connections. Use resin core solder.

ASSEMBLY

Attach the slip-ring end frame to the stator assembly and position the diode connectors above the diode, relay, and stator leads. Tighten the terminal nuts, then slide the front end frame over the rotor. Slide on the spacer, pulley, washer, and nut, and torque the shaft to 50–60 ft lbs. Attach the slip-ring end frame and stator to the rotor and drive end frame assembly and insert and tighten the thru-bolts.

Regulator

There are two types of external regulators used on Corvettes, a standard, double-contact model and an optional, transistorized model. One transistor and two diodes are used in the optional voltage regulator. The transistor assists the conventional voltage regulator in limiting voltage to a pre-set value. The diodes protect the system from transient voltages which may occur. Regulator tests and voltage adjustments may be made on the vehicle. Point cleaning and air gap adjustment must be made with the unit removed from the car.

REGULATOR TESTS

Regulator Check—Double Contact Regulator

Disconnect the battery ground cable and insert a ¼ ohm resistor in the BAT terminal cir-

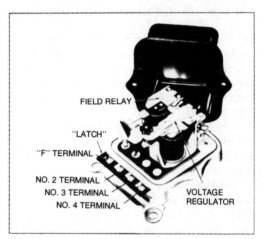

Double-contact voltage regulator

cuit. Separate the wiring harness connector at the regulator and attach a suitable adapter as shown in the accompanying illustration. Insert a 25 watt, 25 ohm variable resistor into the F circuit, then attach a voltmeter between the regulator no. 3 terminal and ground.

Run a jumper lead from the no. 3 regulator to the BAT terminal on the regulator. Fi-

Regulator Ambient Temperature F°	Regulator Normal Range Volts
65	13.9–15.0
85	13.8–14.8
105	13.7–14.6
125	13.5–14.4
145	13.4–14.2
165	13.2–14.0
185	13.1–13.9

nally, connect 1000 ohm impedance headphones between the F terminal on the regulator and ground. Check all connections and reconnect the battery cable.

The following comparison chart should be referred to during the checks:

Open Resistor and Diode Check—Transistorized Regulator

An open resistor check is made by connecting the voltmeter between the F circuit and the regulator base plate. A reading of less than nine volts indicates that either the transistor or a regulator resistor is burned open.

A diode check necessitates removing the regulator from the vehicle and unsoldering the diode leads. Two diodes are exposed when the cover is removed; the suppression diode and the field discharge diode. Attach an ohmmeter to the field discharge diode leads in the manner of the accompanying illustration. Reverse the connections and observe both readings. The diode is defective if both readings are less than two ohms or are infinitely high.

Subject the suppression diode to the same examination. Again, a normal diode will give a high and a low reading when the ohmmeter connections are reversed.

Test the diodes with the ohmmeter at 1½ volts and set on the lowest range scale. If diode replacement is necessary, keep in mind that excessive heat will damage the diode, and adjust the soldering time accordingly. Leave the ohmmeter connected as for the diode check if you desire to test for a shorted transistor, but do not start the engine.

With the cover off and the ignition on, open the voltage points and check the reading. A shorted transistor will cause a reading in excess of nine volts. Remove its attaching screws and unsolder the connections above the transistor to remove it.

Upper Contact Voltage Test—Double Contact Regulator

Turn all vehicle accessories off and close the variable resistor to the "no resistance" setting.

Attach a thermometer to the regulator cover then start the engine and set the idle at 1500 rpm. Let the engine idle for 15 minutes then cycle the generator by opening the variable resistor to "full resistance" and momentarily disconnecting and reconnecting the number four, wiring harness terminal lead.

Finally, close the variable resistor to "no resistance."

Increase the idle speed to 2500 rpm and compare the ambient temperature and voltage readings with the comparison chart. At this time, the headphones should be emitting a steady buzz. Record the temperature and voltage settings as well as the desired settings but make no adjustments.

Lower Contact Voltage Test—Double Contact Regulator

Force the regulator to operate on the lower contact points by increasing the variable field resistance. As the transition from upper to lower points takes place, the earphones will detect a drop in sound to a very weak signal then a return to normal. An accompanying change in voltmeter reading will occur.

Record the voltage setting of the lower contact points and compute the difference between the upper and lower contact point readings. The normal voltage difference should place the lower contact points 0.1 to 0.5 volts less than the uppers.

Compare the upper reading to the comparison chart. If the readings are not concurrent, the regulator must be adjusted.

Field Relay Test—Transistorized Regulator

Separate the wiring harness connector and connect a voltmeter between the R lead of the regulator and the regulator base plate. Insert a 50 ohm, variable resistor in the circuit between the regulator R lead and the wiring harness connector V receptacle. Open the resistor and switch off the ignition. Decrease the resistance slowly and observe the relay closing voltage. Bend the heel iron to adjust to specifications.

VOLTAGE ADJUSTMENT

Double Contact Regulator

The regulator is adjusted when it is functioning on the upper contacts. First remove the regulator cover. To prevent accidental grounds, open the variable resistor to full resistance and disconnect the no. 4 regulator terminal lead. Reconnect the lead and close the resistor after the cover is off.

The large nylon nut adjusts the voltage difference. Turn it clockwise to decrease the difference and counterclockwise to increase. If the correct voltage difference cannot be obtained, replace the regulator. Check the

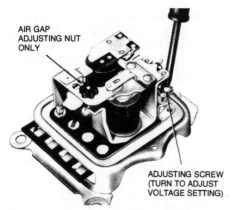

Double-contact voltage regulator adjustment

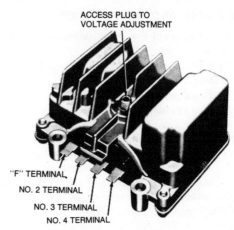

Transistorized voltage regulator

difference adjustment by noting the upper contact reading then increasing the variable field resistance and observing the lower contact voltage reading. As the operation changes from the upper to lower points, the headphones will emit a sound change from normal again. The lower points should show a voltage reading difference as previously specified.

Close the variable resistor, turn off all accessories, and observe the upper-contact voltage reading. Any change is due to the removal of the cover. At the beginning of the voltage tests, the actual voltage setting and the desired setting were recorded. Take the difference between the two figures and add or subtract them to the present voltage reading to derive the adjusted reading. If the adjusted reading is higher than the actual present voltage reading, turn the adjusting screw clockwise to increase the voltage. A lower adjusted voltage is reached by turning the adjusting screw counterclockwise.

Install the regulator cover and operate the engine for five minutes at 2500 rpm before checking the final voltage figures.

Transistorized Regulator

The regulator voltage changes in relation to the ambient temperature. This temperature is measured ¼ in. from the regulator cover. If a regulator setting change is needed, a check of the ambient temperature and a comparison with the accompanying chart will furnish the specified setting for the prevailing temperature.

After selecting the desired voltage setting and checking the existing ambient temperature, disconnect the voltage regulator V lead from the wiring harness connector and run a jumper lead from the V lead to the BAT ter-

minal of the generator. Connect a voltmeter from the V lead to the regulator ground plate. Insert an ammeter into the circuit by attaching one lead to the BAT terminal and the other to the horn relay.

Start the engine and run at 3000 rpm for 15 minutes. Generator output should be between 3 and 30 amps. Leave the cover installed. Stop the engine after 15 minutes and momentarily remove the jumper lead from the generator then reinstall. This cycles the generator. Start the engine and note the voltage setting with the engine at 3000 rpm.

Remove cover and turn the adjusting screw as required. Make the final setting with the screw being turned clockwise to ensure the removal of all slack and proper tensioning of the adjusting screw against the screwholder.

Cycle the generator after adjusting so that a valid final setting is achieved. Operate at 3000 rpm to verify adjustment. Should the generator output drop below 3 amps during the adjustment operation, turn on the accessories to force the required minimum ampere output.

Ambient Temperature vs. Regulator Voltage Setting

Regulator Ambient Temperature	Specified Voltage Range			
45° F	13.9	14.1	14.3	14.5
65° F	13.8	14.0	14.2	14.4
85° F	13.7	13.9	14.1	14.3
105° F	13.5	13.7	13.9	14.1
125° F	13.3	13.5	13.7	13.9
145° F	13.2	13.4	13.6	13.8
165° F	13.0	13.2	13.4	13.6

REMOVAL AND INSTALLATION

1. Disconnect the negative cable from the battery.

2. Disconnect the wiring harness from the regulator.

3. Remove the mounting screws and remove the regulator.

4. Make sure that the regulator base rubber gasket is in place before installation.

5. Clean attaching area for proper grounding.

6. Install the regulator. Do not overtighten the mounting screws, as this will cancel the cushioning effect of the rubber grommets.

7. Attach the wiring harness connector to the regulator.

8. Do not polarize the alternator. Connect the battery negative cable.

CONTACT POINT CLEANING

Double Contact Regulator

A sooty point condition is normal and such points do not require cleaning. Unnecessary cleaning will reduce contact point life. Contacts on this regulator consist of a soft material which, if necessary, may be cleaned with crocus cloth or another fine abrasive. Wash the contacts with tri-chlorethylene after cleaning. Field relay contacts may be cleaned with a thin, fine-cut file. Only enough material to clean the points should be removed. Never use emery cloth to clean the contacts.

Transistorized Regulator

The large contact point may be cleaned with a spoon or riffler file after loosening the upper contact support mounting screws. All oxidation should be removed, but it is not necessary to completely smooth the contact. The smaller contact does not oxidize and may be cleaned with a fine abrasive such as crocus cloth. Wash the contacts with trichloroethylene after cleaning. Field relay contacts may be cleaned with a fine-cut file, remove only enough material to clean the points.

POINT OPENING AND AIR GAP ADJUSTMENT

Double Contact Regulator

The voltage regulator point opening is measured between the upper contacts while the lower contacts are touching. Adjustment may be made by bending the upper contact arm. Air gap is measured with a feeler gauge placed between the armature and core when the lower contacts are touching. The nylon nut located on the contact support adjust the air gap.

Field relay point opening is checked as shown in figure. Carefully bend the armature stop for adjustment. Check the field relay air gap with the points just touching. The air gap rarely needs adjustment. As long as the point opening and closing voltages are within specifications, the relay will operate satisfactorily in spite of an air gap slightly out of the specified dimensions. The flat contact spring may be bent to make an adjustment.

Transistorized Regulator

To adjust the voltage regulator air gap, push the armature (not the flat spring) down against a feeler gauge, and adjust the upper contact support so that the contacts align squarely and just touch when the contact support screws are tightened. The field relay unit air gap is checked with the points just touching. Carefully bend the flat contact support spring for adjustment. Field relay point opening is checked as shown in figure. Point opening very seldom needs adjustment. If air gap and closing voltage are within specifications, the relay will perform satisfactorily although point opening may be out of specifications.

Integrated Alternator/Regulator

The Delcotron 10-SI combination alternator/regulator was used on some 1972 models and all later models. Removal and installation are similar to that for the standard alternator used before 1972. Testing procedures which differ are given below.

This system is an integrated AC generating system containing a built-in voltage regulator. Removal and replacement is essentially the same as for the standard AC generator.

The regulator is mounted inside the slip ring end frame. All regulator components are enclosed in an epoxy molding, and the regulator cannot be adjusted. Rotor and stator tests are the same as for the 5.5 Delcotron, covered previously.

CHARGING SYSTEM TEST—LOW CHARGING RATE

1. After battery condition, drive belt tension, and wiring terminals and connections

have been checked, charge the battery fully and perform the following test:

2. Connect a test voltmeter between the alternator BAT, terminal and ground, ignition switch on. Connect the voltmeter in turn to alternator terminals No. 1 and No. 2, the other voltmeter lead being grounded as before. A zero reading indicates an open circuit between the battery and each connection at the alternator. If this test discloses no faults in the wiring, proceed to Step 3.

3. Connect the test voltmeter to the alternator BAT terminal (the other test lead to ground), start the engine and run at 1,500–2,000 rpm with all lights and electrical accessories turned on. If the voltmeter reads 12.8 volts or greater, the alternator is good and no further checks need be made. If the voltmeter reads less than 12.8 volts, ground the field winding by inserting a screwdriver into the test hole in the end frame.

CAUTION: *Do not force the tab more than ¾ in. into the end frame.*

a. If voltage increases to 13 volts or more, the regulator unit is defective;

b. If voltage does not increase significantly, the generator is defective.

CHARGING SYSTEM TEST–HIGH CHARGING RATE

1. With the battery fully charged, connect a voltmeter between alternator terminal No.

2 and ground. If the reading is zero, No. 2 circuit from the battery is open.

2. If No. 2 circuit is OK, but an obvious overcharging condition still exists, proceed as follows:

a. Remove the alternator and separate the end frames;

b. Connect a low-range ohmmeter between the brush lead clip and the end frame (Test 1), then reverse the connections. If both readings are zero, either the brush lead clip is grounded or the regulator is defective. A grounded brush lead clip can be due to damaged insulating sleeve or omission of the insulating washer.

ALTERNATOR OUTPUT TEST

1. Connect a test voltmeter, ammeter, and a 10-ohm, 6-watt resistor into the charging circuit. Do not connect the carbon pile to the battery posts at this time.

2. Increase alternator speed and observe the voltmeter—if the voltage is uncontrolled with speed and increases to 16 volts or more, check for a grounded brush lead clip as previously covered. If a brush lead clip is not grounded, the voltage regulator is faulty and must be replaced.

3. Connect the carbon pile load to the battery terminals.

4. Operate the alternator at moderate

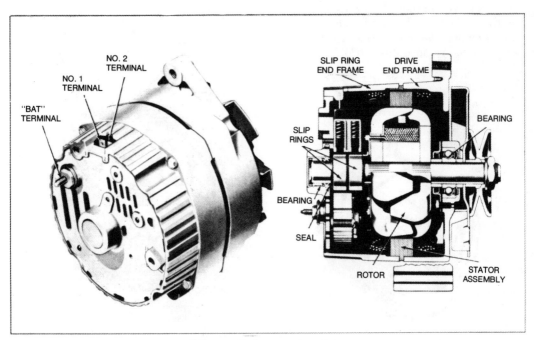

Integrated alternator/regulator

speed and adjust the carbon pile to obtain maximum alternator output as indicated on the ammeter. If output is within 10% of rated output as stamped on the alternator. frame, alternator is O.K. If output is not within specifications, ground the alternator field by inserting a screwdriver into the test hole in the end frame. If output now is within 10% of rating, replace the voltage regulator; if still not within specifications, check field winding, diode trio, rectifier bridge and stator, as described later. Disassembly of alternator up to and including Step 6 is necessary.

DISASSEMBLY AND ASSEMBLY

1. Place alternator in a vise, clamped by the mounting flange only.
2. Remove the four through bolts and separate the slip ring end frame and stator assembly from the drive end and rotor assembly, using a screwdriver to pry the two sections apart. Use the slots provided for the purpose.

NOTE: *Scribe matchmarks on the parts to aid in assembly.*

3. Place a piece of tape over the slip ring end frame bearing to prevent entry of dirt; also tape shaft at slip ring end to prevent scratches.
4. Clean brushes, if they are to be reused, with trichloroethylene or carbon tetrachloride solvent. Use these solvents only in an adequately ventilated area.
5. Remove the stator lead nuts and separate the stator from the end frame.
6. Remove the screw that secures the diode trio and remove diode trio.

NOTE: *At this point, test the rotor, rectifier bridge, stator and diode trio if these tests are necessary.*

7. Remove the rectifier bridge holddown screw and the BAT terminal screw, then disconnect condenser lead. Remove rectifier bridge from end frame.
8. Remove the two securing screws and brush holder and regulator assemblies. Note the insulating sleeves over the screws.
9. Remove the retaining screw and condenser from the end frame.
10. Remove the slip ring end frame bearing, if it is to be replaced, using the procedure given later in this section.
11. Remove the pulley nut, washer, pulley, fan and spacer from the rotor shaft, using a $5/16$ in. allen key to hold the shaft while loosening the nut.
12. Remove rotor and spacers from drive end frame assembly.
13. Remove drive end frame bearing retainer plate, screws, plate, bearing, and slinger from end frame, if necessary.
14. To assemble, reverse order of disassembly. Pulley nut must be tightened to 40–50 ft. lbs.

CLEANING AND INSPECTION

1. Clean all metal parts, except stator and rotor assemblies, in solvent.
2. Wipe off bearings and inspect them for pitting or roughness.

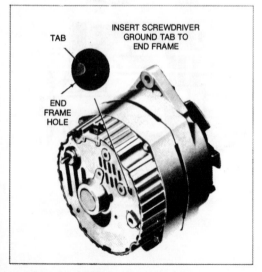

Grounding field winding

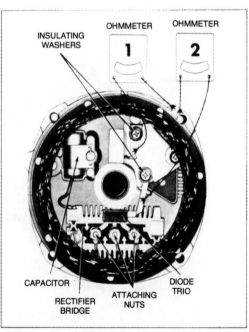

High charging rate test

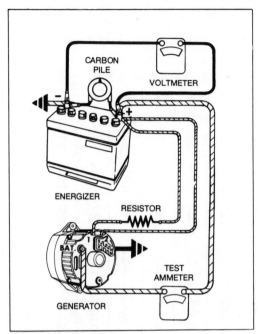

Alternator output test

3. Inspect rotor slip rings for scoring. They may be cleaned with 400 grit sandpaper (not emery), rotating the rotor to make the rings concentric. Maximum out-of-true is 0.001 in. If slip rings are deeply scored, the entire rotor must be replaced as a unit.

4. Inspect brushes for wear; minimum length is ¼ in.

DIODE TRIO INITIAL TESTING

1. Before removing this unit, connect an ohmmeter between the brush lead clip and

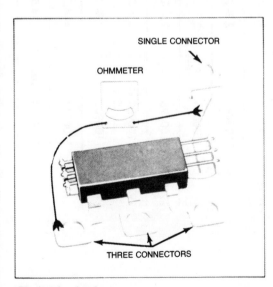

Diode trio check

the end frame. The lowest reading scale should be used for this test.

2. After taking a reading, reverse the lead connections. If the meter reads zero, the brush lead clip is probably grounded, due to omission of the insulating sleeve or insulating washer.

DIODE TRIO REMOVAL

1. Remove the three nuts which secure the stator.

2. Remove stator.

3. Remove the screw which secures the diode trio lead clip, then remove diode trio.

NOTE: *The position of the insulating washer on the screw is critical; make sure that it is returned to the same position on reassembly.*

DIODE TRIO TESTING

1. Connect an ohmmeter, on lowest range, between the single brush connector and one stator lead connector.

2. Observe the reading, then reverse the meter leads. Repeat this test with each of the other two stator lead connectors. The readings on each of these tests should NOT be identical, there should be one low and one high reading for each test. If this is not the case, replace the diode trio.

CAUTION: *Do not use high voltage on the diode trio.*

RECTIFIER BRIDGE TESTING

1. Connect an ohmmeter between the heat sink (ground) and the base of one of the three terminals. Then, reverse the meter leads and take a reading. If both readings are identical, the bridge is defective and must be replaced.

2. Repeat this test with the remaining two terminals, then between the INSULATED heat sink (as opposed to the GROUNDED heat sink in previous test) and each of the three terminals. As before, if any two readings are identical, on reversing the meter leads, the rectifier bridge must be replaced.

RECTIFIER BRIDGE REMOVAL

1. Remove the attaching screw and the BAT terminal screw.

2. Disconnect the condenser lead.

3. Remove the rectifier bridge.

NOTE: *The insulator between the insulated heat sink and the end frame is ex-*

Alternator and Regulator Specifications

Year	Alternator		Output @ Generator RPM		Regulator	Field Relay			Regulator		
	Model	Field Current Draw @ 12V	2000	5000	Model	Air Gap (in.)	Point Gap (in.)	Volts to Close	Air Gap (in.)	Point Gap (in.)	Volts at 125°
1963–64	1100628	1.9–2.3	27A	37A	1119512	0.015	0.030	2.3–3.7	0.067	0.014	13.5–14.4
1965–67	1100693	2.2–2.6	27A	37A	1119515	0.015	0.030	2.3–3.7	0.067	0.014	13.5–14.4
	1100696	2.2–2.6	29A	42A	1119515	0.015	0.030	2.3–3.7	0.067	0.014	13.5–14.4
1968	1100693	2.2–2.6	27A	37A	1119515	0.015	0.030	2.3–3.7	0.067	0.014	13.5–14.4
	1100794	2.2–2.6	27A	37A	1119515	0.015	0.030	2.3–3.7	0.067	0.014	13.5–14.4
	1100696	2.2–2.6	29A	42A	1119515	0.015	0.030	2.3–3.7	0.067	0.014	13.5–14.4
1969	1100696	2.2–2.6	27A	37A	1119515	0.015	0.030	2.3–3.7	0.067	0.014	13.5–14.4
1970	1100900	2.2–2.6	27A	37A	1119515	0.015	0.030	2.3–3.7	0.067	0.014	13.5–14.4
	1100901	2.2–2.6	27A	37A	1119515	0.015	0.030	2.3–3.7	0.067	0.014	13.5–14.4
1971–72	1100544	4–4.5	①	①	1119515	0.015	0.030	1.5–3.2	0.067	0.014	13.8–14.8
	1100543, 1100950	4–4.5	①	37A	1119515	0.015	0.030	1.5–3.2	0.067	0.014	13.8–14.8

1100566	2.2–2.6	25A	35A	1119515	0.015	0.030	1.5–3.2	0.067	0.014	13.8–14.8
1100843	2.2–2.6	—	58A	1119515	0.015	0.030	1.5–3.2	0.067	0.014	13.8–14.8
1100917	2.8–3.2	—	59A	1119519	0.030	0.030	1.5–3.2	0.067	0.014	13.8–14.8
1100567	2.2–2.6	—	40A	1119515	0.015	0.030	1.5–3.2	0.067	0.014	13.8–14.8
1100497	2.8–3.2	—	37A	Integrated with alternator						13.8–14.8
1100934	2.8–3.2	—	37A	Integrated with alternator						13.8–14.8
1973–74 1100544	4.0–4.5	—	61A	Integrated with alternator						13.8–14.8
1102353, 1100573, 1102346, 1100950	4.0–4.5	—	42A	Integrated with alternator						13.8–14.8
1100934, 1100497	4.0–4.5	—	37A	Integrated with alternator						13.8–14.8
1102354, 1100542	4.0–4.5	—	63A	Integrated with alternator						13.8–14.8
1975–76 1102483	4.0–4.5	—	37A	Integrated with alternator						13.8–14.8
1100950	4.0–4.5	—	42A	Integrated with alternator						13.8–14.8
1977–79 1102484	4.0–4.5	—	38A	Integrated with alternator						13.8–14.8
1102474	4.0–4.5	—	57A	Integrated with alternator						13.8–14.8

① Voltmeter not needed for cold output check. Load battery with carbon pile to obtain maximum output.

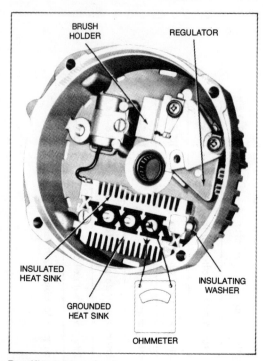

Rectifier bridge check

tremely important to the operation of the unit. It must be replaced in exactly the same position on reassembly.

CAUTION: *Do not use high voltage to test the rectifier bridge.*

BRUSH AND/OR VOLTAGE REGULATOR REMOVAL AND INSTALLATION

1. Remove two brush holder screws and stator lead to strap nut and washer, brush holder screws and one of the diode trio lead strap attaching screws.

NOTE: *The insulating washers must be replaced in the same position on reassembly.*

2. Remove brush holder and brushes. The voltage regulator may also be removed at this time, if desired.

3. Brushes and brush springs must be free of corrosion and must be undamaged and completely free of oil or grease.

4. Insert spring and brushes into holder, noting whether they slide freely without binding. Insert wooden or plastic toothpick into bottom hole in holder to retain brushes.

NOTE: *The brush holder is serviced as a unit; individual parts are not available.*

5. Reassemble in reverse order of disassembly.

SLIP RING END FRAME BEARING AND SEAL REMOVAL AND INSTALLATION

1. With stator removed, press out bearing and seal, using a socket or similar tool that fits inside the end frame housing. Press from outside to inside, supporting the frame inside with a hollow cylinder (large, deep socket) to allow the seal and bearing to pass.

2. The bearings are sealed for life and permanently lubricated. If a bearing is dry, do not attempt to repack it, as it will throw off the grease and contaminate the inside of the generator.

3. Using a flat plate, press the new bearing from the outside toward the inside. A large vise is a handy press, but care must be exercised so that end frame is not distorted or cracked. Again, use a deep socket to support the inside of the end frame.

4. From inside the end frame, insert seal and press flush with housing.

5. Install stator and reconnect leads.

Starting System

The starting system consists of the starting motor, solenoid, and battery. The motor is comprised of a drive mechanism, an armature, brushes, field windings, and a frame. It has four pole shoes and four field shoes, one of which is shunted to the armature. A solenoid is attached to the starting motor frame and this controls the over-running clutch drive.

STARTER REMOVAL AND INSTALLATION

1. Remove the positive cable from the battery to prevent accidental shorting. Remove the heat shield on big block models.

2. Disconnect the solenoid S, R, and battery leads. Mark these wires for correct replacement.

3. Loosen the supporting bracket bolt on the cylinder block and remove the stud nut and lockwasher on the front of the starter. Move the bracket out of the working area.

4. Loosen the mounting bolts while supporting the starter. Remove the mounting bolts and pull the starter out and down from the engine.

5. Reverse this procedure to install the starter.

STARTING MOTOR TESTS

A series of resistance checks may be made with the unit mounted on the vehicle. These

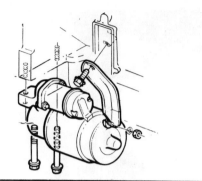

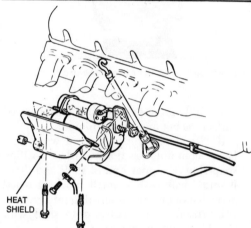

HEAT
SHIELD

Starter mounting—small block (top) and big block (bottom)

require only a voltmeter. Connect the voltmeter between the positive post of the battery and the battery terminal of the solenoid. Ground the primary coil terminal to prevent the engine from starting, then crank the engine with the switch on.

Repeat the test; first with the voltmeter connected between the negative battery terminal and the starting motor housing, and finally with the voltmeter between the solenoid battery terminal and the solenoid motor terminal. A voltage drop in excess of 0.2 volts, indicates excessive resistance in the portion of the circuit being tested.

SOLENOID TESTING

Failure of the solenoid to retract may be due to an excessive voltage drop in the control circuit. Check this by connecting a voltmeter between the solenoid battery terminal and the solenoid switch terminal. A drop in excess of 3.5 volts indicates excessive resistance in the solenoid control circuit.

A voltage figure of less than 7.7 volts between the solenoid switch terminal and ground warrants checks of the solenoid cur-

rent draw, starting motor pinion clearance, or for possible binding of the solenoid linkage.

STARTER DISASSEMBLY

1. Disconnect the field coil connectors from the motor solenoid terminal.
2. Remove the thru-bolts.
3. Remove commutator end frame, field frame, and armature assembly from drive housing.
4. Remove the overrunning clutch from the armature shaft as follows:
   a. Slide the two-piece thrust collar off the end of the armature shaft.
   b. Slide a standard ½ in. pipe coupling or other spacer onto the shaft so that the end of the coupling butts against the edge of the retainer.
   c. Tap the end of the coupling with a hammer, driving retainer toward armature end of snap-ring.
   d. Remove snap-ring from its groove in the shaft using pliers. Slide retainer and clutch from armature shaft.
5. Disassemble brush assembly from field frame by releasing the V-spring and removing the support pin. The brush holders, brushes, and springs now can be pulled out as a unit and the leads disconnected.

ARMATURE TESTS

To test for shorts, place the armature on a growler and hold a hacksaw blade over the

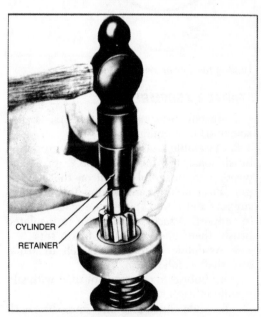

CYLINDER
RETAINER

Driving retainer off snap-ring

armature while rotating the armature. A short will cause the saw blade to vibrate. Clean between the commutator cracks and repeat the test. Replace the armature if no improvement is noted.

To test for grounding, connect one test lamp lead to the armature core and the other to the commutator. A lighted lamp indicates a grounded armature and demands replacement.

FIELD COIL TESTS

To test for an open circuit, attach a test lamp lead to each end of the field coils. An open circuit will prevent the lamp from lighting and will warrant replacement of the field coils.

To test for grounding, attach one test lead to the commutator bar and the other to the field frame. A grounded field coil will light the lamp. The shunt coil must be disconnected before making this check.

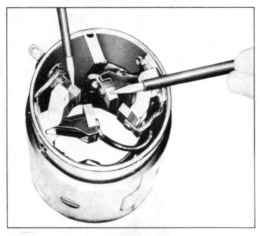

Testing for a grounded field coil

STARTER ASSEMBLY

1. Install brushes into holders. Install solenoid, if so equipped.

2. Assemble insulated and grounded brush holder together using the V-spring and position the assembled unit on the support pin. Push holders and spring to bottom of support and rotate spring to engage the slot in support. Attach ground wire to insulated brush, then repeat for other brush sets.

3. Assemble overruning clutch to armature shaft as follows:

    a. Lubricate drive end of shaft with silicone lubricant.

    b. Slide clutch assembly onto shaft with pinion outward.

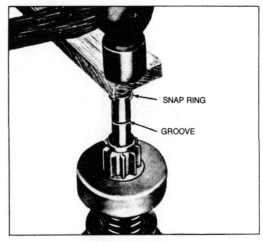

Forcing snap-ring over the armature shaft

    c. Slide retainer onto shaft with cupped surface facing away from pinion.

    d. Stand armature up on a wood surface, commutator downwards. Position snap-ring on upper end of shaft and drive it onto shaft with a small block of wood and a hammer. Slide snap-ring into groove.

    e. Install thrust collar onto shaft with shoulder next to snap-ring.

    f. With retainer on one side of snap-ring and thrust collar on the other side, squeeze together with two sets of pliers until ring seats in retainer.

4. Lubricate drive end bushing with silicone lubricant, then slide armature and clutch assembly into place, at the same time engaging shift lever with clutch.

5. Position field frame over armature and apply sealer (silicone) between frame and

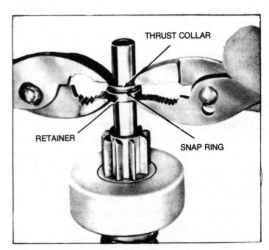

Forcing the snap-ring into the retainer

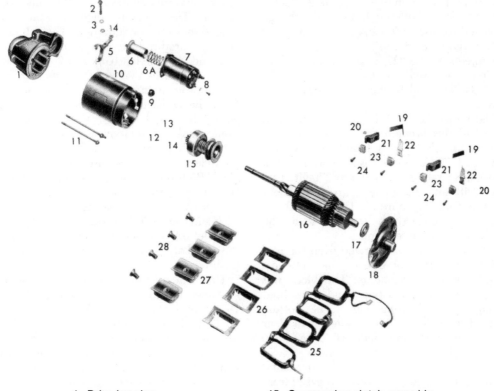

1. Drive housing
2. Shift lever bolt
3. Shift lever nut and lockwasher
4. Pin
5. Shift lever
6. Solenoid plunger
6A. Solenoid return spring
7. Solenoid case
8. Screw and lockwasher
9. Grommet
10. Field frame
11. Through-bolts
12. Thrust collar
13. Snap-ring
14. Retainer
15. Overrunning clutch assembly
16. Armature
17. Braking washer
18. Commutator end frame
19. Brush springs
20. Washer
21. Insulated brush holders
22. Grounded brush holder
23. Brushes
24. Screws
25. Field coils
26. Insulators
27. Pole shoes
28. Screws

Exploded view of starter

solenoid case. Position frame against drive housing, making sure brushes are not damaged in the process.

6. Lubricate commutator end bushing with silicone lubricant, place a leather brake washer on the armature shaft and slide commutator end frame onto shaft. Install thrubolts and tighten to 65 in. lbs.

7. Reconnect field coil connector /s to the solenoid motor terminal. Install solenoid mounting screws, if so equipped.

8. Check pinion clearance; it should be 0.010–0.140 in. Excessive clearance will force the replacement of worn parts since there is no method of adjusting the pinion.

ENGINE MECHANICAL

Design

The success of the Corvette is largely due to the lengthy option lists that permit an owner to literally tailor his car to a specific type of driving or competition. For this reason, the engines that power the 1963–1976 models have been offered in five internal displacements and approximately 14 performance levels.

Induction systems for these engines are varied and range from a single, four-barrel configuration of three, two-barrels, and fuel injection.

The most common engine is the 327 cubic inch V8. It was offered from 1963 through 1968 and spanned a horsepower range of 250 to 375; the latter figure being obtained with fuel injection. The 327, in addition to fuel injection, has used the Carter WCFB and AFB, Holley, and Rochester Quadrajet carburetors.

The stroke of the 327 was lengthened in 1969 and this brought the displacement to 350 cu in. The 350 as found in the 1969 through 1979 Corvettes has been available in horsepower ratings from 165 to 370. It is offered with either a single, four-barrel Rochester or Holley carburetor. The 327 and 350 engines are collectively referred to as the small block Corvette engines.

The 327 engine was derived from the earlier 265 and 283 Corvette engines, but featured many improvements. The block was completely new casting and provided stronger main bearing webs. The bottom ends of the cylinders were relieved to clear the longer stroke crankshaft. All 327 and 350 cubic inch engines, except base power plants, are equipped with forged crankshafts. Main bearing diameters were increased from 2.30 to 2.45 inches in 1968.

The large block engines were introduced to provide more torque and more flexible horsepower than the peakier small blocks. The cylinder block is quite conventional, the heads are where the innovation lies. Intake and exhaust valves are canted away from each other for optimum gas flow and port configuration. The seemingly strange angles at which the valves point gave rise to the nickname of "Porcupine" which was applied to these heads when they first appeared on NASCAR racing Chevrolets in 1963.

The large block Corvette engine was introduced in 1965 with an initial offering of 396 cubic inches and 425 hp. The 396 was enlarged to 427 cubic inches with a bore increase in 1966, although the top rated horsepower remained at 425. The 427, optional from 1966 through 1969, was offered in 390, 400, 425, 430, and 435 horsepower versions. Carburetors used on the large blocks included four-barrel Holley and Rochester carburetors and three, two-barrel carburetors. The 427 recieved a stroke increase in 1970 and became the 454. It reached its highest performance rating in 1970 with an output of 460 horsepower for the rare LS-7.

Generally speaking, the small and large block Corvette engines are of the same basic design. They feature eight cylinders arranged in a vee configuration. The cylinders are numbered front to rear with cylinders 1, 3, 5, and 7 on the left bank and 2, 4, 6, and 8 on the right, when viewed from the rear. Firing order for both engines is 1-8-4-3-6-5-7-2. Both the crankshaft and camshaft are supported by five bearings. Viewed from the front, crankshaft rotation is clockwise. Lubrication is full pressure, and a gear type oil pump feeds the system through a full flow oil filter. Both the oil pump and the distributor are driven by the camshaft. The main oil gallery pressurizes the bearings via the crankshaft and camshaft. The valve lifter oil gallery provides oil to the lifters which, in turn, feed the rocker arms through the hollow pushrods.

The standard bearer of Corvette high performance models was established, with the 1967 introduction of the 430 horsepower L-88 limited production option engine. This unit was furnished with a Tuft-rided and cross-drilled heavy duty crankshaft, magnafluxed and shotpeened connecting rods with $7/16$ inch connecting bolts, forged pistons with pop-up domes, and aluminum cylinder heads.

The peak of large block development was reached in 1969 with the ZL-1 engine. This was the basic L-88 engine but with an aluminum cylinder block.

ENGINE REMOVAL AND REPLACEMENT

This procedure is basically the same for all engines regardless of size and model year. Certain pieces of optional equipment require minor specific changes but the overall operation remains the same.

1. The engine may be removed separately from the transmission, through the top of the engine compartment. Begin by draining the cooling system and the engine crankcase. If a suitable plug is not available for the propeller shaft opening after the shaft has been removed, then drain the transmission.

2. Disconnect the battery cables from the battery terminals and remove the air cleaner and ignition shields. Remember to cover the carburetor.

3. Disconnect wiring at the alternator, temperature sending unit, oil pressure switch, primary coil lead, and CEC solenoid

when applicable. Also disconnect the engine ground wires and the accelerator rod at the bellcrank.

4. Disconnect the power brake hose at the carburetor end when applicable. Disconnect the tachometer drive cable at the distributor and the throttle valve if so equipped. Scribe the hood hinge locations on the support brackets and remove the hood.

5. Remove the radiator shroud and radiator, then the fan and fan assembly. If the car is equipped with power steering, remove the pump mounting bolts and push the pump into the vacant radiator opening. An alternate method is to disconnect the pump lines and plug both ends.

6. Remove the heater hose from the clip at the alternator bracket, then disconnect the hose from the engine connections and move back for extra clearance. Remove the rocker arm covers and place the vehicle on jack stands.

7. Remove the center head bolt on each head, and install the lift tool to the engine. Unhook the distributor cap and move it forward. Cover the distributor with a clean cloth.

8. Remove the propeller shaft and disconnect the speedometer cable. Disconnect the exhaust pipes at the manifold flanges. On cars equipped with large block engines, the front stud on each manifold must be removed before the exhaust pipes can be removed.

9. Disconnect the wire leads at the starter solenoid. Remove the gas tank line at the fuel pump and plug the line to prevent fuel siphoning.

10. Block the clutch pedal in the return position and remove the clutch cross-shaft. Remove the oil filter and oil cooler lines if so equipped. Remove the starting motor. If the Corvette is equipped with a manual transmission, remove the flywheel cover plate. If equipped with an automatic transmission, remove the converter underpan.

11. Remove the front engine mount thrubolts. Support the transmission with a floor jack and remove the transmission-to-engine bolts. If the car has Powerglide, remove the converter-to-flywheel bolts and install the converter holding bracket to the transmission.

12. Move the engine forward and upward as needed to clear the engine compartment.

13. Replacement is the reversal of this procedure.

Cylinder Heads
REMOVAL AND INSTALLATION

1. Remove the intake manifold as described. Remove the alternator lower mounting bolt, and lay the unit aside.

2. Remove the exhaust manifolds. If the vehicle has A/C, dismount the compressor and position it out of the way. Do not disconnect the refrigerant lines.

3. Back off the rocker arm nuts and pivot the rocker arms out of the way so that the pushrods can be removed. Identify the pushrods so that they can be reinstalled in their original locations.

4. Remove the cylinder head bolts and cylinder heads.

5. Install using new gaskets. The head gasket is installed with the bead up.

NOTE: *Coat a steel gasket, thinly and evenly, on both sides with sealer. If a steel asbestos gasket is used, do not apply sealer. Clean the bolt threads, apply sealing compound and install the bolts finger tight.*

6. Tighten the head bolts a little at a time in the sequence illustrated to the specified torque.

7. Install the exhaust and intake manifolds.

8. Adjust the valves.

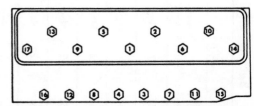

Small block V8 cylinder head bolt tightening sequence

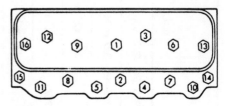

Big block V8 cylinder head bolt tightening sequence

Rocker Arms and Studs
REMOVAL AND INSTALLATION

NOTE: *Some engines are assembled using RTV silicone sealant in place of rocker arm*

Battery and Starter Specifications

| Year | Model | Battery | | | Starters | | | | | | Brush Spring Tension (oz) |
| | | Ampere Hour Capacity | Volts | Terminal Grounded | Lock Test | | | No-Load Test | | | |
					Amps	Volts	Torque	Amps	Volts	rpm	
1963–64	327 cu in.	61	12	Neg	330	3.5	—	65–100	10.6	3,600–5,100	35
1965–66	327 cu in.	61	12	Neg	330	3.5	—	83	10.6	4,350	35
	396, 427 cu in.	61	12	Neg	Not Recommended			83	10.6	4,350	35
1967	327 cu in.	61	12	Neg	Not Recommended			83	10.6	4,250	35
	427 cu in	61	12	Neg	Not Recommended			85	10.6	9,900	35
1968	All Engines	62	12	Neg	Not Recommended			85	10.6	10,000	35
1969	All Engines	62	12	Neg	Not Recommended			85	9.0	10,000	35
1970	All Engines	62	12	Neg	Not Recommended			55–80	9.0	3,500–6,000	35
1971–72	350	62	12	Neg	Not Recommended			65–95	9.0	7,500–10,500	35
	454	76	12	Neg	Not Recommended			65–95	9.0	7,500–10,500	35
1973–74	350	62	12	Neg	Not Recommended			65–95	9.0	7,500–10,500	35
	454	76	12	Neg	Not Recommended			65–95	9.0	7,500–10,500	35
1975	350	110①	12	Neg	Not Recommended			65–95	9.0	7,500–10,500	35
1976–79	350	100	12	Neg	Not Recommended			65–95	9.0	7,500–10,500	35

① 125 w/H.D. battery

General Engine Specifications

Year	Engine Displacement (cu in.)	Carburetor Type	Horsepower @ rpm ■	Torque @ rpm (ft lbs) ■	Bore and Stroke (in.)	Compression Ratio	Oil Pressure @ 2000 rpm
1963–64	327	4 bbl	250 @ 4400	350 @ 2800	4.00 x 3.25	10.5 : 1	45
	327	4 bbl	300 @ 5000	360 @ 2800	4.00 x 3.25	10.5 : 1	45
1963	327	4 bbl	340 @ 6000	344 @ 4000	4.00 x 3.25	11.25 : 1	45
	327	Fuel Inj	360 @ 6000	352 @ 5000	4.00 x 3.25	11.0 : 1	45
1964	327	4 bbl	365 @ 6200	360 @ 3600	4.00 x 3.25	11.0 : 1	45
	327	Fuel Inj	375 @ 6200	350 @ 4000	4.00 x 3.25	11.0 : 1	45
1965	327	4 bbl	250 @ 4400	350 @ 2800	4.00 x 3.25	10.5 : 1	45
	327	4 bbl	300 @ 5000	360 @ 3200	4.00 x3. 25	10.5 : 1	45
	327	4 bbl	350 @ 5800	360 @ 3800	4.00 x 3.25	11.0 : 1	45
	327	4 bbl	375 @ 6200	350 @ 4000	4.00 x 3.25	11.0 : 1	45
	327	Fuel Inj	365 @ 6200	350 @ 4600	4.00 x 3.25	11.0 : 1	45
	396	4 bbl	425 @ 6400	415 @ 4000	4.094 x 3.760	11.0 : 1	45
1966	327	4 bbl	300 @ 5000	360 @ 3200	4.00 x3. 25	10.5 : 1	45
	327	4 bbl	350 @ 5800	360 @ 3600	4.00 x 3.25	11.0 : 1	45
	427	4 bbl	390 @ 5200	460 @ 3600	4.25 x 3.76	10.25 : 1	60
	427	4 bbl	425 @ 5600	460 @ 4000	4.25 x 3.76	11.0 : 1	60
1967–68	327	4 bbl	300 @ 5000	360 @ 3400	4.00 x 3.25	10.0 : 1	45
	327	4 bbl	350 @ 5800	360 @ 3600	4.00 x 3.25	11.0 : 1	45
	427	4 bbl	390 @ 5400	460 @ 3600	4.25 x 3.76	10.25 : 1	65
	427	3–2 bbl	400 @ 5400	460 @ 3600	4.25 x 3.76	10.25 : 1	65
	427	3–2 bbl	435 @ 5800	460 @ 4000	4.25 x 3.76	11.0 : 1	65
	427①	4 bbl	430 @ 5200	450 @ 4400	4.25 x 3.76	12.0 : 1	65

General Engine Specifications (cont.)

Year	Engine Displacement (cu in.)	Carburetor Type	Horsepower @ rpm ■	Torque @ rpm (ft lbs) ■	Bore and Stroke (in.)	Compression Ratio	Oil Pressure @ 2000 rpm
1969	350	4 bbl	300 @ 4800	380 @ 3200	4.00 x 3.48	10.25 : 1	45
	350	4 bbl	350 @ 5600	380 @ 3200	4.00 x 3.48	11.0 : 1	45
	427	4 bbl	390 @ 5400	460 @ 3600	4.25 x 3.76	10.25 : 1	65
	427	3–2 bbl	400 @ 5400	460 @ 3600	4.25 x 3.76	10.25 : 1	65
	427	3–2 bbl	435 @ 5800	460 @ 4000	4.25 x 3.76	11.0 : 1	65
	427①	4 bbl	430 @ 5200	450 @ 4400	4.25 x 3.76	12.0 : 1	65
1970	350	4 bbl	300 @ 4800	380 @ 3200	4.00 x 3.48	10.25 : 1	40
	350	4 bbl	350 @ 5600	380 @ 3600	4.00 x 3.48	11.0 : 1	40
	350	4 bbl	370 @ 6000	380 @ 4000	4.00 x 3.48	11.0 : 1	40
	454	4 bbl	390 @ 4800	500 @ 3400	4.251 x 4.000	10.25 : 1	40
	454	4 bbl	460 @ 5600	490 @ 3000	4.251 x 4.000	11.25 : 1	40
1971	350	4 bbl	270 @ 4800	360 @ 3200	4.00 x 3.48	8.5 : 1	40
	350	4 bbl	330 @ 5600	360 @ 4000	4.00 x 3.48	9.0 : 1	40
	454	4 bbl	365 @ 4800	465 @ 3200	4.251 x 4.000	8.5 : 1	40
	454	4 bbl	425 @ 5600	475 @ 4000	4.251 x 4.000	8.5 : 1	40
1972	350	4 bbl	200 @ 4400	300 @ 2800	4.00 x 3.48	8.5 : 1	40
	350	4 bbl	255 @ 5600	280 @ 4000	4.00 x 3.48	9.0 : 1	40
	454	4 bbl	270 @ 4000②	390 @ 3200	4.251 x 4.000	8.5 : 1	40
1973	350	4 bbl	190 @ 4400	270 @ 2800	4.000 x 3.480	8.5 : 1	40
	350	4 bbl	250 @ 5200	285 @ 4000	4.000 x 3.480	9.0 : 1	40
	454	4 bbl	275 @ 4400	395 @ 2800	4.251 x 4.000	8.25 : 1	40
1974	350	4 bbl	195 @ 4400	275 @ 2800	4.000 x 3.480	8.5 : 1	40

General Engine Specifications (cont.)

Year	Engine Displacement (cu in.)	Carburetor Type	Horsepower @ rpm ■	Torque @ rpm (ft lbs) ■	Bore and Stroke (in.)	Compression Ratio	Oil Pressure @ 2000 rpm
1974	350	4 bbl	250 @ 5200	285 @ 4000	4.000 x 3.480	9.0 : 1	40
	454	4 bbl	270 @ 4400	380 @ 2800	4.251 x 4.000	8.25 : 1	40
1975–76	350	4 bbl	165 @ 3800	255 @ 2400	4.000 x 3.480	8.5 : 1	40
	350	4 bbl	205 @ 4800	255 @ 3600	4.000 x 3.480	9.0 : 1	40
1977	350	4 bbl	180 @ 4000	270 @ 2400	4.000 x 3.480	8.5 : 1	40
	350	4 bbl	210 @ 5200	255 @ 3600	4.000 x 3.480	9.0 : 1	40
1978	350	4 bbl	185 @ 4000	280 @ 2400	4.000 x 3.480	8.2 : 1	40
	350	4 bbl	220 @ 5200	260 @ 2600	4.000 x 3.480	8.9 : 1	40
1979	350	4 bbl	195 @ 4000	285 @ 3200	4.000 x 3.480	8.2 : 1	45
	350	4 bbl	225 @ 5200	270 @ 3600	4.000 x 3.480	8.9 : 1	45

■ Beginning 1972, horsepower and torque are SAE net figures. They are measured at the rear of of the transmission with all accessories installed and operating. Since the figures vary when a given engine is installed in different models, some are representative rather than exact.
① Limited production engine L88, for special purposes
② Not available in California

cover gasket. If the engine was assembled using RTV, never use a gasket when reassembling. Conversely, if the engine was assembled using a rocker arm cover gasket, never replace it with RTV.

When using RTV, an ⅛ inch bead is sufficient. Always run the bead on the inside of the bolt holes.

Rocker arms are removed by removing the adjusting nut. But sure to adjust valve lash after replacing rocker arms.

NOTE: When replacing an exhaust rocker, move an old intake rocker to the exhaust rocker arm stud and install the new rocker arm on the intake stud.

Rocker arm studs that have damaged threads or are loose in the cylinder heads may be replaced with new studs available in 0.003 in. and 0.013 in. oversize or the bores may be tapped and screw-in replacement studs used. Do not attempt to install an over-size stud without reaming the stud bore. Studs are press-fit. Mark IV (big block V8) and late high performance small-block engines use screw-in studs and pushrod guide plates.

NOTE: If engine is equipped with the A.I.R. exhaust emission control system, the interfering components of the system must be removed. Disconnect the lines at the air injection nozzles in the exhaust manifolds.

Valve Clearance Adjustment
HYDRAULIC LIFTERS

On V8 engines, crank the engine until the No. 1 piston is at TDC of its compression stroke (the compression can be felt by placing a finger over the spark plug hole or by feeling the valves as the timing mark passes "0"—if the valves don't move, the No. 1 piston is at the top of its compression stroke). With the

Valve Specifications

Year	Engine Displacement (cu in.)	Seat Angle (deg)	Face Angle (deg)	Spring Test Pressure (lbs @ in.)	Spring Installed Height (in.)	STEM TO GUIDE Clearance (in.)		STEM Diameter (in.)	
						Intake	Exhaust	Intake	Exhaust
1963–64	327	46	45	175 @ 1.26	1.66	0.0010–0.0027	0.0016–0.0033	0.3404–0.3417	0.3410–0.3417
	327 (High Perf)	46	45	175 @ 1.26	1.66	0.0010–0.0027	0.0016–0.0033	0.3404–0.3417	0.3410–0.3417
1965–66	327	46	45	175 @ 1.26	1.66	0.0010–0.0027	0.0016–0.0033	0.3404–0.3417	0.3410–0.3417
	327 (350 hp)	46	45	175 @ 1.26	1.66	0.0010–0.0027	0.0016–0.0033	0.3410–0.3417	0.3410–0.3417
	327 (fuel inj)	46	45	175 @ 1.26	1.66	0.0010–0.0027	0.0016–0.0033	0.3410–0.3417	0.3410–0.3417
	396	46	45	315 @ 1.38	$1\frac{7}{8}$	0.0005–0.0024	0.0012–0.0029	0.3715–0.3722	0.3713–0.3720
	427	46	45	315 @ 1.38	1.88	0.0010–0.0027	0.0015–0.0032	0.3715–0.3722	0.3713–0.3720
	427 (425 hp)	46	45	315 @ 1.38	1.88	0.0010–0.0027	0.0015–0.0032	0.3715–0.3722	0.3713–0.3720
1967	327 (300 hp)	46	45	200 @ 1.25	$1\frac{5}{32}$	0.0010–0.0027	0.0015–0.0032	0.3410–0.3417	0.3410–0.3417
	327 (350 hp)	46	45	200 @ 1.25	$1\frac{5}{32}$	0.0010–0.0027	0.0015–0.0032	0.3410–0.3417	0.3410–0.3417
	427 (390, 400 hp)	46	45			0.0010–0.0027	0.0015–0.0032	0.3715–0.3722	0.3713–0.3720
	427 (435 hp)	46	45	315 @ 1.38	$1\frac{7}{8}$	0.0010–0.0027	0.0015–0.0032	0.3715–0.3722	0.3713–0.3720
1968	327 (exc 350 hp)	46	45	198 @ 1.25	1.70	0.0010–0.0027	0.0017–0.0027	0.3410–0.3417	0.3410–0.3417

Year	Engine								
	327 (350 hp)	46	45	198 @ 1.25	1.70	0.0010–0.0027	0.0017–0.0027	0.3410–0.3417	0.3410–0.3417
	427 (exc 435 hp)	46	45	315 @ 1.38	1.88	0.0010–0.0027	0.0015–0.0032	0.3715–0.3722	0.3713–0.3722
	427 (435 hp)	46	45	315 @ 1.38	1.88	0.0010–0.0027	0.0015–0.0032	0.3715–0.3722	0.3713–0.3722
1969	350	46	45	200 @ 1.25	1.70	0.0010–0.0027	0.0010–0.0027	0.3410–0.3417	0.3410–0.3417
	350 (350 hp)	46	45	200 @ 1.25	1.70	0.0010–0.0027	0.0010–0.0027	0.3410–0.3417	0.3410–0.3417
	427 (390, 400 hp)	46	45	312 @ 1.38	1.88	0.0010–0.0027	0.0010–0.0027	0.3715–0.3722	0.3713–0.3722
	427 (435 hp)	46	45	312 @ 1.38	1.88	0.0010–0.0027	0.0010–0.0027	0.3715–0.3722	0.3713–0.3722
1970	350	46	45	80 @ 1.70	$1\,23/32$	0.0010–0.0037	0.0010–0.0047	0.3414	0.3414
	454	46	45	75 @ 1.88①	$1\,7/8$	0.0010–0.0037	0.0010–0.0047	0.3718	0.3718
	454②	46	45	75 @ 1.88③	$1\,7/8$	0.0010–0.0037	0.0010–0.0047	0.3718	0.3718
1971	350	46	45	80 @ 1.70	$1\,23/32$	0.0010–0.0037	0.0010–0.0047	0.3414	0.3714
	454	46	45	75 @ 1.88①	$1\,7/8$	0.0010–0.0037	0.0010–0.0047	0.3719	0.3717
1972	350	46	45	80 @ 1.70	$1\,23/32$	0.0010–0.0037	0.0010–0.0047	0.3414	0.3414
	454	46	45	75 @ 1.88①	$1\,7/8$	0.0010–0.0037	0.0010–0.0047	0.3719	0.3717
1973	350	46	45	80 @ 1.70④	$1\,23/32$	0.0010–0.0027	0.0010–0.0027	0.3414	0.3414
	454	46	45	80 @ 1.88	$1\,7/8$	0.0010–0.0027	0.0010–0.0027	0.3719	0.3717

Valve Specifications (cont.)

Year	Engine Displacement (cu in.)	Seat Angle (deg)	Face Angle (deg)	Spring Test Pressure (lbs @ in.)	Spring Installed Height (in.)	STEM TO GUIDE Clearance (in.)		STEM Diameter (in.)	
						Intake	Exhaust	Intake	Exhaust
1974	350	46	45	80 @ 1.70④	1 23/32	0.0010–0.0027	0.0010–0.0027	0.3414	0.3414
	454	46	45	80 @ 1.88	1 7/8	0.0010–0.0027	0.0010–0.0027	0.3719	0.3717
1975–79	350	46	45	80 @ 1.70④	1 23/32 ⑤	0.0010–0.0027	0.0010–0.0027	0.3414	0.3414

① Inner spring 30 @ 1.78
② 460 hp
③ Inner spring 41 @ 1.78
④ Intake given; 80 @ 1.61 for exhaust spring
⑤ 1977–79—exhaust—1 19/32

Crankshaft and Connecting Rod Specifications

All measurements are given in in.

Year	Engine	CRANKSHAFT					CONNECTING ROD	
		Main Brg Journal Dia	Main Brg Oil Clearance	Shaft End-Play	Thrust on No.	Journal Diameter	Oil Clearance	Side Clearance
1963–65	All	2.2978–2.2988	0.0008–0.0034	0.002–0.006	5	1.999–2.000	0.0007–0.0028	0.0017–0.0038
1966–67	All 327 cu in.	2.2978–2.2988	0.0008–0.0034	0.002–0.006	5	1.999–2.000	0.0007–0.0028	0.009–0.013
1966–67 1968	390 hp 400 hp	2.7481–2.7490	0.0013–0.0025	0.006–0.010	5	2.199–2.200	0.0009–0.0025	0.015–0.021
1966 1967 1968	425 hp 430 hp 435 hp	2.7481–2.7490	0.0013–0.0025	0.006–0.010	5	2.198–2.199	0.0014–0.0030	0.019–0.025
1968	327 cu in.	2.4484–2.4493	0.0008–0.0034	0.002–0.006	5	2.099–2.100	0.0007–0.0028	0.009–0.013
1969	350 cu in.	2.4474–2.4488	no. 1–2–3–4 0.0008–0.0020 no. 5 0.0018–0.0034	0.003–0.011	5	2.099–2.100	0.0007–0.0028	0.009–0.013
1969	390 & 400 hp	no. 1–2–3–4 2.7481–2.7490 no. 5 2.7478–2.7488	no. 1–2–3–4 0.0013–0.0025 no. 5 0.0015–0.0031	0.006–0.010	5	2.199–2.200	0.0009–0.0025	0.015–0.021
1967–69	L88	no. 1–2–3–4 2.7418–2.7490 no. 5 2.7478–2.7488	no. 1–2–3–4 0.0013–0.0025 no. 5 0.0015–0.0031	0.006–0.010	5	2.1985–2.1995	0.0014–0.0030	0.019–0.025

Crankshaft and Connecting Rod Specifications (cont.)

All measurements are given in in.

Year	Engine	CRANKSHAFT				CONNECTING ROD		
		Main Brg Journal Dia	Main Brg Oil Clearance	Shaft End-Play	Thrust on No.	Journal Diameter	Oil Clearance	Side Clearance
1969	435 hp	no. 1–4 2.7481–2.7490 no. 5 2.7478–2.7488	no. 1-2-3-4 0.0013–0.0025 no. 5 0.0015–0.0031	0.006–0.010	5	2.1985–2.1995	0.0014–0.0030	0.019–0.025
1970	350	2.4484–2.4493③	0.0003–0.0015④	0.002–0.006	5	2.0990–2.1000	0.0007–0.0028	0.008–0.014
	454	2.7485–2.7494①	0.0013–0.0025⑥	0.006–0.010	5	2.1990–2.2000	0.0009–0.0025	0.015–0.021
	454 (460 hp)	2.7481–2.7490②	0.0013–0.0025⑦	0.006–0.010	5	2.1985–2.1995	0.0014–0.0030	0.019–0.025
1971	350	2.4484–2.4493③	0.0008–0.0020⑤	0.002–0.006	5	2.0990–2.1000	0.0013–0.0035	0.008–0.014
	350 (330 hp)	2.4484–2.4493③	0.0013–0.0025⑨	0.002–0.006	5	2.0990–2.1000	0.0013–0.0035	0.008–0.014
	454 (365 hp)	2.7485–2.7494⑪	0.0013–0.0025⑥	0.006–0.010	5	2.1990–2.2000	0.0009–0.0025	0.015–0.021
	454 (425 hp)	2.7481–2.7490②	0.0013–0.0025⑦	0.006–0.010	5	2.1985–2.1995	0.0009–0.0025	0.019–0.025
1972	350	2.4484–2.4493⑧	0.0008–0.0020⑤	0.002–0.006	5	2.0990–2.1000	0.0013–0.0035	0.008–0.014
	350 (255 hp)	2.4484–2.4493⑧	0.0013–0.0025⑨	0.002–0.006	5	2.0990–2.1000	0.0013–0.0035	0.008–0.014
	454 (270 hp)	2.7485–2.7494⑪	0.0013–0.0025⑥	0.006–0.010	5	2.1990–2.2000	0.0009–0.0025	0.015–0.021

1973–74	350	2.4502⑫	0.0013–0.0025⑨	0.002–0.006	5	2.0990–2.1000	0.0013–0.0035	0.008–0.014
	454	2.7504⑬	0.0007–0.0019⑩	0.006–0.010	5	2.1990–2.2000	0.0009–0.0025	0.015–0.021
1975–76	350	2.4502⑫	0.0013–0.0025⑨	0.002–0.006	5	2.0990–2.1000	0.0013–0.0035	0.008–0.014
1977–79	350	2.4484–2.4493⑧	0.0008–0.0020⑤	0.002–0.006	5	2.0988–2.0998	0.0013–0.0035	0.008–0.014

① Nos. 3, 4—2.7481–2.7490; No. 5—2.7478–2.7488
② No. 5—2.7478–2.7488
③ No. 5—2.4479–2.4488
④ Nos. 2, 3, 4—0.0006–0.0018; No. 5—0.0008–0.0023
⑤ Nos. 2, 3, 4—0.0011–0.0023; No. 5—0.0017–0.0033
⑥ No. 5—0.0024–0.0040
⑦ No. 5—0.0029–0.0045
⑧ Nos. 2, 3, 4—2.4481–2.4490; No. 5—2.4479–2.4488
⑨ No. 5—0.0023–0.0033; with auto. trans. No. 1—0.0019–0.0031
⑩ Nos. 2, 3, 4—0.0013–0.0025; No. 5—0.0019–0.0035
⑪ Nos. 2, 3, 4—2.7481–2.7490; No. 5—2.7478–2.7488
⑫ No. 5—2.4508
⑬ Nos. 1, 5—2.7499

Piston Clearance

Year	Engine Displacement (cu in.)	Advertised Horsepower	Piston-to-Bore Clearance (in.) ●
1963–79	327	All	0.0005–0.0025
	350	165, 180, 185, 190, 195, 250, 300	0.0007–0.0027
		350	0.0020–0.0036
		245, 370	0.0036–0.0061
		210, 220, 225	0.0046–0.0061
	396	425	0.0036–0.0065

Piston Clearance (cont.)

Year	Engine Displacement (cu in.)	Advertised Horsepower	Piston-to-Bore Clearance (in.) ●
1963–79	427	390	0.0024–0.0045
		400	0.0024–0.0045
		430	0.0058–0.0080
		435	0.0040–0.0065
	454	245, 275	0.0018–0.0035
		345	0.0024–0.0049
		360	0.0024–0.0049
		390	0.0024–0.0049
		450	0.0040–0.0065

● Service range—minimum to maximum

Torque Specifications
All readings are given in ft lbs

Year	Engine Displacement (cu in.)	Cylinder Head Bolts	Rod Bearing Bolts	Main Bearing Bolts	Crankshaft Balancer Bolt	Flywheel-To-Crankshaft Bolts	Manifold	
							Intake	Exhaust
1963–67	327	60–70	35	80	60⑤	60	30	18–22
1968–76	327, 350	60–70	45	75②	60⑤	60	30	18–22
1977–79	350	65	45	80	60⑥	60	30	20⑦
1965	396	80	50	115	85	65	30	20
1966–76	427, 454	80①	50④	100③	85	65	30	20

① Aluminum heads—short bolts 65; long bolts 75
② Engines with 4-bolt mains—outer bolts 65
③ Engines with 4-bolt mains—short bolts 95; long bolts 105
④ $7/16$ rod bolts—70
⑤ Where applicable
⑥ Outer bolts—High Perf.—70 ft lbs
⑦ Inboard bolts—30 ft lbs

Ring Gap

All measurements are given in inches

Year	Engine Displacement (cu in.)	Top Compression	Bottom Compression
1963–68	327	0.013–0.023	0.013–0.025
1969–71	350	0.010–0.020①	0.013–0.025①
1965–74	396, 427, 454	0.010–0.020	0.010–0.020
1973–76	350	0.010–0.020	0.013–0.025②
1977	350	0.010–0.020	0.010–0.023③
1978–79	350	0.010–0.020	0.010–0.023④

① 250, 300 hp 350 cu in.
Top—0.013–0.023
2nd—0.013–0.025

② 250, 255 hp 350 cu in.—0.013–0.023
③ 180 hp—0.013–0.025
④ 185, 195 hp—0.010–0.025

Ring Side Clearance

All measurements are given in inches

Year	Engine Displacement (cu in.)	Top Compression	Bottom Compression
1963–68	327	0.0012–0.0032①	0.0012–0.0027①
1969	350	0.0012–0.0032	0.0012–0.0027
1970–77	350	0.0012–0.0032	0.0012–0.0027
1978–79	350	0.0012–0.0032	0.0012–0.0032
1965	396	0.0017–0.0032	0.0017–0.0032
1967–69	427	0.0017–0.0032	0.0017–0.0032
1971–76	454	0.0017–0.0032	0.0017–0.0032

① 250, 275 hp 327 cu in.
Top—0.0012–0.0027
2nd—0.0012–0.0032

Ring Side Clearance (cont.)

Year	Engine Displacement (cu in.)	Oil Control
1963–74	All engines except 396, 427	0.015–0.055
	396, 427	0.010–0.030
1975–79	350	0.015–0.055
1963–68	327	0.000–0.005
1969–76	350	0.000–0.005
1977–79	350	0.002–0.007
1965	396	0.0005–0.0065
1967–69	427	0.0005–0.0065
1970–76	454	0.0005–0.0065

crankshaft in this position the following valves may be adjusted.

Exhaust—1, 3, 4, 8
Intake—1, 2, 5, 7

Rotate the crankshaft one full revolution until the timing pointer is again aligned with the "0". With the crankshaft thus in No. 6 cylinder firing position, the following valves may be adjusted:

Exhaust—2, 5, 6, 7
Intake—3, 4, 6, 8

Adjustment is made by backing off the rocker arm adjusting nut until there is play in the pushrod. Tighten the nut to remove the pushrod clearance (this can be felt by rotating the pushrod with the fingers while tightening the adjusting nut). When the pushrod cannot be freely turned, tighten the nut one additional turn to place the hydraulic lifter in the center of its travel. No further adjustment is required.

MECHANICAL LIFTERS

Position the crankshaft for No. 1, then No. 6 cylinder firing positions as described for adjusting hydraulic lifters above. In the case of mechanical lifters, however, use a feeler gauge between the rocker arm and the valve stem to obtain the correct clearance. The final valve lash setting is made with the engine running at normal operating temperature. Specified valve lash (hot) can be found in the Tune-Up Specifications.

Intake Manifold

REMOVAL AND INSTALLATION

NOTE: *Some engines will require the use of RTV silicone sealant during installation of the manifold.*

1. Remove the air cleaner.
2. Drain the radiator.
3. Disconnect:
   a. Battery cables at the battery.
   b. Upper radiator and heater hoses at the manifold.
   c. Crankcase ventilation hoses as required.
   d. Fuel line at the carburetor.
   e. Accelerator linkage at the pedal lever.
   f. Vacuum hose at the distributor.
   g. Power brake hose at the carburetor base or manifold, if applicable.
   h. Ignition coil and temperature sending switch wires.
4. Remove the distributor cap and scribe the rotor position relative to distributor body.
5. Remove the distributor.
6. If applicable, remove the Delcotron upper bracket.
7. Remove the manifold to head attaching bolts, then remove the manifold and carburetor as an assembly.

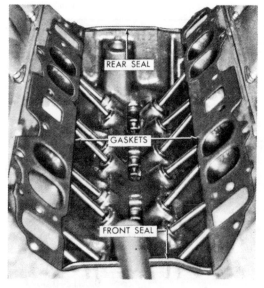

Intake manifold gasket and seal placement

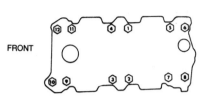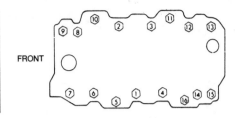

Intake manifold tightening sequence (small block V8, left; big block V8 right)

8. If the manifold is to be replaced, transfer the carburetor (and mounting studs), water outlet and thermostat (use a new gasket), heater hose adapter and, if applicable, the choke coil and EGR valve with its vacuum line.

9. Before installing the manifold, thoroughly clean the gasket and seal surfaces of the cylinder heads and manifold.

10. Install the manifold end seals, folding the tabs if applicable, and the manifold/head gaskets, using a sealing compound around the water passages. Make sure the gaskets are firmly cemented in place before installing the manifold.

NOTE: *On those engines not having front and rear manifold seals, place a $3/16$ inch bead of RTV silicone sealant on the front and rear ridges of the cylinder case. Extend the bead $1/2$ inch up each cylinder head to seal and retain the manifold side gaskets.*

11. When installing the manifold, care should be taken not to dislocate the end seals. It is helpful to use a pilot in the distributor opening. Tighten the manifold bolts in the sequence illustrated.

12. Install the ignition coil.

13. Install the distributor with the rotor in its original location as indicated by the scribe line. If the engine has been disturbed, refer to Distributor Removal and Installation.

14. If applicable, install the Delcotron upper bracket and adjust the belt tension.

15. Connect all components disconnected in Step 3 above.

16. Fill the cooling system, start the engine, check for leaks and adjust the ignition timing and carburetor idle speed.

Exhaust Manifold

REMOVAL AND INSTALLATION

Through 1973

1. If equipped with A.I.R., remove the air injector manifold assembly. The $1/4$ in. pipe threads in the manifold are straight threads. Do not use a $1/4$ in. tapered pipe tap.

2. Disconnect the battery.

3. If applicable, remove the air cleaner pre-heater shroud.

4. Remove the exhaust pipe flange nuts, then hang the pipe with wire.

5. Remove the manifold mounting bolts (end bolts first); then remove the manifold.

6. To install, clean the mating surfaces, then install the manifold with the center bolts first. Install the end bolts, then tighten all bolts.

7. To complete installation, reverse Steps 1 through 3.

1974 and Later Left Side

1. Disconnect the battery ground cable and raise the car. Disconnect the exhaust pipe at the manifold.

2. Remove the front manifold to exhaust pipe flange stud, and then remove the rear spark plug shield; lower the car.

3. Disconnect the spark plug wires and their holder, the temperature sending unit lead and the dipstick.

4. Remove the attaching bolts and remove the manifold.

5. To install, reverse the removal procedure.

1974 and Later Right Side

1. Disconnect the ground cable, and remove the fan shroud upper bolts and loosen the fan shroud. Remove the air cleaner intake pipe. Remove and set aside the air conditioning compressor and then remove the compressor lower mounting bracket. Do not disconnect any air conditioning lines. On. models to 1974, if equipped with an air pump, remove the air injector manifold assembly.

2. Raise the car and disconnect the exhaust pipe at the manifold.

3. Remove the right side engine mounting bracket through bolt, and loosen the left side mounting bracket through bolt. Jack up the

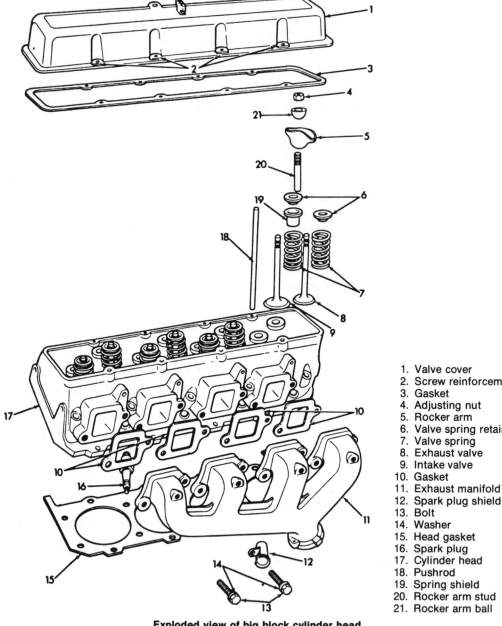

1. Valve cover
2. Screw reinforcements
3. Gasket
4. Adjusting nut
5. Rocker arm
6. Valve spring retainer
7. Valve spring
8. Exhaust valve
9. Intake valve
10. Gasket
11. Exhaust manifold
12. Spark plug shield
13. Bolt
14. Washer
15. Head gasket
16. Spark plug
17. Cylinder head
18. Pushrod
19. Spring shield
20. Rocker arm stud
21. Rocker arm ball

Exploded view of big block cylinder head

right side of the engine, reinstall the right side through bolt, and lower the engine until the through bolt is resting on the mounting bracket.

4. Remove the rear spark plug shield bolt. Disconnect the AIR tube from the exhaust pipe and move it aside; also remove the rear spark plug shield and the three rear manifold attaching bolts.

5. Lower the vehicle and remove the spark plug wires, air cleaner heat stove pipe, and the air cleaner intake pipe. Remove the rear spark plug shield.

6. Remove the manifold to engine bolts,

and remove the manifold, the EFE valve and the vacuum can.

7. To install, reverse the removal procedure.

Timing Chain

REMOVAL AND INSTALLATION

To replace the chain, remove the radiator core, water pump, the harmonic balancer and the crankcase front cover. This will allow access to the timing chain. Crank the engine until the timing marks on both sprockets are nearest each other and in line between the shaft centers. Then take out the three bolts that hold the camshaft gear to the camshaft. This gear is a light press fit on the camshaft and will come off easily. It is located by a dowel.

The chain comes off with the camshaft gear.

A gear puller will be required to remove the crankshaft gear.

Without disturbing the position of the engine, mount the new crankshaft gear on the shaft, and mount the chain over the camshaft gear. Arrange the camshaft gear in such a way that the timing marks will line up between the shaft centers and the camshaft locating dowel will enter the dowel hole in the cam sprocket.

Place the cam sprocket, with its chain mounted over it, in position on the front of the car and pull up with the three bolts that hold it to the camshaft.

After the gears are in place, turn the engine two full revolutions to make certain that the timing marks are in correct alignment between the shaft centers.

End-play of the V8 camshaft is zero.

Timing Gear Cover and Oil Seal Replacement

NOTE: *The timing case cover oil seal may be replaced without removing the case cover on all Corvettes.*

After gaining access to the oil seal, pry the old seal out of the cover with a screwdriver. Then, lubricate the new seal and drive it into place with a seal installer.

454 Engine

1. Remove the radiator, fan belts and, using a puller, remove the crankshaft pulley. On V8 engines, remove the water pump.

2. Remove the timing case-to-engine attaching bolts and remove the two oil pan-to-timing case bolts.

3. Slide the front cover forward until a knife can be positioned behind the cover, then cut the ends of the oil pan front seal off flush with the cylinder block on the two ends of the front cover.

4. Remove the front cover and clean all gasket mounting surfaces on the front cover, the block and the exposed portion of the oil pan.

5. Temporarily position a new oil pan front seal on the front of the oil pan and trim off the edges of the new seal so that it will fit flush with the engine block.

6. Remove the new front seal, coat it with sealer and install it on the front cover. Apply a bead of silicone rubber sealer to the place on the front of the oil pan where the cut off portion of the old seal will mate with the new oil pan front seal.

7. Install a centering tool in the crankshaft snout hole in the front cover and install the front cover on the engine.

8. Install the front cover bolts finger tight, remove the centering tool and tighten the

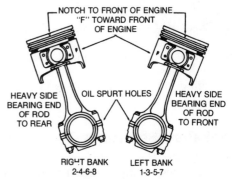

Correct piston/connecting rod positioning for 327 and 350 cu in. engines

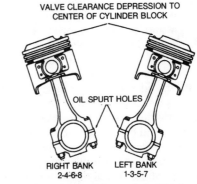

Correct piston/connecting rod positioning for 396, 427, and 454 cu in. engines

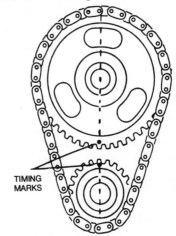

Timing mark alignment

cover bolts. Install the pulley, fan belts and radiator.

All Except 454 Engine

1. Remove the crankshaft pulley. Remove the oil pan on engines through 1974. Remove the water pump. Remove the screws holding the timing case cover to the block and remove the cover and gaskets.

2. Use a large screwdriver to pry the old seal out of the front face of the cover.

3. Install the new seal so that open end is toward the inside of the cover.

4. Check that the timing chain oil slinger is in place against the crankshaft sprocket.

5. Install the cover carefully onto the locating dowels.

6. Tighten the attaching screws to 6–8 ft lbs.

Crankshaft Servicing

Crankshaft servicing literally makes or breaks any engine; especially a high performance one such as the Corvette.

The most critical maintenance operation is the replacement of the crankshaft main bearings. These bearings are of the precision insert design and do not require adjustment through shims. They are offered in undersizes of 0.001 in., 0.002 in., 0.009 in., 0.010 in., 0.020 in., and 0.030 in.

Despite the advent of these inserts and accompanying precision machine work, it does happen that sizing mistakes are made and no crankshaft should be installed in a block without checking clearances. One of the simplest means of doing so is to use plastigage. This is a wax-like plastic material that is formed into precision threads. It will compress evenly between two surfaces, without damage, and when measured, will indicate the actual clearance. Certain precautions should be observed, however, and the following method should be used for accuracy.

It is easiest to check bearing clearance with the engine removed from the car and the block inverted. This ensures that the crank is resting against the upper bearing shells. If plastigage is to be used on an engine still in the vehicle, it will be necessary to support the crankshaft at both ends so that clearance between the crankshaft and the upper bearing shells is eliminated.

For demonstration purposes, assume that the engine is inverted on a work stand. Position the replacement upper bearing halves in the block and carefully lay the crank in place. Both the upper and lower bearing halves must be free of oil for the test. Beginning with the rear main bearing, cut a piece of plastigage sufficient to span the width of the crankshaft journal when placed in line with the longitudinal axis of the crankshaft.

Position the rear main bearing cap, with bearing half in place, into its proper placement. Insert the main bearing bolts and, with a torque wrench, evenly tighten them to specifications. Do not rotate the crankshaft with the plastigage between the journal and bearing. If this happens, the plastic thread will smear and reveal nothing.

When the correct torque has been achieved, loosen the bolts and carefully remove the bearing cap. The plastigage will be found either on the journal or the bearing surface. Regardless of its location, measure the compressed width of the plastic against the gauge printed on the packaging envelope. The flattened width will indicate the actual clearance between the bearing and the journal. Clearances beyond specifications will require bearing substitution and/or crankshaft grinding. Repeat the procedure

Checking main bearing clearance with Plastigage®

Checking crankshaft end-play

for the remaining bearings. If the flattened plastigage tapers either in the middle or at the ends, or exhibits any unusual patterns, it indicates that something is amiss and a close check with a micrometer is called for before continuing assembly.

When all the bearings have been satisfactorily checked, remove the plastigage and check the crankshaft for excessive drag by rotating it. Finally, check the crankshaft endplay. Force the crankshaft toward the front of the block and measure the clearance between the crankshaft and the front of the rear main bearing with a feeler gauge. Replace the bearing if it exceeds specifications.

With all clearances checked, the crankshaft is ready for placement in the block. Begin by installing the rear main seal halves in the rear main bearing cap and cylinder block grooves. The seal is correctly installed when the lips face the front of the engine. Lubricate these lips but keep oil off the mating surfaces. Insert the main bearing halves in the block and the bearing caps and lubricate the bearing surfaces with clean engine oil. Carefully lay the crankshaft in place.

Coat the mating surfaces of the rear main bearing and the block with a thin layer of oil sealing compound. Keep the sealer off the crankshaft and seal lips. Position the main bearing caps with their arrows aimed at the front of the block. Torque the front four bearings to specifications. Tighten the rear main bearing cap bolts to 12 ft lbs and tap the crankshaft first backward then forward, using a soft hammer. This aligns the rear main bearing and crankshaft thrust surfaces. Complete the installation by torquing all main bearing caps to specifications.

Connecting Rods and Bearings

The method of checking connecting rod bearing clearance is basically the same as for the crankshaft. Exercise the same precautionary steps to protect the connecting rod journals from damage and do not rotate the connecting rod on the journal with plastigage in place. To aid accuracy, pull the connecting rod up snug against the journal so that all clearance will be reflected in the bearing cap.

To remove the piston and rod assemblies from the block, force the piston downward in the block and use a ridge cutter to remove the ridge from the top of the cylinder. This done, carefully remove the assemblies. It is a good idea to place a rag in the cylinder, during the cutting operation so that loose chips will be caught. Also, when removing the bearing caps, slip pieces of rubber hose over the connecting rod bolts so they will not scratch the connecting rod journal when they exit the cylinder block.

It is cheap insurance to replace connecting rod bolts if the engine has seen extended service or is used for competition. Use a ring compressor to prevent the rings from catching on the block during reassembly. Lubricate the inside of the compressor liberally. Position the piston/rod assembly in the cylinder. They are correctly positioned when the connecting rod bearing tang slots are opposite the camshaft.

Be sure that the rod bolts are protected by tape or scrap pieces of hose to prevent damaging the rod journals. Use a wood mallet handle and lightly tap the piston into the cylinder. Attach the rod caps and torque the rod bolts to specification.

Pistons, Pins, and Rings

Corvette pistons are made of aluminum alloy and should not be exposed to careless treatment. Never use a wire brush to clean these pistons. Use cleaning solvent to remove varnish or carbon. Clean the ring grooves with a groove cleaner tool. Be sure the oil holes in the grooves are clear. Check for cracks, scuff marks, etc., and replace any piston that is suspect. Check the piston skirt measurement with a micrometer and compare to specifications.

Piston pins are matched to an individual piston and should be replaced with the piston as a set, not separately. Clean the pin with solvent and with a micrometer, check the pin external size and the piston pin bore size. Replace both if wear tolerance exceeds the specifications by 0.001 in.

Two compression rings and an oil ring assembly are used on Corvette pistons. The compression rings are marked on their top

Measuring ring end-gap

side and should always be assembled to the piston with this mark upward. Before assembling the rings to the piston, they should be fitted to their individual cylinder bore. To do this, place a compression ring in its cylinder and press it into the cylinder about ¼ inch above normal ring travel. A piston may be used to keep the ring even in the bore. If the gap between the ring ends exceeds tolerances, replace it, or, if the gap is too small, carefully widen the gap with a file. Repeat this procedure until rings are matched to their bores. Now check for ring/piston interference by placing the outer edge of the compression rings in their respective grooves and rolling them around the piston. Investigate any interference.

To install rings on a piston, first slip the oil control ring spacer into its groove and secure its tang in an oil hole. Butt the ends of the spacer together and install the lower spacer ring with its gap installed according to the enclosed chart. Install the upper ring in the same manner, then check the assembly for binding. Install the second compression ring expander and then the ring. The second ring is identified by a chamfer or step on its lower edge. Be sure the gap is correctly spaced. Install the top compression ring. This ring has its chamfer on its upper edge and is chrome faced.

Corvette rings are furnished in oversizes of 0.020 in., 0.030 in., and 0.040 in.

Camshaft Removal and Replacement

Remove the radiator and shroud. Remove the fan and fan pulley. Use a gear puller to remove the harmonic balancer. Remove the oil pan, water pump, and the timing chain cover.

On top of the engine, remove the battery

Camshaft removal

cables, carburetor(s)/fuel injection unit, distributor shielding, and distributor. Be sure to mark the distributor so that it will not be necessary to retime the engine.

When the intake manifold has been cleared of obstructions, remove it to expose the valve lifters. Cover the open area and remove the fuel pump and push rod.

Remove the rocker arm covers and rocker arms and withdraw the pushrods and lifters. Keep the pushrods and lifters in order so that they can be returned to their original positions. Remove the grille, timing chain, and camshaft sprocket. Loosen the engine side mount through bolts and jack up the front of the engine slightly. This is necessary for the camshaft to clear the radiator brace. Run two $5/16$–18 x 4 in. bolts into the camshaft bolt holes and carefully remove the camshaft from the engine. Do not rotate the crankshaft until the camshaft has been replaced and the sprocket and chain correctly installed and aligned. Alignment procedures are the same as those in the engine assembly section.

Reverse the operation to complete the replacement. Lubricate the cam and lifters with E.O.S. additive before installation. Make an initial and final valve adjustment as previously described.

Valve Lifters

Two types of lifters are employed in the Corvette engine: mechanical and hydraulic. Mechanical lifters require no maintenance and in fact should not be disassembled. Wash the lifter in solvent, then dry and clear its oil holes with compressed air. If the lifter is scored or damaged, replace it. If the bottom of the lifter is scored, it is a good idea to check the corresponding camshaft lobe for damage. Whenever a lifter is replaced, E.O.S. additive should be used for a reasonable break-in period.

There are two hydraulic lifters available for Corvette engines. Their principles are the same and they are interchangeable as a unit but their parts are not interchangeable. They are simply identified as types A and B.

To disassemble either, depress the plunger with a pushrod and remove the pushrod retainer seat with a thin screwdriver blade. If the lifter is an A type, remove the pushrod seat and the metering valve. If a B, take out the seat and the inertia valve assembly. Pull out the plunger, check valve assembly and plunger spring. Pry the ball re-

LIFTER "A"   LIFTER "B"

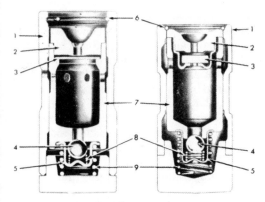

1. Lifter body
2. Pushrod seat
3. Metering valve (lifter A)
   Intertia valve (lifter B)
4. Check ball
5. Check ball retainer
6. Pushrod seat retainer
7. Plunger
8. Check ball spring
9. Plunger spring

Hydraulic valve lifters

tainer loose and shake out the check valve and a spring.

Wash the disassembled lifter in solvent and replace the entire unit if damage or excessive wear is evident.

To assemble the lifter, invert the plunger and place the check ball over the hole in the plunger's end. Position the check ball spring inside the ball so that the spring contacts the ball. Press-fit the retainer into the plunger. Place the plunger spring over the retainer, then slip the lifter body over the entire assembly. Make sure that the oil feed holes in the plunger and lifter body align.

Now turn the lifter over and fill it with SAE 10 oil. Depress the plunger with an ⅛ in. drift pin until the plunger seats and the oil holes are lined up. Slip the end of a 1/16 in. drift through the aligned oil holes to secure the plunger.

Withdraw the ⅛ in. drift pin and continue filling the assembly with oil. Refit the pushrod seat and metering valve assembly on A types, and the seat and inertia valve assembly on B types.

ENGINE LUBRICATION

Oil Pan

REMOVAL AND INSTALLATION

1. Disconnect the battery and remove the dipstick and its tube.
2. Raise the car and support the front on stands.
3. Remove the starter and flywheel shield.
4. Disconnect the steering idler arm and lower it out of the way.
5. Remove the oil pan and discard the side gaskets and end seals.
6. On high performance engines, the oil splash shield must be removed before further operations can be carried out.
7. Glue the side gaskets and end seals to the oil pan.
8. Install the pan on the engine and tighten the bolts in a criss-cross pattern. Do not overtighten these bolts.

Rear Main Oil Seal

REPLACEMENT

The rear main bearing seal may be replaced without removing the crankshaft. Both upper and lower seals must be replaced at the same time.

1. Remove the oil pan and oil pump.
2. Remove the rear main bearing cap, and pry the seal out from the bottom with a small screwdriver.
3. Remove the upper seal with a small hammer and a brass pin punch. Tap on one end of the seal until the opposite end can be gripped with pliers.
4. Clean the bearing cap and crankshaft.
5. Coat the lips and bead of the seal with a light engine oil. Do not get oil on the seal ends.
6. Insert the new seal into the bearing cap, rolling it into place with your finger and thumb. Press lightly on the seal, so that the

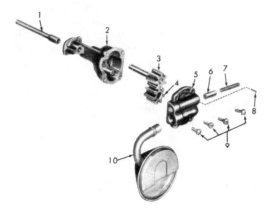

1. Shaft extension
2. Pump body
3. Drive gear and shaft
4. Idler gear
5. Pump cover
6. Pressure regulator valve
7. Pressure regulator spring
8. Retaining pin
9. Screws
10. Pickup screen and pipe

Exploded view of small block oil pump

1. Shaft extension
2. Shaft coupling
3. Pump body
4. Drive gear and shaft
5. Idler gear
6. Pickup screen and pipe
7. Pump cover
8. Pressure regulator valve
9. Pressure regulator spring
10. Washer
11. Retaining pin
12. Screws

Exploded view of big block oil pump

seal tangs on the cap don't cut the bead on the back of the seal.

7. Lubricate the lip of the new oil seal and slowly push it into place while turning the crankshaft. Make sure that the seal tangs don't cut the bead on the back of the seal.

8. Install the main bearing cap and torque to specifications.

Oil Pump

The oil pump is a two-piece housing containing a pressure regulator valve and the two pump gears. It is driven by the distributor shaft, which is in turn driven off the camshaft.

REMOVAL AND INSTALLATION

1. Remove the oil pan.
2. Remove the oil pump-to-rear main bearing cap bolt. Remove the pump and the extension shaft.
3. Installation is the reverse of removal.

ENGINE COOLING

The cooling system consists of a radiator, expansion tank, viscous drive fan, thermostat, and mechanical water pump. Small block and certain special-performance large block Corvettes use an aluminum cross-flow radiator. Most large block Corvettes utilize a larger capacity radiator of conventional copper-brass alloy. The viscous drive fan restricts operation at 1500 rpm in cold weather and 3500 rpm during warmer temperatures. This fan requires less horsepower to drive during high rpm operation and reduces under-hood noise.

Corvettes equipped with aluminum radiators demand certain precautions during normal operation and maintenance. Caution is advised when removing and replacing the filler cap, to avoid denting or scratching the sealing surfaces of the filler neck. Do not use replacement filler caps that use brass in their construction. Extended use will damage the radiator and necessitate extensive repair or replacement. The same precautionary measure should be taken with replacement drain cocks. A ⅛ in. cast iron plug may be substituted only for an extremely short period of time. Use only antifreezes and cleaners that are recommended for aluminum cooling systems.

Radiator

REMOVAL AND INSTALLATION
1963–68

1. Drain the radiator and cylinder block.
2. Remove upper and lower hoses and expansion tank hose.
3. Remove radiator shroud(s).
4. Remove retaining clamps and carefully pull radiator up and out of vehicle.

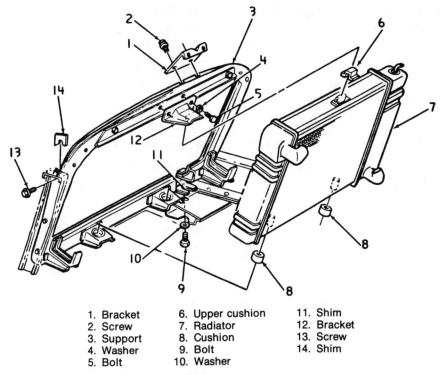

1. Bracket	6. Upper cushion	11. Shim
2. Screw	7. Radiator	12. Bracket
3. Support	8. Cushion	13. Screw
4. Washer	9. Bolt	14. Shim
5. Bolt	10. Washer	

1971–74 standard radiator and mounting

5. Reverse this procedure to install the radiator. Be sure that the two rubber cushions are correctly seated under the radiator before tightening.

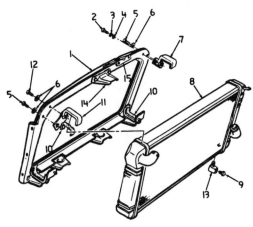

1. Support	9. Plug
2. Bolt	10. Insulator
3. Washer	11. Plate
4. Washer	12. Bolt
5. Bolt	13. Elbow
6. Washer	14. Bracket
7. Plate	15. Bracket
8. Radiator	

1971 heavy-duty 454 radiator and mounting

6. Refill the cooling system and check for leaks.

1969–74

1. Drain the radiator.

2. Raise the hood and insert a bolt in the hole of the hood support. Remove the hood.

3. Remove the radiator inlet and outlet hoses and, if applicable, the transmission coolant hoses.

4. If applicable, remove the supply tank hose at the radiator connection.

5. Remove the shroud to radiator support bracket screws (the L88 engine does not have a fan shroud).

6. Remove the shroud to radiator baffle bracket screws and let the shroud rest on the fan.

7. Remove the radiator upper support bracket screws and carefully lift the radiator from the car.

8. Install in the reverse order of removal.

1975–76

1. Drain the radiator and disconnect the battery ground cable. Disconnect cooler lines on automatic transmission models.

2. Remove the hood. This is a two-man job.

3. Remove the radiator support brackets attached to the fan shroud.

4. Remove the two front hood hinge bolts.

5. From inside the wheel well, remove the six radiator side support bolts.

6. Remove the two bottom radiator support bolts and the center brace.

7. Pull the radiator support forward and use a clamp to retain it to the right hood hinge.

8. Disconnect the two radiator hoses and the overflow hose.

9. Carefully lift the radiator out of the car.

10. If replacing the radiator, remove the shrouds and mount them on the new unit.

11. Installation is the reverse of removal.

1977–79

1. Disconnect the negative battery cable at the battery.

2. Drain the cooling system.

3. If necessary remove the air cleaner snorkel.

4. Raise the front of the vehicle and support it with jack stands.

5. Disconnect the fan shroud from the radiator support bracket.

6. If so equipped disconnect the automatic transmission cooler lines from the radiator.

7. Remove the radiator support brackets.

8. Disconnect the radiator upper and lower hoses and the overflow tube from the radiator.

9. Remove the radiator.

10. Installation is the reverse of removal. When installing the radiator make sure it is seated in the mounting pads. When replacing the radiator cap make sure the arrows line up with the overflow tube.

Water Pump

REMOVAL AND INSTALLATION

1. Drain the radiator.

2. Remove the fan.

3. Loosen the alternator mounting, rotate the alternator, and remove the fan belt. Remove power steering belt, A.I.R. belt, and idler belt, if so equipped.

4. Disconnect radiator and heater hoses.

5. Remove the water pump retaining bolts and remove the pump.

6. Reverse this procedure to install.

Thermostat

REMOVAL AND INSTALLATION

1. Drain enough coolant from the radiator to bring the level below the thermostat.

2. Remove the two bolts retaining the water neck to the manifold.

3. Lift the water neck (with radiator hose attached) and remove the thermostat.

4. Reverse this procedure to install, using a new gasket.

ENGINE REBUILDING

Most procedures involved in rebuilding an engine are fairly standard, regardless of the type of engine involved. This section is a guide accepted rebuilding procedures. Examples of standard rebuilding practices are illustrated and should be used along with specific details concerning your particular engine, found earlier in this chapter.

The procedures given here are those used by any competent rebuilder. Obviously some of the procedures cannot be performed by the do-it-yourself mechanic, but are provided so that you will be familiar with the services that should be offered by rebuilding or machine shops. As an example, in most instances, it is more profitable for the home mechanic to remove the cylinder heads, buy the necessary parts (new valves, seals, keepers, keys, etc.) and deliver these to a machine shop for the necessary work. In this way you will save the money to remove and install the cylinder head and the mark-up on parts.

On the other hand, most of the work involved in rebuilding the lower end is well within the scope of the do-it-yourself mechanic. Only work such as hot-tanking, actually boring the block or Magnafluxing (invisible crack detection) need be sent to a machine shop.

Tools

The tools required for basic engine rebuilding should, with a few exceptions, be those included in a mechanic's tool kit. An accurate torque wrench, and a dial indicator (reading in thousandths) mounted on a universal base should be available. Special tools, where required, are available from the major tool suppliers. The services of a competent automotive machine shop must also be readily available.

Precautions

Aluminum has become increasingly popular for use in engines, due to its low weight and excellent heat transfer characteristics. The following precautions must be observed when handling aluminum (or any other) engine parts:

—Never hot-tank aluminum parts.
—Remove all aluminum parts (identification tags, etc.) from engine parts before hot-tanking (otherwise they will be removed during the process).

—Always coat threads lightly with engine oil or anti-seize compounds before installation, to prevent seizure.
—Never over-torque bolts or spark plugs in aluminum threads. Should stripping occur, threads can be restored using any of a number of thread repair kits available (see next section).

Inspection Techniques

Magnaflux and Zyglo are inspection techniques used to locate material flaws, such as stress cracks. Magnaflux is a magnetic process, applicable only to ferrous materials. The Zyglo process coats the matrial with a fluorescent dye penetrant, and any material may be tested using Zyglo. Specific checks of suspected surface cracks may be made at lower cost and more readily using spot check dye. The dye is sprayed onto the suspected area, wiped off, and the area is then sprayed with a developer. Cracks then will show up brightly.

Overhaul

The section is divided into two parts. The first, Cylinder Head Reconditioning, assumes that the cylinder head is removed from the engine, all manifolds are removed, and the cylinder head is on a workbench. The camshaft should be removed from overhead cam cylinder heads. The second section, Cylinder Block Reconditioning, covers the block, pistons, connecting rods and crankshaft. It is assumed that the engine is mounted on a work stand, and the cylinder head and all accessories are removed.

Procedures are identified as follows:

Unmarked—Basic procedures that must be performed in order to successfully complete the rebuilding process.

Starred (*)—Procedures that should be performed to ensure maximum performance and engine life.

Double starred (**)—Procedures that may be performed to increase engine performance and reliability.

When assembling the engine, any parts that will be in frictional contact must be prelubricated, to provide protection on initial start-up. Any product specifically formulated for this purpose may be used. NOTE: *Do not use engine oil.* Where semi-permanent (locked but removable) installation of bolts or nuts is desired, threads should be cleaned and located with Loctite® or a similar product (non-hardening).

Repairing Damaged Threads

Several methods of repairing damaged threads are available. Heli-Coil® (shown here), Keenserts® and Microdot® are among the most widely used. All involve basically the same principle—drilling out stripped threads, tapping the hole and installing a pre-wound insert—making welding, plugging and oversize fasteners unnecessary.

Two types of thread repair inserts are usually supplied—a standard type for most Inch Coarse, Inch Fine, Metric Coarse and Metric Fine thread sizes and a spark plug type to fit most spark plug port sizes. Consult the individual manufacturer's catalog to determine exact applications. Typical thread repair kits will contain a selection of pre-wound threaded inserts, a tap (corresponding to the outside diameter threads of the insert) and an installation tool. Spark plug inserts usually differ because they require a tap equipped with pilot threads and a combined reamer/tap section. Most manufacturers also supply blister-packed thread repair inserts separately in addition to a master kit containing a variety of taps and inserts plus installation tools.

Before effecting a repair to a threaded hole, remove any snapped, broken or damaged bolts or studs. Penetrating oil can be used to free frozen threads; the offending item can be removed with locking pliers or with a screw or stud extractor. After the hole is clear, the thread can be repaired, as follows:

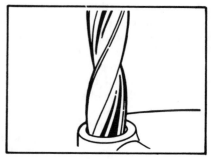

Drill out the damaged threads with specified drill. Drill completely through the hole or to the bottom of a blind hole

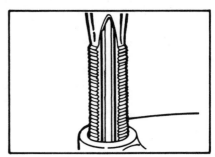

With the tap supplied, tap the hole to receive the thread insert. Keep the tap well oiled and back it out frequently to avoid clogging the threads

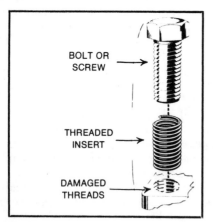

BOLT OR SCREW

THREADED INSERT

DAMAGED THREADS

Damaged bolt holes can be repaired with thread repair inserts

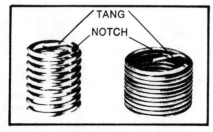

TANG

NOTCH

Standard thread repair insert (left) and spark plug thread insert (right)

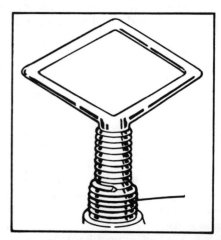

Screw the threaded insert onto the installation tool until the tang engages the slot. Screw the insert into the tapped hole until it is ¼–½ turn below the top surface. After installation break off the tang with a hammer and punch

Standard Torque Specifications and Fastener Markings

The Newton-metre has been designated the world standard for measuring torque and will gradually replace the foot-pound and kilogram-meter. In the absence of specific torques, the following chart can be used as a guide to the maximum safe torque of a particular size/grade of fastener.

- There is no torque difference for fine or coarse threads.
- Torque values are based on clean, dry threads. Reduce the value by 10% if threads are oiled prior to assembly.
- The torque required for aluminum components or fasteners is considerably less.

U. S. BOLTS

SAE Grade Number	1 or 2			5			6 or 7		

Bolt Markings

Manufacturer's marks may vary—number of lines always 2 less than the grade number.

Usage	Frequent			Frequent			Infrequent		
Bolt Size (inches)—(Thread)	Maximum Torque			Maximum Torque			Maximum Torque		
	Ft-Lb	kgm	Nm	Ft-Lb	kgm	Nm	Ft-Lb	kgm	Nm
¼—20	5	0.7	6.8	8	1.1	10.8	10	1.4	13.5
—28	6	0.8	8.1	10	1.4	13.6			
⁵⁄₁₆—18	11	1.5	14.9	17	2.3	23.0	19	2.6	25.8
—24	13	1.8	17.6	19	2.6	25.7			
⅜—16	18	2.5	24.4	31	4.3	42.0	34	4.7	46.0
—24	20	2.75	27.1	35	4.8	47.5			
⁷⁄₁₆—14	28	3.8	37.0	49	6.8	66.4	55	7.6	74.5
—20	30	4.2	40.7	55	7.6	74.5			
½—13	39	5.4	52.8	75	10.4	101.7	85	11.75	115.2
—20	41	5.7	55.6	85	11.7	115.2			
⁹⁄₁₆—12	51	7.0	69.2	110	15.2	149.1	120	16.6	162.7
—18	55	7.6	74.5	120	16.6	162.7			
⅝—11	83	11.5	112.5	150	20.7	203.3	167	23.0	226.5
—18	95	13.1	128.8	170	23.5	230.5			
¾—10	105	14.5	142.3	270	37.3	366.0	280	38.7	379.6
—16	115	15.9	155.9	295	40.8	400.0			
⅞— 9	160	22.1	216.9	395	54.6	535.5	440	60.9	596.5
—14	175	24.2	237.2	435	60.1	589.7			
1— 8	236	32.5	318.6	590	81.6	799.9	660	91.3	894.8
—14	250	34.6	338.9	660	91.3	849.8			

METRIC BOLTS

NOTE: *Metric bolts are marked with a number indicating the relative strength of the bolt. These numbers have nothing to do with size.*

Description	Torque ft-lbs (Nm)			
Thread size x pitch (mm)	Head mark—4		Head mark—7	
6 x 1.0	2.2–2.9	(3.0–3.9)	3.6–5.8	(4.9–7.8)
8 x 1.25	5.8–8.7	(7.9–12)	9.4–14	(13–19)
10 x 1.25	12–17	(16–23)	20–29	(27–39)
12 x 1.25	21–32	(29–43)	35–53	(47–72)
14 x 1.5	35–52	(48–70)	57–85	(77–110)
16 x 1.5	51–77	(67–100)	90–120	(130–160)
18 x 1.5	74–110	(100–150)	130–170	(180–230)
20 x 1.5	110–140	(150–190)	190–240	(160–320)
22 x 1.5	150–190	(200–260)	250–320	(340–430)
24 x 1.5	190–240	(260–320)	310–410	(420–550)

NOTE: *This engine rebuilding section is a guide to accepted rebuilding procedures. Typical examples of standard rebuilding procedures are illustrated. Use these procedures along with the detailed instructions earlier in this chapter, concerning your particular engine.*

Cylinder Head Reconditioning

Procedure	Method
Remove the cylinder head:	See the engine service procedures earlier in this chapter for details concerning specific engines.
Identify the valves:	Invert the cylinder head, and number the valve faces front to rear, using a permanent felt-tip marker.
Remove the rocker arms:	Remove the rocker arms with shaft(s) or balls and nuts. Wire the sets of rockers, balls and nuts together, and identify according to the corresponding valve.
Remove the valves and springs:	Using an appropriate valve spring compressor (depending on the configuration of the cylinder head), compress the valve springs. Lift out the keepers with needlenose pliers, release the compressor, and remove the valve, spring, and spring retainer. See the engine service procedures earlier in this chapter for details concerning specific engines.
Check the valve stem-to-guide clearance: 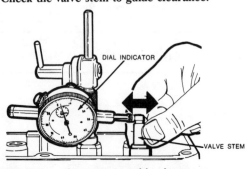 **Check the valve stem-to-guide clearance**	Clean the valve stem with lacquer thinner or a similar solvent to remove all gum and varnish. Clean the valve guides using solvent and an expanding wire-type valve guide cleaner. Mount a dial indicator so that the stem is at 90° to the valve stem, as close to the valve guide as possible. Move the valve off its seat, and measure the valve guide-to-stem clearance by rocking the stem back and forth to actuate the dial indicator. Measure the valve stems using a micrometer, and compare to specifications, to determine whether stem or guide wear is responsible for excessive clearance. NOTE: *Consult the Specifications tables earlier in this chapter.*

Cylinder Head Reconditioning

Procedure	Method

De-carbon the cylinder head and valves:

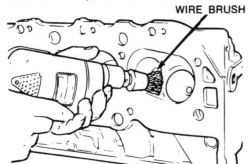

WIRE BRUSH

Remove the carbon from the cylinder head with a wire brush and electric drill

Chip carbon away from the valve heads, combustion chambers, and ports, using a chisel made of hardwood. Remove the remaining deposits with a stiff wire brush.
NOTE: *Be sure that the deposits are actually removed, rather than burnished.*

Hot-tank the cylinder head (cast iron heads only):
CAUTION: *Do not hot-tank aluminum parts.*

Have the cylinder head hot-tanked to remove grease, corrosion, and scale from the water passages.
NOTE: *In the case of overhead cam cylinder heads, consult the operator to determine whether the camshaft bearings will be damaged by the caustic solution.*

Degrease the remaining cylinder head parts:

Clean the remaining cylinder head parts in an engine cleaning solvent. Do not remove the protective coating from the springs.

Check the cylinder head for warpage:

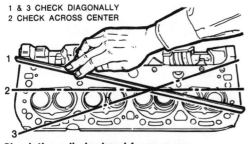

1 & 3 CHECK DIAGONALLY
2 CHECK ACROSS CENTER

Check the cylinder head for warpage

Place a straight-edge across the gasket surface of the cylinder head. Using feeler gauges, determine the clearance at the center of the straight-edge. If warpage exceeds .003″ in a 6″ span, or .006″ over the total length, the cylinder head must be resurfaced.
NOTE: *If warpage exceeds the manufacturer's maximum tolerance for material removal, the cylinder head must be replaced.*
When milling the cylinder heads of V-type engines, the intake manifold mounting position is altered, and must be corrected by milling the manifold flange a proportionate amount.

---

*Knurl the valve guides:

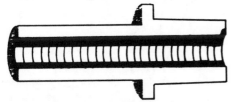

Cut-away view of a knurled valve guide

*Valve guides which are not excessively worn or distorted may, in some cases, be knurled rather than replaced. Knurling is a process in which metal is displaced and raised, thereby reducing clearance. Knurling also provides excellent oil control. The possibility of knurling rather than replacing valve guides should be discussed with a machinist.

Replace the valve guides:
NOTE: *Valve guides should only be replaced if damaged or if an oversize valve stem is not available.*

See the engine service procedures earlier in this chapter for details concerning specific engines. Depending on the type of cylinder head, valve guides may be pressed, hammered, or shrunk in. In cases where the guides are shrunk into the head, replacement should be left to an equipped machine shop. In other

Cylinder Head Reconditioning

Procedure	Method

A—VALVE GUIDE I.D. B—LARGER THAN THE VALVE GUIDE O.D.

WASHERS

B — A

A—VALVE GUIDE I.D. B—LARGER THAN THE VALVE GUIDE O.D.

Valve guide installation tool using washers for installation

cases, the guides are replaced using a stepped drift (see illustration). Determine the height above the boss that the guide must extend, and obtain a stack of washers, their I.D. similar to the guide's O.D., of that height. Place the stack of washers on the guide, and insert the guide into the boss.

NOTE: *Valve guides are often tapered or beveled for installation.* Using the stepped installation tool (see illustration), press or tap the guides into position. Ream the guides according to the size of the valve stem.

Replace valve seat inserts:

Replacement of valve seat inserts which are worn beyond resurfacing or broken, if feasible, must be done by a machine shop.

Resurface (grind) the valve face:

FOR DIMENSIONS, REFER TO SPECIFICATIONS

CHECK FOR BENT STEM

DIAMETER

VALVE FACE ANGLE

1/32″ MINIMUM

THIS LINE PARALLEL WITH VALVE HEAD

Critical valve dimensions

Using a valve grinder, resurface the valves according to specifications given earlier in this chapter.

CAUTION: *Valve face angle is not always identical to valve seat angle.* A minimum margin of $1/32''$ should remain after grinding the valve. The valve stem top should also be squared and resurfaced, by placing the stem in the V-block of the grinder, and turning it while pressing lightly against the grinding wheel.

NOTE: *Do not grind sodium filled exhaust valves on a machine. These should be hand lapped.*

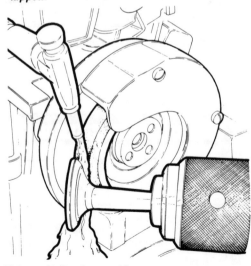

Valve grinding by machine

Cylinder Head Reconditioning

Procedure	Method

Resurface the valve seats using reamers of grinder:

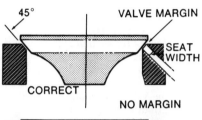

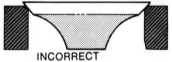

Valve seat width and centering

Reaming the valve seat with a hand reamer

Select a reamer of the correct seat angle, slightly larger than the diameter of the valve seat, and assemble it with a pilot of the correct size. Install the pilot into the valve guide, and using steady pressure, turn the reamer clockwise.

CAUTION: *Do not turn the reamer counterclockwise.* Remove only as much material as necessary to clean the seat. Check the concentricity of the seat (following). If the dye method is not used, coat the valve face with Prussian blue dye, install and rotate it on the valve seat. Using the dye marked area as a centering guide, center and narrow the valve seat to specifications with correction cutters.

NOTE: *When no specifications are available, minimum seat width for exhaust valves should be* $5/64''$, *intake valves* $1/16''$.

After making correction cuts, check the position of the valve seat on the valve face using Prussian blue dye.

To resurface the seat with a power grinder, select a pilot of the correct size and coarse stone of the proper angle. Lubricate the pilot and move the stone on and off the valve seat at 2 cycles per second, until all flaws are gone. Finish the seat with a fine stone. If necessary the seat can be corrected or narrowed using correction stones.

Check the valve seat concentricity:

Coat the valve face with Prussian blue dye, install the valve, and rotate it on the valve seat. If the entire seat becomes coated, and the valve is known to be concentric, the seat is concentric.

*Install the dial gauge pilot into the guide, and rest of the arm on the valve seat. Zero the gauge, and rotate the arm around the seat. Run-out should not exceed .002″.

Check the valve seat concentricity with a dial gauge

Cylinder Head Reconditioning

Procedure	Method

*Lap the valves:
NOTE: *Valve lapping is done to ensure efficient sealing of resurfaced valves and seats.*

Invert the cylinder head, lightly lubricate the valve stems, and install the valves in the head as numbered. Coat valve seats with fine grinding compound, and attach the lapping tool suction cup to a valve head.
NOTE: *Moisten the suction cup.* Rotate the tool between the palms, changing position and lifting the tool often to prevent grooving. Lap the valve until a smooth, polished seat is evident. Remove the valve and tool, and rinse away all traces of grinding compound.

** Fasten a suction cup to a piece of drill rod, and mount the rod in a hand drill. Proceed as above, using the hand drill as a lapping tool.
CAUTION: *Due to the higher speeds involved when using the hand drill, care must be exercised to avoid grooving the seat.* Lift the tool and change direction of rotation often.

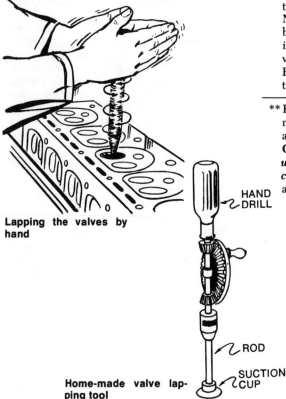

Lapping the valves by hand

HAND DRILL

ROD

SUCTION CUP

Home-made valve lapping tool

Check the valve springs:

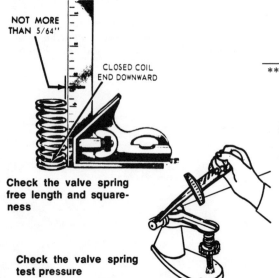

NOT MORE THAN 5/64"

CLOSED COIL END DOWNWARD

Check the valve spring free length and squareness

Check the valve spring test pressure

Place the spring on a flat surface next to a square. Measure the height of the spring, and rotate it against the edge of the square to measure distortion. If spring height varies (by comparison) by more than $1/16''$ or if distortion exceeds $1/16''$, replace the spring.

** In addition to evaluating the spring as above, test the spring pressure at the installed and compressed (installed height minus valve lift) height using a valve spring tester. Springs used on small displacement engines (up to 3 liters) should be $\mp$ 1 lb of all other springs in either position. A tolerance of $\mp$ 5 lbs is permissible on larger engines.

Cylinder Head Reconditioning

Procedure	Method

*Install valve stem seals:

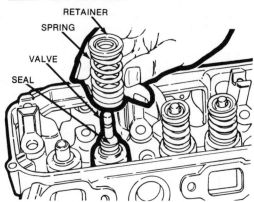

RETAINER

SPRING

VALVE

SEAL

Install valve stem seals

*Due to the pressure differential that exists at the ends of the intake valve guides (atmospheric pressure above, manifold vacuum below), oil is drawn through the valve guides into the intake port. This has been alleviated somewhat since the addition of positive crankcase ventilation, which lowers the pressure above the guides. Several types of valve stem seals are available to reduce blow-by. Certain seals simply slip over the stem and guide boss, while others require that the boss be machined. Recently, Teflon guide seals have become popular. Consult a parts supplier or machinist concerning availability and suggested usages.

NOTE: *When installing seals, ensure that a small amount of oil is able to pass the seal to lubricate the valve guides; otherwise, excessive wear may result.*

Install the valves:

See the engine service procedures earlier in this chapter for details concerning specific engines.

Lubricate the valve stems, and install the valves in the cylinder head as numbered. Lubricate and position the seals (if used) and the valve springs. Install the spring retainers, compress the springs, and insert the keys using needlenose pliers or a tool designed for this purpose.

NOTE: *Retain the keys with wheel bearing grease during installation.*

Check valve spring installed height:

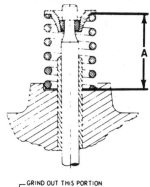

Valve spring installed height (A)

GRIND OUT THIS PORTION

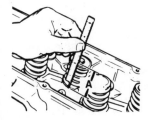

Measure the valve spring installed height (A) with a modified steel rule

Measure the distance between the spring pad the lower edge of the spring retainer, and compare to specifications. If the installed height is incorrect, add shim washers between the spring pad and the spring.

CAUTION: *Use only washers designed for this purpose.*

Cylinder Head Reconditioning

Procedure	*Method*
Inspect the rocker arms, balls, studs, and nuts: 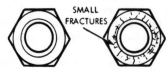 **Stress cracks in the rocker nuts**	Visually inspect the rocker arms, balls, studs, and nuts for cracks, galling, burning, scoring, or wear. If all parts are intact, liberally lubricate the rocker arms and balls, and install them on the cylinder head. If wear is noted on a rocker arm at the point of valve contact, grind it smooth and square, removing as little material as possible. Replace the rocker arm if excessively worn. If a rocker stud shows signs of wear, it must be replaced (see below). If a rocker nut shows stress cracks, replace it. If an exhaust ball is galled or burned, substitute the intake ball from the same cylinder (if it is intact), and install a new intake ball. NOTE: *Avoid using new rocker balls on exhaust valves.*
Replace rocker studs: 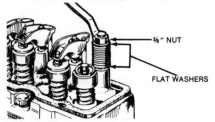 **Extracting a pressed-in rocker stud** 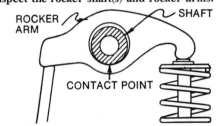 **Ream the stud bore for oversize rocker studs**	In order to remove a threaded stud, lock two nuts on the stud, and unscrew the stud using the lower nut. Coat the lower threads of the new stud with Loctite, and install. Two alternative methods are available for replacing pressed in studs. Remove the damaged stud using a stack of washers and a nut (see ilustration). In the first, the boss is reamed .005–.006″ oversize, and an oversize stud pressed in. Control the stud extension over the boss using washers, in the same manner as valve guides. Before installing the stud, coat it with white lead and grease. To retain the stud more positively drill a hole through the stud and boss, and install a roll pin. In the second method, the boss is tapped, and a threaded stud installed.
Inspect the rocker shaft(s) and rocker arms: 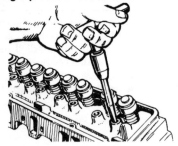 **Check the rocker arm-to-rocker shaft contact area**	Remove the rocker arms, springs and washers from rocker shaft. NOTE: *Lay out parts in the order as they are removed.* Inspect rocker arms for pitting or wear on the valve contact point, or excessive bushing wear. Bushings need only be replaced if wear is excessive, because the rocker arm normally contacts the shaft at one point only. Grind the valve contact point of rocker arm smooth if necessary, removing as little material as possible. If excessive material must be removed to smooth and square the arm, it should be replaced. Clean out all oil holes and passages in rocker shaft. If shaft is grooved or worn, replace it. Lubricate and assemble the rocker shaft.

Cylinder Head Reconditioning

Procedure	Method
Inspect the pushrods:	Remove the pushrods, and, if hollow, clean out the oil passages using fine wire. Roll each pushrod over a piece of clean glass. If a distinct clicking sound is heard as the pushrod rolls, the rod is bent, and must be replaced.
	*The length of all pushrods must be equal. Measure the length of the pushrods, compare to specifications, and replace as necessary.
*Inspect the valve lifters: 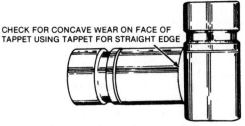 CHECK FOR CONCAVE WEAR ON FACE OF TAPPET USING TAPPET FOR STRAIGHT EDGE **Check the lifter face for squareness**	Remove lifters from their bores, and remove gum and varnish, using solvent. Clean walls of lifter bores. Check lifters for concave wear as illustrated. If face is worn concave, replace lifter, and carefully inspect the camshaft. Lightly lubricate lifter and insert it into its bore. If play is excessive, an oversize lifter must be installed (where possible). Consult a machinist concerning feasibility. If play is satisfactory, remove, lubricate, and reinstall the lifter.
*Testing hydraulic lifter leak down:	Submerge lifter in a container of kerosene. Chuck a used pushrod or its equivalent into a drill press. Position container of kerosene so pushrod acts on the lifter plunger. Pump lifter with the drill press, until resistance increases. Pump several more times to bleed any air out of lifter. Apply very firm, constant pressure to the lifter, and observe rate at which fluid bleeds out of lifter. If the fluid bleeds very quickly (less than 15 seconds), lifter is defective. If the time exceeds 60 seconds, lifter is sticking. In either case, recondition or replace lifter. If lifter is operating properly (leak down time 15–60 seconds), lubricate and install it.

Cylinder Block Reconditioning

Procedure	Method
Checking the main bearing clearance: 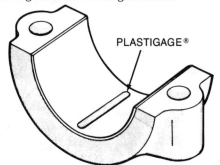 PLASTIGAGE® **Plastigage® installed on the lower bearing shell**	Invert engine, and remove cap from the bearing to be checked. Using a clean, dry rag, thoroughly clean all oil from crankshaft journal and bearing insert. NOTE: *Plastigage® is soluble in oil; therefore, oil on the journal or bearing could result in erroneous readings.* Place a piece of Plastigage along the full length of journal, reinstall cap, and torque to specifications. **NOTE: Specifications are given in the engine specifications earlier in this chapter.** Remove bearing cap, and determine bearing clearance by comparing width of Plastigage to the scale on Plastigage envelope. Journal taper is determined by comparing width of the Plas-

Cylinder Block Reconditioning

Procedure	Method

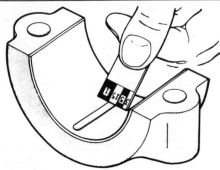

Measure Plastigage® to determine main bearing clearance

tigage strip near its ends. Rotate crankshaft 90° and retest, to determine journal eccentricity. NOTE: *Do not rotate crankshaft with Plastigage installed.* If bearing insert and journal appear intact, and are within tolerances, no further main bearing service is required. If bearing or journal appear defective, cause of failure should be determined before replacement.

* Remove crankshaft from block (see below). Measure the main bearing journals at each end twice (90° apart) using a micrometer, to determine diameter, journal taper and eccentricity. If journals are within tolerances, reinstall bearing caps at their specified torque. Using a telescope gauge and micrometer, measure bearing I.D. parallel to piston axis and at 30° on each side of piston axis. Subtract journal O.D. for bearing I.D. to determine oil clearance. If crankshaft journals appear defective, or do not meet tolerances, there is no need to measure bearings; for the crankshaft will require grinding and/or undersize bearings will be required. If bearing appears defective, cause for failure should be determined prior to replacement.

Check the connecting rod bearing clearance:

Connecting rod bearing clearance is checked in the same manner as main bearing clearance, using Plastigage. Before removing the crankshaft, connecting rod side clearance also should be measured and recorded.

* Checking connecting rod bearing clearance, using a micrometer, is identical to checking main bearing clearance. If no other service is required, the piston and rod assemblies need not be removed.

Remove the crankshaft:

Using a punch, mark the corresponding main bearing caps and saddles according to position (i.e., one punch on the front main cap and saddle, two on the second, three on the third, etc.). Using number stamps, identify the corresponding connecting rods and caps, according to cylinder (if no numbers are present). Remove the main and connecting rod caps, and place

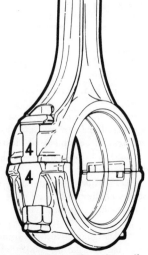

Match the connecting rod to the cylinder with a number stamp

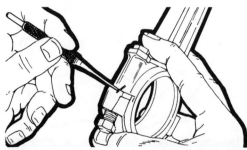

Match the connecting rod and cap with scribe marks

Cylinder Block Reconditioning

Procedure	Method
	sleeves of plastic tubing or vacuum hose over the connecting rod bolts, to protect the journals as the crankshaft is removed. Lift the crankshaft out of the block.
Remove the ridge from the top of the cylinder: RIDGE CAUSED BY CYLINDER WEAR CYLINDER WALL TOP OF PISTON **Cylinder bore ridge**	In order to facilitate removal of the piston and connecting rod, the ridge at the top of the cylinder (unworn area; see illustration) must be removed. Place the piston at the bottom of the bore, and cover it with a rag. Cut the ridge away using a ridge reamer, exercising extreme care to avoid cutting too deeply. Remove the rag, and remove cuttings that remain on the piston. **CAUTION:** *If the ridge is not removed, and new rings are installed, damage to rings will result.*
Remove the piston and connecting rod: **Push the piston out with a hammer handle**	Invert the engine, and push the pistons and connecting rods out of the cylinders. If necessary, tap the connecting rod boss with a wooden hammer handle, to force the piston out. **CAUTION:** *Do not attempt to force the piston past the cylinder ridge* (see above).
Service the crankshaft:	Ensure that all oil holes and passages in the crankshaft are open and free of sludge. If necessary, have the crankshaft ground to the largest possible undersize.
	** Have the crankshaft Magnafluxed, to locate stress cracks. Consult a machinist concerning additional service procedures, such as surface hardening (e.g., nitriding, Tuftriding) to improve wear characteristics, cross drilling and chamfering the oil holes to improve lubrication, and balancing.
Removing freeze plugs:	Drill a small hole in the middle of the freeze plugs. Thread a large sheet metal screw into the hole and remove the plug with a slide hammer.
Remove the oil gallery plugs:	Threaded plugs should be removed using an appropriate (usually square) wrench. To remove soft, pressed in plugs, drill a hole in the plug, and thread in a sheet metal screw. Pull the plug out by the screw using pliers.

Cylinder Block Reconditioning

Procedure	Method
Hot-tank the block: NOTE: *Do not hot-tank aluminum parts.*	Have the block hot-tanked to remove grease, corrosion, and scale from the water jackets. NOTE: *Consult the operator to determine whether the camshaft bearings will be damaged during the hot-tank process.*

Check the block for cracks:	Visually inspect the block for cracks or chips. The most common locations are as follows:
	    Adjacent to freeze plugs.
	    Between the cylinders and water jackets.
	    Adjacent to the main bearing saddles.
	    At the extreme bottom of the cylinders.
	Check only suspected cracks using spot check dye (see introduction). If a crack is located, consult a machinist concerning possible repairs.

	** Magnaflux the block to locate hidden cracks. If cracks are located, consult a machinist about feasibility of repair.
Install the oil gallery plugs and freeze plugs:	Coat freeze plugs with sealer and tap into position using a piece of pipe, slightly smaller than the plug, as a driver. To ensure retention, stake the edges of the plugs. Coat threaded oil gallery plugs with sealer and install. Drive replacement soft plugs into block using a large drift as a driver.
	* Rather than reinstalling lead plugs, drill and tap the holes, and install threaded plugs.
Check the bore diameter and surface: 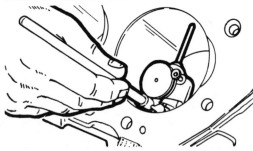 **Measure the cylinder bore with a dial gauge**	Visually inspect the cylinder bores for roughness, scoring, or scuffing. If evident, the cylinder bore must be bored or honed oversize to eliminate imperfections, and the smallest possible oversize piston used. The new pistons should be given to the machinist with the block, so that the cylinders can be bored or honed exactly to the piston size (plus clearance). If no flaws are evident, measure the bore diameter using a telescope gauge and micrometer, or dial gauge, parallel and perpendicular to the engine centerline, at the top (below the ridge) and bottom of the bore. Subtract the bottom measurements from the top to determine taper, and the parallel to

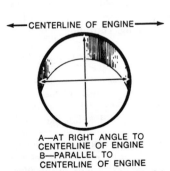

A—AT RIGHT ANGLE TO CENTERLINE OF ENGINE
B—PARALLEL TO CENTERLINE OF ENGINE

Cylinder bore measuring points

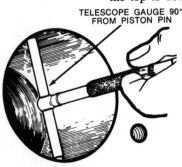

Measure the cylinder bore with a telescope gauge

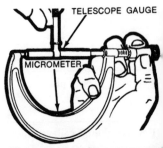

Measure the telescope gauge with a micrometer to determine the cylinder bore

Cylinder Block Reconditioning

Procedure	Method
	the centerline measurements from the perpendicular measurements to determine eccentricity. If the measurements are not within specifications, the cylinder must be bored or honed, and an oversize piston installed. If the measurements are within specifications the cylinder may be used as is, with only finish honing (see below). NOTE: *Prior to submitting the block for boring, perform the following operation(s).*
Check the cylinder block bearing alignment: **Check the main bearing saddle alignment**	Remove the upper bearing inserts. Place a straightedge in the bearing saddles along the centerline of the crankshaft. If clearance exists between the straightedge and the center saddle, the block must be alignbored.
*Check the deck height:	The deck height is the distance from the crankshaft centerline to the block deck. To measure, invert the engine, and install the crankshaft, retaining it with the center main cap. Measure the distance from the crankshaft journal to the block deck, parallel to the cylinder centerline. Measure the diameter of the end (front and rear) main journals, parallel to the centerline of the cylinders, divide the diameter in half, and subtract it from the previous measurement. The results of the front and rear measurements should be identical. If the difference exceeds .005″, the deck height should be corrected. NOTE: *Block deck height and warpage should be corrected at the same time.*
Check the block deck for warpage:	Using a straightedge and feeler gauges, check the block deck for warpage in the same manner that the cylinder head is checked (see Cylinder Head Reconditioning). If warpage exceeds specifications, have the deck resurfaced. NOTE: *In certain cases a specification for total material removal (cylinder head and block deck) is provided. This specification must not be exceeded.*
Clean and inspect the pistons and connecting rods: RING EXPANDER **Remove the piston rings**	Using a ring expander, remove the rings from the piston. Remove the retaining rings (if so equipped) and remove piston pin. NOTE: *If the piston pin must be pressed out, determine the proper method and use the proper tools; otherwise the piston will distort.* Clean the ring grooves using an appropriate tool, exercising care to avoid cutting too deeply. Thoroughly clean all carbon and varnish from the piston with solvent. CAUTION: *Do not use a wire brush or caustic solvent on pistons.* Inspect the pistons for scuffing, scoring, cracks, pitting, or excessive ring

Cylinder Block Reconditioning

Procedure	Method

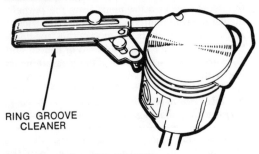

RING GROOVE
CLEANER

Clean the piston ring grooves

groove wear. If wear is evident, the piston must be replaced. Check the connecting rod length by measuring the rod from the inside of the large end to the inside of the small end using calipers (see illustration). All connecting rods should be equal length. Replace any rod that differs from the others in the engine.

* Have the connecting rod alignment checked in an alignment fixture by a machinist. Replace any twisted or bent rods.

* Magnaflux the connecting rods to locate stress cracks. If cracks are found, replace the connecting rod.

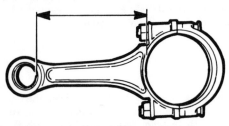

Check the connecting rod length (arrow)

Fit the pistons to the cylinders:

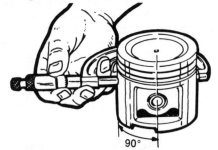

90°

Measure the piston prior to fitting

Using a telescope gauge and micrometer, or a dial gauge, measure the cylinder bore diameter perpendicular to the piston pin, 2½″ below the deck. Measure the piston perpendicular to its pin on the skirt. The difference between the two measurements is the piston clearance. If the clearance is within specifications or slightly below (after boring or honing), finish honing is all that is required. If the clearance is excessive, try to obtain a slightly larger piston to bring clearance within specifications. Where this is not possible, obtain the first oversize piston, and hone (or if necessary, bore) the cylinder to size.

Assemble the pistons and connecting rods:

Install the piston pin lock-rings (if used)

Inspect piston pin, connecting rod small end bushing, and piston bore for galling, scoring, or excessive wear. If evident, replace defective part(s). Measure the I.D. of the piston boss and connecting rod small end, and the O.D. of the piston pin. If within specifications, assemble piston pin and rod.
CAUTION: *If piston pin must be pressed in, determine the proper method and use the proper tools; otherwise the piston will distort.*
    Install the lock rings; ensure that they seat properly. If the parts are not within specifications, determine the service method for the type of engine. In some cases, piston and pin are serviced as an assembly when either is defective. Others specify reaming the piston and connecting rods for an oversize pin. If the connecting rod bushing is worn, it may in many cases be replaced. Reaming the piston and replacing the rod bushing are machine shop operations.

Cylinder Block Reconditioning

Procedure	Method
Clean and inspect the camshaft:	Degrease the camshaft, using solvent, and clean out all oil holes. Visually inspect cam lobes and bearing journals for excessive wear. If a lobe is questionable, check all lobes as indicated below. If a journal or lobe is worn, the camshaft must be reground or replaced. **NOTE:** *If a journal is worn, there is a good chance that the bushings are worn.* If lobes and journals appear intact, place the front and rear journals in V-blocks, and rest a dial indicator on the center journal. Rotate the camshaft to check straightness. If deviation exceeds .001", replace the camshaft.

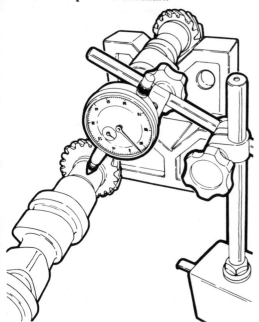

Check the camshaft for straightness

* Check the camshaft lobes with a micrometer, by measuring the lobes from the nose to base and again at 90° (see illustration). The lift is determined by subtracting the second measurement from the first. If all exhaust lobes and all intake lobes are not identical, the camshaft must be reground or replaced.

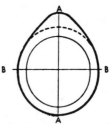

Camshaft lobe measurement

Procedure	Method
Replace the camshaft bearings:	If excessive wear is indicated, or if the engine is being completely rebuilt, camshaft bearings should be replaced as follows: Drive the camshaft rear plug from the block. Assemble the removal puller with its shoulder on the bearing to be removed. Gradually tighten the puller nut until bearing is removed. Remove remaining bearings, leaving the front and rear for last. To remove front and rear bearings, reverse position of the tool, so as to pull the bearings in toward the center of the block. Leave the tool in this position, pilot the new front and rear bearings on the installer, and pull them into position: Return the tool to its original position and pull remaining bearings into position. **NOTE:** *Ensure that oil holes align when installing bearings.* Replace camshaft rear plug, and stake it into position to aid retention.

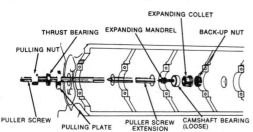

Camshaft bearing removal and installation tool (OHV engines only)

Procedure	Method
Finish hone the cylinders:	Chuck a flexible drive hone into a power drill, and insert it into the cylinder. Start the hone, and remove it up and down in the cylinder at a rate which will produce approximately a 60° cross-hatch pattern. **NOTE:** *Do not extend the hone below the cylinder bore.* After developing the pattern, remove

Cylinder Block Reconditioning

Procedure	Method

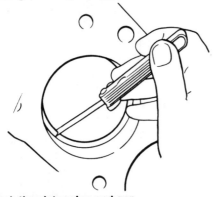

CROSS HATCH PATTERN

50°-60°

Cylinder bore after honing

the hone and recheck piston fit. Wash the cylinders with a detergent and water solution to remove abrasive dust, dry, and wipe several times with a rag soaked in engine oil.

Check piston ring end-gap:

Compress the piston rings to be used in a cylinder, one at a time, into that cylinder, and press them approximately 1″ below the deck with an inverted piston. Using feeler gauges, measure the ring end-gap, and compare to specifications. Pull the ring out of the cylinder and file the ends with a fine file to obtain proper clearance.
CAUTION: *If inadequate ring end-gap is utilized, ring breakage will result.*

Check the piston ring end gap

Install the piston rings:

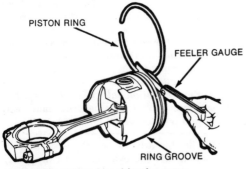

PISTON RING

FEELER GAUGE

RING GROOVE

Check the piston ring side clearance

Inspect the ring grooves in the piston for excessive wear or taper. If necessary, recut the groove(s) for use with an overwidth ring or a standard ring and spacer. If the groove is worn uniformly, overwidth rings, or standard rings and spacers may be installed without recutting. Roll the outside of the ring around the groove to check for burrs or deposits. If any are found, remove with a fine file. Hold the ring in the groove, and measure side clearance. If necessary, correct as indicated above.
NOTE: *Always install any additional spacers above the piston ring.*
The ring groove must be deep enough to allow the ring to seat below the lands (see illustration). In many cases, a "go-no-go" depth gauge will be provided with the piston rings. Shallow grooves may be corrected by recutting, while deep grooves require some type of filler or expander

Cylinder Block Reconditioning

Procedure	Method
	behind the piston. Consult the piston ring supplier concerning the suggested method. Install the rings on the piston, lowest ring first, using a ring expander. NOTE: *Position the rings as specified by the manufacturer.* Consult the engine service procedures earlier in this chapter for details concerning specific engines.
Install the camshaft:	Liberally lubricate the camshaft lobes and journals, and install the camshaft. CAUTION: *Exercise extreme care to avoid damaging the bearings when inserting the camshaft.* Install and tighten the camshaft thrust plate retaining bolts.
	See the engine service procedures earlier in this chapter for details concerning specific engines.
Check camshaft end-play (OHV engines only): **Check the camshaft end-play with a feeler gauge**	Using feeler gauges, determine whether the clearance between the camshaft boss (or gear) and backing plate is within specifications. Install shims behind the thrust plate, or reposition the camshaft gear and retest endplay. In some cases, adjustment is by replacing the thrust plate. See the engine service procedures earlier in this chapter for details concerning specific engines.
DIAL INDICATOR CAMSHAFT **Check the camshaft end-play with a dial indicator**	*Mount a dial indicator stand so that the stem of the dial indicator rests on the nose of the camshaft, parallel to the camshaft axis. Push the camshaft as far in as possible and zero the gauge. Move the camshaft outward to determine the amount of camshaft endplay. If the endplay is not within tolerance, install shims behind the thrust plate, or reposition the camshaft gear and retest. See the engine service procedures earlier in this chapter for details concerning specific engines.
Install the rear main seal:	See the engine service procedures earlier in this chapter for details concerning specific engines.
Install the crankshaft: 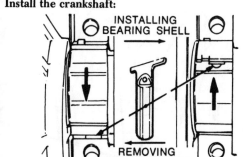 INSTALLING BEARING SHELL REMOVING BEARING SHELL **Remove or install the upper bearing insert using a roll-out pin**	Thoroughly clean the main bearing saddles and caps. Place the upper halves of the bearing inserts on the saddles and press into position. NOTE: *Ensure that the oil holes align.* Press the corresponding bearing inserts into the main bearing caps. Lubricate the upper main bearings, and lay the crankshaft in position. Place a strip of Plastigage on each of the crankshaft journals, install the main caps, and torque to specifications. Remove the main caps, and compare the Plastigage to the scale on the Plastigage envelope. If clearances are within tolerances, remove the Plastigage, turn the crankshaft 90°, wipe off all oil and retest. If all clearances are correct,

Cylinder Block Reconditioning

Procedure	Method

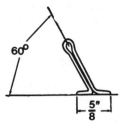

Home-made bearing roll-out pin

remove all Plastigage, thoroughly lubricate the main caps and bearing journals, and install the main caps. If clearances are not within tolerance, the upper bearing inserts may be removed, without removing the crankshaft, using a bearing roll out pin (see illustration). Roll in a bearing that will provide proper clearance, and retest. Torque all main caps, excluding the thrust bearing cap, to specifications. Tighten the thrust bearing cap finger tight. To properly align the thrust bearing, pry the crankshaft the extent of its axial travel several times, the last movement held toward the front of the engine, and torque the thrust bearing cap to specifications. Determine the crankshaft end-play (see below), and bring within tolerance with thrust washers.

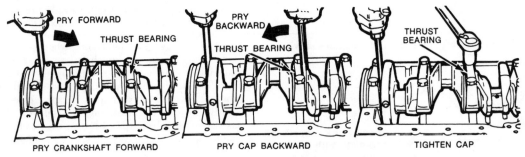

Aligning the thrust bearing

Measure crankshaft end-play:

Mount a dial indicator stand on the front of the block, with the dial indicator stem resting on the nose of the crankshaft, parallel to the crankshaft axis. Pry the crankshaft the extent of its travel rearward, and zero the indicator. Pry the crankshaft forward and record crankshaft end-play.

NOTE: *Crankshaft end-play also may be measured at the thrust bearing, using feeler gauges (see illustration).*

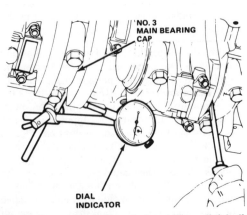

Check the crankshaft end-play with a dial indicator

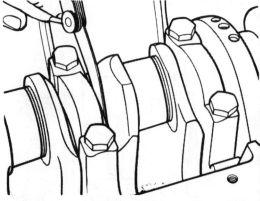

Check the crankshaft end-play with a feeler gauge

Cylinder Block Reconditioning

Procedure	Method
Install the pistons:	Press the upper connecting rod bearing halves into the connecting rods, and the lower halves into the connecting rod caps. Position the piston ring gaps according to specifications (see car section), and lubricate the pistons. Install a ring compresser on a piston, and press two long (8″) pieces of plastic tubing over the rod bolts. Using the tubes as a guide, press the pistons into the bores and onto the crankshaft with a wooden hammer handle. After seating the rod on the crankshaft journal, remove the tubes and install the cap finger tight. Install the remaining pistons in the same manner. Invert the engine and check the bearing clearance at two points (90° apart) on each journal with Plastigage. **NOTE:** *Do not turn the crankshaft with Plastigage installed.* If clearance is within tolerances, remove *all* Plastigage, thoroughly lubricate the journals, and torque the rod caps to specifications. If clearance is not within specifications, install different thickness bearing inserts and recheck. **CAUTION:** *Never shim or file the connecting rods or caps.* Always install plastic tube sleeves over the rod bolts when the caps are not installed, to protect the crankshaft journals.

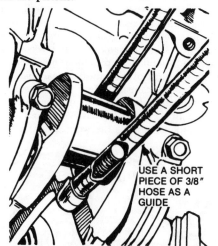

USE A SHORT
PIECE OF 3/8″
HOSE AS A
GUIDE

Use lengths of vacuum hose or rubber tubing to protect the crankshaft journals and cylinder walls during piston installation

RING COMPRESSOR

Install the piston using a ring compressor

Procedure	Method
Check connecting rod side clearance:	Determine the clearance between the sides of the connecting rods and the crankshaft using feeler gauges. If clearance is below the minimum tolerance, the rod may be machined to provide adequate clearance. If clearance is excessive, substitute an unworn rod, and recheck. If clearance is still outside specifications, the crankshaft must be welded and reground, or replaced.

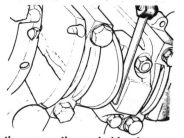

Check the connecting rod side clearance with a feeler gauge

Procedure	Method
Inspect the timing chain (or belt):	Visually inspect the timing chain for broken or loose links, and replace the chain if any are found. If the chain will flex sideways, it must be replaced. Install the timing chain as specified. Be sure the timing belt is not stretched, frayed or broken. **NOTE:** *If the original timing chain is to be reused, install it in its original position.*

Cylinder Block Reconditioning

Procedure	Method
Check timing gear backlash and runout (OHV engines):	Mount a dial indicator with its stem resting on a tooth of the camshaft gear (as illustrated). Rotate the gear until all slack is removed, and zero the indicator. Rotate the gear in the opposite direction until slack is removed, and record gear backlash. Mount the indicator with its stem resting on the edge of the camshaft gear, parallel to the axis of the camshaft. Zero the indicator, and turn the camshaft gear one full turn, recording the runout. If either backlash or runout exceed specifications, replace the worn gear(s).

Check the camshaft gear backlash

Check the camshaft gear run-out

Completing the Rebuilding Process

Follow the above procedures, complete the rebuilding process as follows:

Fill the oil pump with oil, to prevent cavitating (sucking air) on initial engine start up. Install the oil pump and the pickup tube on the engine. Coat the oil pan gasket as necessary, and install the gasket and the oil pan. Mount the flywheel and the crankshaft vibration damper or pulley on the crankshaft. NOTE: *Always use new bolts when installing the flywheel.* Inspect the clutch shaft pilot bushing in the crankshaft. If the bushing is excessively worn, remove it with an expanding puller and a slide hammer, and tap a new bushing into place.

Position the engine, cylinder head side up. Lubricate the lifters, and install them into their bores. Install the cylinder head, and torque it as specified. Insert the pushrods and install the rocker shaft(s) or position the rocker arms on the pushrods. Adjust the valves.

Install the intake and exhaust manifolds, the carburetor(s), the distributor and spark plugs. Adjust the point gap and the static ignition timing. Mount all accessories and install the engine in the car. Fill the radiator with coolant, and the crankcase with high quality engine oil.

Break-in Procedure

Start the engine, and allow it to run at low speed for a few minutes, while checking for leaks. Stop the engine, check the oil level, and fill as necessary. Restart the engine, and fill the cooling system to capacity. Check the point dwell angle and adjust the ignition timing and the valves. Run the engine at low to medium speed (800–2500 rpm) for approximately ½ hour, and retorque the cylinder head bolts. Road test the car, and check again for leaks.

Follow the manufacturer's recommended engine break-in procedure and maintenance schedule for new engines.

Emission Controls and Fuel System

EMISSION CONTROLS

Positive Crankcase Ventilation

In this system, crankcase vapors are drawn into the intake manifold and burned as part of the engine combustion. The "closed positive" system draws clean air from the carburetor air cleaner. The ventilation flow is regulated by a PCV valve located in the valve cover. Maintenance is covered in Chapter 1.

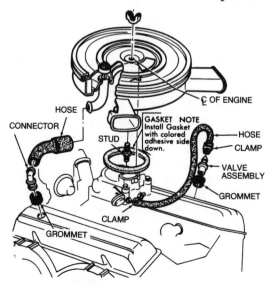

Typical PCV system components

Air Injection Reactor

The A.I.R. system injects compressed air into the exhaust system, close enough to the exhaust valves to continue the burning of the normally unburned segment of the exhaust gases. To do this it employs an air injection pump and a system of hoses, valves, tubes, etc., necessary to carry the compressed air from the pump to the exhaust manifolds. Carburetors and distributors for A.I.R. engines have specific modifications to adapt them to the air innjection system; these components should not be interchanged with those intended for use on engines that do not have the system.

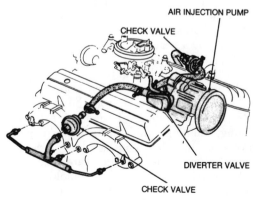

Typical 350 cu in. engine A.I.R. system components

A diverter valve is used to prevent backfiring. The valve senses sudden increases in manifold vacuum and ceases the injection of air during fuel-rich periods. During coasting, this valve diverts the entire air flow through the muffler and during high engines speeds, expels it through a relief valve. Check valves in the system prevent exhaust gases from entering the pump.

On models with catalytic converters, it is not necessary to inject the air close to the exhaust valves. For this reason, not all models are equipped with manifolds on the exhaust manifolds for air injection as in previous years. Instead, one large pipe is used to inject air into the exhaust pipe ahead of the converter. Some models use part of the old system, but utilize only two or three of the injection nozzles on the exhaust manifold.

AIR PUMP REMOVAL AND INSTALLATION

1. Disconnect the air hoses at the pump.
2. Hold the pump pulley from turning and loosen the pulley bolts.
3. Loosen the pump mounting bolt and adjustment bracket bolt. Remove the drive belt.
4. Remove the mounting bolts and then remove the pump.
5. Install the pump using a reverse of the removal procedure.

Thermostatic Air Cleaner

This system is designed to warm the air entering the carburetor when underhood temperatures are low. This allows more precise calibration of the carburetor.

The thermostatically-controlled air cleaner is composed of the air cleaner body, a filter, sensor unit, vacuum diaphragm, damper door and associated hoses and connections. Heat radiating from the exhaust manifold is trapped by a heat stove and is ducted to the air cleaner to supply heated air to the carburetor. A movable door in the air cleaner snorkel allows air to be drawn in from the heat stove (cold operation) or from the underhood air (warm operation). Periods of extended idling, climbing a grade or high-speed operation is followed by a considerable increase in engine compartment temperature. Excessive fuel vapors enter the intake manifold causing an over-rich mixture, resulting in a rough idle. To overcome this, some engines may be equipped with a hot idle compensator.

Service

1. Either start with a cold engine or remove the air cleaner from the engine for at least half an hour. While cooling the air cleaner, leave the engine compartment hood open.
2. Tape a thermometer, of known accuracy, to the inside of the air cleaner so that it is near the temperature sensor unit. Install the air cleaner on the engine but do not fasten its securing nut.
3. Start the engine. With the engine cold and the outside temperature less than 90° F., the door should be in the "heat on" position (closed to outside air).

NOTE: *Due to the position of the air cleaner on some models, a mirror may be necessary when observing the position of the air door.*

4. Operate the throttle lever rapidly to ½–¾ of its opening and release it. The air door should open to allow outside air to enter and then close again.
5. Allow the engine to warm up to normal temperature. Watch the door. When it opens to the outside air, remove the cover from the air cleaner. The temperature should be over 90° F and no more than 130° F; 115° F is about normal. If the door does not work within these temperature ranges, or fails to work at all, check for linkage or door binding.

If binding is not present and the air door is not working, proceed with the vacuum tests, given below. If these indicate no faults in the vacuum motor and the door is not working, the temperature sensor is defective and must be replaced.

Vacuum Motor Test

Be sure that the vacuum hose which runs between the temperature switch and the vacuum motor is not pinched by the retaining clip under the air cleaner. This could prevent the air door from closing.

1. Check all of the vacuum lines and fittings for leaks. Correct any leaks. If none are found, proceed with the test.
2. Remove the hose which runs from the sensor to the vacuum motor. Run a hose directly from the manifold vacuum source to the vacuum motor.
3. If the motor closes the air door, it is functioning properly and the temperature sensor is defective.
4. If the motor does *not* close the door and no binding is present in its operation, the

vacuum motor is defective and must be replaced.

NOTE: *If an alternate vacuum source is applied to the motor, insert a vacuum gauge in the line by using a T-fitting. Apply at least 7 in. Hg of vacuum in order to operate the motor.*

VACUUM MOTOR

Removal

1. Remove the air cleaner.
2. Disconnect the vacuum hose from the motor.
3. Drill out the spot welds with a 1/6″ hole, then enlarge as necessary to remove the retaining strap.
4. Remove the retaining strap.
5. Lift up the motor and cock it to one side to unhook the motor linkage at the control damper assembly.

Installation

1. Drill a 7/64″ hole in the snorkel tube at the center of the vacuum motor retaining strap.
2. Insert the vacuum motor linkage into the control damper assembly.
3. Use the motor retaining strap and a sheet metal screw to secure the retaining strap and motor to the snorkel tube.

NOTE: *Make sure the screw does not interfere with the operation of the damper assembly. Shorten the screw if necessary.*

SENSOR

Removal and Installation

1. Remove the air cleaner.
2. Disconnect the hoses at the air cleaner.
3. Pry up the tabs on the sensor retaining clip and remove the clip and sensor from the air cleaner.
4. Installation is the reverse of removal.

Evaporative Emission Control

Introduced on California cars in 1970, and nationwide in 1971, this system reduces the amount of escaping gasoline vapors. Float bowl emissions are controlled by internal carburetor modifications. Redesigned bowl vents, reduced bowl capacity, heat shields, and improved intake manifold-to-carburetor insulation serve to reduce vapor loss into the atmosphere. The venting of fuel tank vapors

into the air has been stopped. Fuel vapors are now directed through lines to a canister containing an activated charcoal filter. Unburned vapors are trapped here until the engine is started. When the engine is running, the canister is purged by air drawn in by manifold vacuum. The air and fuel vapors are then directed into the engine to be burned. This system is designed to reduce fuel vapor emission. The canister filter should be replaced every 12 months or 12,000 miles on Models 1970–74, on Models 1975–79 the interval was extended to 24 months or 30,000 miles. To replace the filter, proceed as follows:

The filter is located in the bottom of the canister. Pull out the old filter and work the new filter into place. It may be necessary, on earlier models, to remove the bottom of the canister for access.

Anti-Dieseling Solenoid

Some models may have an idle speed solenoid on the carburetor. All 1972–74 models have idle solenoids. Due to the leaner carburetor settings required for emission control, the engine may have a tendency to "diesel" or "run-on" after the ignition is turned off. The carburetor solenoid, energized when the ignition is on, maintains the normal idle speed. When the ignition is turned off, the solenoid is de-energized and permits the throttle valves to fully close, thus preventing run-on. For adjustment of carburetors with idle solenoids see Carburetor Adjustments.

Transmission Controlled Spark

Introduced in 1970, this system controls exhaust emissions by eliminating vacuum advance in the lower forward gears.

1970

The 1970 system consists of a transmission switch, solenoid vacuum switch, time delay relay, and a thermostatic water temperature switch. The solenoid vacuum switch is energized in the lower gears via the transmission switch and closes off distributor vacuum. The two-way transmission switch is activated by the shifter shaft on manual transmissions, and by oil pressure on automatic transmissions. The switch deenergizes the solenoid in high gear, the plunger extends and uncovers the vacuum port, and the distributor receives

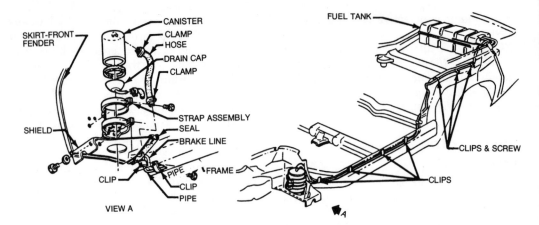

Evaporative emission control system components

full vacuum. The temperature switch overrides the system when engine temperature is below 63° or above 232°. This allows vacuum advance in all gears. A time delay relay opens 15 seconds after the ignition is switched on. Full vacuum advance during this delay eliminates the possibility of stalling.

1971

The 1971 system is similar, except that the vacuum solenoid (now called a Combination Emissions Control solenoid) serves two functions. One function is to control distributor vacuum; the added function is to act as a deceleration throttle stop in high gear. This cuts down on emissions when the vehicle is coming to a stop in high gear. The CEC solenoid is controlled by a temperature switch, a transmission switch, and a 20 second time delay relay. This system also contains a reversing relay, which energizes the solenoid when the transmission switch, temperature switch or time delay completes the CEC cir-

cuit to ground. This system is directly opposite the 1970 system in operation. The 1970 vacuum solenoid was normally open to allow vacuum advance and when energized, closed to block vacuum. The 1971 system is normally closed blocking vacuum advance and when energized, opens to allow vacuum advance. The temperature switch completes the CEC circuit to ground when engine temperature is below 82°. Corvettes also have a high temperature terminal on the switch to complete the CEC circuit when coolant temperature reaches 232°. The time delay relay allows vacuum advance (and raised idle speed) for 20 seconds after the ignition key is turned to the "on" position. Models with an automatic transmission and air conditioning also have a solid state timing device which engages the air conditioning compressor for three seconds after the ignition key is turned to the "off" position to prevent the engine from running-on. Two throttle settings are necessary; one for curb idle and one for emis-

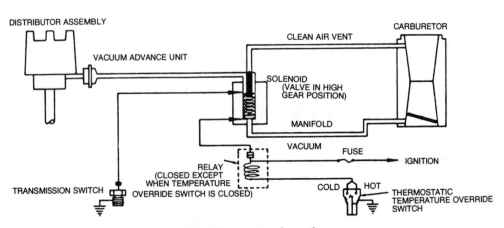

1970 TCS system schematic

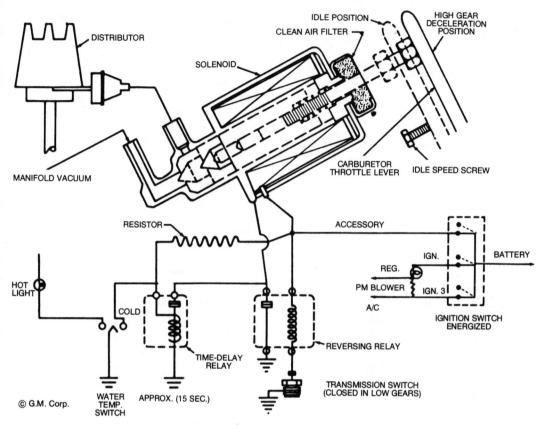

1971 TCS system schematic

sion control on coast. Both settings are described in the tune-up chapter.

1972–74

A vacuum advance solenoid similar to that
sued in 1970 is used. The CEC valve is not
used. This relay is normally closed to block
vacuum and opens when energized to allow
vacuum advance. The solenoid controls distributor vacuum advance and performs no
throttle positioning function. The 1973–74
TCS system differs from the 1972 system in
three ways. The 23 second uplift delay has
been replaced by a 20 second starting relay.
This relay closes to complete the TCS circuit
and open the TCS solenoid, allowing vacuum
advance, for 20 seconds after the key is
turned to the "on" position. The operating
temperature of the temperature override
switch has been raised to 93°, and the switch
that was used to engage the A/C compressor
when the key was turned "off" has been
eliminated. All models are equipped with an
electric throttle control solenoid to prevent
run-on. The 1974 TCS system is used only on
manual transmission models. System components remain unchanged from 1973. The vac-

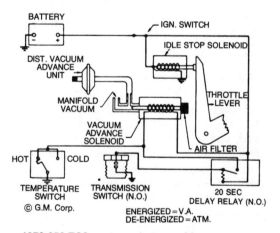

1972 350 TCS system—hot override on

uum advance solenoid is located on the coil
bracket.

All 1973–74 Corvette models are equipped
with a Thermo-Override system instead of
the normal TCS system. This system consists
of a three-position temperature switch,
which is mounted in the right cylinder head
and a two-position vacuum advance solenoid.
Three vacuum lines are connected to the

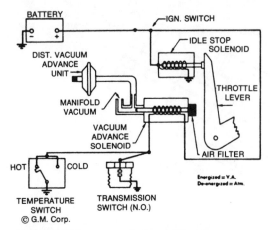

1972 454 TCS system—hot override on

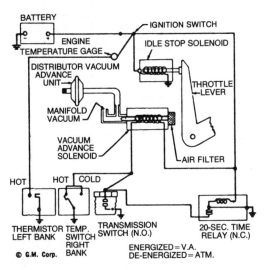

1973 4-speed TCS system

Exhaust Gas Recirculation

All 1973–79 engines are equipped with exhaust gas recirculation (EGR). This system consists of a metering valve, a vacuum line to the carburetor, and cast-in exhaust gas passages in the intake manifold. The EGR valve is controlled by carburetor vacuum, and exhaust gases into the fuel/air mixture. The exhaust gases lower the combustion temperature, and reduce the amount of oxides of nitrogen (NO_x) produced. The valve is closed at idle and wide open throttle, but is open between the two extreme throttle positions.

As the car accelerates, the carburetor throttle plate uncovers the vacuum port for the EGR valve. At 3–5 in. Hg, the EGR valve opens and then some of the exhaust gases are allowed to flow into the air/fuel mixture to lower the combustion temperature. At full-throttle the valve closes again.

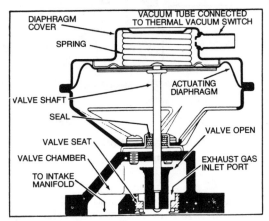

EGR valve cross-section

EGR VALVE REMOVAL AND INSTALLATION

1. Detach the vacuum line from the EGR valve.

2. Unfasten the two bolts which attach the valve to the manifold. Withdraw the valve.

3. Installation is the reverse of removal. Always use a new gasket between the valve and the manifold.

Early Fuel Evaporation System

1975–79 models are equipped with this system to reduce engine warm-up time, improve driveability, and reduce emissions. On start-up, a vacuum motor acts to close a heat valve in the exhaust manifold which causes exhaust gases to enter the intake manifold

solenoid, a ported vacuum line from the carburetor, a vacuum line from the intake manifold, and a vacuum line that runs to the distributor vacuum advance unit. When the engine temperature is between 92° F and 232° F, the temperature switch contacts are open and the vacuum solenoid is de-energized. This causes carburetor-ported vacuum to control the operation of the distributor vacuum advance unit. When the engine temperature is below 93° F or above 232° F, the temperature switch contacts are closed and the vacuum solenoid is energized. This moves the plunger in the solenoid to block the ported vacuum opening and connect manifold vacuum to the distributor. When the engine reaches normal temperature, the temperature switch contacts open and ported vacuum is restored to the distributor. TCS is not used on 1975–79 models.

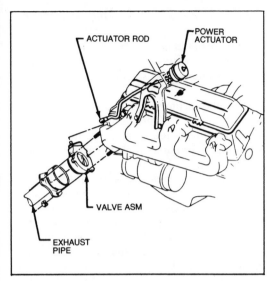

350 V8 EFE system

heat riser passages. Incoming fuel mixture is then heated and more complete fuel evaporation is provided during warm-up.

Catalytic Converter

All 1975–79 models are equipped with a catalytic converter. The converter is located midway in the exhaust system. Stainless steel exhaust pipes are used ahead of the converter. The converter is stainless steel with an aluminized steel cover and a ceramic felt blanket to insulate the converter from the floorpan. The catalyst pellet bed inside the converter consists of noble metals which cause a reaction that converts hydrocarbons and carbon monoxide into water and carbon dioxide.

FUEL SYSTEM

Fuel Pump

The Corvette fuel pump is a diaphragm type, actuated by an eccentric on the engine camshaft. A pushrod connects the camshaft eccentric and the fuel pump rocker arm. A rubber gasket is used between the mating surfaces.

Check the operation of the fuel pump with the unit on the engine and gas in the tank. The inlet (or suction) line transfers fuel from the tank to the pump. The pump outlet (or pressure) line furnishes fuel to the carburetor(s).

REMOVAL AND INSTALLATION

1. Disconnect the fuel inlet and outlet lines.

2. On small block engines, remove the upper bolt from the right front mounting boss. Insert a longer bolt (⅜-16x2 in.) in this hole to hold the fuel pump pushrod.

3. Remove the fuel pump mounting bolts and remove the fuel pump. The pushrod may be retained in position on large block engines with either mechanical fingers or heavy grease.

4. Install the fuel pump using a reverse procedure and check for leaks.

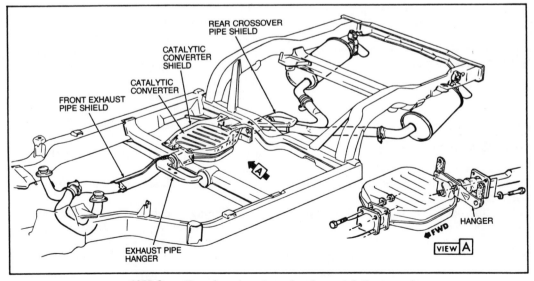

1975 Corvette exhaust system showing catalytic converter

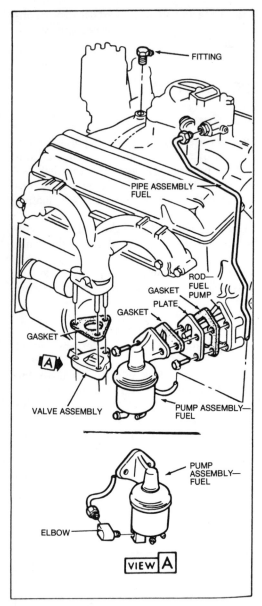

1974 350 fuel pump mounting

Carburetor Overhaul & Adjustments—All Types

Efficient carburetor depends greatly on careful cleaning and inspection during overhaul, since dirt, gum, varnish, water in or on the carburetor parts are mainly responsible for poor performance.

Carburetor overhaul should be performed in a clean, dust-free area. Carefully disassemble the carburetor, keeping look-alike parts segregated. Note all jet sizes.

NOTE: *The carburetor Specifications*

Chart at the end of the chapter gives the various carburetor applications. Determine which carburetor you are dealing with and refer to the following sections. The sections are divided by carburetor type.

Once the carburetor is disassembled, wash all parts (except diaphragms, electric choke units, pump plunger and any other plastic, leather or fiber parts) in clean carburetor solvent. Do not leave the parts in solvent any longer than necessary to sufficiently loosen the deposits. Excessive cleaning may remove the special finish from the float bowl and choke valve bodies, leaving them unfit for service. Rinse all parts in clean solvent and blow dry with compressed air. Wipe all plastic, leather or fiber parts with a clean, lint-free cloth.

Blow out all passages and jets with compressed air and be sure there are no restrictions or blockages. Never use wire to clean jets, fuel passages or air bleeds.

Check all parts for wear or damage. If wear or damage is found, replace the complete assembly. Especially check the following:

1. Check the float and needle seat for wear. If any is found, replace the assembly.

2. Check the float hinge pin for wear and the floats for distortion or dents. Replace the float if fuel has leaked into it.

3. Check the throttle and choke shaft bores for out-of-round. Damage or wear to the throttle arm, shaft or shaft bore will often require replacement of the throttle body. These parts require close tolerances and an air leak here can cause poor starting and idling.

4. Inspect the idle mixture adjusting needles for burrs or grooves. Burrs or grooves will usually require replacement of the needles since a satisfactory idle cannot be obtained.

5. Test the accelerator pump check valves. They should pass air one way only. Test for proper seating by blowing and sucking on the valve. If the valve is satisfactory, wash the valve again to remove breath moisture.

6. Check the bowl cover for warping with a straightedge.

7. Closely inspect the valves and seats for wear or damage, replacing as necessary.

8. After the carburetor is assembled, check the choke valve for freedom of operation.

Carburetor overhaul kits are recommended for each overhaul. These kits contain all gaskets and new parts to replace those that deteriorate most rapidly. Failure to replace all parts supplied with the kit (especially gaskets) can result in poor performance later.

Overhaul kits contain specific procedures for the model carburetor the kit applies too. Some carburetor manufacturers supply overhaul kits of three types—minor repair, major repair and gasket kits. They basically consist of:

Minor Repair Kits:
- All gaskets
- Float needle valve
- Volume control screw
- All diaphragms
- Pump diaphragm spring

Major Repair Kits:
- All jets and gaskets
- All diaphragms
- Float needle valve
- Volume control screw
- Pump ball valve
- Main jet carrier
- Float
- Complete intermediate rod
- Intermediate pump lever
- Complete injector tube
- Assorted screws and washers

Gasket Kits:
- All gaskets.

After cleaning and checking all components, reassemble the carburetor using new parts, using the exploded views in the car sections, if necessary. Make sure that all screws and jets are tight in their seats, but do not overtighten needle valves into their seats or uneven jetting will result. Always use new gaskets and adjust the float.

Carter WCFB Carburetor

The Carter WCFB is the standard carburetor on 1963–1965 Corvettes.

Functionally, it is two, dual carburetors mounted in a single housing and is comprised of four basic components: choke housing, top cover, main body, and throttle flange. The metering rods, accelerator pump, and choke are located in the primary side of the carburetor body. It has the five conventional systems: float, low speed, high speed, accelerator pump, and choke.

IDLE SPEED AND MIXTURE ADJUSTMENTS

Idle speed and mixture adjustments are best accomplished using a tachometer and vac-

uum gauge. Make this adjustment with the air cleaner installed.

Bring the engine to operating temperature, check to see that the choke is fully off, and adjust the idle-speed adjustment screw to give 475 rpm (450 on automatic transmissions in Drive range). Adjust the idle-mixture adjustment screws separately until peak vacuum and rpm are indicated on the vacuum gauge and tachometer.

An alternative method is to set the idle-mixture screws lean to a beginning, rough idle, then back screws out (enrichen) ¼ turn. Never bottom the idle-mixture adjustment screws or possible damage to the needle seat may result.

AUTOMATIC CHOKE ADJUSTMENT

The choke is correctly set when the index mark on the plastic cover aligns with the corresponding mark on the choke housing. The introduction of dirt, gum, water or carbon into the choke housing or vacuum passage can detrimentally affect engine performance. Check this system periodically and clean if necessary.

INTERMEDIATE CHOKE ROD ADJUSTMENT

The intermediate choke rod adjustment requires the removal of the choke coil housing assembly, gasket, and baffle plate. Open the choke valve and position a 0.026 in. wire gauge between the botton of the slot in the piston and the top of the slot in the choke piston housing. Seat the choke piston on the gauge. The measurement between the top of the choke valve and the air horn divider should be 0.096 in. Adjustment is made by bending the intermediate choke rod.

FLOAT ADJUSTMENT

To make the float adjustment, remove the top cover then disassemble and reassemble the floats without the cover gasket. Make the lateral adjustment by placing the ¼ in. float gauge (supplied in the carburetor overhaul kit) under the center of the secondary float so that the notched portion of the gauge fits over the edge of the casting. Bend the floats until their sides just clear the vertical uprights of the gauge. Repeat the adjustment on the primary float using either the ⅛ in. float gauge or a ⅛ in. drill bit.

The vertical adjustment is correct when the floats just clear the horizontal bar of the gauges when the gauges are positioned as described above. The required clearance be-

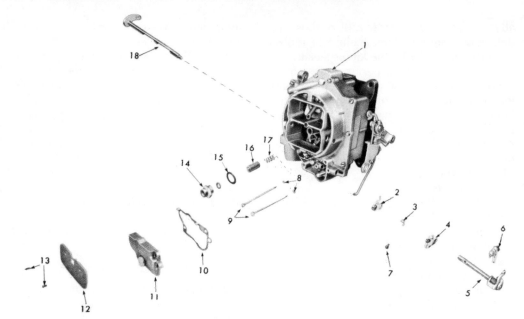

1. Bowl cover
2. Metering rod arm
3. Vent arm
4. Pump operating arm and link
5. Pump countershaft assembly
6. Choke shaft lever
7. Vent arm screw
8. Metering rod discs
9. Metering rods
10. Dust cover gasket
11. Dust cover
12. Choke valve
13. Choke valve screw
14. Inlet fitting nut
15. Filter gaskets
16. Filter
17. Filter spring
18. Choke valve shaft

WCFB bowl cover upper parts

tween the top of the floats and the bowl cover is ⅛ in. on the primary floats and ¼ in. on the secondary floats.

Float drop measurement must be made with the top cover gasket removed. Measure between the lowest point of the floats and the bottom of the top cover. This should be 2 in.

for both primary and secondary floats. Adjust the accelerator pump by backing off the idle-speed adjustment screw and positioning the float-drop adjustment gauge (supplied in rebuilding kits) on the dust cover boot. Bend the top flat of the pump arm so that it is parallel to the gauge.

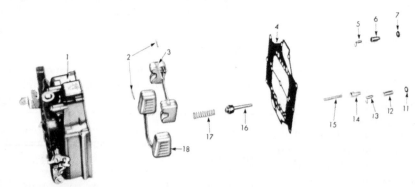

1. Carburetor body
2. Float hinge pins
3. Secondary float
4. Bowl cover gasket
5. Secondary float needle
6. Secondary float needle seat
7. Needle seat gasket
8. Bowl cover
9. Vacuum piston link
10. Bowl cover attaching screw
11. Needle seat gasket
12. Primary float needle seat
13. Primary float needle
14. Vacuum piston
15. Vacuum piston spring
16. Pump plunger assembly
17. Pump plunger return spring
18. Primary float

WCFB lower bowl cover parts

METERING ROD ADJUSTMENT

To adjust the metering rods, back off the idle-speed adjusting screw until the throttle valves are fully seated, then loosen the screw in the metering arm. Depress the metering rod arm upward until it just touches the hanger. Secure the arm with the set screw.

UNLOADER AND SECONDARY THROTTLE LEVER ADJUSTMENT

Make the unloader adjustment with the throttle valves wide open. Measure between the inboard edge of the choke valve and the center wall of the top cover. Bend the unloader tang to obtain a $3/16$ in. clearance.

Turn the carburetor upside down to adjust the secondary throttle lever. With the primary valves wide open, the secondary valves should be within 4° to 7° of the wide open position. Bend the connector rod at its upper angle until actuation of the throttle linkage fully opens the primary valves. Bend the tang on the secondary throttle dog so that with the primary throttle valves open, the secondary throttle-to-bore angle will be 5½°. There should be 0.017 in.–0.022 in. clearance between the positive closing shoes on the primary and secondary throttle levers with the throttle valves closed.

DISSASSEMBLY AND ASSEMBLY

1. Remove the carburetor from the engine but do not drain the fuel in the bowl. Tap the filter nut lightly with a hammer then remove the inlet nut and gasket and lift out the filter.

2. Disconnect the choke connector rod, intermediate choke rod, and throttle rod. Remove the metering-rod dust cover and vapor vent arm. Loosen the pump operating arm and metering-rod arm securing screws, and withdraw the countershaft.

3. Remove the metering rod arm and link. Turn each metering rod 180° and lift them from the hanger. Do not lose the two, metering rod discs.

4. Remove the top cover, lifting straight up so as to avoid damaging the floats, vacuum piston, or plunger assembly. Be sure the cover gasket is free of the bowl before lifting the cover. Mark the floats before removing them from the cover, to avoid unnecessary bending during assembly adjustments.

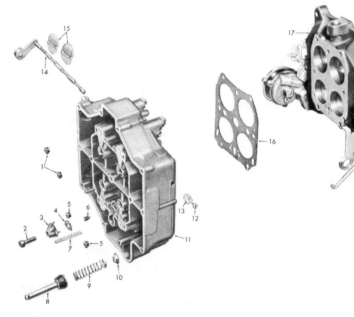

1. Secondary jets	9. Pump plunger return spring
2. Pump jet cluster attaching screw	10. Pump inlet ball retainer
3. Pump jet cluster	11. Carburetor body
4. Cluster gasket	12. Screw
5. Metering rod jets	13. Auxiliary throttle valve cam
6. Pump discharge needle	14. Auxiliary throttle valve shaft
7. Vacuum piston spring	and weight assembly
8. Pump plunger assembly	

15. Auxiliary throttle valves
16. Carburetor body basket
17. Throttle flange
18. Throttle flange attaching screw

WCFB throttle body parts

5. Remove the secondary float needle, seat, and gasket, and group together. Remove the pump plunger assembly and spring and soak the leather pump plunger in gasoline or kerosine to prevent it from drying out. Turn the vacuum piston ¼ turn to disconnect and remove the piston link.

6. At this time, check the fuel in the bowl for contamination. Sweep the bottom of the bowl with a magnet while the fuel is still present. This will pick up iron oxide dust or metallic particles. Water contamination will appear as milky globules at the bottom of the bowl.

7. Invert the carburetor body and remove the pump jet cluster and gasket. Tap out the pump discharge needle. Attach a ⁵/₁₆ in. six-point socket to a six-inch extension and pry the pump inlet ball retainer and check ball from the bottom of the pump cylinder well.

8. Remove the primary metering rod jets from the pump side of the carburetor. Remove the secondary main jets but do not mix them as their orifices are not the same size. Check the low speed jets to see that they are angled slightly on installation. The antipercolator plugs and bushings and main discharge nozzles are a press fit and should not be removed.

9. Separate the throttle flange and carburetor body. Remove the idle-mixture screws and springs, throttle-lever adjusting screw, washer, and spring. Remove the fast-idle cam assembly and lockout arm. Remove the primary/secondary throttle valve connector rod. Back out the primary throttle shaft screw and washer and remove the throttle levers. Dislodge the secondary throttle return spring. Remove the primary and secondary-throttle valves and shafts. It will be necessary to file the staked ends of the throttle valve securing screws before they can be removed. Remove the choke housing and baffle.

10. Clean and inspect the disassembled components. Use a carburetor cleaning solution to wash everything but the coil housing assembly and pump plunger. Clean the choke housing assembly in gasoline. Reassembly is the reverse of this procedure.

Carter AFB Carburetor

The Carter AFB (aluminum four-barrel) carburetor is a high performance option found on the 327 cubic inch Corvette engine from 1963–1965. It is a four-throat downdraft type and offers improved flow rates over the standard carburetor. A clean air system reduces contamination of the choke vacuum circuit and linkage, and subsequent malfunctioning.

IDLE SPEED AND MIXTURE ADJUSTMENT

Idle speed and mixture are adjusted with the engine thoroughly warmed and idling and with the aid of a tachometer and vacuum gauge attached to the engine. With the choke fully off, adjust the idle-speed adjustment screw to give 475 rpm (450 for automatic transmission models in Drive). Adjust each idle-mixture screw until peak steady vacuum is achieved at the specified rpm.

AUTOMATIC CHOKE ADJUSTMENT

The automatic choke is correctly adjusted when the scribe mark on the coil housing is aligned with the center notch in the choke housing for Powerglide models and one notch lean with synchromesh.

FLOAT ADJUSTMENTS

Remove the metering rods and the bowl cover. Align the float by sighting down its side to determine if it is parallel with the outer edge of the air horn. Bend to adjust. The float level is adjusted with the air horn inverted and the air horn gasket in place. Clearance between each float (at the outer end) and the air horn gasket should be ⁵/₁₆ in. Bend to adjust.

The float drop is adjusted by holding the air horn in the upright position and bending the float arm until the vertical distance from the air horn gasket to the outer end of each float measures ¾ in.

AFB float drop adjustment

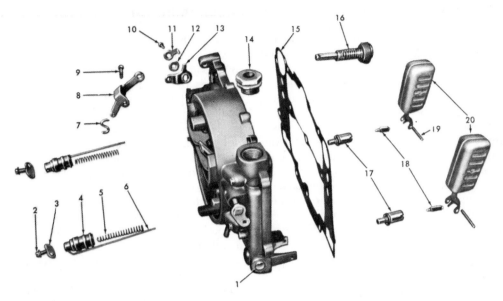

1. Bowl cover assembly
2. Screw
3. Piston cover plate
4. Power piston
5. Spring
6. Metering rod
7. Pump link

8. Pump lever
9. Pump lever pivot screw
10. Screw
11. Choke shaft outer lever
12. Washer (spacer)
13. Choke shaft kick lever
14. Fuel inlet fitting

15. Cover gasket
16. Pump plunger assembly
17. Float needle seat
18. Float needle
19. Float hinge
20. Float

AFB bowl cover parts

INTERMEDIATE CHOKE ROD ADJUSTMENT

The intermediate choke rod adjustment begins with the removal of the choke coil housing assembly, gasket and baffle plate. Position a 0.026 in. wire gauge between the bottom of the slot in the piston and the top of the slot in the choke piston housing. Close the choke piston against the gauge and secure it with a rubber band. Now bend the intermediate choke rod so that the distance between the top edge of the choke valve and the air horn divider measures 0.070 in.

ACCELERATOR PUMP ADJUSTMENT

The first step in adjusting the accelerator pump is to push aside the fast-idle cam and seat the throttle valves firmly. Bend the pump rod at the lower angle to obtain a ½ in. measurement between the air horn and the top of the plunger shaft.

UNLOADER, CLOSING SHOE, AND SECONDARY THROTTLE ADJUSTMENT

To adjust the unloader, hold the throttle wide open and bend the unloader tang to obtain a ³/₁₆ in. clearance between the upper edge of the choke valve and inner wall of the air horn.

Clearance between the positive closing shoes on the primary and secondary throttle valves is checked with the valves closed. Bend the secondary closing as required to obtain a clearance of 0.20 in.

The secondary throttle opening is governed by the pick-up lever on the primary throttle shaft. It has two points of contact with the loose lever on the primary shaft. If the contact points do not simultaneously engage, bend the pick-up lever to obtain proper engagement. The primary and secondary throttle valve opening must be synchronized.

DISASSEMBLY AND ASSEMBLY

1. Remove the pump rod and intermediate choke rod. Remove the outer lever and washer from the choke shaft, then remove the inner lever and fast-idle rod as an assembly. Remove the step-up position cover plates, piston, and step-up rod and spring. Lightly tap the fuel inlet fitting. Before removing it, remove its gasket and strainer then carefully lift the top cover to protect the floats and pump plunger from damage.

2. Remove the float lever pins, floats, float needles, seats, and gaskets. Keep separate to avoid unnecessary adjustment. Remove the pump plunger lever, S link, plunger, and cover gasket.

3. Do not remove the choke valve and shaft(s) unless there is obvious shaft binding or damage to the valve.

4. Remove the accelerator-pump lower spring and, after checking the fuel for contamination, drain the bowl. Sweep a magnet around the bottom of the bowl while fuel is still present to capture iron oxide dust or metal particles which may damage the needle seats. Water contamination will appear as milky globules at the bottom of the fuel bowl.

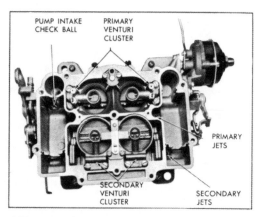

AFB main body components

5. Remove the choke housing cover, gasket, and baffle. Remove the O-ring seal from the vacuum opening in the mounting boss. Remove the choke piston, levers, pump cluster and gasket, and pump discharge needle. Remove the venturi cluster. The venturi assemblies are dissimilar and cannot be assembled in the wrong location. Primary venturi gaskets differ from secondary.

6. Remove the secondary auxiliary valves, idle-mixture screws and springs, and all four metering jets. Metering rods are used in the primary metering jets and these jets are visibly larger than their secondary counterparts. Remove the pump intake check valve and seat assembly.

7. Wash all parts except the choke coil housing and the pump plunger in carburetor cleaning solution. Clean the choke housing in gasoline.

8. Reassembly is the reversal of this procedure.

Rochester 4MV Quadrajet

The Rochester 4MV is a four-throat unit which serves as standard carburetor on the 327, 350, 427, and 454 cu in. engines. The 4MV is designed as an all-purpose carburetor. Its primary throats feature small bores and a triple venturi configuration for better fuel control and corresponding gas mileage at idle and normal operational speeds. The secondary throats are quite a bit larger and are designed to meet the greater air flow demands of harder driving.

The float chamber is centrally located and has a pressure-balanced float valve which allows the use of a small, single float. This combination greatly reduces erratic fuel delivery during acceleration. The 4MV is used in combination with a temperature-sensing choke coil mounted on the intake manifold.

FLOAT ADJUSTMENT

Remove the top cover and gasket, and use an adjustable T-scale to measure the distance from the top of the float bowl gasket surface to the top of the float at a point $3/16$ in. back from the toe of the float. Bend the float tang to specifications.

ACCELERATOR PUMP ADJUSTMENT

Close the throttle valves and position the pump rod in the specified hole of the pump lever. Use an adjustable T-scale to measure from the top of the choke valve wall, nearest the vent stack, to the top of the pump stem. Bend the pump lever to obtain the specified distance.

IDLE VENT ADJUSTMENT

Close the vent valve and open the primary throttle until the vent valve arm touches the bi-metallic strip next to the valve. Measure the distance between the top of the choke valve wall and the top of the pump stem. Bend to adjust.

FAST IDLE ADJUSTMENT

Close the primary throttles and position the cam follower above the high step of the fast-idle cam. Turn the fast-idle screw clockwise until it touches the lever then turn it down three full turns.

CHOKE ROD ADJUSTMENT

Position the cam follower on the second step of the fast-idle cam, touching the high step. Close the choke valve and gauge the clear-

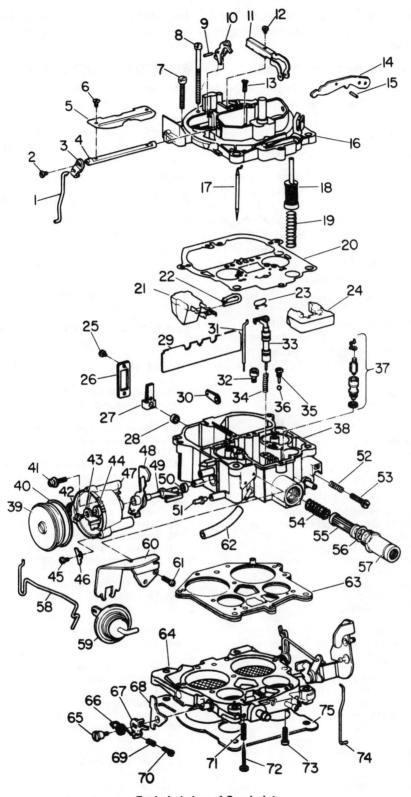

Exploded view of Quadrajet

ance between the lower edge of the valve and the body. Bend choke rod to obtain the specified clearance.

AIR VALVE DASHPOT ADJUSTMENT

Seat the vacuum break diaphragm and gauge the clearance between the dashpot rod and the end of the slot in the air valve lever. Bend rod to adjust.

VACUUM BREAK ADJUSTMENT

Close the choke valve and secure it with a rubber band. Place the cam follower on the highest step of the fast-idle cam and position the break diaphragm stem against its seat with the vacuum link at the end of the slot. Bend the tang so that the measurement between the lower edge of the choke valve and the air horn meets specifications.

UNLOADER ADJUSTMENT

Close the choke valve and secure it with a rubber band placed on the vacuum break lever. Completely open the primary throttle and measure the distance between the air

horn and the lower edge of the throttle valve. Bend the fast-idle lever tang to achieve specifications.

SECONDARY LOCKOUT ADJUSTMENT

Completely open the choke valve and rotate the vacuum break lever clockwise. Bend the lever if the measurement between the lever and the secondary throttle shaft exceeds specifications. Close the choke and gauge the distance between the lever and secondary throttle shaft pin. Bend the lever to adjust.

AIR VALVE SPRING ADJUSTMENT

Remove all spring tension by loosening the locking screw and backing out the spring adjusting screw. Close the air valve and turn in the adjusting screw until the torsion spring touches the pin on the shaft then turn it the additional turns specified. Secure the locking screw.

SECONDARY OPENING ADJUSTMENT

With the primary throttle valves open and the actuating link touching the secondary

1. Choke rod
2. Choke lever screw
3. Choke lever
4. Choke shaft
5. Choke valve
6. Choke valve screw
7. Short air horn screw
8. Long air horn screw
9. Roll pin
10. Lever
11. Secondary metering rod holder
12. Secondary metering rod holder screw
13. Air horn screw
14. Pump actuating lever
15. Pump lever roll pin
16. Air horn assembly
17. Secondary metering rod
18. Pump assembly
19. Pump return spring
20. Air horn gasket
21. Float assembly
22. Float assembly hinge pin
23. Primary metering rod retainer spring
24. Float bowl
25. Idle compensator cover screw
26. Idle compensator cover
27. Idle compensator
28. Idle compensator seal
29. Float bowl baffle
30. Choke rod lever
31. Primary metering rod
32. Primary main metering jet
33. Power piston assembly
34. Power piston spring
35. Pump discharge ball retainer
36. Pump discharge ball
37. Needle and seat assembly, gasket, and pull clip

38. Float bowl assembly
39. Thermostatic cover and coil assembly
40. Thermostatic cover gasket
41. Choke housing-to-bowl screw
42. Choke coil lever screw
43. Choke coil lever
44. Intermediate choke shaft
45. Stat cover screw
46. Stat cover retainer
47. Choke housing
48. Fast idle cam
49. Inter choke shaft lever assembly
50. Intermediate choke shaft seal
51. Choke housing-to-bowl seal
52. Idle adjust screw spring
53. Idle adjusting screw
54. Filter relief spring
55. Fuel inlet filter
56. Filter nut gasket
57. Fuel inlet filter nut
58. Vacuum break rod
59. Vacuum break diaphragm assembly
60. Vacuum break control bracket
61. Bracket attaching screw
62. Vacuum control hose
63. Throttle body-to-bowl gasket
64. Throttle body assembly
65. Cam and fast idle lever screw
66. Fast idle lever spring
67. Fast idle lever
68. Cam follower lever
69. Fast idle screw spring
70. Fast idle adjusting screw
71. Idle mixture needle spring
72. Idle mixture needle
73. Throttle body-to-bowl attaching screw
74. Pump rod
75. Flange gasket

lever, the bottom of the link should be in the center of the secondary lever slot and clearance between the tang and link should be 0.070 in.

SECONDARY CLOSING ADJUSTMENT

With the curb idle-speed set to specified rpm and the cam follower free of the fast-idle cam, there should be 0.020 in. clearance between the actuation link and the front of the secondary lever slot. The tang must touch the tang on the primary shaft's actuating lever. Bend to adjust.

DISASSEMBLY AND ASSEMBLY

1. Remove the idle vent valve, and choke rod, then disconnect the accelerator pump rod from the pump lever. Back out the nine retaining screws and separate the top cover from the carburetor body. Lift the cover straight up so that the two, main well air-bleed tubes will not be damaged. These tubes are pressed into the top cover and should not be removed.

2. Completely open the secondary air valves and extract the secondary metering rods. Remove the choke valve and shaft, then the accelerator pump lever roll pin and lever. Do not disturb the calibrated air valves and shaft.

3. Remove the accelerator pump plunger and the float bowl gaskets. Remove the accelerator pump spring and the plastic filler over the float valve. Grasp the metering rod hanger with needle nose pliers and withdraw the hanger, power piston, and primary metering rods, then rotate and slip the rods from the power piston.

4. Remove the float retaining pin and slide the float assembly forward and up to free. Remove the float needle and seat assembly, discarding the gasket. Remove the primary metering jets but leave the secondary metering discs in place. Remove the accelerator pump check ball retainer and ball.

5. Remove the secondary float bowl baffle and the vacuum break assembly hose. Remove the choke assembly and secondary lock-out link. Remove the vacuum break lever rod and the vacuum break assembly. Remove the fast-idle cam, lower choke rod, and actuating lever found inside the float bowl. Remove the inlet fuel filter and spring, then remove the attaching screws and separate the bowl from the throttle plate.

6. Rotate the pump rod free of the pri-

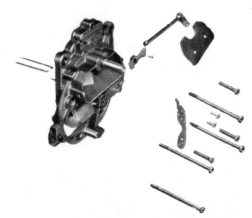

Quadrajet top cover (refer to the exploded view of Quadrajet)

mary throttle lever and remove the idle mixture screws and springs.

7. Clean the carburetor parts in a cold, immersion type cleaner. Do not put the vacuum break assembly, pump plungers, diaphragms, or plastic parts in the cleaner.

8. Clean and blow dry with compressed air, then reassemble by reversing the disassembly procedure.

C.E.C. VALVE MAINTENANCE—1971 QUADRAJET

The Rochester 4MV Quadrajet has a number of revisions for 1971 which include: calibration changes, greater capacity accelerator pump, increase in the size of the vacuum break diaphragm restriction to 0.020 in., a beefed-up, choke-closing assist spring, removal of the wide open kick lever from the choke unloader mechanism and its replacement with a tang on the fast-idle lever that contacts the fast-idle cam and forces the choke valve to admit more air under flooded engine conditions, and the adaption of a combination emission control valve (C.E.C. valve). This valve increases the idle speed during high gear overrun and helps to control normally unburned hydrocarbons. The mixture is set at the factory and the idle-mixture screws are capped to prevent adjustment in the field.

When disassembling the carburetor, remove the C.E.C. valve from the carburetor but leave the valve bracket attached to the carburetor. Do not immerse the C.E.C. valve in carburetor cleaner. Disassembly practices differ in the 1971 4MV due to calibration changes. Of primary importance is the revised procedure for removing the power piston. Do not use pliers but press the

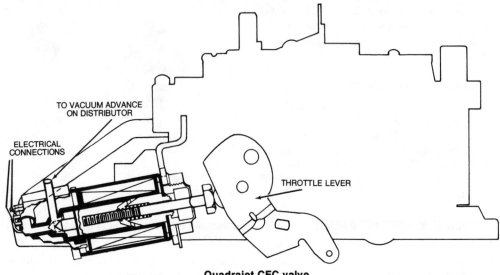

TO VACUUM ADVANCE
ON DISTRIBUTOR

ELECTRICAL
CONNECTIONS

THROTTLE LEVER

Quadrajet CEC valve

piston down and release it. Do not remove the idle mixture screws.

If it should be necessary to replace the idle-mixture adjustment screws, carefully bottom the old screws and count the turns so that the replacement screws will retain the same mixture.

If the throttle body is replaced it will be necessary to adjust the idle-mixture screws. Before making the adjustment, read and follow the instructions on the inner fender tune-up sticker on each 1971 and later Corvette. Lightly bottom the mixture screws and back out four turns. Set the idle-speed adjusting screw to obtain the specified initial idle speed, then make equal adjustments to the mixture screws until the required carbon monoxide level is reached in the exhaust gas. Adjust the idle-speed screw until the final

idle setting is achieved. Install the idle-mixture screws' limiter caps and reconnect the distributor vacuum hose and the fuel tank vapor hose.

An alternate method is available if access to exhaust gas analyzing equipment is not practical. Follow the same procedure until the mixture admustment stage. Adjust the mixture screws equally leaner until the final idle speed is achieved. Install the limiter cap, vacuum hose, and tank vapor hose.

Holley 2300 and 2300C Carburetors

The Holley 2300 and 2300C are used as the three, two-barrel high performance option on the 427 engine from 1967 through 1969. This configuration uses one 2300C as the

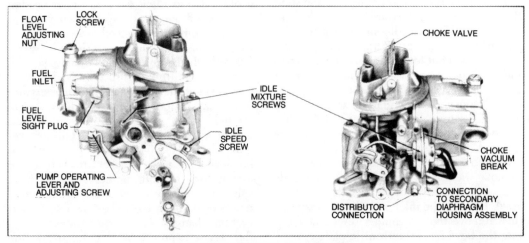

FLOAT
LEVEL
ADJUSTING
NUT

LOCK
SCREW

CHOKE VALVE

FUEL
INLET

IDLE
MIXTURE
SCREWS

FUEL
LEVEL
SIGHT PLUG

IDLE
SPEED
SCREW

CHOKE
VACUUM
BREAK

PUMP OPERATING
LEVER AND
ADJUSTING SCREW

DISTRIBUTOR
CONNECTION

CONNECTION
TO SECONDARY
DIAPHRAGM
HOUSING ASSEMBLY

Holley 2300C primary carburetor

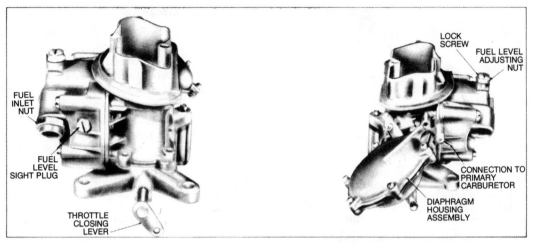

Holley 2300 secondary carburetor

primary carburetor and two 2300 models as the two secondary units. The two models differ in that the C model contains the choke, power, and accelerator pump systems while the straight 2300 does not. The C model is operated through conventional linkage while the two secondaries are vacuum actuated.

IDLE ADJUSTMENT

Adjust the idle-speed screw until it touches the throttle lever. Add one and ½ turns to obtain the preliminary adjustment.

Fast-idle adjustment on the primary carburetor is made as follows: crack the throttle, and with the choke closed, place the fast-idle lever against the top step of the fast-idle cam. Bend the fast-idle lever so that the specified opening of the throttle plate on the idle transfer slot of the carburetor is achieved.

FLOAT LEVEL ADJUSTMENT

Position the car on a flat, level surface and start the engine. Remove the sight plugs and check to see that the fuel level reaches the bottom threads of the sight plug port. A plus or minus tolerance of $1/32$ in. is acceptable. To change the level, loosen the fuel inlet-needle locking screw and adjust the nut. Clockwise lowers the fuel level and counterclockwise raises it. Turn the nut $1/16$ of a turn for each $1/16$ in. desired change. Open the primary throttle slightly to assure a stabilized adjusting condition on the secondaries. There is no required float drop adjustment.

ACCLERATOR PUMP ADJUSTMENT— PRIMARY CARB

Secure the throttle plate fully open and depress the pump lever, fully. Gauge the dis-

tance between the pump lever arm and the spring adjusting nut. Turn the nut or screw to adjust. The slightest movement of the throttle lever will actuate the correctly adjusted pump lever.

VACUUM BREAK ADJUSTMENT— PRIMARY CARB

Secure the choke valve closed and restrain the vacuum break against its stop. Bend the break rod to achieve the specified measurement between the lower edge of the choke valve and the body.

CHOKE UNLOADER ADJUSTMENT— PRIMARY CARB

Fully open the throttle valve and secure it. Close the choke valve against the throttle shaft unloader tang and bend the choke rod to obtain the specified measurement between the lower edge of the choke valve and the body.

DISASSEMBLY AND ASSEMBLY

Primary Carburetor

1. Remove the fuel bowl, metering body, and splash shield. Disconnect the vacuum break hose, remove the throttle body attachment screws, and separate the throttle body from the primary carburetor body.

2. Remove the fuel inlet baffle, float hinge screws, and the brass float. Remove the needle and seat assembly lock screw, then back out the adjusting nut and remove the seat assembly.

3. Remove the sight plug and gasket, fuel inlet fitting, filter, spring and gasket. Re-

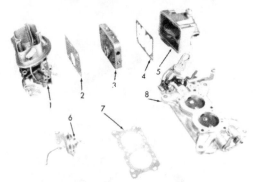

1. Carburetor body
2. Metering body gasket
3. Metering body
4. Fuel bowl gasket
5. Fuel bowl assembly
6. Vacuum break
7. Throttle body gasket
8. Throttle body

Primary carburetor components

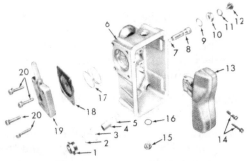

1. Nut—fuel inlet
2. Gasket—fuel filter
3. Gasket—inlet nut
4. Fuel filter
5. Spring fuel filter
6. Fuel bowl
7. Seal—inlet needle and seat assembly
8. Inlet needle and seat assembly
9. Gasket—inlet adjusting nut
10. Nut—inlet adjusting
11. Gasket—inlet lockscrew
12. Screw—inlet lock
13. Float assembly
14. Screw—float hinge
15. Fuel lever sight plug
16. Gasket—sight plug
17. Spring—pump diaphragm
18. Pump diaphragm
19. Cover assembly—pump diaphragm
20. Screw—pump diaphragm cover

Primary carburetor float bowl; secondary has no accelerator pump

move the accelerator pump cover, diaphragm, and spring.

4. Check the acclerator pump inlet ball. If damage is evident, replace the bowl assembly.

5. Remove the main metering jets, power valve, vacuum fitting, and the idle-mixture needles and screws.

6. Remove the choke vacuum break, choke lever and fast-idle cam. Remove the accelerator pump discharge nozzle and its check valve.

7. Reverse the above procedure to assemble.

Secondary Carburetors

1. Remove the fuel bowl and metering block. Disconnect the secondary diaphragm housing from the throttle lever and separate the housing from the carburetor body.

2. Remove the throttle body attaching screws and separate the throttle body from the main body. Remove the fuel inlet baffle hinge screws and plastic float.

3. Remove the needle and seat assembly, sight plug, fuel inlet fitting, filter, and spring. Remove the metering body plate and gaskets. Remove the diaphragm cover and diaphragm.

4. Reverse this procedure to reassemble.

Holly 4150, 4160 Series Carburetors

Holley four-barrel carburetors first appeared on the Corvette in 1964. The 4160 used is an end-inlet carburetor, while the 4150 carburetors used have been both end and center-inlet designs. The secondary metering body on the 4150 carburetor is similar to the primary metering body. The 4160 secondary metering body is a cast body and a plate attached to the main body by six screws. The center-inlet 4150 has been utilized on the higher performance versions of the Corvette. In 1971, the Holley carburetor has revised calibration and a C.E.C. valve. Holley part numbers are located on the carburetor air horn.

CHOKE ADJUSTMENT

The early model 4150 uses a bi-metallic choke mounted on the carburetor. It is correctly set when the cover scribe mark aligns with the specified notch mark. The later model 4150 and 4160 employ a remotely located choke. To adjust, disconnect the choke rod at the choke lever and secure the choke lever closed. Bend the rod so that when the rod is depressed to the contact stop, the top is even with the bottom of the hole in the choke lever.

FLOAT LEVEL ADJUSTMENT

Position the car on a flat, level surface and start the engine. Remove the sight plugs and check to see that the fuel level reaches the bottom threads of the sight plug port. A plus or minus tolerance of $1/32$ in. is acceptable. To change the level, loosen the fuel-inlet needle locking screw and adjust the nut.

Holley float level adjustment

Holley accelerator pump adjustment

Clockwise lowers the fuel level and counterclockwise raises it. Turn the nut $1/16$ of a turn for each $1/16$ in. desired change. Open the primary throttle slightly to assure a stabilized adjusting condition on the secondaries. There is no required float drop adjustment.

FAST-IDLE ADJUSTMENT

Early 4150

Bring the engine to normal operating temperature with the air cleaner off. Open the throttle. Place the fast-idle cam on its high step and close the throttle. Adjust the fast-idle screw to reach the specified idle speed.

Late Model 4150 and 4160

Open the throttle and place the choke plate fast-idle lever against the top step of the fast-idle cam. Bend the fast-idle lever to achieve the specified throttle plate opening.

CHOKE UNLOADER ADJUSTMENT

Adjustment should be made with the engine not running. Fully open and secure the throttle plate. Force the choke valve toward a closed position, so that contact is made with the unloader tang. Bend the choke rod to gain the specified clearance between the main body and the lower edge of the choke valve.

ACCELERATOR PUMP ADJUSTMENT

Turn off the engine. Block open the throttle and push down the pump lever. Clearance between the pump lever arm and the spring adjusting nut should be 0.015 in. minimum.

Turn the screw or nut to adjust this clearance.

SECONDARY THROTTLE VALVE ADJUSTMENT

Late Model 4150 and 4160

Close the throttle plates then turn the adjustment screw until it contacts the throttle lever. Advance the screw ½ turn more.

AIR VENT VALVE ADJUSTMENT

Late Model 4150 and 4160

Close the throttle valve and open the choke valve so that the throttle arm is free of the idle screw. Bend the air vent valve rod to obtain the specified clearance between the choke valve and seat. Advance the idle-speed screw until it touches the throttle lever then advance it 1½ turns.

VACUUM BREAK ADJUSTMENT

Late Model 4150 and 4160 Holley

Secure the choke valve closed and the vacuum break against the stop. Bend the vacuum break link to gain the specified clearance between the main body and the lower edge of the choke valve.

C.E.C. VALVE ADJUSTMENT

1971 4150 Holley

This adjustment is made only when it has been necessary to remove the throttle plate, overhaul the carburetor, or replace the sole-

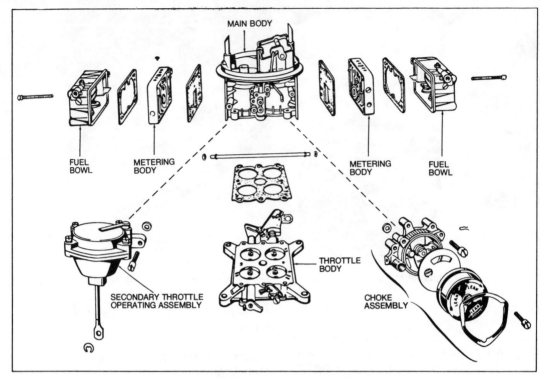

Exploded view of Holley 4150

noid. To adjust, warm the engine and place the transmission in Neutral for manual transmissions or Drive for automatic transmissions. If so equpped, turn off the air conditioner. Disconnect the vapor-canister fuel tank hose and remove and plug the distributor vacuum hose. Extend the C.E.C. valve plunger until it touches the throttle lever and then adjust its length until the specified idle speed is reached.

DISASSEMBLY AND ASSEMBLY

Disassembly and assembly are similar for the 4150 and 4160 series carburetors although there are minor differences from model to model. The following is a generalized disassembly and assembly procedure for all Corvette, four-barrel Holley carburetors.

1. Remove the primary and secondary fuel bowls, metering bodies, plates, splash shields, and fuel tubes.

2. Disconnect the secondary throttle-operating rod from the throttle lever. Remove the secondary throttle-operating assembly and gasket from the main body of the carburetor.

3. Remove the float hinge pin retainer and remove the float and spring from the bowl. If so equipped, remove the inlet baffle.

4. Loosen the inlet needle and seat lock screw and remove the assembly. Remove the sight plug and gasket.

5. Remove the inlet fitting(s), gaskets, fuel filter, and spring.

6. On the primary bowl: remove the air vent assembly (except early 4150); remove the pump diaphragm screws and lift the pump housing, diaphragm, and spring from the fuel bowl; check that the pump inlet ball

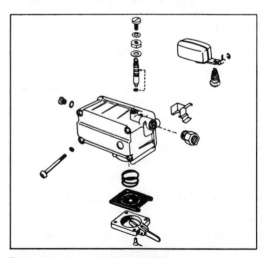

Exploded view of Holley 4150 bowl

can move freely. Replace the bowl assembly if ball movement is restricted or if either the ball or passage are damaged.

7. To disassemble the metering body (all except 4160 secondary): remove the main metering jets.

CAUTION: *Use a jet wrench or very wide screwdriver to prevent damaging the jets.* Use a one-inch, twelve-point socket to remove the power valves. On the primary side, remove the idle mixture screws and seals.

8. On the 4160 secondary: remove the plate and gasket from the metering body dowel pins.

9. On the early model 4150: remove the choke housing, retainer, and gasket. Remove the choke housing shaft, fast-idle cam, and choke piston.

10. On late model 4150 and 4160 carburetors: remove the choke vacuum break disconnecting link, fast-idle cam, and choke lever.

11. Remove the discharge nozzle, invert the carburetor, and shake the discharge needle out.

12. Replace gaskets, seals, and small parts with those provided in the rebuilding kit. Reverse the disassembly procedure to assemble the carburetor.

Fuel Injection

The Rochester fuel injection system was a performance option on 1963 through 1965 327 cubic inch engines. It delivers a constantly regulated air/fuel flow regardless of the engine requirements and eliminates carburetion difficulties caused by cornering or braking. While the fuel injection system is more complex than the ordinary carburetor, it is not beyond the repair capabilities of that average owner/mechanic—provided he adheres to procedure and specification recommendations.

The first hurdle is understanding the design of the fuel injector and this is best done by thinking of the unit as three separate systems, interlocked to accomplish a common function. The first system is the air meter and this simultaneously furnishes the fuel meter with an assessment of the load demands of the engine and feeds air to the intake manifold. The intake manifold is designed to ram charge the air as it distributes it to the cylinders. The fuel meter evaluates the air meter signal and furnishes the correct amount of fuel to the nozzles where it is injected into the engine.

DESCRIPTION AND OPERATION

Air Meter

The 1963–1964 air meter consists of three sub-components: the throttle valve, cold enrichment valve and diffuser cone assembly, and the meter housing. The 1965 air meter was modified to the extent that a choke piston was added and the choke valve stop was relocated in the diffuser cone. This allows an initial choke opening of 10° which increases to 30° after an initial cold start. The throttle valve regulates the flow of air into the manifold and is mechanically actuated by the accelerator pedal. The diffuser cone, suspended in the bore of the air meter inlet, functions as an annular venturi and accelerates the air flow between the cone and the meter housing. The air meter houses the previously mentioned components plus the idle and main venturi signal systems.

The main venturi vacuum signals are generated at the venturi as the incoming air rushes over an annular opening formed between the air meter body and piezometer ring. They are then transmitted through a tube to the main control diaphragm in the fuel meter. The venturi vacuum signal measures the flow of air into the engine and automatically controls the air/fuel ratio. The one exception to this is at idle speeds.

Idle air requirements are handled differently by the fuel injection method. Approximately 40% of the idle-speed air flow enters the engine through the nozzle block air connections tapped into the air meter body. Part of the remaining 60% flows past

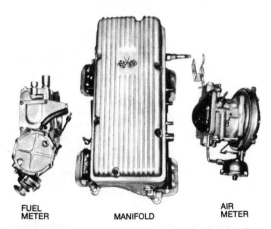

FUEL METER   MANIFOLD   AIR METER

Three major components of the fuel injection system

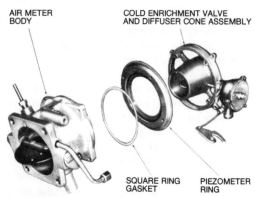

AIR METER BODY

COLD ENRICHMENT VALVE AND DIFFUSER CONE ASSEMBLY

SQUARE RING GASKET

PIEZOMETER RING

Exploded view of the air meter

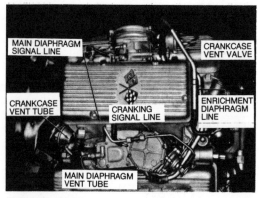

MAIN DIAPHRAGM SIGNAL LINE

CRANKCASE VENT VALVE

CRANKCASE VENT TUBE

CRANKING SIGNAL LINE

ENRICHMENT DIAPHRAGM LINE

MAIN DIAPHRAGM VENT TUBE

Fuel injection lines

the throttle valve which is pre-set against a fixed stop. The remainder enters through the idle air, by-pass passage that is controlled by the large, idle-speed adjusting screw. Idle speed is adjusted by turning this screw in or out.

Fuel Meter

The fuel meter's float-controlled fuel reservoir is basically the same as that found in conventional carburetion. The fuel meter receives fuel from the regular engine fuel pump. The incoming fuel is routed through a 10 micron filter before entering the main reservoir of the fuel meter, where the high pressure gear pump picks it up. This, high pressure, spur-gear type pump is completely submerged in the lower part of the fuel meter main reservoir. A distributor-powered, flexible shaft drives the pump at ½ engine speed. Fuel pressures span a range of near zero to 200 psi, according to engine speed. Fuel not used by the engine reenters the fuel meter through a fuel control system. The 1965 fuel meter contains a vent screen and baffle which helps to stabilize the air/fuel mixture.

Fuel Control System

A fuel control system regulates fuel pressure (flow) from the fuel pump to the nozzles. This flow is controlled by the amount of fuel that is spilled or recirculated from the high pressure pump, through the nozzle block, back to the fuel meter spill ports. This is accomplished by a three-piece spill plunger or disc that is located between the gear pump and the nozzles.

When high fuel flow is required, it moves downward, closing the spill ports to the fuel meter reservoir and concentrating the flow to the nozzle circuits. Correspondingly, the spill plunger or disc must be raised to allow the spill ports to be exposed when a low fuel flow is required. This causes the main output of the gear pump to by-pass the nozzle circuits and reenter the meter reservoir through the now-opened spill ports.

The spill plunger is not mechanically controlled by the accelerator pedal. Fuel control is accomplished by a precisely counter-balanced linkage system sensitive to fuel pressure and diaphragm vacuum. Thus the slightest change in venturi vacuum signal on the main control diaphragm will activate the linkage. One end of the fuel control lever rests against the spill plunger head while the other end connects by a link to the main control diaphragm. The control lever pivots on the roller end of an arm called the ratio lever. When the increased vacuum above the diaphragm forces the control lever upward, the lever pivots on the ratio lever's roller and pushes the spill plunger or disc downward. This closes the spill ports and steps up fuel flow to the nozzles. When decreased vacuum above the diaphragm reverses the pivot action, fuel pressure forces the spill plunger

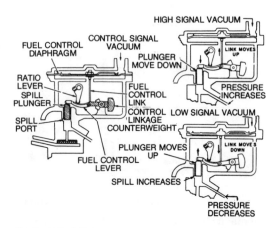

HIGH SIGNAL VACUUM

CONTROL SIGNAL VACUUM

FUEL CONTROL DIAPHRAGM

PLUNGER MOVE DOWN

LINK MOVES UP

RATIO LEVER

FUEL CONTROL LINK

PRESSURE INCREASES

SPILL PLUNGER

CONTROL LINKAGE

LOW SIGNAL VACUUM

SPILL PORT

COUNTERWEIGHT

PLUNGER MOVES UP

LINK MOVES DOWN

FUEL CONTROL LEVER

SPILL INCREASES

PRESSURE DECREASES

Fuel control linkage

upward and permits the spill ports to by-pass fuel into the reservoir, thus fuel flow to the nozzles is reduced.

The diaphragm vacuum-to-fuel pressure ratio, and subsequent fuel/air ratio, is regulated by the position of the ratio lever. As the ratio lever changes position, the mechanical advantage of the linkage system also changes, thus providing the correct fuel/air ratio for each driving condition. As long as engine manifold vacuum exceeds 8 in. Hg (mercury), the ratio lever remains at the economy stop and fuel flow follows the dictates of the main control diaphragm vacuum. A sudden decrease in manifold vacuum moves the ratio lever to the power stop. The resulting increase in the mechanical advantage of the linkage system closes the spill ports and increases full flow to the nozzles.

Starting System

Cold engine starting conditions require richer fuel/air mixtures to compensate for poor fuel evaporation. The absence of an accelerator pump prevents the driver from providing extra fuel by pumping the accelerator pedal. The correct method is to depress the pedal once and then release. This pre-sets the throttle for starting by the fast-idle cam. The vacuum signal generated at cranking rpm is very low and must be boosted. This boost is provided by a spring-loaded, open-cranking signal valve located at the enrichment diaphragm housing. This open valve allows the manifold cranking vacuum to react directly on, and lift, the main control diaphragm. This closes the spill valve. In addition, the spring-loaded enrichment diaphragm holds the ratio lever at the rich or power stop, thus providing maximum fuel flow to the nozzles. As soon as the engine starts, manifold vacuum overcomes the springs in the cranking signal valve and enrichment diaphragm, and the regular idle system is brought into operation.

The vacuum-controlled, cranking-signal valve circuit was eliminated on 1965 model injectors and replaced by a solenoid-controlled, by-pass fuel circuit. This system delivers the entire output engine fuel pump to the fuel distributor via a by-pass line. The fuel is then routed through a check valve and finally arrives at the individual nozzles. The control solenoid is energized when the ignition switch is held in the start position and the accelerator pedal is depressed less than 1/3 of its travel. Depressing the accelerator

pedal further trips a micro-switch on the throttle linkage and stops fuel delivery to the by-pass circuit.

Idle System

Correct injector operation at idle speed is highly dependent upon the generation of a strong venturi signal and its subsequent transmittal to the control diaphragm. To ensure this signal during cold engine idle, the fast-idle cam holds the throttle valve cracked open. This increases the velocity of air flowing through the venturi which in turn strengthens the venturi vacuum signal being transported to the main control diaphragm. The electrically heated choke valve remains closed during initial cold engine operation, and this requires the entire air flow to pass through the venturi. This rerouting of the air flow generates a usable venturi signal even at relatively low engine speeds. Intake manifold vacuum acts directly on the enrichment diaphragm. The diaphragm's response movement adjusts the ratio lever to the economy stop as soon as manifold vacuum is sufficient to overcome the diaphragm spring. As the electric heating element senses a rise in engine temperature, it relaxes the thermostat and permits the choke valve to open. Air flow through the venturi decreases and the signal generated here drops. The idle signal system now becomes the more dominant signal.

Fuel control during warm engine idle is a result of main control diaphragm response to the idle circuit signal. With the ratio lever already positioned at the economy stop, air now enters through the idle air circuit and the nozzle blocks.

Acceleration

Acceleration is instantaneous at normal driving speeds. Opening the throttle valve increases both air flow and the venturi signal at the main diaphragm. The momentary drop in manifold vacuum causes the ratio lever to move to the power stop position. A calibrated restriction in the main control signal circuit stabilizes the idle signal and adds this to the total signal as long as it is present.

Ratio Lever—Power Stop

The air/fuel ratio requirements for power are basically the same as those necessary for acceleration. The drop in manifold vacuum, caused by a wide-open throttle condition, moves the ratio lever to the power stop. The open throttle also provides a stronger venturi signal through the increased air flow.

Hot Starting/Unloading

Rich mixtures must be prevented during hot starting/unloading situations. Depressing the accelerator pedal to fully open the throttle valve during starting will prevent high vacuum from reaching the cranking signal valve and will facilitate starting.

Hot Idle Compensator

Extremely hot operation conditions can cause rich mixture conditions that detrimentally affect engine smoothness and idling. To remedy this, a thermostatically controlled valve on the top side of the air meter throttle valve allows additional air to bleed into the manifold and restore the idle mixture to a correct ratio.

Idle Speed and Fuel Adjustments

Idle speed and fuel adjustments require presetting of the idle-speed and idle-fuel adjust-

Idle speed adjustment

Idle mixture adjustment

ing screws 1½ turns out from their fully closed position. Start the engine and adjust the idle-speed screw until 800–850 rpm is obtained. Adjust the idle-fuel screw until the smoothest engine idle is attained. Should the two idle-adjusting screws become completely out of phase, purge the system or stop the engine and repeat the entire preceding procedure.

FAST IDLE-SPEED AND COLD ENRICHMENT ADJUSTMENTS

Adjust the fast idle-speed by bending the enrichment linkage until clearance between the fast-idle cam and the adjusting screw resembles the illustration. With the engine stopped, crack the throttle valve and manually close the cold enrichment valve. Release the throttle linkage and check to see that the fast-idle is now positioned for cold engine operation. Release the cold enrichment valve, warm the engine, and adjust the fast-idle screw to obtain 2200 rpm. Make the cold enrichment adjustment by setting the cold enrichment cover to 3 notches lean. Be sure that the valve linkage operates freely.

RATIO LEVER STOP SETTINGS

This series of adjustments requires the use of a manometer. Attach the manometer in a convenient place on the vehicle and use the two-position bracket so that the most vertical position may be obtained. After the unit has been leveled by means of the leveling vial, open both water manometer valves and see if a zero reading exists. If not, adjust the oil leveling screw. If this fails to zero the indicator, add red oil (specific gravity 0.826). Back off the leveling screw for this procedure.

Remove both hose adapters on the mercury (Hg) manometer and plugs located in the adapters. Install the tee fitting in the most easily accessible fuel nozzle circuit. Attach the fuel pressure line to the tee fitting and the mercury manometer. Check the fuel trap inlet to see that it is properly positioned in the line. Clamp the venturi signal line to the cranking signal valve line and the water manometer. Check the clamp to be sure it is tightly closed on the line. If it isn't, high vacuum during engine cranking will cause the red oil to be lost. Replace the main diaphragm vent tube with the large rubber tube. Adjust the scale of the mercury manometer to read zero inches. Recheck the manometer leveling vial and make any neces-

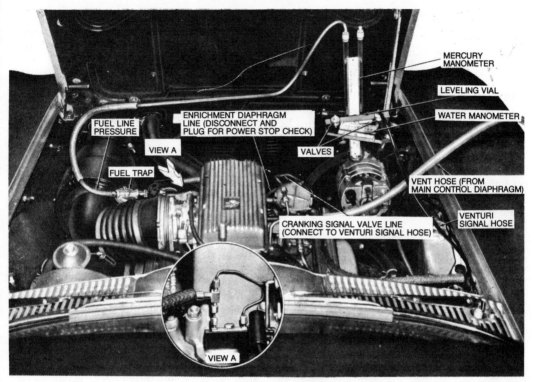

Manometer installation

sary adjustments. This completes the installation.

The economy stop adjustment procedure begins with a visual check of the unit for physical defects. With the engine warmed up, check to see that the unit is operating on the economy stop. Some injectors may be difficult to start with the cranking-signal valve line disconnected. The line may be reconnected during the initial starting procedure.

Increase engine rpm until a 0.5 in. signal is registered on the water manometer. Check the mercury manometer and record its reading. Decrease the engine rpm and repeat the above procedure. Average three readings for best accuracy. To adjust, loosen the locknut and turn the economy stop screw in or out until the mercury manometer reads 0.8 in. (±0.1 in.) when the water manometer reads 0.5 in.

The power stop readings are obtained with the manometer hooked up as in the previous procedure. Disconnect and plug the vacuum line going to the enrichment diaphragm and the injection unit will operate only on the power stop. Do not prolong this operation or spark plug fouling will result.

Increase the engine rpm until a 0.5 in. signal is reached on the water manometer and check and record the mercury manometer reading. Reduce engine speed and repeat the above operation. Average three readings for the best results. Check the enrichment diaphragm to see that it is not bottoming in the housing. To adjust the power stop, loosen the locknut and turn the adjusting screw until a reading of 1.2 in. (±0.1 in.) is reached on the mercury manometer when the water manometer reads 0.5 in.

Economy and power stop adjusting screws

REMOVAL AND INSTALLATION

1. Disconnect the washer vacuum line, accelerator linkage, electric choke lead wire, and the bellcrank return spring.

2. Loosen the flexible hose clamp and slide the hose from the air meter adapter.

3. Disconnect the fuel line at the filter and the drive cable coupling at the distributor by sliding the cable into the pump housing to disengage it from the distributor, and then pulling it clear. Don't lose the fiber washer on the end of the cable.

4. Remove the engine/manifold adapter-plate retaining nuts and lift the assembly from the engine.

5. Install a ⅜ in. x 2 in. bolt and nut in each manifold outer mounting-hole to allow the unit to be placed upright on a workbench without damaging the nozzles.

6. Reverse the above procedure to install.

Removing fuel pressure lines

DISASSEMBLY AND ASSEMBLY

1. The first step in disassembly is to separate the fuel injection unit into its three main components: fuel meter, air meter, and manifold.

2. Separate the air meter from the injector unit by disconnecting the bellcrank from the pivot shaft and leaving it attached to the air meter. Disconnect the main control signal tube at both ends and remove. Remove the retaining nuts and washers and carefully lift the air meter while simultaneously disconnecting the rubber, nozzle balance tube elbow at the air meter.

3. Disconnect the enrichment diaphragm tube at both ends, disengaging the tube at the manifold end first. Disconnect the main control diaphragm vent tube at both ends. Invert the injector and drain the fuel reservoir through the cover vent, then disconnect the fuel pressure lines. Remove the lower retaining screws, the single upper bolt, and the short vent tube. Discard the rubber O-ring at the fuel meter end of the fuel line. Remove the fuel meter from the injector unit.

4. Disassemble the air meter by removing the air cleaner adapter, fast-idle cam pivot screw, diffuser cone assembly, and piezometer ring from the air meter.

5. Remove the idle-speed and idle-fuel adjusting screws. The throttle valve need not be removed unless shaft binding exists.

6. Disassemble the fuel meter by removing the diaphragm cover and shield. Carefully remove the diaphragm retaining nut and diaphragm from the control link. The control link must be kept from rotating to prevent damaging the control link.

7. Remove the nylon splash shield, the fuel bowl cover attaching screws and carefully lift the cover, upper support bracket, and gasket from the meter body. Do not bend the control link. Start the link into the slot, then pry the opposite side upward and turn the shield over the link.

8. Remove the fuel pump, enrichment housing, and cranking signal valve. Remove the spill plunger cover and filter, spill plunger and sleeve assembly from the fuel meter bore. If the spill plunger separates

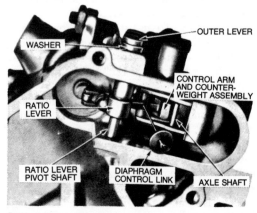

Ratio lever control linkage

Fuel pump piston and valve assembly

from the sleeve, use a hooked wire to pull the sleeve out.

9. Remove the ratio lever and shaft. Rotate the control arm and counterweights on the axle and remove the axle. Remove the control arm and counterweight assembly from the meter body. This will also remove the lead sealing ball on the outer end of the axle shaft.

10. The fuel pump is secured to the fuel meter by 5 screws. Remove these, noting that the shortest screw is positioned in the 9 o'clock position. With pump separated from the fuel meter, scribe reassembly marks on the pump housing.

11. Remove the cover attaching screws and the cover. Hand pressure is sufficient to pull the drive shaft from the pump drive gear and housing. Use a suitable driver to remove the drive shaft seal from the pump housing. Bear in mind, the fuel meter contains 48 parts in addition to screws. Be careful. Reassembly is the reverse of this procedure.

12. Nozzles may be disassembled for cleaning but care should be taken to ensure correct reassembly. Never clean nozzle orifices with wire. If a nozzle is dirty, replace it. Should more than one nozzle be found exceptionally dirty, replace the fuel meter filter. Replace nozzles only as complete assemblies and according to the following chart:

Nozzle Code	Part Number
W17 or 18	7017323
X18 or 19	7017324
Y19 or 20	7017325

13. Begin disassembly by carefully disconnecting and lifting the fuel lines out of the way. Disconnect either the throttle bell crank or fuel pump drive cable when removing nozzles in their vicinity. Remove the nozzles and nozzle blocks as complete assemblies. Invert the blocks and remove the individual nozzles. Carefully remove the old nozzle gaskets. Disassemble the unit by securing the nozzle body and inserting a drift punch in the head to turn it. Avoid damaging, losing, or mixing parts. Remember: the nozzle orifice discs are assembled with the bright side toward the engine. After cleaning or replacing nozzle assemblies, reinstall them in the nozzle block, using new gaskets. Check to see that the nozzle gaskets remain in position during reinstallation and that the nozzles are properly placed in the nozzle shields. Reassembly is the reversal of this procedure.

14. A fuel nozzle spray-pattern check should be made whenever a complete nozzle cleaning is made. Drive the gear pump with an electric drill while applying oral vacuum at the main control diaphragm. The latter ensures that all fuel is routed through the nozzle circuit. The spray pattern is correct when each bank of nozzles appears as a single spray when viewed from the end of the assembly.

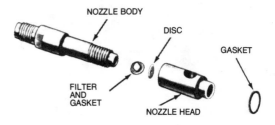

Nozzle assembly

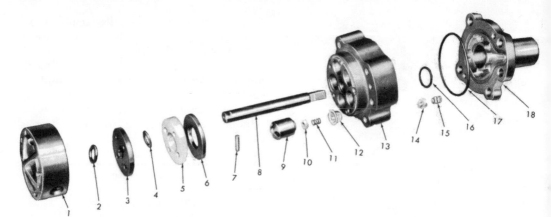

1. Inlet housing cover
2. Thrust washer
3. Drive plate
4. Thrust washer
5. Wobble plate
6. Bearing plate

7. Drive pin
8. Driveshaft
9. Inlet piston (5)
10. Inlet valve (5)
11. Valve spring (5)
12. Valve retainer (5)

13. Main housing
14. Discharge valve (5)
15. Valve spring (5)
16. O-ring seal
17. O-ring seal
18. Discharge housing

Fuel injection pump

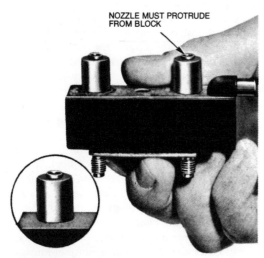

NOZZLE MUST PROTRUDE FROM BLOCK

Nozzle block assembly

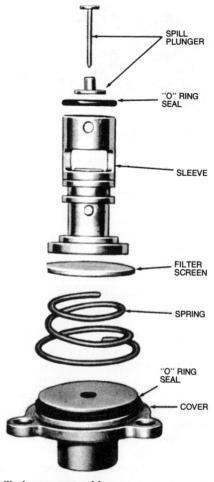

SPILL PLUNGER

"O" RING SEAL

SLEEVE

FILTER SCREEN

SPRING

"O" RING SEAL

COVER

Spill plunger assembly

APPLY ORAL VACUUM HERE

Checking spray pattern

CHILTON'S
FUEL ECONOMY
& TUNE-UP TIPS

Tune-Up • Spark Plug Diagnosis • Emission Controls

Fuel System • Cooling System • Tires and Wheels

General Maintenance

CHILTON'S FUEL ECONOMY & TUNE-UP TIPS

Fuel economy is important to everyone, no matter what kind of vehicle you drive. The maintenance-minded motorist can save both money and fuel using these tips and the periodic maintenance and tune-up procedures in this Repair and Tune-Up Guide.

There are more than 130,000,000 cars and trucks registered for private use in the United States. Each travels an average of 10-12,000 miles per year, and, in total they consume close to 70 billion gallons of fuel each year. This represents nearly ⅔ of the oil imported by the United States each year. The Federal government's goal is to reduce consumption 10% by 1985. A variety of methods are either already in use or under serious consideration, and they all affect your driving and the cars you will drive. In addition to "down-sizing", the auto industry is using or investigating the use of electronic fuel delivery, electronic engine controls and alternative engines for use in smaller and lighter vehicles, among other alternatives to meet the federally mandated Corporate Average Fuel Economy (CAFE) of 27.5 mpg by 1985. The government, for its part, is considering rationing, mandatory driving curtailments and tax increases on motor vehicle fuel in an effort to reduce consumption. The government's goal of a 10% reduction could be realized — and further government regulation avoided — if every private vehicle could use just 1 less gallon of fuel per week.

How Much Can You Save?

Tests have proven that almost anyone can make at least a 10% reduction in fuel consumption through regular maintenance and tune-ups. When a major manufacturer of spark plugs sur-

TUNE-UP

1. Check the cylinder compression to be sure the engine will really benefit from a tune-up and that it is capable of producing good fuel economy. A tune-up will be wasted on an engine in poor mechanical condition.

2. Replace spark plugs regularly. New spark plugs alone can increase fuel economy 3%.

3. Be sure the spark plugs are the correct type (heat range) for your vehicle. See the Tune-Up Specifications.

Heat range refers to the spark plug's ability to conduct heat away from the firing end. It must conduct the heat away in an even pattern to avoid becoming a source of pre-ignition, yet it must also operate hot enough to burn off conductive deposits that could cause misfiring.

The heat range is usually indicated by a number on the spark plug, part of the manufacturer's designation for each individual spark plug. The numbers in bold-face indicate the heat range in each manufacturer's identification system.

Periodically, check the spark plugs to be sure they are firing efficiently. They are excellent indicators of the internal condition of your engine.

Manufacturer	Typical Designation
AC	R **45** TS
Bosch (old)	WA **145** T30
Bosch (new)	HR **8** Y
Champion	RBL **15** Y
Fram/Autolite	**4**15
Mopar	P-**62** PR
Motorcraft	BRF-**42**
NGK	BP **5** ES-15
Nippondenso	W **16** EP
Prestolite	14GR **5** 2A

On AC, Bosch (new), Champion, Fram/Autolite, Mopar, Motorcraft and Prestolite, a higher number indicates a hotter plug. On Bosch (old), NGK and Nippondenso, a higher number indicates a colder plug.

4. Make sure the spark plugs are properly gapped. See the Tune-Up Specifications in this book.

5. Be sure the spark plugs are firing efficiently. The illustrations on the next 2 pages show you how to "read" the firing end of the spark plug.

6. Check the ignition timing and set it to specifications. Tests show that almost all cars

veyed over 6,000 cars nationwide, they found that a tune-up, on cars that needed one, increased fuel economy over 11%. Replacing worn plugs alone, accounted for a 3% increase. The same test also revealed that 8 out of every 10 vehicles will have some maintenance deficiency that will directly affect fuel economy, emissions or performance. Most of this mileage-robbing neglect could be prevented with regular maintenance.

Modern engines require that all of the functioning systems operate properly for maximum efficiency. A malfunction anywhere wastes fuel. You can keep your vehicle running as efficiently and economically as possible, by being aware of your vehicles operating and performance characteristics. If your vehicle suddenly develops performance or fuel economy problems it could be due to one or more of the following:

PROBLEM	POSSIBLE CAUSE
Engine Idles Rough	Ignition timing, idle mixture, vacuum leak or something amiss in the emission control system.
Hesitates on Acceleration	Dirty carburetor or fuel filter, improper accelerator pump setting, ignition timing or fouled spark plugs.
Starts Hard or Fails to Start	Worn spark plugs, improperly set automatic choke, ice (or water) in fuel system.
Stalls Frequently	Automatic choke improperly adjusted and possible dirty air filter or fuel filter.
Performs Sluggishly	Worn spark plugs, dirty fuel or air filter, ignition timing or automatic choke out of adjustment.

Check spark plug wires on conventional point type ignition for cracks by bending them in a loop around your finger.

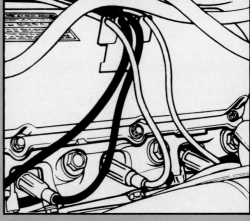

Be sure that spark plug wires leading to adjacent cylinders do not run too close together. (Photo courtesy Champion Spark Plug Co.)

have incorrect ignition timing by more than 2°.

7. If your vehicle does not have electronic ignition, check the points, rotor and cap as specified.

8. Check the spark plug wires (used with conventional point-type ignitions) for cracks and burned or broken insulation by bending them in a loop around your finger. Cracked wires decrease fuel efficiency by failing to deliver full voltage to the spark plugs. One misfiring spark plug can cost you as much as 2 mpg.

9. Check the routing of the plug wires. Misfiring can be the result of spark plug leads to adjacent cylinders running parallel to each other and too close together. One wire tends to pick up voltage from the other causing it to fire "out of time".

10. Check all electrical and ignition circuits for voltage drop and resistance.

11. Check the distributor mechanical and/or vacuum advance mechanisms for proper functioning. The vacuum advance can be checked by twisting the distributor plate in the opposite direction of rotation. It should spring back when released.

12. Check and adjust the valve clearance on engines with mechanical lifters. The clearance should be slightly loose rather than too tight.

SPARK PLUG DIAGNOSIS

Normal

APPEARANCE: This plug is typical of one operating normally. The insulator nose varies from a light tan to grayish color with slight electrode wear. The presence of slight deposits is normal on used plugs and will have no adverse effect on engine performance. The spark plug heat range is correct for the engine and the engine is running normally.

CAUSE: Properly running engine.

RECOMMENDATION: Before reinstalling this plug, the electrodes should be cleaned and filed square. Set the gap to specifications. If the plug has been in service for more than 10-12,000 miles, the entire set should probably be replaced with a fresh set of the same heat range.

Oil Deposits

APPEARANCE: The firing end of the plug is covered with a wet, oily coating.

CAUSE: The problem is poor oil control. On high mileage engines, oil is leaking past the rings or valve guides into the combustion chamber. A common cause is also a plugged PCV valve, and a ruptured fuel pump diaphragm can also cause this condition. Oil fouled plugs such as these are often found in new or recently overhauled engines, before normal oil control is achieved, and can be cleaned and reinstalled.

RECOMMENDATION: A hotter spark plug may temporarily relieve the problem, but the engine is probably in need of work.

Incorrect Heat Range

APPEARANCE: The effects of high temperature on a spark plug are indicated by clean white, often blistered insulator. This can also be accompanied by excessive wear of the electrode, and the absence of deposits.

CAUSE: Check for the correct spark plug heat range. A plug which is too hot for the engine can result in overheating. A car operated mostly at high speeds can require a colder plug. Also check ignition timing, cooling system level, fuel mixture and leaking intake manifold.

RECOMMENDATION: If all ignition and engine adjustments are known to be correct, and no other malfunction exists, install spark plugs one heat range colder.

Photos Courtesy Champion Spark Plug Co.

Carbon Deposits

APPEARANCE: Carbon fouling is easily identified by the presence of dry, soft, black, sooty deposits.

CAUSE: Changing the heat range can often lead to carbon fouling, as can prolonged slow, stop-and-start driving. If the heat range is correct, carbon fouling can be attributed to a rich fuel mixture, sticking choke, clogged air cleaner, worn breaker points, retarded timing or low compression. If only one or two plugs are carbon fouled, check for corroded or cracked wires on the affected plugs. Also look for cracks in the distributor cap between the towers of affected cylinders.

RECOMMENDATION: After the problem is corrected, these plugs can be cleaned and reinstalled if not worn severely.

MMT Fouled

APPEARANCE: Spark plugs fouled by MMT (Methycyclopentadienyl Maganese Tricarbonyl) have reddish, rusty appearance on the insulator and side electrode.

CAUSE: MMT is an anti-knock additive in gasoline used to replace lead. During the combustion process, the MMT leaves a reddish deposit on the insulator and side electrode.

RECOMMENDATION: No engine malfunction is indicated and the deposits will not affect plug performance any more than lead deposits (see Ash Deposits). MMT fouled plugs can be cleaned, regapped and reinstalled.

High Speed Glazing

APPEARANCE: Glazing appears as shiny coating on the plug, either yellow or tan in color.

CAUSE: During hard, fast acceleration, plug temperatures rise suddenly. Deposits from normal combustion have no chance to fluff-off; instead, they melt on the insulator forming an electrically conductive coating which causes misfiring.

RECOMMENDATION: Glazed plugs are not easily cleaned. They should be replaced with a fresh set of plugs of the correct heat range. If the condition recurs, using plugs with a heat range one step colder may cure the problem.

Ash (Lead) Deposits

APPEARANCE: Ash deposits are characterized by light brown or white colored deposits crusted on the side or center electrodes. In some cases it may give the plug a rusty appearance.

CAUSE: Ash deposits are normally derived from oil or fuel additives burned during normal combustion. Normally they are harmless, though excessive amounts can cause misfiring. If deposits are excessive in short mileage, the valve guides may be worn.

RECOMMENDATION: Ash-fouled plugs can be cleaned, gapped and reinstalled.

Detonation

APPEARANCE: Detonation is usually characterized by a broken plug insulator.

CAUSE: A portion of the fuel charge will begin to burn spontaneously, from the increased heat following ignition. The explosion that results applies extreme pressure to engine components, frequently damaging spark plugs and pistons.

Detonation can result by over-advanced ignition timing, inferior gasoline (low octane) lean air/fuel mixture, poor carburetion, engine lugging or an increase in compression ratio due to combustion chamber deposits or engine modification.

RECOMMENDATION: Replace the plugs after correcting the problem.

Photos Courtesy Fram Corporation

EMISSION CONTROLS

13. Be aware of the general condition of the emission control system. It contributes to reduced pollution and should be serviced regularly to maintain efficient engine operation.

14. Check all vacuum lines for dried, cracked or brittle conditions. Something as simple as a leaking vacuum hose can cause poor performance and loss of economy.

15. Avoid tampering with the emission control system. Attempting to improve fuel econ-

FUEL SYSTEM

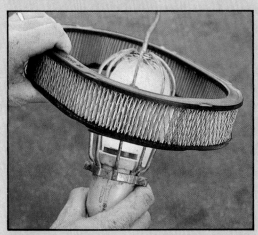

Check the air filter with a light behind it. If you can see light through the filter it can be reused.

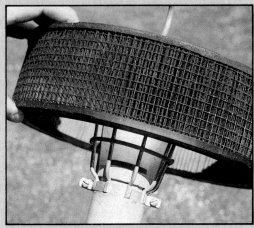

Extremely clogged filters should be discarded and replaced with a new one.

18. Replace the air filter regularly. A dirty air filter richens the air/fuel mixture and can increase fuel consumption as much as 10%. Tests show that 1/3 of all vehicles have air filters in need of replacement.

19. Replace the fuel filter at least as often as recommended.

20. Set the idle speed and carburetor mixture to specifications.

21. Check the automatic choke. A sticking or malfunctioning choke wastes gas.

22. During the summer months, adjust the automatic choke for a leaner mixture which will produce faster engine warm-ups.

COOLING SYSTEM

29. Be sure all accessory drive belts are in good condition. Check for cracks or wear.

30. Adjust all accessory drive belts to proper tension.

31. Check all hoses for swollen areas, worn spots, or loose clamps.

32. Check coolant level in the radiator or expansion tank.

33. Be sure the thermostat is operating properly. A stuck thermostat delays engine warm-up and a cold engine uses nearly twice as much fuel as a warm engine.

34. Drain and replace the engine coolant at least as often as recommended. Rust and scale

TIRES & WHEELS

38. Check the tire pressure often with a pencil type gauge. Tests by a major tire manufacturer show that 90% of all vehicles have at least 1 tire improperly inflated. Better mileage can be achieved by over-inflating tires, but never exceed the maximum inflation pressure on the side of the tire.

39. If possible, install radial tires. Radial tires deliver as much as 1/2 mpg more than bias belted tires.

40. Avoid installing super-wide tires. They only create extra rolling resistance and decrease fuel mileage. Stick to the manufacturer's recommendations.

41. Have the wheels properly balanced.

omy by tampering with emission controls is more likely to worsen fuel economy than improve it. Emission control changes on modern engines are not readily reversible.

16. Clean (or replace) the EGR valve and lines as recommended.

17. Be sure that all vacuum lines and hoses are reconnected properly after working under the hood. An unconnected or misrouted vacuum line can wreak havoc with engine performance.

---

23. Check for fuel leaks at the carburetor, fuel pump, fuel lines and fuel tank. Be sure all lines and connections are tight.

24. Periodically check the tightness of the carburetor and intake manifold attaching nuts and bolts. These are a common place for vacuum leaks to occur.

25. Clean the carburetor periodically and lubricate the linkage.

26. The condition of the tailpipe can be an excellent indicator of proper engine combustion. After a long drive at highway speeds, the inside of the tailpipe should be a light grey in color. Black or soot on the insides indicates an overly rich mixture.

27. Check the fuel pump pressure. The fuel pump may be supplying more fuel than the engine needs.

28. Use the proper grade of gasoline for your engine. Don't try to compensate for knocking or "pinging" by advancing the ignition timing. This practice will only increase plug temperature and the chances of detonation or pre-ignition with relatively little performance gain.

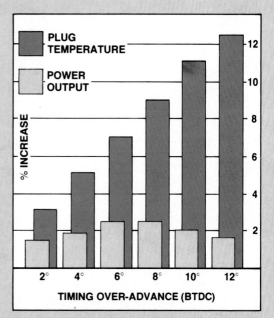

Increasing ignition timing past the specified setting results in a drastic increase in spark plug temperature with increased chance of detonation or preignition. Performance increase is considerably less. (Photo courtesy Champion Spark Plug Co.)

---

that form in the engine should be flushed out to allow the engine to operate at peak efficiency.

35. Clean the radiator of debris that can decrease cooling efficiency.

36. Install a flex-type or electric cooling fan, if you don't have a clutch type fan. Flex fans use curved plastic blades to push more air at low speeds when more cooling is needed; at high speeds the blades flatten out for less resistance. Electric fans only run when the engine temperature reaches a predetermined level.

37. Check the radiator cap for a worn or cracked gasket. If the cap does not seal properly, the cooling system will not function properly.

---

42. Be sure the front end is correctly aligned. A misaligned front end actually has wheels going in different directions. The increased drag can reduce fuel economy by .3 mpg.

43. Correctly adjust the wheel bearings. Wheel bearings that are adjusted too tight increase rolling resistance.

Check tire pressures regularly with a reliable pocket type gauge. Be sure to check the pressure on a cold tire.

GENERAL MAINTENANCE

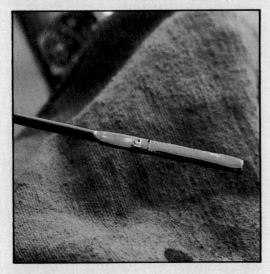

Check the fluid levels (particularly engine oil) on a regular basis. Be sure to check the oil for grit, water or other contamination.

A vacuum gauge is another excellent indicator of internal engine condition and can also be installed in the dash as a mileage indicator.

44. Periodically check the fluid levels in the engine, power steering pump, master cylinder, automatic transmission and drive axle.

45. Change the oil at the recommended interval and change the filter at every oil change. Dirty oil is thick and causes extra friction between moving parts, cutting efficiency and increasing wear. A worn engine requires more frequent tune-ups and gets progressively worse fuel economy. In general, use the lightest viscosity oil for the driving conditions you will encounter.

46. Use the recommended viscosity fluids in the transmission and axle.

47. Be sure the battery is fully charged for fast starts. A slow starting engine wastes fuel.

48. Be sure battery terminals are clean and tight.

49. Check the battery electrolyte level and add distilled water if necessary.

50. Check the exhaust system for crushed pipes, blockages and leaks.

51. Adjust the brakes. Dragging brakes or brakes that are not releasing create increased drag on the engine.

52. Install a vacuum gauge or miles-per-gallon gauge. These gauges visually indicate engine vacuum in the intake manifold. High vacuum = good mileage and low vacuum = poorer mileage. The gauge can also be an excellent indicator of internal engine conditions.

53. Be sure the clutch is properly adjusted. A slipping clutch wastes fuel.

54. Check and periodically lubricate the heat control valve in the exhaust manifold. A sticking or inoperative valve prevents engine warm-up and wastes gas.

55. Keep accurate records to check fuel economy over a period of time. A sudden drop in fuel economy may signal a need for tune-up or other maintenance.

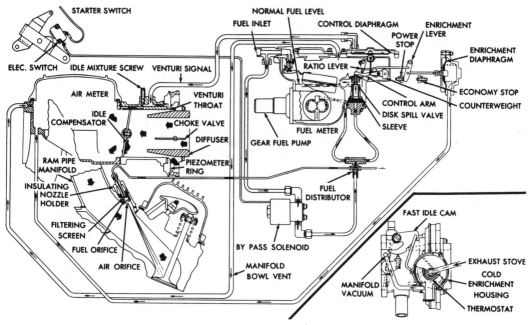

Fuel injection system diagram

15. Spill plunger assemblies are basically the same for all fuel injection units. After removing the assembly from the fuel meter, lubricate with fuel, and check the valve action. Clean or replace the assembly as required.

16. Reassembly of the air meter is the reversal of the disassembly procedure. At this time, check for throttle shaft binding. If such a condition exists, attempt to remedy by soaking in solvent. If the throttle shaft still binds, disconnect the throttle shaft from the linkage, remove the throttle plate screws, and file the burrs on the shaft. Remove the shaft, clean, rebush and then reassemble. During reassembly, preset the idle-speed and idle-fuel adjusting screws 1½ turns out from the bottom.

17. Fuel meter reassembly is the reversal of the disassembly procedure. When installing the main control diaphragm, keep in mind that the slots in the diaphragm should readily align with the cover attaching screw holes located in the bowl cover. Repeat the reassembly steps until the diaphragm holes line up naturally. Do not force this alignment. If the diaphragm seemed tight when removed, it is defective. The replacement diaphragm should not be installed in the same condition. At this time check the clearance between the housing and the enrichment diaphragm. A minimum of 0.040 in. is required

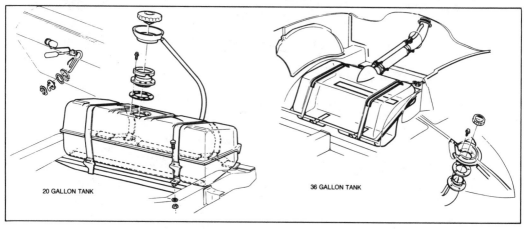

Fuel tank assembly—1963–67 (20 gal.), 1966–67 (optional 36 gal.) (© Chevrolet Motor Division)

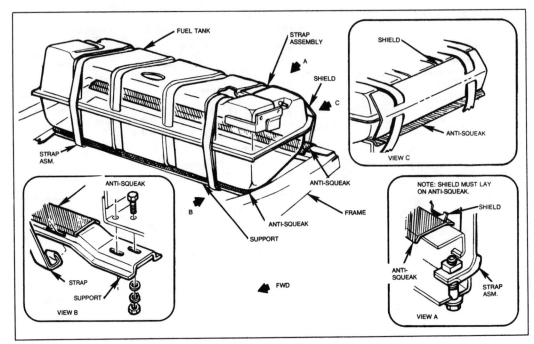

Fuel tank assembly—1968–77 (© Chevrolet Motor Division)

to prevent interference during power stop operation. Adjust the diaphragm shaft length to gain proper clearance.

Check the fuel reservoir float settings before replacing the top cover. Float level should be $2^9/_{32}$ in. while float drop should be $2^{27}/_{32}$ in. Bend to adjust.

FUEL TANK

REMOVAL AND INSTALLATION

1. Disconnect the battery ground cable.
2. Remove the fuel line and drain the tank.

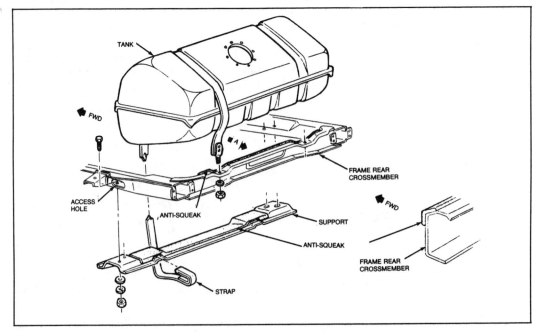

Fuel tank assembly—1978–79 (© Chevrolet Motor Division)

3. Remove the spare tire compartment.

4. Remove the exhaust pipe-to-tailpipe U-bolts at the crossmember.

5. Remove the tailpipe extensions.

6. Disconnect the muffler brackets and drop the entire assembly out of the way.

7. Remove the two retaining straps from the tank.

8. Disconnect fuel gauge wiring.

9. Remove the gas cap and rubber neck boot. Disconnect the filler drain line.

10. Unbolt and remove the frame gas tank support.

11. Lower the tank and turn to remove.

12. Reverse the removal procedure to install.

Carter WCFB & AFB

Year	Application	Identification No.	Float Level (in.)	Float Drop (in.)	Pump Rod (in.)	Automatic Choke Setting	Main Metering Jet (in.)		Metering Rod (in.)		Throttle Bore (in.)		Fast Idle (rpm)
							Prim	Sec	Prim	Sec	Prim	Sec	
1963–65	250 hp	3501S (M.T.) 3500S (A.T.)	$7/_{32}$ ①	$3/_4$	$1/_2$	index	0.086	0.0635	0.042	0.067	$1 7/_{16}$	$1 7/_{16}$	1750
	300, 340 hp	3461S (M.T.) 3460S (A.T.)	$7/_{32}$	$3/_4$	$1/_2$	1 lean	0.104	0.0689	0.060	0.069	$1 9/_{16}$	$1 11/_{16}$	1750

① $3/_4$" for secondary

Holley Model 2100 & 2300

Year	Engine H.P.	Identification No.①	Float Level	Accelerator Pump Lever Adjustment	Choke Unloader Clearance	Vacuum Break (in.)	Fast Idle RPM	Choke Setting
1967	400, 435	R3660A (Prim.)	②	.015	.275	.250	2,200	④
		R3659A (Sec.)	②	.015	—	—	2,200	④
		R3888A (Prim.)	②	.015	.275	.250	2,200	④
1968	400, 435	R4055A (Prim.)	.350	.015	.275	.250	2,200	③
		R4056A (Sec.)	.50	.015	—	—	2,200	③
		R3659A (Prim.)	.350	.015	.275	.250	2,200	③
1969	400, 435	R40551A (Prim.)	.350	.015	.250	.275	2,200	③
		R36591A (Sec.)	.50	.015	—	—	2,200	③
		R40561A (Prim.)	.350	.015	.250	.250	2,200	③

① Located on tag attached to carburetor
② Bottom of sight plug port plus or minus $\frac{1}{32}''$
③ Hold the choke valve closed and push downward on the coil rod to the end of travel. The top of the rod should be even with the top of the hole in the choke lever. Bend the rod to adjust.
④ Hold the choke valve closed and pull upward on the coil rod to the end of travel. The bottom of the rod end which slides into the hole should be even with the top of the hole. Bend the rod to adjust.

Holley 4150 and 4160 Specifications

Year	Identification No.①	Engine (H.P.)	Float Level (Dry) (in.)	Accelerator Pump Lever Adjustment (in.)	Choke Setting (in.)	Choke Unloader Clearance (in.)	Fast Idle On Car (rpm)	Choke Vacuum Break (in.)
1966	R3367A	300, 350	③	.015	④	.260	2,200	.170
	R3416A②	300, 350	③	.015	④	.260	2,200	.170
	R3370A	390	③	.015	⑤	.260	2,000	.180
	R3433A②	390	③	.015	⑤	.260	2,000	.180
	R3247A	425	⑥	.015	⑤	.350	2,000	.350
1967	R3810A	300, 350	③	.015	⑤	.265	2,000	.190

Holley 4150 and 4160 Specifications (cont.)

Year	Identification No.①	Engine (H.P.)	Float Level (Dry) (in.)	Accelerator Pump Lever Adjustment (in.)	Choke Setting (in.)	Choke Unloader Clearance (in.)	Fast Idle On Car (rpm)	Choke Vacuum Break (in.)
1967	R3814A②	300, 350	③	.015	⑤	.265	2,000	.175
	R3811A	390	③	.015	⑤	.265	2,200	.175
	R3815A②	390	③	.015	⑤	.265	2,200	.175
	R3418A	430	⑥	.015	⑤	.350	2,200	.350
1968	R4054A	430	⑦	.015	④	.350	2,200	.300
1969	R4296A	430	⑦	.015	④	.350	2,200	.350
1970	R4346	370	⑦	.015	⑤	.350	2,200	.300
	R4296A	430	⑦	.015	④	.350	2,200	.350
1971	R4801A⑧	330	⑩	.015	⑪	.350	2,200	.350
	R4800A⑨	330	⑩	.015	⑪	.350	2,200	.350
	R4803A⑧	425	⑩	.015	⑪	.350	2,200	.350
	R4802A⑨	425	⑩	.015	⑪	.350	2,200	.350
1972	R6239A⑧	255	⑩	.015	⑪	.350	2,350	.350
	R6238A⑨	255	⑩	.015	⑪	.350	2,350	.350

① Located on the tag attached to the carburetor, or on the casting or choke plate
② A.I.R.—Air Injector Reactor System
③ Prim.—.170″, Sec.—.300″
④ Hold the choke valve closed and push downward on the coil rod to the end of travel. The top of the rod should be even with the top of the hole in the choke lever. Bend the rod to adjust.
⑤ Hold the choke valve closed. Pull upward on the coil rod to the end of travel. The bottom of the rod end which slides into the hole in the choke lever should be in line with the notch. Bend the rod to adjust.
⑥ Prim.—.350″, Sec.—.450″
⑦ Prim.—.350″, Sec.—.500″
⑧ Man. Trans.
⑨ Auto. Trans.
⑩ Float centered in bowl
⑪ Hold the choke valve open. Pull downward on the coil rod to the end of travel. The bottom of the rod end which slides into the hole in the choke lever should be in line with the notch. Bend the rod to adjust.

Rochester 4MC & 4MV Carburetor Specifications

Year	Engine (H.P.)	Carburetor Identification①	Float Level (in.)	Air Valve Spring	Pump Rod (in.)	Idle Vent (in.)	Vacuum Break (in.)	Choke Setting	Choke Rod (in.)	Choke Unloader (in.)	Fast Idle Speed (rpm)
1966	390②	7026205	9/32	1 11/32	13/32④	3/8	.245	⑤	.100	.300	2,000
	390③	7026204	9/32	1 11/32	13/32④	3/8	.160	⑤	.100	.300	2,000
1968	300②	7028207	9/32	3/8	9/32	3/8	.245	⑥	.100	.300	2,400
	300③	7028208	9/32	3/8	9/32	3/8	.160	⑥	.100	.260	2,400
	350	7028219	9/32	7/8	9/32	3/8	.245	⑥	.100	.300	2,400
	390②	7028209	3/16	7/8	9/32	3/8	.245	⑤	.100	.300	2,400
	390③	7028216	3/16	7/8	9/32	3/8	.160	⑤	.100	.300	2,400
1969	300②	7029203	7/32	7/16	5/16	3/8	.245	⑥	.100	.450	2,400
	300③	7029202	7/32	7/16	5/16	3/8	.180	⑥	.100	.450	2,400
	350	7029207	3/16	13/16	5/16	3/8	.245	⑥	.100	.450	2,400
	390②	7029215	1/4	13/16	5/16	3/8	.245	⑥	.100	.450	2,400
	390③	7029204	1/4	13/16	5/16	3/8	.180	⑥	.100	.450	2,400
1970	300②	7040203	1/4	7/16	5/16	—	.275	⑥	.100	.450	2,400
	300③	7040202	1/4	7/16	5/16	—	.245	⑥	.100	.450	2,400

Rochester 4MC & 4MV Carburetor Specifications (cont.)

Year	Engine (H.P.)	Carburetor Identification ①	Float Level (in.)	Air Valve Spring	Pump Rod (in.)	Idle Vent (in.)	Vacuum Break (in.)	Choke Setting	Choke Rod (in.)	Choke Unloader (in.)	Fast Idle Speed (rpm)
	350	7040207	1/4	13/16	5/16	—	.275	⑥	.100	.450	2,400
	390②	7040205	1/4	13/16	5/16	—	.275	⑥	.100	.450	2,400
	390③	7040204	1/4	13/16	5/16	—	.245	⑥	.100	.450	2,400
1971	270②	7041213	1/4	7/16	—	—	.275	⑥	.100	—	2,400
	270③	7041212	1/4	7/16	—	—	.260	⑥	.100	—	2,400
	365②	7041205	1/4	7/16	—	—	.275	⑥	.100	—	2,400
	365③	7041204	1/4	7/16	—	—	.260	⑥	.100	—	2,400
1972	200②	7042203	1/4	1/2	3/8	—	.215	⑥	.100	.450	1,350
	200③	7042202	1/4	1/2	3/8	—	.215	⑥	.100	.450	1,500
	200②⑦	7042903	1/4	1/2	3/8	—	.215	⑥	.100	.450	1,350
	200③⑦	7042902	1/4	1/2	3/8	—	.215	⑥	.100	.450	1,500
	270②	7042217	1/4	7/16	3/8	—	.250	⑥	.100	.450	1,350
	270③	7042216	1/4	7/16	3/8	—	.250	⑥	.100	.450	1,500

Year											
1973	190[2]	7043203	7/32	1/2	13/32	—		[8]	.430	.450	1,300
	190[3]	7043202	7/32	1/2	13/32	—	.250	[8]	.430	.450	1,600
	250, 270[2]	7043201	1/4	11/16	13/32	—	.250	[8]	.430	.450	1,600
	250, 270[3]	7043200	1/4	11/16	13/32	—	.250	[8]	.430	.450	1,600
1974	195[2]	7044207	1/4	7/8	13/32	—	.230	[9]	.430	.450	1,300[10]
	195[3]	7044206	1/4	7/8	13/32	—	.230	[9]	.430	.450	1,600[11]
	195[2] [7]	7044507	1/4	7/8	13/32	—	.230	[9]	.430	.450	1,300[10]
	195[3], [7]	7044506	1/4	7/8	13/32	—	.230	[9]	.430	.450	1,600[11]
	250, 270[2]	7044211	1/4	1	13/32	—	.230	[9]	.430	.450	1,300[10]
	250, 270[3]	7044210	1/4	1	13/32	—	.230	[9]	.430	.450	1,600[11]
1975	165[2]	7045223	15/32		.275	—	[12]	Index	.300	.325	1,600
	165[3]	7045222	15/32		.275	—	[12]	Index	.300	.325	1,600
	205[2]	7045211	15/32		.275	—	[12]	Index	.300	.325	1,600
	205[3]	7045210	15/32		.275	—	[12]	Index	.300	.325	1,600
1976	165[2]	17056203	13/32	7/8	9/32	—	.185	3NL	.325	.325	1,600
	165[3]	17056202	13/32	7/8	9/32	—	.185	2NL	.325	.325	1,600

Rochester 4MC & 4MV Carburetor Specifications (cont.)

Year	Engine (H.P.)	Carburetor Identification①	Float Level (in.)	Air Valve Spring	Pump Rod (in.)	Idle Vent (in.)	Vacuum Break (in.)	Choke Setting	Choke Rod (in.)	Choke Unloader (in.)	Fast Idle Speed (rpm)
1977	205②	17056211	13/32	1	9/32	—	.170	2NL	.325	.325	1,600
	205③	17056210	13/32	1	9/32	—	.185	2NL	.325	.325	1,600
	180②	17057203	15/32	7/8	15/32	—	.180	3NL	.325	.280	1,600
	180③	17057202	15/32	7/8	15/32	—	.180	2NL	.325	.280	1,600
	180③⑦	17057502	15/32	7/8	15/32	—	.165	2NL	.325	.280	1,600
	210②	17057211	15/32	1	15/32	—	.180	3NL	.325	.280	1,300
	210③	17057210	15/32	1	15/32	—	.180	2NL	.325	.280	1,600
	210③⑦	17057510	15/32	1	15/32	—	.180	2NL	.325	.280	1,600
1978	185②	17058203	15/32	7/8	9/32	—	.179	2NL	.314	.277	—
	185③	17058202	15/32	7/8	9/32	—	.179	2NL	.314	.277	—
	185②③	17058502	15/32	7/8	9/32	—	.187	2NL	.314	.277	—
	220②	17058211	15/32	—	9/32	—	.203	2NL	.314	.277	—
	220③	17058210	15/32	—	9/32	—	.203	2NL	.314	.277	—

1979 195②	17059203	15/32	7/8	—	2NL	—
195③	17059202	15/32	7/8	—	1NL	—
195③⑦	17059502	15/32	7/8	—	2NL	—
195③⑬	17059582	15/32	7/8	—	1NL	—
225②	17059211	15/32	—	—	2NL	—
225③	17059210	15/32	—	—	1NL	—

① The carburetor identification number is stamped on the float bowl, near the secondary throttle lever.
② Man. Trans.
③ Auto. Trans.
④ Inner hole
⑤ Hold the choke valve closed. Pull upward on the coil rod to the end of travel. The bottom of the rod end which slides into the hole in the choke lever should be even with the top of the hole. Bend the coil rod to adjust.
⑥ Hold the choke valve closed and push downward on the coil rod to the end of travel. The top of the rod should be even with the top of the hole in the choke lever. Bend the rod to adjust.
⑦ California
⑧ Hold the choke valve open. Pull downward on the coil rod to the end of travel. The bottom of the rod end which slides into the hole in the choke lever should be in line with the notch. Bend the rod to adjust.
⑨ Hold the choke valve closed. Pull upward on the coil rod to the end of travel. The bottom of the rod end which slides into the hole in the choke lever should be in line with the notch. Bend the rod to adjust.
⑩ Without vacuum advance
⑪ With vacuum advance, without EGR signal
⑫ Front—0.180, rear—0.170
⑬ High altitude

Fuel Injection Specifications

		1963	Early 1964[1]	Late 1964[2]	1965
Fuel pressure @ 0.5 H_2O ($\pm$ Hg)	Power Stop	1.2	1.9	1.9	1.9
	Economy Stop	0.8	1.0	1.0	1.0
Fast idle speed (rpm-engine hot)		2000	2200	2200	2600
Float level (in.)		$2\frac{9}{32}$	$2\frac{9}{32}$	$2\frac{9}{32}$	$2\frac{9}{32}$
Float drop (in.)		$2\frac{27}{32}$	$2\frac{27}{32}$	$2\frac{27}{32}$	$2\frac{27}{32}$
Vacuum to apply—Enrichment Diaphragm (in. Hg)	Economy Stop	9	6	6	6
	Travel Center	NA	4	4	4
	Power Stop	3	2	2	2
Minimum Enrichment Diaphragm Clearance (in.)		0.040	0.010	0.010	0.010
Cold Enrichment Setting		Index	3 notches lean	3 notches lean	Index
Maximum vacuum to apply—Cranking signal valve (in. Hg)		1	1	—	—
Vacuum to apply—Main signal diaphragm (in. H_2O)		$\frac{1}{2}$	$\frac{1}{2}$	$\frac{1}{2}$	$\frac{1}{2}$

[1] Part No. 7017375-R   [2] Part No. 7017380

Chassis Electrical

HEATER

Blower

REMOVAL AND INSTALLATION

1963–1967 With or Without A/C

1. It is not necessary to drain the cooling system to remove the heater blower. Remove the radiator expansion-tank retaining straps and move the tank from the work area.

2. Disconnect the ground cable from the battery.

3. Remove the blower motor leads.

4. Mark the blower motor mounting plate and blower motor assembly for correct reassembly.

5. Remove the five retaining screws and remove the blower assembly.

6. Reverse the removal procedure to reinstall, being careful to reposition the blower according to the marks previously made.

1968–1972 Without A/C

1. Disconnect the ground cable from the battery.

2. If so equipped, remove the radiator expansion-tank retaining screws and move the tank out of the way.

3. Remove the blower motor leads.

4. Remove the case mounting screws and remove the blower assembly. Gentle pry on

the flange, should the sealer hold the motor in place.

5. Use the reverse procedure to install the motor.

1968–72 With A/C

1. Disconnect the battery ground cable.

2. Disconnect the blower motor wire and the rubber air cooling tube.

3. Remove the three sill plate molding screws and pry it out to gain access to the right splash shield retaining bolts.

4. Remove the splash shield retaining bolts and remove the splash shield.

5. Remove the motor to case mounting screws and lower the motor through the splash shield opening.

6. It may be necessary to pry the flange gently if the sealer acts as an adhesive.

7. Reverse the above procedure to install the motor.

1973–79 With or Without A/C

1. Disconnect the ground cable from the battery.

2. If so equipped, remove the radiator expansion tank retaining screws and move the tank out of the way.

3. Remove the blower motor leads.

4. Remove the case mounting screws and remove the blower assembly. Gently pry on

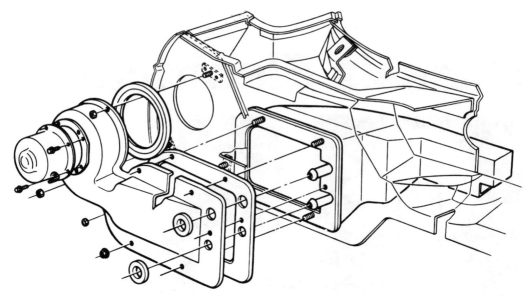

Heater and blower assembly-wo/AC—typical (© Chevrolet Motor Division)

the flange, should the sealer hold the motor in place.

5. Reverse the above procedure to install the motor.

Core

REMOVAL AND INSTALLATION

1963–1967 With or Without A/C

1. Drain the radiator, remove the radiator expansion-tank retaining straps, and move it from the work area.

2. Remove the battery.

3. Remove the water hoses from the heater assembly.

4. Remove the seven stud nuts attaching the blower and an inlet assembly to the firewall. Remove the assembly.

5. Remove the glove compartment and panels on both sides of the console.

6. As a precaution, place a plastic sheet or other waterproof covering over the passenger-side carpet.

7. Remove the two control cables from the instrument panel.

8. Disconnect the wire leads from the lower switch and the resistor.

9. Carefully remove the heater assembly from under the dashboard.

10. Remove the four, core cover retaining screws.

11. Loosen the four screws holding the core retaining yokes and the core to the retainer cover.

12. Remove the rear cover and core.

13. To install, reverse this procedure.

1968–1979 Without A/C

1. Disconnect the battery ground cable.

2. Drain the cooling system and remove and plug the water hoses from the heater connections.

3. Remove the air-distributor duct stud nuts on the firewall.

4. Remove the right instrument panel pad, right-hand dashboard braces, center dash console duct, and the floor outlet duct.

5. Remove the radio and center dashboard console.

6. Pull the distributor duct from the firewall and remove the resistor wires when clearance is sufficient.

7. Remove the heater-core retaining springs and remove the core.

8. Installation is the reverse of removal. If core-to-case sealer was damaged during removal, replace with new sealer.

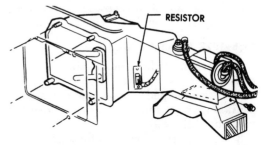

Heater and distributor assembly—1968–79 wo/AC (© Chevrolet Motor Division)

1968–79 With A/C

1. Disconnect the battery ground cable.
2. Drain the cooling system. It is not necessary to evacuate the A.C. refrigerant.
3. Disconnect the heater hoses at the firewall and plug the pipes.
4. Remove the nuts from the distributor studs protruding through the firewall.
5. Remove the right side dash pad and center dash cluster (described under "Instruments").
6. Disconnect the right dash outlet from the center duct.
7. Remove the center duct from the selector duct.
8. Remove the selector duct to the dash panel and pull it to the right and to the rear.
9. Remove the cables and wiring connectors from the selector and remove it from the car.
10. Remove the temperature door cam plate from the selector duct.
11. Remove the heater core and housing from the selector.
12. Reverse the removal procedure to install.

RADIO

REMOVAL AND INSTALLATION

1963–67

1. Remove both console side panels and trim strip(s).
2. Remove the radio knobs, washers, bezels, and nuts.
3. Disconnect the antenna lead-in, the radio-to-electrical harness, and radio-to-speaker connectors.
4. Remove the one attaching bolt located on the lower, right side of the radio.
5. Turn the radio on its side and remove it from the left side of the console.

1968–71 Coupe

1. Disconnect battery.
2. Remove right and left door sill plates and kick pads.
3. Disconnect right and left side radio-to-speaker connectors.
4. Remove right side dash pad.
5. Remove right and left console forward trim pads.
6. Remove bolt and remove the heater floor outlet duct by pulling it through left hand opening.
7. From front of console, tape radio push buttons in depressed position. From rear of console, disconnect electrical connector, brace and antenna lead-in.
8. Remove radio knobs and bezel retaining nuts. Push radio assembly forward and remove from rear through right side opening.
9. Install by reversing procedure above.

1969–71 Convertible

1. Disconnect battery.
2. Remove right instrument panel pad.
3. Disconnect speaker connectors.
4. Remove wiper switch trim plate screws to gain access to switch connector and remove connector and trim plate from cluster assembly.
5. Unclip and remove right and left console forward trim pads and remove forwardmost screw on right and left side of console.
6. Inserting a flexible drive socket between the console and metal horseshoe brace, remove the nuts from the two studs on the lower edge of the console cluster. Remove the remaining screws that retain the cluster assembly to the instrument panel.
7. From rear of console, disconnect electric connector, brace and antenna lead-in.
8. Remove radio knobs and bezel retaining nuts.
9. Pull radio assembly forward and remove through right side opening.
10. Install by reversing procedure above.

1972–76

1. Disconnect the negative battery cable and remove the right instrument panel pad.

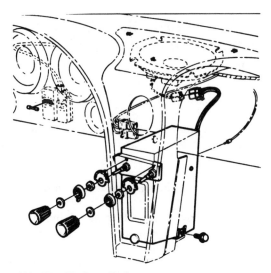

1963–67 radio Installation

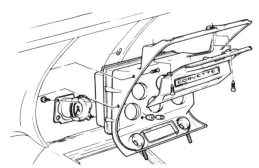

1968–76 center instrument cluster (© Chevrolet Motor Division)

2. Disconnect the radio speaker connectors.

3. Remove the wiper switch trim plate screws and tip the plate forward to gain access to the switch connector. Remove the switch connector and trim plate from the dash.

4. Unclip and remove the right and left forward console trim pads. Remove the forwardmost screw on the left and right sides of the console.

5. Working with a flexible drive socket between the console and the metal horseshoe brace, remove the nuts from the studs on the lower edge of the console cluster.

6. Remove the remaining console attaching screws and disconnect the radio electrical connectors, antenna wire and radio

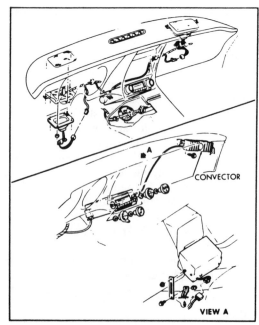

CONVECTOR

VIEW A

1974–79 radio installation (© Chevrolet Motor Division)

brace from the rear of the console. Remove the radio knobs and nuts.

7. Pull the top of the console rearward and separate the radio from the console and remove it from the right side opening.

NOTE: *The center instrument cluster trim panel is designed to collapse under impact. Do not deflect the panel to gain access to the radio. Also, the remotely located radio heat sink should be removed with the radio when servicing is required.*

1977–79

1. Disconnect the battery ground cable.
2. Remove the console tunnel side panels.
3. Pull the radio control knobs from the shaft.
4. Remove the two screws that secures the console trim plate to the instrument cluster.
5. Remove the rear defogger switch if so equipped.
6. Remove the five screws from around the upper perimeter of the instrument cluster.
7. Pull the instrument cluster enough to disconnect the electrical connector from the rear of the cluster.
8. Remove the screw holding the radio bracket reinforcement to the floor pan.
9. Pull the radio outward and disconnect the wiring from the back.
10. Installation is the reverse of removal. If a new radio is being installed, save the mounting bracket from the rear of the old one.

INSTRUMENT CLUSTER

REMOVAL AND INSTALLATION

1963–67

All instruments are contained in one cluster.

1. Disconnect the negative battery cable. Remove the instrument panel harness from the lower steering column switch and disconnect the switch.

2. Remove the steering wheel cap and the center nut and washer.

3. Pull off the steering wheel with a suitable puller.

4. Remove the steering column escutcheon screws and the nuts from the column support U-bolt.

5. Loosen the lower column clamp at the firewall.

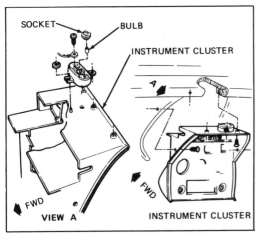

1977–79 center instrument cluster (© Chevrolet Motor Division)

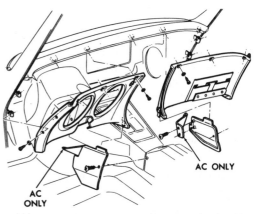

1968–76 instrument panels and lower trim assembly (© Chevrolet Motor Division)

6. Loosen the lower, spring stop-clamp and slide the stop and spring down on the shaft.

7. Paint or mark the steering shaft and coupling with chalk. Remove the upper coupling clamp bolt.

8. Pull the jacket and steering shaft assembly from the coupling and very carefully pull it out through the dash, at the same time sliding the lower spring stop, spring, bearing, and seat off the steering shaft.

9. Disconnect the tachometer drive cable, cowl-vent control cable brackets, and headlight motor switch from the instrument cluster.

10. Disconnect the parking brake lever support bracket from the cowl crossmember.

11. Pull the headlight switch on. Reach under the instrument cluster and push in the detent pin on the switch; remove the knob and shaft.

12. Screw out the retaining nut with a wide bladed screwdriver. Remove the bezel and switch assembly from the instrument cluster. Disconnect the wiring connector from the switch.

13. Remove the lock cylinder from the ignition switch by turning it to the "Lock" position and inserting a wire in the small cylinder face hole. Push the wire in while turning the ignition key counterclockwise, until the lock cylinder can be removed.

14. Carefully remove ignition-switch escutcheon nut using a screwdriver held in the escutcheon slot and tapping it with a small hammer.

15. Remove the ignition switch from the instrument cluster and remove all wiring

connectors. Unsnap the two locking tangs with a screwdriver and unplug the ignition connector. Disconnect the ignition switch lamp support.

16. Disconnect the oil pressure line and the instrument and lamp lead wires. Disconnect the trip odometer cable.

17. Remove the cluster retaining screws and pull the cluster slightly forward for access to the speedometer and tachometer cables and the remaining wires.

18. Remove cluster. All instruments are now easily accessible for service. Installation uses a reverse of the removal procedure.

1968–77

1. To service instruments other than the speedometer and tachometer, follow radio removal procedures. Small instruments are easily removed, after the center cluster is removed from the console.

2. To remove the driver's-side instrument cluster, first disconnect the negative battery cable.

3. Lower the steering column.

4. Remove retaining screws and washers at the door opening, dash top, and leftside of the center panel.

5. Unclip and remove the left, front console trim-panel.

6. Pull the cluster slightly forward for access to speedometer and tachometer cables, headlight switch connectors, and lamp wires.

7. Remove the cluster. Speedometer and tachometer may now be serviced.

8. Install using a reversal of the removal procedure.

1978–79

1. Disconnect the negative battery cable.
2. Remove the left air distribution duct.
3. Remove the screws attaching the lens to the bezel and remove the lens.
4. Remove the cluster attaching screws and pull the cluster slightly forward.
5. Disconnect the speedometer cable and lamp connectors as necessary.
6. Installation is the reverse of removal.

SPEEDOMETER CABLE REMOVAL

Reach behind the speedometer and depress the retaining clip. Pull the cable from the casing. If the cable is broken, raise the car and disconnect the cable at the transmission. Lubricate only the bottom ¾ of the cable core with speedometer cable lubricant. Reconnect all parts.

WINDSHIELD WIPERS

Motor

REMOVAL AND INSTALLATION

1963–67

1. Remove the negative cable from the battery.
2. Remove distributor and left-side ignition shields. Remove the left-side, spark plug wire bracket and position out of the way.
3. Disconnect the ballast resistor on the firewall, then remove washer inlet and outlet hoses at the pump valve assembly.
4. Remove the distributor cap and position one side.
5. Disconnect washer pump and wiper-motor lead wires.
6. Remove the glove compartment.
7. Ensure that the wipers and motor are parked, then remove the wiper linkage re-

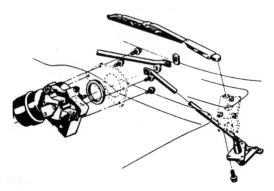

1963–67 windshield wiper motor and linkage

taining clip and disconnect both linkage and spacer from the crank arm.

8. Remove the wiper motor-to-firewall bolts and remove the motor.
9. To install, have an assistant aid in positioning and mount the wiper motor to the firewall. Ensure that the motor is in the parked position.
10. Position the left linkage, spacer, and right linkage on the crank arm and install the retaining clip in the groove in the crank arm.
11. Install remaining parts in a reverse order of removal.
12. Connect battery and test wipers and washers.

1968–79

1. Ensure that the wiper motor is in the Park position.
2. Disconnect washer hoses and wire leads from the motor.

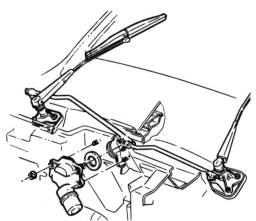

1968–79 windshield wiper motor and linkage (© Chevrolet Motor Division)

3. Remove the plenum chamber grille.
4. Remove the crank arm-to-motor retaining nut.
5. Remove the ignition shielding and distributor cap.
6. Remove the three, motor retaining screws or nuts and remove the motor.
7. Check gaskets and replace if necessary. Ensure that the motor is in Park position.
8. Reverse removal steps to install.

Wiper Blades And Inserts
REMOVAL AND INSTALLATION

In most cases the wiper rubber insert need only be replaced when it appears the wipers are worn out however, if the wiper blade assembly becomes bent, broken or distorted

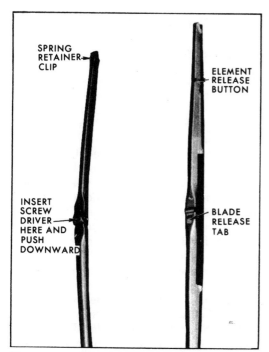

The two methods of releasing wiper blade assemblies and inserts (© Chevrolet Motor Division)

and does not lay against the windshield correctly it must be replaced. Two methods are used to retain the blades to the arms. One uses a press release tab. By pressing the tab, the blade can be slid off the arm. The other method uses a coil spring retainer. A screwdriver must be inserted on top of the spring and the spring pushed downward. The blade can then be slid off.

There are also two types of releases for the rubber inserts. One is a push button on the top of the blade which when pushed enables the insert to be slid out of the blade. The other is a clip at one end of the blade which when squeezed enables the insert to be pulled out the end of the blade.

Wiper Transmission

REMOVAL AND INSTALLATION

1963–67

1. Remove the wiper block and arm assembly from the transmission.
2. Remove the glove box door and compartment assembly.
3. Remove the three transmission-to-cowl retaining screws.
4. Remove the wiper transmission retaining clip and remove the transmission from the crank arm.

5. Remove the transmission through the glove box opening.
6. To install, reverse the above procedure.

1968–72

1. Make sure the wiper is in the park position.
2. Open the hood and disconnect the battery ground cable.
3. Remove the rubber plug from the front of the wiper door actuator, insert a screwdriver and push the internal piston rearward to actuate the wiper door open.
4. Remove the wiper arm and blade assemblies from the transmission.
5. Remove the plenum chamber air intake grille, or screen, if so equipped.
6. Loosen the nuts retaining the drive rod ball stud to the crank arm and detach the drive rod from the crank arm.
7. Remove the transmission retaining screws, or nuts, then lower the drive rod assemblies into the plenum chamber.
8. Remove the transmission and linkage from the plenum chamber through the cowl opening.
9. To install reverse the above procedure. Make sure the wiper assemblies are installed in the park position.

1973–79

1. Make sure the wiper is in the park position.
2. Disconnect the battery ground cable.
3. Open the hood and remove the plenum chamber screen.
4. Loosen the nuts retaining the ball sockets to the crank arm and detach the drive rod from the crank arm.
5. Remove the transmission nuts, then lift the rod assemblies from the plenum chamber.
6. Remove the transmission linkage from the plenum chamber.
7. To install reverse the removal procedure. Make sure the wipers are in the park position.

IGNITION SWITCH

REMOVAL AND INSTALLATION

1964–67

See Chapter 8 for "1969–79 Ignition Switch Removal and Installation."

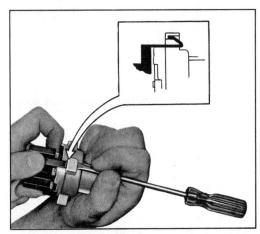

Unlocking the ignition switch connector—1964-68 (© Chevrolet Motor Division)

1. Disconnect the ground cable from the battery.

2. Remove the cylinder by placing it in the lock position and inserting a stiff wire in a small hole to depress the plunger. Turn the cylinder counter-clockwise until the cylinder can be removed.

3. Remove the holding nut (Tool J-7607 will assist).

4. Pull the switch from under the dash and remove the connector.

5. Using a screwdriver, unsnap the locking tangs.

6. To install reverse the above procedure.

1968

1. Open the battery storage compartment and disconnect the ground cable from the battery.

2. Remove the screws securing the "Corvette" cover plate in the top center of the cluster assembly.

3. Remove the ash tray and retainer.

4. Remove the radio and bracket.

5. Remove the lock cylinder by positioning the switch in the "ACC" position and inserting a wire in the cylinder face small hole. Push in on the wire to depress the plunger and continue turning the key counter-clockwise until the lock cylinder can be removed.

6. Remove the ignition switch bezel nut and pull the ignition switch out from under the dash.

7. Using a screwdriver unsnap the "theft resistant" locking tangs on the connector and unplug the connector.

8. To install reverse the above procedure.

SEAT BELTS

Warning System

1972-73

The seat belt warning system consists of lap belt retractor switches, a pressure-sensitive switch underneath the right-hand front passenger's seat, a warning lamp and a buzzer.

On manual transmission-equipped cars, the circuit is wired through the ignition switch, the parking brake warning light switch, and a relay, which is located between the instrument cluster wiring and the switch on the parking brake. A diode is used to prevent feedback into the parking brake warning circuit.

On cars having automatic transmissions, the seat belt warning circuit is wired through the ignition switch and the combination back-up lamp/neutral safety switch.

With the ignition key in the "RUN" position, a weight of 40-50 lbs on the driver's or passenger's seat pressure-sensitive switch) energizes the circuit when the parking brake is released (M/T) or the gear selector placed in a forward drive range (A/T).

A warning light will glow and a buzzer will sound with the circuit energized, unless the seat belts are withdrawn from the retractors and fastened over the laps of the two outboard front seat occupants.

Seat Belts/Starter Interlock System

As required by law, all 1974 and some 1975 Chevrolet passenger cars cannot be started until the front seat occupants are seated and have fastened their seat belts. If the proper sequence is not followed, e.g., the occupants fasten their seat belts and then sit on them, the engine cannot be started.

If, after the car is started, the seat belts are unfastened, a warning buzzer and light will be activated in a similar manner to that described for 1972-73 models.

The shoulder harness and lap belt are permanently fastened together, so that they both must be worn. The shoulder harness uses an inertia-lock reel to allow freedom of movement under normal driving conditions.

NOTE: *This type of reel locks up when the car decelerates rapidly, as during a crash.*

The lap belts use the same ratchet-type retractors that the 1972-73 models use.

The switches for the interlock system have been removed from the lap belt retractors and placed in the belt buckles. The seat sensors remain the same as those used in 1972–73.

For ease of service, the car may be started from outside, by reaching in and turning the key, but without depressing the seat sensors.

In case of system failure or for service, an override switch is located under the hood. This is a "one start" switch and it must be reset each time it is used.

DISABLING THE INTERLOCK SYSTEM

Since the requirement for the interlock system was dropped during the 1975 model year, these systems may now be legally disabled. The seat warning light is still required.

1. Disconnect the battery ground cable.

2. Locate the interlock harness connector under the left-side of the instrument panel on or near the fuse block. It has orange, yellow, and green leads.

3. Cut and tape the ends of the green wire on the body side of the connector.

4. Remove the buzzer from the fuse block or connector.

LIGHTING

Headlight Sealed Beams

REMOVAL AND INSTALLATION

1. Open the headlight panel to the open position.

2. Remove the headlight bezel retaining screws and remove the bezel.

3. Disengage the spring from the retaining ring and remove the two attaching screws.

NOTE: *Do not touch the adjusting screws. The retaining ring screws are the screws which go through the closed holes in the retaining ring. The adjusting screws go through the slotted open holes in the retaining ring and adjust the angle of the mounting ring behind the headlight sealed beam.*

4. Remove the retaining ring and disconnect the sealed beam unit at the wiring connector.

5. When installing the sealed beam unit make sure the number which is moulded into the lens is at the top. The number 1 inboard unit takes a double connector plug and the

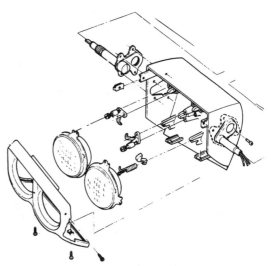

Headlamp assembly—1963–67 (© Chevrolet Motor Division)

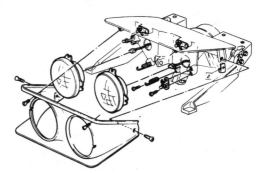

Headlamp assembly—1968–79 (© Chevrolet Motor Division)

number 2 outboard unit takes a triple connector plug.

CIRCUIT PROTECTION

Fusible Links

In addition to fuses, the wiring harness incorporates fusible links to protect the wiring. Fusible links are sections of wire, with special insulation, designed to melt under electrical overload. There are four different gauge sizes used. The links are marked on the insulation with the wire gauge size because of the heavy insulation which makes the link appear a heavier gauge than it actually is. Whenever it is necessary to splice a new wire in always bond the splice with rosin core solder then cover with electrical tape.

Refer to the Fusible Link Chart at the end of this chapter to find which circuits use fusible links to protect them.

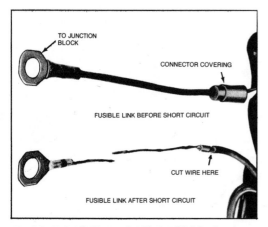

Fusible link (© Chevrolet Motor Division)

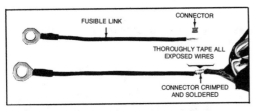

Fusible link replacement (© Chevrolet Motor Division)

Circuit Breakers

A circuit breaker is an electrical switch which breaks the circuit in case of an overload. The circuit breaker is located at the top of the fuse panel. The circuit breaker will remain open until the short or overload condition in the circuit is corrected. Refer to the Circuit Breaker Chart at the end of this chapter to find which circuits they protect.

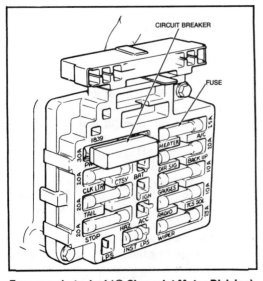

Fuse panel—typical (© Chevrolet Motor Division)

Fuses and Flashers

Fuses are located in the junction box below the instrument panel to the left of the steering column. The turn signal flasher and hazard warning flasher also plug into the fuse block. Each fuse recepticle is marked as to the circuit it protects and the correct amperage of the fuse. In line fuses are also used. Refer to the Fuse Chart at the end of this chapter for their location.

Thermal Limiter Fuse

The thermal fuse consists of a temperature sensitive fuse link and a wire wound resistor enclosed in a plastic housing. There are three spade-type electrical terminals which plug into an in-line connection at the wiring harness to the air conditioning compressor.

A blown thermal fuse indicates that the air conditioning system is either low or com-

Thermal limiter fuse (© Chevrolet Motor Division)

pletely out of refrigerant charge, a malfunctioning POA or expansion valve or an improperly located thermal limiter.

Light Bulb Specifications

Year	Usage	Number
1963	Headlamp (outer)	4002
	Headlamp (inner)	4001
	Parking lamp and directional signal	1034
	Tail, stop, and turn signal lamps	1034
	Directional signal indicator lamps	1816
	High beam indicator lamp	53
	Lighter lamp	53
	Ignition switch lamp	53
	Instrument panel lamps	1816
	Courtesy and/or dome lamps	90

Light Bulb Specifications (cont.)

Year	Usage	Number
1963	License plate lamp	67
	Radio lamp	1816
	Clock lamp	1816
	Parking brake alarm lamp	257
	Headlamp position warning lamp	257
1964	Headlamp (outer)	4002L
	Headlamp (inner)	4001L
	Parking lamp and directional signal	1157
	Tail, stop, and turn signal lamps	1157
	Directional signal indicator lamps	1816
	High beam indicator lamp	1445
	Lighter lamp	1445
	Ignition lamp	1445
	Instrument panel lamps	1816
	Courtesy and/or dome lamps	90
	License plate lamp	1155
	Radio lamp	1816
	Clock lamp	1816
	Parking brake alarm lamp	257
	Headlamp position warning lamp	257
1965–68	Headlamp (outer)	4002
	Headlamp (inner)	4001
	Parking and front directional, tail and stop and rear directional	1157
	Back-up lamp	1156
	Instrument lamps, panel compartment, temperature, oil pressure, generator, hi-beam indicator, clock lamp	1895
	A.T. quadrant, directional signal, ignition lock, heater control panel	1145
	Dome lamp	1004
	License plate lamp	1155
	Radio dial lamp	1893
	Brake alarm lamp	257
1969–72	Headlamp (outer)	
	(outer)—high beam	4002
	(outer)—low beam	4002
	(inner)—high beam only	4001

Light Bulb Specifications (cont.)

Year	Usage	Number
1969–72	Parking lamp and directional signal	1157NA
	Tail, stop and directional signal	1157
	Backing lamp	1156
	Instrument illumination lamps	1895
	Temperature indicator	194
	Oil pressure indicator	194
	Generator indicator	194
	Hi-beam indicator	1895
	Directional indicator	1895
	Cigarette lighter lamp	1445
	Warning lamps	
	Door ajar	1895
	Headlamps up	1895
	Seat belts	1895
	Heater or A/C control panel	1816
	Glove box lamps	1895
	Dome and courtesy lamps	
	Cartridge type	211
	Bayonet type	90
	Seat separator-courtesy lamp	212
	Side marker-front	194
	Side marker-rear	194
	License plate lamp	97
	All tape players and FM radios	1893
	Tape player lens illumination lamp	216
	Stereo indicator lamp	2182D
	Brake alarm lamp	1895
	Luggage compartment lamp	1003
	Map lamp (mirror)	563
1973	AC and heater controls	1816
	Alternator light	—
	Back-up	1156
	Brake system warning	1895
	Cargo	1895
	Cigar lighter	1445
	Clock	1895
	Courtesy	631
	Dome	90
	Door ajar	1895
	Gearshift indicator	1895
	Glove box	—
	Hi-beam indicator	1895
	Head lamps-UP	1895

Light Bulb Specifications (cont.)

Year	Usage	Number
1973	Instrument and speedometer	1895
	License	67
	Map	563
	Oil pressure	—
	Park and directional	1157NA
	Radio	1893
	Radio stereo	564
	Sealed beam	
	High	4001
	Low-High	4002
	Seat belt indicator	1895
	Side marker	
	front	168
	rear	168
	Tail and stop	1157
	Trunk/engine	93
	Turn signal indicators	1895
	Temperature indicators	—
	Washer fluid level	—
	Washer and wiper switch	1445
1974	AC and heater controls	1816
	Alternator light	—
	Back-up	1156
	Brake system warning	1895
	Cargo	1895
	Cigarette lighter	1445
	Clock	1895
	Courtesy	631
	Dome	212
	Door ajar	1895
	Gearshift indicator	1895
	Glove box	—
	High-beam indicator	1895
	Head light door-UP	1895
	Instrument and speedometer	1895
	License	168
	Map	563
	Oil pressure	—
	Park and directional	1157NA
	Radio	1893
	Radio stereo	564
	Sealed beam	
	High	5001
	Low-High	4000
	Seat belt indicator	1895
	Side marker	
	front	168
	rear	168
	Tail and stop	1157
	Trunk/engine	93

Light Bulb Specifications (cont.)

Year	Usage	Number
1974	Turn signal indicators	1895
	Temperature indicators	—
	Washer fluid level	168
	Wiper washer control	1445
1975	AC and heater controls	1816
	Alternator light	—
	Back-up	1156
	Brake system warning	1895
	Cargo	—
	Clock	1895
	Cigarette lighter	1445
	Courtesy	631
	Dome	212
	Door ajar	1895
	Gearshift indicator	1895
	Glove box	1895
	High-beam indicator	—
	Headlamp-UP	1895
	Instrument and speedometer	1895
	License	168
	Map	563
	Oil pressure	—
	Park and directional	1157
	Radio	1893
	Radio stereo	564
	Sealed beam	
	High	5001
	Low-High	4000
	Seat belt indicator	1895
	Side marker	
	front	168
	rear	168
	Tail and stop	1157
	Trunk/engine	93
	Turn signal indicators	1895
	Temperature indicators	—
	Washer fluid level	168
	Wiper washer control	1445
1976	A/C or heater control panel	1816
	Back-up	1156
	Cigarette lighter	1445
	Clock	1895
	Courtesy lamp—front	631
	Courtesy lamp—rear	212-1 or 2
	Door ajar	1895
	Directional signal indicator	1895
	Electro Clear indicator	2102-D

Light Bulb Specifications (cont.)

Year	Usage	Number
1976	Glove box	1895
	Headlamp—outer	4000
	Headlamp—inner	5001
	Headlamp beam indicator	1895
	Headlamp door warning	1895
	Instrument panel cluster	1895
	License	168
	Map/mirror	563
	Parking and directional	1157
	Seat belt warning	1895
	Side marker—front	168
	Side marker—rear	168
	Stereo indicator	2182
	Tail and stop	1157
	Transmission control	1895
	Radio dial	1893
	Windshield washer switch	1445
1977	A/C or heater control panel	558
	Back-up	1156
	Clock	1895
	Courtesy lamp—front	631
	Courtesy lamp—overhead	212-2
	Directional signal indicator	1895
	Electro Clear indicator	2102-D
	Headlamp—outer	4000
	Headlamp—inner	5001
	Headlamp beam indicator	1895
	Instrument panel cluster	1895
	Instrument center cluster	194
	License	168
	Parking and directional	1157
	Seat belt warning	194
	Side marker—front	168

Light Bulb Specifications (cont.)

Year	Usage	Number
1977	Side marker—rear	168
	Stereo indicator	2182
	Tail and stop	1157
	Transmission control	1895
	Radio dial	1893
1978–79	A/C or heater control panel	558
	Back-up	1156
	Brake warning	194
	Cigarette lighter	194
	Courtesy lamp—front	906
	Courtesy lamp—overhead	214-2
	Directional signal indicator	194
	Electro Clear indicator	2102-D
	Generator	194
	Headlamp—outer	4000
	Headlamp—inner	5001
	Headlamp beam indicator	194
	Instrument center cluster	192
	Instrument panel cluster	194
	License	168
	Low fuel	194
	Parking and directional	1157
	Seat belt warning	194
	Side marker—front	168
	Side marker—rear	168
	Spare tire	93
	Stereo indicator	DS410
	Tail and stop	1157
	Radio dial	1
	Underhood	93
	W/shield washer and light switch	

Fuses, Circuit Breakers, and Fusible Links

Year	Circuit	Type
1963–66	Headlamp circuit	15 amp circuit breaker
	Headlamp motors and power windows	40 amp circuit breaker
	Instrument, clock, and radio lamps	4 amp fuse
	Taillights	10 amp fuse
	Radio	2½ amp fuse
	Heater	10 amp fuse
	Stop, license, courtesy, and dome lamps	15 amp fuse (1963, 20 amp)
	Parking brake alarm, back-up lamp, and gas gauge	10 amp fuse
	Air conditioning	30 amp fuse
	AC high blower speed	30 amp fuse (in-line)

Fuses, Circuit Breakers, and Fusible Links (cont.)

Year	Circuit	Type
1967	Back-up lamp and gauges	10 amp fuse
	Heater and air conditioning	25 amp fuse
	Radio and wipers	20 amp fuse
	Instrument lamps	4 amp fuse
	Stop and taillights	20 amp fuse
	Clock, lighter, courtesy lamps, and flasher	20 amp fuse
	AC high blower speed	30 amp fuse
	Solenoid Bat terminal	14 gauge fusible link
	Horn relay	16 gauge fusible link
	Voltage regulator No. 3 terminal	20 gauge fusible link
	Voltage circuit (both sides of meter)	20 gauge fusible link
	Headlamp circuit	15 amp circuit breaker
	Headlamp motors and power windows	40 amp circuit breaker
1968–69	Headlamp circuit breaker	15 amp circuit breaker
	Power window circuit	30 amp circuit breaker
	Wiper/washer	25 amp fuse
	Back-up lights and turn signals	20 amp fuse
	Heater and air conditioning	25 amp fuse
	Radio and power windows	10 amp fuse
	Tail and side marker lamps	20 amp fuse
	Instrument lamps	5 amp fuse
	Gauges	10 amp fuse
	Stop light and flasher	20 amp fuse
	Clock, lighter, courtesy and dome lamps	20 amp fuse
	AC high blower speed	30 amp fuse (in-line)
	Solenoid Bat terminal	14 gauge fusible link
	Horn relay	16 gauge fusible link
	Voltage regulator No. 3 terminal	20 gauge fusible link
	Ammeter circuit (both sides of meter)	20 gauge fusible link
1970	Headlamp circuit	15 amp circuit breaker
	Power window circuit	30 amp circuit breaker
	Wiper/washer	25 amp fuse
	Back-up lights, turn signal, heater	25 amp fuse
	Air conditioning and TCS solenoid	25 amp fuse
	Radio and power windows	10 amp fuse
	Taillights and side marker lights	20 amp fuse
	Instrument lamps	5 amp fuse
	Gauges	20 amp fuse
	Clock, lighter, courtesy and dome lights	20 amp fuse
	AC high blower speed	30 amp fuse (in-line)
	Solenoid Bat terminal	14 gauge fusible link
	Horn relay	16 gauge fusible link
	Voltage regulator No. 3 terminal	20 gauge fusible link
	Ammeter circuit (Both sides of meter)	20 gauge fusible link
1971–72	Headlamp circuit	15 amp circuit breaker
	Power window circuit	30 amp circuit breaker
	Radio, TCS system, and power windows	10 amp fuse
	Wiper/washer	25 amp fuse

Fuses, Circuit Breakers, and Fusible Links (cont.)

Year	Circuit	Type
1971–72	Stop lights and flasher	20 amp fuse
	Heater and air conditioning	25 amp fuse
	Directional signals, back-up lights, and AC blocking relay	20 amp fuse
	Instrument lamps	5 amp fuse
	Gauges	10 amp fuse
	Clock, lighter, courtesy and dome lights	25 amp fuse
	Anti-diesel control and anti-theft alarm	25 amp fuse
	Tail, side marker, and back-up lights	20 amp fuse
	AC high blower speed	30 amp fuse (in-line)
	Solenoid Bat terminal	14 gauge fusible link
	Horn relay	16 gauge fusible link
	Voltage regulator No. 3 terminal	20 gauge fusible link
	Ammeter circuit (both sides of meter)	20 gauge fusible link
1973–76	Headlamp circuit	circuit breaker
	Power window circuit	30 amp circuit breaker
	Back-up lamps and turn signals	
	Power window relay	25 amp AGC fuse
	Heater/air conditioning	25 amp 3AG fuse
	Radio, automatic trans, downshift switch, TCS solenoid, rear defogger	20 amp AGC fuse
	Rear window defogger (low speed)	3 amp AGC fuse (in-line)
	Instrument lamps	5 amp AGC fuse
	Taillamps (side marker and parking lamps)	20 amp SFE fuse
	Clock, lighter, courtesy, anti-theft alarm	20 amp SFE fuse
	Stop/hazard warning, key warning buzzer	20 amp SFE fuse
	Gauges/telltale lamps, seat belt buzzer lamp	10 amp AGC fuse
	High blower speed (air conditioning)	30 amp AGC fuse (in-line)
	Wipers/washers	25 amp AGC fuse
1977	Headlamp circuit	circuit breaker
	Power window circuit	30 amp circuit breaker
	Back-up lamp and turn signals	25 amp AGC fuse
	Heater/air conditioner	25 amp 3AG fuse
	Radio, automatic trans., downshift switch, rear defogger	20 amp AGC fuse
	Instrument lamps	5 amp AGC fuse
	Tail lamps (side marker and parking lamps)	20 amp SFE fuse
	Clock, lighter, courtesy, anti-theft alarm, glove box	20 amp SFE fuse
	Stop/hazard warning, key warning buzzer	20 amp SFE fuse
	Gauges/teletale lamps, seat belt buzzer lamp, and relays (power window relay)	10 amp AGC fuse
	High blower speed (air conditioning)	30 amp AGC (in line) fuse
	Wipers/washers	25 amp AGC fuse
1978	Headlamp circuit	circuit breaker
	Power window circuit	30 amp circuit breaker
	Back-up lamp and turn signals	20 amp AGC fuse

Fuses, Circuit Breakers, and Fusible Links (cont.)

Year	Circuit	Type
1978	Heater/air conditioner	25 amp 3AG fuse
	Radio, rear defogger	20 amp AGC fuse
	Instrument lamps	5 amp AGC fuse
	Tail lamps (side marker and parking lamps), underhood lamps	20 amp SFE fuse
	Clock, lighter, courtesy, anti-theft alarm, glove box, dome	20 amp SFE fuse
	Stop/hazard warning, key warning buzzer	20 amp SFE fuse
	Gauges/teletale lamps, seat belt buzzer lamp, and relays (power window relay), cruise control	10 amp AGC fuse
	Wipers/washers	25 amp AGC fuse
1979	Headlamp circuit	circuit breaker
	Power window circuit	30 amp circuit breaker
	Back-up lamp and turn signals	20 amp AGC fuse
	Heater/air conditioning	25 amp 3AG fuse
	Radio	20 amp AGC fuse
	Rear defogger	35 amp fuse
	Instrument lamps	6 amp AGC fuse
	Tail lamps (side marker and parking lamps), underhood lamp	20 amp SFE fuse
	Clock, lighter, courtesy, anti-theft alarm, glove box, dome	20 amp SFE fuse
	Stop/hazard warning, key warning buzzer	20 amp SFE fuse
	Gauges/teletale lamps, seat belt buzzer lamp and relays (power window relay), cruise control	10 amp AGC fuse
	Auxiliary fan	30 amp fuse
	Wipers/washers	25 amp AGC fuse

WIRING DIAGRAMS

Wiring diagrams have been left out of this book. As cars have become more complex, and available with longer and longer option lists, wiring diagrams have grown in size and complexity also. It has become virtually impossible to provide a readable reproduction in a reasonable number of pages.

Clutch and Transmission

CLUTCH

Two types of clutch assemblies have been available on Stingray. The standard clutch is a bent-finger, centrifugal diaphragm unit first introduced in 1963. This design permits heavy plate loads, yet allows low pedal effort without resorting to center booster springs. The second type of clutch is a dual-plate, bent-finger diaphragm model that was available in 1969 and 1970. It was optional on the 427/454 high performance engines and requires a 14 in. diameter ring gear. The throwout bearing used with both models is 1¼ in. in overall length and should not be replaced by the longer 1⅞ in. unit.

REMOVAL AND INSTALLATION

1. Remove the transmission from the car as outlined in this chapter.
2. Disconnect the clutch-fork push rod and spring.
3. Remove the bell housing.
4. Install a clutch pilot tool (wooden versions available at most automotive parts stores) to hold the clutch plate during removal.
5. The flywheel and clutch cover are marked with x's for correct assembly, if these are not visible, scribe new marks.
6. Gradually loosen the clutch-to-flywheel bolts one turn at a time until all spring pressure is released.
7. Remove the bolts and remove the clutch assembly.
8. To install, crank the engine over by hand until the x-mark on the flywheel is on the bottom.
9. Position the clutch disc and pressure plate in the same relative location as removed and suppprt with the clutch pilot tool.

   NOTE: *The clutch disc is installed with the damper springs and slinger toward the transmission.*

10. Rotate the clutch assembly until the x-marks on the flywheel and clutch assembly align. Align the cover bolt holes with those in the flywheel.
11. Install bolts in every other hole and tighten down evenly. Install the remaining bolts.
12. Remove the clutch pilot tool.
13. Lubricate the ball socket on the clutch fork and reinstall on the ball stud.
14. Pack the recess on the inside of the throwout bearing collar and the throwout groove with graphite grease.
15. Install the bell housing.
16. Install the throwout bearing on the fork.
17. Install the transmission as previously outlined.

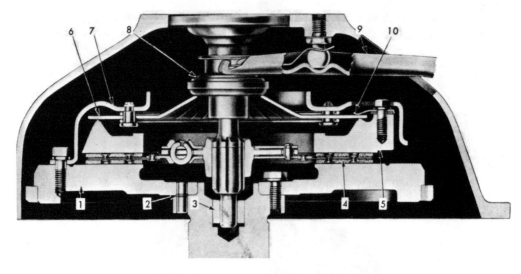

1. Flywheel
2. Dowel hole
3. Pilot bushing
4. Driven disc
5. Pressure plate
6. Diaphragm spring
7. Cover
8. Throwout bearing
9. Fork
10. Retracting spring

Cutaway of single disc clutch

18. Connect the fork push rod and spring.

19. Adjust the free pedal play and check the clutch release position.

PEDAL REPOSITIONING

Earlier Corvette clutch linkage includes a provision for a second clutch setting which reduces total pedal travel approximately 1½ in. The reduced travel will make the release faster and permit faster gear shifting.

1. Remove the clutch return spring at the cross-shaft and the pedal push rod at the pedal.

2. Loosen the pedal bracket lower bolt, remove the upper bolt, and rotate the bracket so that it will align with the extra upper bolt hole. Install the upper bolt.

3. Disconnect the pedal push rod at the cross-shaft and turn it ½ turn. Reconnect the push rod at the cross-shaft.

4. Tighten the bracket bolts and connect the pedal push rod.

CLUTCH ADJUSTMENT

1963–74

1. Disconnect the spring between the clutch push rod and cross shaft lever.

2. While holding the clutch pedal against the stop, loosen the two locknuts enough to allow the adjusting rod to move against the

clutch fork until the throwout bearing lightly touches the pressure plate springs.

3. Turn the upper nut against the swivel and then back it off 4½ turns. Tighten the bottom locknut to lock the swivel against the top nut.

4. Reinstall the return spring. Pedal free travel, the distance the pedal can be moved before the throwout bearing contacts the pressure plate spring, should be:

1963–64 Corvette—¾–1 in.

1965–71 Corvette—1¼–2 in.

1969–70 Corvette with HD clutch—2–2½ in.

1972 Corvette—1¼–1¾ in.

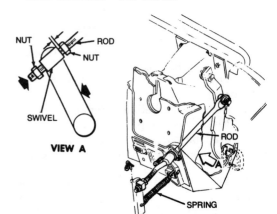

Clutch linkage

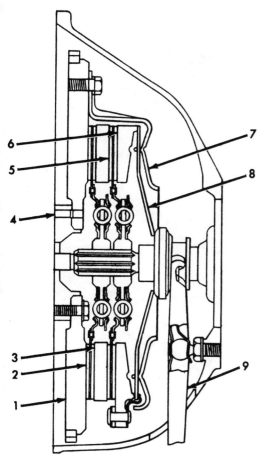

1. Flywheel
2. Front driven disc
3. Front pressure plate
4. Dowel hole
5. Rear driven disc
6. Rear pressure plate
7. Cover
8. Retracting spring
9. Fork

Cutaway of dual disc clutch

1973 Corvette—1¼–1½ in.
1974 Corvette—1–1½ in.

1975–79

1. Disconnect the return spring between the floor and the cross shaft.
2. Push the clutch lever and shaft assembly until the clutch pedal is tightly against the rubber stop under the dash.
3. Loosen the two locknuts on the shaft.
4. Push the shaft until the throwout bearing just touches the pressure plate spring.
5. Tighten the top locknut toward the swivel until the distance between it and the swivel is 0.4 in.
6. Tighten the bottom locknut against the swivel.
7. Check pedal free travel. It should be 1–1½ in.

MANUAL TRANSMISSION

Identification

The manual transmissions used in the Corvettes are the Muncie 3-speed, Saginaw 3-speed, Saginaw 4-speed, Muncie 4-speed, and the Warner 4-speed. Identification is determined by the side cover design and linkage. The 3-speed Muncie side cover has two bolts on the side cover top edge and the Saginaw 3-speed one. The Saginaw 4-speed linkage arms are all mounted through the side cover. The Muncie and Warner 4-speeds have the reverse fork mounted in the tailshaft. These two may be differentiated by the shape of the side cover; the Warner has a nine bolt curved bottom and the Muncie a seven bolt straight bottom.

REMOVAL AND INSTALLATION

1963–65 Muncie Three-Speed and 1963 Borg-Warner T-10, Four-Speed

1. Jack the car high enough to provide working clearance.
2. Disconnect the speedometer cable from the transmission.
3. Disconnect the shift linkage from the shift rods on the transmission. Remove the shift lever assembly and linkage.
4. Remove the driveshaft as described in the driveshaft section of Chapter 7.
5. Support the engine at the rear of the oil pan with a jack.
6. Remove the left and right exhaust pipes.
7. Remove the transmission tailshaft-to-crossmember attaching bracket.
8. Remove the two, top transmission-to-bell housing bolts and replace them with two guide pins; these may be fabricated from studs. This will prevent damaging the clutch disc.
9. Remove the bottom two bolts and slide the transmission straight back on the guide pin until the input shaft is clear of the clutch splines.
10. Move the transmission back to clear the bell housing. Tilt the forward end of the transmission down and withdraw from the car.
11. To install, insert a guide pin in the upper right bell housing bolt hole.
12. Raise the transmission and support it on the guide pin.
13. Rotate the transmission and engage

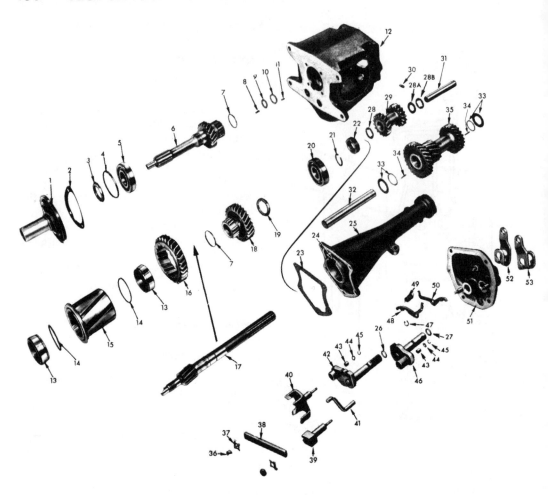

1. Clutch gear bearing retainer
2. Bearing retainer gasket
3. Bearing nut and oil slinger
4. Bearing snap-ring
5. Clutch gear bearing
6. Clutch gear
7. Energizing spring
8. Front pilot bearing roller
9. Thrust washer
10. Thrust washer
11. Rear pilot bearing rollers
12. Transmission case
13. Synchronizer ring
14. Snap-ring
15. Second and third speed clutch
16. First and Reverse sliding gear
17. Mainshaft
18. Second speed gear
19. Thrust washer
20. Mainshaft rear bearing

21. Snap-ring
22. Speedometer drive gear
23. Case extension gasket
24. Rear bearing snap-ring
25. Case extension
26. First and Reverse shifter shaft O-ring
27. Second and Third shifter shaft O-ring
28. Thrust washer
28a. Thrust bearing
28b. Thrust bearing washer
29. Reverse idler gear
30. Reverse idler shaft pin
31. Reverse idler shaft
32. Countershaft
33. Countergear and roller thrust washers
34. Bearing roller
35. Countergear
36. Shifter interlock retainer stud nut

37. Shifter interlock retainer stud nut lock
38. Shifter interlock retainer
39. Second and Third shifter fork
40. First and Reverse shifter fork
41. Shifter interlock shaft
42. First and Reverse shifter shaft and plate assembly
43. Shifter fork spacer
44. Shifter fork washer
45. Shifter fork retainer
46. Second and Third shifter shaft and plate assembly
47. Detent cam retainer
48. First and Reverse detent cam
49. Detent cam spring
50. Second and Third detent cam
51. Side cover
52. First and Reverse shifter lever (outer)
53. Second and Third shifter lever (outer)

Exploded view of Muncie 3-speed

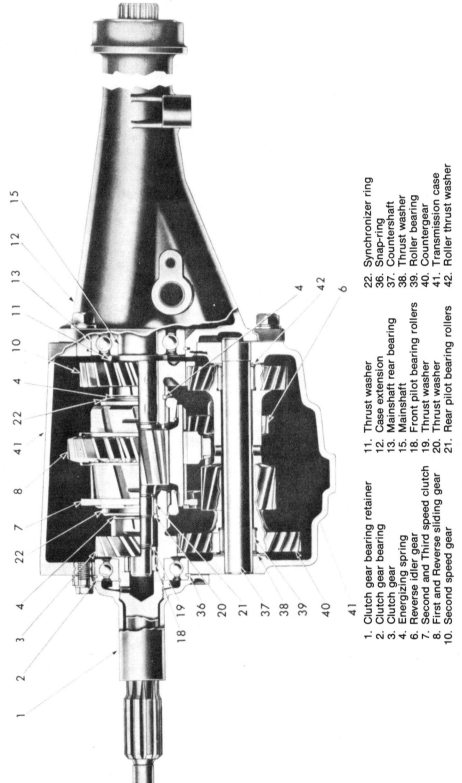

Cross-section of Munice 3-speed

1. Clutch gear bearing retainer
2. Clutch gear bearing
3. Clutch gear
4. Energizing spring
6. Reverse idler gear
7. Second and Third speed clutch
8. First and Reverse sliding gear
10. Second speed gear
11. Thrust washer
12. Case extension
13. Mainshaft rear bearing
15. Mainshaft
18. Front pilot bearing rollers
19. Thrust washer
20. Thrust washer
21. Rear pilot bearing rollers
22. Synchronizer ring
36. Snap-ring
37. Countershaft
38. Thrust washer
39. Roller bearing
40. Countergear
41. Transmission case
42. Roller thrust washer

the input shaft with the clutch disc. Slide the transmission forward until it bottoms against the clutch housing.

14. Install the two, bottom transmission-to-bell housing bolts. Remove the guide pin, and install the top two bolts. Torque all four bolts to 40–50 ft lbs.

15. Position the tailshaft mount-to-frame crossmember bracket and install the bolts hand tight. Install the bracket-to-extension mount bolts.

16. Tighten the support bracket-to-frame retaining bolts. Remove the jack from under the oil pan and tighten the bracket-to-extension mount bolts.

17. Install the driveshaft.

18. Install the speedometer cable to the transmission.

19. Install the shift lever assembly onto the transmission and connect the shift linkage.

20. Refill the transmission with lubricant. Check and adjust the shift pattern, if necessary.

1963–79 Four-Speed and 1966–69 Three-Speed

1. Disconnect the negative cable from the battery.

2. Disassemble the shift lever. Unscrew the ball from the lever, lift out the "T" handle return spring and "T" handle, and remove the anti-rattle bushings. On 1968 and later cars, remove the console trim plate.

3. Jack the car high enough to provide working clearance.

4. Remove the driveshaft as described in the driveshaft section of Chapter 7.

5. Remove the exhaust pipe heat deflectors and remove the left and right exhaust pipes. On a large block engine it is necessary to remove the forward stud on each manifold.

6. Remove the two rear-mount, cushion-to-bracket attaching bolts. Support the rear of the oil pan with a jack to take off the load from the rear mount cushion.

CAUTION: *Place a board between the oil pan and jack to prevent damage.*

7. Remove the three transmission mount bracket-to-crossmember bolts and remove the bracket.

8. Remove the two mount pad-to-transmission bolts and remove the rubber mount cushion and the exhaust pipe.

9. Disconnect the shift linkage by removing the shift levers at the transmission side cover.

10. Disconnect the speedometer cable at the tailshaft. Disconnect the TCS switch wiring, on cars so equipped.

11. Remove the two shift lever-and-bracket bolts; lower and remove the assembly.

12. Remove the four transmission-to-bell housing bolts and lower left extension bolts on later models.

13. Pull the transmission rearward until it clears the bell housing. Turn the transmission to the left while pulling to the rear.

14. Slowly lower the rear of the engine until the tachometer drive cable on the distributor just clears the horizontal ledge across the front of the firewall.

CAUTION: *The tachometer cable can be easily damaged.*

15. Slide the transmission rearward out from the clutch. Lower the front end of the transmission and remove it from the car.

16. Perform the above steps in reverse order to install the transmission.

LINKAGE ADJUSTMENT

1963 Muncie Three-Speed

1. Position both transmission side-cover selector fork levers and the shift lever in Neutral.

2. Attach rod to lever then adjust the clevis on its opposite end until the clevis pin will freely enter the side cover lever.

3. Insert the pin and secure it with a cotter pin.

4. Position the shift lever so that it ac-

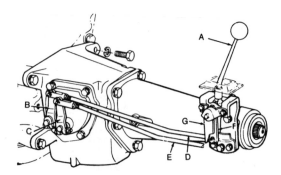

A. Shift lever
B. 2–3 fork lever
C. First/Reverse fork lever
D. 2–3 shift rod
E. First/Reverse shift rod
F. 2–3 shift lever
G. First/Reverse shift lever

1963–64 3-speed linkage

tivates the first and reverse lever, but still remains in Neutral.

5. Attach the first/reverse shift rod to the shift lever, adjust the clevis as done with the other shift rod, and secure it to selector lever.

6. Tighten the locknuts on both shift rod clevis fittings, and check the shift pattern for correct operation.

1964–68 Three-Speed

1. Set the side cover selector levers in Neutral and position the shift lever in Neutral and lock it in place with a $5/16$ in. (early models) or $41/64$ in. (late models) locating pin.

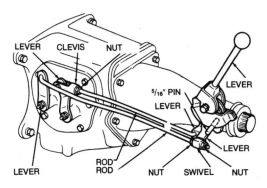

1965–68 3-speed linkage

2. Attach the first and reverse rod as with earlier transmissions and secure it.

3. Attach the second/third shift rod and attach it in the same manner.

4. Secure the locknuts on the clevis of each rod, then withdraw the locating pin and check the shift pattern.

1969 Three-Speed with Backdrive

1. Place the ignition switch in the "off" position and the side cover selector levers in Neutral.

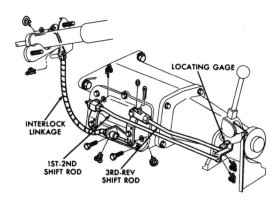

1969 3-speed linkage

2. Position the shift lever in Neutral and secure it with a $41/64$ in. locating gauge, between the shift lever notch and the linkage bracket.

3. Adjust the clevis of each rod so that they freely enter the attachment locations on their respective ends. Secure the locknuts, remove the gauge, and shift the transmission into Reverse.

4. Loosen the bracket assembly on the dash and allow any tension in the backdrive cable to position the bracket.

5. Secure the bracket and switch the key from "off" to "lock." Binding of the key will necessitate readjustment of the interlock mechanism.

6. Check the shift pattern.

1963 Borg-Warner, T-10 Four-Speed

The illustrated wooden gauge, if made, will greatly aid in shift linkage adjustment.

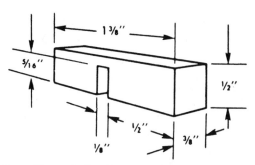

Borg-Warner T-10 adjustment gauge

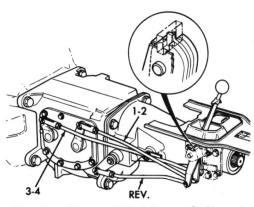

1963—Borg Warner T-10 linkage (© Chevrolet Motor Division)

1. Put the shift lever in Neutral, install the block gauge, and remove the clevis pin from the clevis of each shift rod.

2. Adjust the threaded clevis until thre clevis pin freely enters the holes in the clevis and the selector levers.

3. Secure the pins and lock the clevis securing nuts.

Remove the gauge block and check the shift pattern. Minor adjustment of the rods may be necessary to remove all traces of shifting roughness.

1963–68 Muncie Four-Speed

1. Position the individual selector levers and the shift lever in Neutral.

2. Construct a block gauge ⅛ in. thick by $^{41}/_{64}$ in. wide and install it in the shift lever bracket assembly.

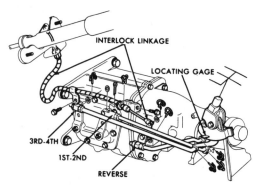

1964–77 4-speed linkage—typical (© Chevrolet Motor Division)

3. Attach the first/second shift rod to the lever. Hold the lever against the gauge block and adjust the threaded swivel on the shift rod until the clevis pin freely enters the clevis hold and the hole in selector lever. Secure the locking nuts.

4. Repeat the procedure and attach the reverse rod to the selector lever, and the bracket lever. Repeat again to adjust the third/fourth rod.

5. Remove the block gauge, check the pattern for correct shifting, and adjust, if necessary, to correct minor shifting difficulties.

6. An alternate clevis pin hole is placed on each selector lever below the regular pattern hole. This lower placement of the shift rods will tighten the pattern and permit shorter shift lever movement for a faster shift. Bear in mind, however, that this adjustment will increase the shifting effort.

1969–77 Warner or Saginaw Four Speed

1. Place the ignition switch in "lock."

2. Loosen locknuts at swivels on shift rods and reverse control rod.

3. Set transmission shift levers in neutral positions.

4. Shift lever into neutral. Insert locating gauge, ⅛ thick x $^{41}/_{64}$ wide x 3 in. long, into control lever bracket assembly.

5. Hold each lever against the gauge and adjust in turn. Tighten shift rod locknuts and remove gauge.

6. Loosen the interlock bracket assembly bolts at the bottom of the steering column. Make sure that the bracket is not stuck to the dash and then tighten the bracket again.

7. Move the ignition key through "off" and "lock" positions. If there is any binding, readjust the interlock linkage.

1978–79 Warner or Saginaw Four Speed

1. Place the ignition switch in Lock.

2. Loosen the swivels on the shift rods.

3. Place the transmission shift levers in Neutral. Neutral may be found by moving the levers all the way forward (counterclockwise), then back one detent.

4. Place the shift lever in Neutral.

5. Align the notches in the shift control levers with the notch in the lever and bracket assembly. Install a locating gauge, ⅛ inch thick by $^{41}/_{64}$ inch wide by 3 inches long into the control lever bracket assembly.

6. Attach the 3–4 shift rod to the shift control lever with a cotter pin.

7. Insert the 3–4 rod swivel into the transmission lever and attach the washer and cotter pin.

8. Push the 3–4 lever rearward to take up the slack and tighten the rear adjusting nut against the swivel.

9. Repeat this procedure for the 1–2 and reverse levers.

NOTE: *After the adjustments have been made, the centerlines of the levers must be aligned to prevent rubbing.*

AUTOMATIC TRANSMISSION

Identification

The two speed Powerglide transmission was used in the Corvette from 1963–67. The Turbo Hydra-Matic 350, 400 three speed transmission was used from 1967–77. From 1978–79 only the Turbo Hydra-Matic 350 has been available. Identification can be made by the shape of the pan.

OIL PAN AND FILTER REPLACEMENT

NOTE: *It is best to drain the fluid immediately after operation before it has the opportunity to cool however, use caution as the fluid temperature can exceed 350° F.*

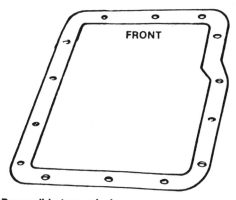

Powerglide transmission

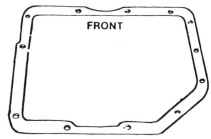

Turbo Hydra-Matic 350

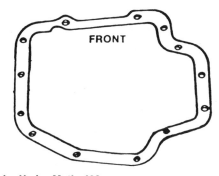

Turbo Hydra-Matic 400

1. Jack the car up and support it with jack stands.

NOTE: *On some models it may be necessary to support the transmission with the proper jack and remove the transmission crossmember support.*

2. Place a suitable drain pan under the transmission oil pan.

3. Remove the pan attaching bolts from the front and side of the pan.

4. Loosen the rear attaching bolts approximately four turns.

5. Carefully pry the transmission pan loose with a screwdriver, allowing the fluid to drain.

6. Remove the remaining screws and remove the oil pan and gasket.

7. Remove the strainer or filter.

8. Install a new gasket or o-ring seal on the new filter and install the filter.

9. Clean the oil pan with solvent and dry throughly.

10. Install a new gasket on the oil pan and install the oil pan. Tighten the pan attaching bolts to the following torque specifications: Powerglide 8 ft lbs, Turbo Hydra-Matic 350-110 in. lbs, Turbo Hydra-Matic 400-12 ft lbs.

11. Lower the vehicle and add the correct amount of DEXRON or DEXRON II automatic transmission fluid. See the Capacities and Pressure Chart in Chapter 1.

12. Put the Selector lever in the PARK position, apply the hand brake, start the engine and let idle. Do not race the engine.

13. Check the fluid level on a level surface and add additional fluid to bring the level to ¼" below the ADD mark on the dipstick.

NOTE: *The fluid level is set at ¼" below the add mark on the dipstick to allow for expansion of the fluid which occurs as transmission temperatures reach normal operating temperature of 180° F.*

SHIFT LINKAGE ADJUSTMENT

1963–67 Powerglide

All Powerglides are adjusted in the same manner, although the shift pattern was changed in 1965 from the staggered pattern of 1963–64 to a straight pattern.

1. Disconnect the control rod from the shift lever.

2. Position both the shift lever and the control rod bell crank in Park, then loosen the clevis locknut and rotate the rod until it freely enters the shift lever.

3. Secure the rod to the shift lever and lock the clevis nut.

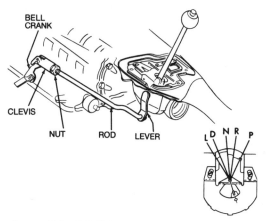

Powerglide shift linkage

1968–72

1. Disconnect the pushrod at the transmission lever.

2. With the transmission lever in Drive detent and the selector lever in Drive, rotate the push-rod until the hole lines up with the lever pin.

3. Install the pushrod on the pin and install the retainer clip.

4. Check operation of the linkage in all positions.

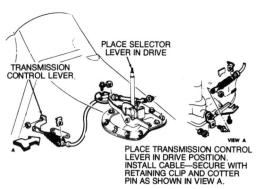

PLACE SELECTOR LEVER IN DRIVE

TRANSMISSION CONTROL LEVER

VIEW A

PLACE TRANSMISSION CONTROL LEVER IN DRIVE POSITION. INSTALL CABLE—SECURE WITH RETAINING CLIP AND COTTER PIN AS SHOWN IN VIEW A.

1968–72 Turbo Hydra-Matic shift linkage

1973–77 Turbo Hydra-Matic 400

1. Loosen the nut on the transmission lever so that the pin can move in the slot. Remove the console cover.

2. Move the transmission lever counterclockwise to the L1 position and then clockwise five detents to Park.

3. Place the shift lever in Park and insert a 0.40 in. spacer in front of the pawl.

4. Tighten the nut on the transmission lever to 20 ft lbs.

5. Turn the ignition switch to Lock with the shift lever in Park.

6. Remove the cotter pin and washer from the backdrive cable at the column lever. Disconnect the cable.

7. Working under the dash, remove the two nuts at the steering column-to-dash bracket.

8. Turn the lock tube lever counterclockwise (when viewed from the front of the column) to remove any freeplay from the column.

9. Move the bracket until the cable eye passes freely over the retaining pin on the bracket.

10. While holding the bracket in place, have an assistant tighten the bracket retaining nuts.

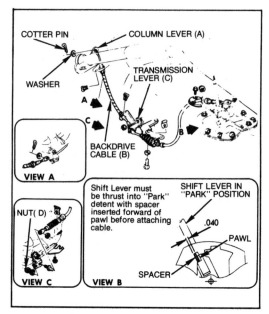

COTTER PIN   COLUMN LEVER (A)

WASHER

TRANSMISSION LEVER (C)

A

C

BACKDRIVE CABLE (B)

VIEW A

NUT(D)

VIEW C

Shift Lever must be thrust into "Park" detent with spacer inserted forward of pawl before attaching cable.

SHIFT LEVER IN "PARK" POSITION

.040

PAWL

SPACER

VIEW B

1973–77 Turbo Hydra-Matic shift linkage (© Chevrolet Motor Division)

11. Install the cotter pin and washer to retain the cable to the lever retaining pin.

1978–79 Turbo Hydra-Matic 350

1. Loosen the screw from the swivel so the rod moves within the swivel.

2. Put the transmission control lever in drive (D) and loosen the nut so that the pin moves in the slot of the transmission lever.

3. Position the transmission lever in the "Drive" position by moving the lever coun-

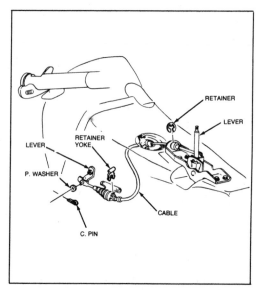

RETAINER

LEVER

LEVER

RETAINER YOKE

P. WASHER

CABLE

C. PIN

1978–79 Turbo Hydra-Matic shift linkage (© Chevrolet Motor Division)

terclockwise to the L1 detent and then clockwise three detent positions to "Drive".

4. Tighten the nut to 20 ft lbs.

5. Position the transmission control lever in the park (P) position and the ignition switch in the "Lock" position.

6. Pull down on the rod slightly against the lock stop and tighten the screw to 20 ft lbs.

THROTTLE VALVE ADJUSTMENT

1963–67 Powerglide

1. Fully open the lever and pull the rod forward until it contacts the internal transmission stop.

2. Adjust the swivel on the rod until the rod freely enters the lever, and then lengthen three full turns.

3. Secure the swivel then remove the toe panel carpeting.

4. Fully depress the accelerator pedal until the carburetor lever contacts the firewall.

5. Hold in position and adjust the swivel on the rod for freedom of entry into the lever, then lengthen 2 turns.

6. Check by returning the linkage to idle position and then rotating the lever to fully open.

7. Push the lever down to see if the rod deflects. If it does, or if the lever fails to open fully, repeat the adjustment.

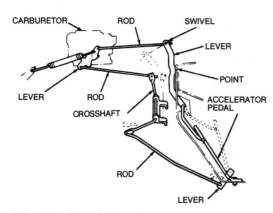

Throttle valve adjustment

DETENT SWITCH ADJUSTMENT

1968–72 Turbo Hydra-Matic 400

The detent switch is located on the carburetor.

1. Pull the detent switch driver rearward until the hole in the switch body aligns with the hole in the driver.

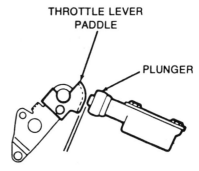

1968–72 detent switch adjustment—Turbo Hydra-Matic 400 (© Chevrolet Motor Division)

2. Insert a 0.092 in. pin through the aligned holes to a depth of 0.10 in. to hold the driver in position.

3. Loosen the switch mounting bolt.

4. With the throttle held in wide open position, move the switch forward until the driver contacts the accelerator lever.

5. Tighten the mounting bolt and remove the pin.

1973–77 TURBO HYDRA-MATIC 400

The switch is located over the accelerator pedal. After installing a new switch, adjustment is made by pressing the plunger in. This presets the switch and it will self-adjust the first time the pedal is fully depressed.

NEUTRAL SAFETY SWITCH ADJUSTMENT

1963–65 Powerglide

Adjustment is made by varying the length of the bellcrank-to-switch control rod. One end of the rod has a swivel to allow adjustment.

1966–67 Powerglide and 1968–71 Turbo Hydra-Matic 400

In all models the adjustment is made with the shift lever in Drive position. Loosen the switch mounting screws. Align the slot in the contact support with the hole in the switch and insert a $3/32$ in. pin to hold the support in place.

The shift control lever must be disconnected from the control rod and the shift control knob removed. Then remove the trim plate to get at the switch. Proceed as described in the first paragraph above, then place the contact support drive slot over the drive tang. Tighten the switch mounting screws, then remove the pin. Reinstall the shift control lever and trim plate.

1972

1. Disconnect the shift control lever arm from the control rod.

2. Remove the shift knob.

3. Remove the trim plate.

4. Remove the control assembly retaining screws and lift the assembly away from the seal.

5. Remove the neutral switch from the control assembly.

To install:

6. On early 1972 models put the shifter into Drive or Neutral on later models.

7. Align the hole in the contact support with the hole in the switch and insert a $^3/_{32}$ in. pin to hold the support in place.

8. Place the contact support drive slot over the drive tang and tighten the switch mounting screws. Remove the pin.

9. Install the control assembly mounting screws. Connect the switch wiring and check the switch operation.

10. Install the trim plate and shift knob.

11. Connect the shift lever arm to the transmission control rod.

1973–77 Turbo Hydra-Matic 400

Use the procedure outlined previously except that during installation, the shift lever is positioned in Drive. It is only necessary to use the $^3/_{32}$ in. pin for alignment when the original switch pin has been sheared off.

LOW BAND ADJUSTMENT

1963–67 Powerglide

Low band adjustment should be performed at 12,000 mile intervals, or if slipping is encountered.

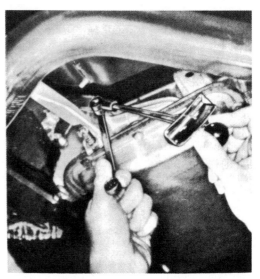

Low band adjustment (Powerglide)

1. Place the selector lever in Neutral.

2. Jack the car up to the required working height.

3. Remove the cap from the adjusting screw.

4. Lower the left exhaust pipe for clearance.

5. Loosen the adjusting screw ¼ turn and hold with a wrench.

6. Using an in. lbs torque wrench, adjust the band to 70 in. lb and back-off exactly four turns for a band in use over 6,000 miles and three turns for one in use less than 6,000 miles.

NOTE: *The locknut must be held at exactly ¼ turn loose during the adjustment. The number of back-off turns must be exactly as stated here.*

7. Tighten the locknut to 15 ft lbs.

Drive Train

DRIVELINE

The Stingray driveline consists of the drive-shaft, differential carrier, and axle drive-shafts. The driveshaft is of conventional tubular design with a universal joint at each end. The differential is mounted directly to a suspension crossmember. Power is transmitted to the wheels through universal-jointed axle driveshafts.

Driveshaft and Universal Joints
REMOVAL AND INSTALLATION

1. Jack the car to a convenient working height.
2. Wedge a block of wood between the top of the differential carrier and the car floor to keep the carrier from twisting on its rubber mounts when the front support bracket is disconnected.
3. Loosen and remove the carrier support-bracket front bolt. Remove the two rubber biscuits and large washer. Discard and replace the rubber biscuits if they show any deterioration.
4. Remove the two side bolts or front thru-bolt on later models from the carrier support bracket. Loosen, but do not remove, the rear thru-bolt and swivel the bracket down and away.

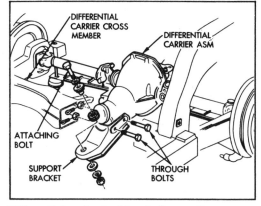

Differential and axle driveshaft mounting

5. Remove the U-bolts from both ends of the driveshaft.
6. Push the front yoke into the transmission and remove the driveshaft by pulling it down and to the rear.
7. Check the universal joints and replace damaged or worn units. Grease both universal joints before reinstalling them.
8. Install the driveshaft and attach to the transmission yoke and carrier flange.
9. Install the front bolt biscuits and flat washer and raise the bracket to the crossmember.
NOTE: *At this point it may be necessary to install a jack under the carrier. This will*

aid in lining up the side-bracket bolt holes and compressing the rubber biscuits.

10. Install the front crossmember bolt and nut. Install the side bolts. Front bolt torque is 30 lbs. Torque the two side bolts to 45–55 and the long thru-bolt to 40–60 ft lbs.

NOTE: *The carrier support bracket bolts frequently work loose, causing vibration and rear axle hop. Periodic torquing of these four bolts will eliminate this problem.*

UNIVERSAL JOINT OVERHAUL

Except for early Stingrays, Corvettes are equipped with lubed-for-life universal joints without grease fittings. Whenever universal joints are removed from the car, they should be checked and regreased.

1. Remove the joints from the driveshaft. These can sometimes be tapped out, but stubborn joints must be pressed out.

2. Remove the bearing cups and seals, being careful not to lose any rollers.

3. Inspect the cups and trunnion ends for damage or wear. Ensure that all bearing rollers are present. Replace the rubber seals.

4. Clean the cups and rollers. Repack the cup with grease and reassemble the joint.

REAR AXLE

Axle Driveshaft

REMOVAL AND INSTALLATION

1. Jack the rear of the car up.

2. Disconnect the inside trunnion from the carrier yoke.

3. On the outer end, bend down the french locktabs and wire-brush the bolts.

4. Scratch a mark on the camber adjusting cam and the bracket to permit realignment.

5. Loosen the camber adjustment nut and turn the cam so that the eccentric end points inward. Doing this will push the trailing arm out and give more room for driveshaft removal.

6. Remove the driveshaft, outside end first.

7. To install, position the inside end of the driveshaft in the carrier yoke and assemble U-bolts or clamp and bolts. Torque the bolts to 14–18 ft lbs.

NOTE: *When removing and installing both axle driveshafts, be certain to position the carrier side yokes so that the trunnion seats are at 90° angles to each other.*

8. Install the outside end of the driveshaft into the spindle drive flange. Install the french locks and bolts. Torque the bolts to 70–90 lbs and bend the locktabs up.

9. Realign the camber adjusting cam and bracket. Torque the nut to 15–22 ft lbs.

Differential Carrier

REMOVAL AND INSTALLATION

1. Remove the transverse spring endlink bolts using the procedures for spring removal.

2. Disconnect the axle driveshafts at the carrier. Disconnect the front carrier support bracket from the frame and the carrier and remove.

3. Remove the driveshaft as previously described.

4. Mark the camber cam/bolt for proper indexing with the strut rod bracket and loosen the cam bolts.

5. Remove the bracket-to-carrier bolts and lower the bracket.

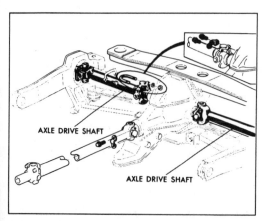

Axle driveshaft installation

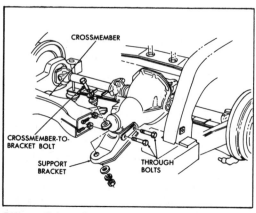

Differential carrier support bracket mounting

Rear Axle Identification

NOTE: *Axle identification is stamped on the differential carrier along with the date of manufacture.*

Type	Plant Identification
1963	
3-Speed (3.36 ratio)	CA
Positraction (3.08 ratio)	CJ
Positraction (3.36 ratio)	CB
Positraction (3.55 ratio)	CC
Positraction (3.70 ratio)	CD
Positraction (4.11 ratio)	CE
Positraction (4.56 ratio)	CF
4-Speed (3.08 ratio)	CZ
4-Speed (3.70 ratio)	CX
1964	
3-Speed (3.36 ratio)	CA
Positraction (3.08 ratio)	CJ
Positraction (3.36 ratio)	CB
Positraction (3.55 ratio)	CC
Positraction (3.70 ratio)	CD
Positraction (4.11 ratio)	CE
Positraction (4.56 ratio)	CF
4-Speed (3.08 ratio)	CZ
4-Speed (3.70 ratio)	CX
1965	
(3.36 ratio)	AK
Positraction (3.08 ratio)	AL
Positraction (3.36 ratio)	AM
Positraction (3.55 ratio)	AN
Positraction (3.70 ratio)	AO
Positraction (4.11 ratio)	AP
Positraction (4.56 ratio)	AQ
(3.08 ratio)	AR
4-Speed (3.70 ratio)	AS
Positraction (3.08 ratio) "396"	AT
Positraction (3.36 ratio) "396"	AU
Positraction (3.55 ratio) "396"	AZ
Positraction (3.70 ratio)	FA
Positraction (4.11 ratio) "396"	FB
Positraction (4.56 ratio) "396"	FC
1966	
(3.36 ratio)	AK
Positraction (3.08 ratio)	AL
Positraction (3.36 ratio)	AM
Positraction (3.55 ratio)	AN
Positraction (3.70 ratio)	AO
Positraction (4.11 ratio)	AP
Positraction (3.08 ratio)	AR
4-Speed (3.70 ratio)	AS

Rear Axle Identification (cont.)

NOTE: *Axle identification is stamped on the differential carrier along with the date of manufacture.*

Type	Plant Identification
1966	
Positraction (3.08 ratio) "396"	AT
Positraction (3.36 ratio) "396"	AU
Positraction (3.55 ratio) "396"	AZ
Positraction (3.70 ratio) "396"	FA
Positraction (4.11 ratio) "396"	FB
Positraction (4.56 ratio) "396"	FC
1967	
(3.36 ratio)	AK
Positraction (3.08 ratio)	AL
Positraction (3.36 ratio)	AM
Positraction (3.55 ratio)	AN
Positraction (3.70 ratio)	AO
Positraction (4.11 ratio)	AP
4-Speed (3.70 ratio)	AS
Positraction (3.08 ratio) "427"	AT
Positraction (3.36 ratio) "427"	AU
Positraction (3.55 ratio) "427"	AZ
Positraction (3.70 ratio) "427"	FA
Positraction (4.11 ratio) "427"	FB
Positraction (4.56 ratio)	FC
1968	
(3.36 ratio)	AK
Positraction (3.08 ratio)	AL
Positraction (3.36 ratio)	AM
Positraction (3.55 ratio)	AN
Positraction (3.70 ratio)	AO
Positraction (4.11 ratio)	AP
(3.70 ratio)	AS
Positraction (3.08 ratio) (H.D.)	AT
Positraction (3.36 ratio) (H.D.)	AU
Positraction (3.08 ratio)	AV
Positraction (3.08 ratio) (H.D.)	AW
1969	
(3.36 ratio)	AK
Positraction (3.08 ratio)	AL
Positraction (3.36 ratio)	AM
Positraction (3.55 ratio)	AN
Positraction (3.70 ratio)	AO
Positraction (4.11 ratio)	AP
(3.70 ratio)	AS
Positraction (3.08 ratio) (H.D.)	AT
Positraction (3.36 ratio) (H.D.)	AU
Positraction (3.08 ratio)	AV
Positraction (3.08 ratio) (H.D.)	AW

Rear Axle Identification (cont.)

NOTE: *Axle identification is stamped on the differential carrier along with the date of manufacture.*

Type	Plant Identification
1969	
Positraction (2.73 ratio) (H.D.)	AY
Positraction (3.55 ratio) (H.D.)	AZ
Positraction (3.70 ratio) (H.D.)	FA
Positraction (4.11 ratio) (H.D.)	FB
Positraction (4.56 ratio)	FC
1970	
(3.36 ratio)	CAK
Positraction (3.08 ratio)	CAL
Positraction (3.36 ratio)	CAM
Positraction (3.55 ratio)	CAN
Positraction (3.70 ratio) 350 H/Per., 4-Speed Closed Ratio	CAO
Positraction (4.11 ratio)	CAP
Positraction (3.70 ratio) 350 H/Per., 4-Speed Closed Ratio	CAS
Positraction (3.08 ratio)	CAT
Positraction (3.36 ratio)	CAU
Positraction (3.08 ratio)	CAV
Positraction (3.08 ratio) 4-Speed Automatic	CAW
Positraction (2.73 ratio)	CAY
Positraction (3.36 ratio) 4-Speed Automatic	CAX
Positraction (3.55 ratio)	CAZ
Positraction (3.70 ratio)	CFA
Positraction (4.11 ratio)	CFB
Positraction (4.56 ratio)	CFC
Positraction (3.36 ratio)	CLR
1971	
Positraction (3.55 ratio)	AA
Positraction (3.70 ratio)	AB
Positraction (4.11 ratio)	AC
Positraction (4.56 ratio)	AD
Positraction (3.08 ratio)	AW
Positraction (3.36 ratio)	AX
Positraction (3.36 ratio)	LR
1972–75	
Positraction (3.36 ratio)	AX
Positraction (3.36 ratio)	LR
Positraction (4.11 ratio)	AC
Positraction (3.70 ratio)	AB
Positraction (3.55 ratio)	AA
Positraction (3.08 ratio)	AW
Positraction (2.73 ratio)	AV

Rear Axle Identification (cont.)

NOTE: *Axle identification is stamped on the differential carrier along with the date of manufacture.*

Type	Plant Identification
1976–77	
Positraction (3.08 ratio)	OA
Positraction (3.36 ratio)	LR-OD
Positraction (3.55 ratio)	OB
Positraction (3.70 ratio)	OC
1978	
Positraction (3.08 ratio)	OK
Positraction (3.36 ratio)	OM
Positraction (3.55 ratio)	OH
Positraction (3.70 ratio)	OJ
1979	
Positraction (3.36 ratio)	OM
Positraction (3.55 ratio)	OH
Positraction (3.70 ratio)	OJ

6. Remove the cam bolts and swing the struts up. Loosen the carrier cover bolts and gradually drain the fluid.

7. Remove the bolts, slide the carrier back and down, and remove.

8. Before reinstalling the carrier, clean the inside of the cover and grease the gasket surface. Install a new gasket on the cover.

9. Fabricate two aligning studs by cutting the heads off from two ¼ in.–13 x 1¼ in. bolts and slotting the unthreaded end. Install the two studs into two lower bolt holes, one to a side.

10. Using the studs as support, position the carrier to align the carrier-to-cover bolt holes. Install the bolts and tighten to 35–55 ft lbs.

11. Install the driveshaft as previously outlined.

12. Position the carrier front support bracket on the carrier and install the thru-bolt.

13. Install the rubber biscuits and rotate the bracket up into position. Install the front bolt and nut and torque to 30 ft lbs. Install the two side bolts in the bracket and torque to 45–55 ft lbs. Torque the thru-bolt to 40–60 ft lbs.

14. Assemble the axle drive shafts to the carrier side yokes. Torque the bolts to 14–18 ft lbs.

Differential carrier installation utilizing locating studs

15. Connect the strut rods to the bracket and install the bracket to the carrier. Torque the four bolts to 15–22 ft lbs. Adjust the camber cams with reference to the marks previously scribed on the cams and bracket. Tighten cam nuts to 15–22 ft lbs.

16. Install the spring end links as described under spring removal.

17. Remove the filler plug and fill the differential with the correct gear lubricant.

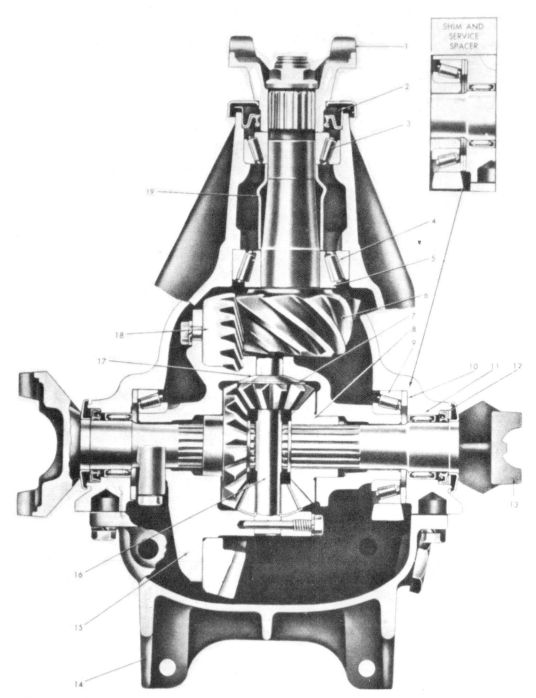

1. Companion flange
2. Pinion seal
3. Front pinion bearing
4. Rear pinion bearing
5. Pinion shim
6. Pinion
7. Differential pinion
8. Differential side gear
9. Differential bearing
10. Differential bearing shim
11. Yoke bearing
12. Yoke bearing seal
13. Side gear yoke
14. Carrier cover
15. Differential case
16. Differential pinion shaft
17. Thrust washer
18. Ring gear
19. Pinion bearing spacer

Cutaway of the differential (© Chevrolet Motor Division)

Suspension and Steering

FRONT SUSPENSION

The Corvette Stingray front suspension is an unequal length arm, independent design. Springing action is provided by coil springs. Ball joints connect the steering knuckles to the control arms. The upper and lower control arms have their cross-shafts bolted to fixed frame members. The upper arm cross-shaft has shims to provide the means for setting caster and camber. The front shock absorbers have their bottom ends attached to the lower control arm while the upper end extends through the frame member. The shock absorbers are double action and fit inside the front coil springs. A stabilizer bar connects the lower control arms to the front frame rails. Tapered roller bearings are used in the front wheels.

Springs

REMOVAL AND INSTALLATION

CAUTION: *Great care should be exercised when removing springs, as the compressed force of a coil spring is potentially very dangerous.*

1. Support the car so that the control arms hang loosely.
2. Remove the wheel and tire, stabilizer bar, and shock absorber.

3. Loosen the lower ball joint-to-steering knuckle nut and the two, lower control arms, cross-shaft bushing bolts.
4. Wrap a safety chain around the lower arm and the coil spring.
5. Install a floor jack under the spring and slightly compress the spring.
6. Disconnect the lower ball joint from the steering knuckle.
7. Very slowly and carefully, lower the control arm and release the spring. It may be necessary to pry the spring out of the tower.
8. To install, position the spring on the control arm and jack up the arm.
9. Install the ball joint on the steering knuckle, and remaining components in a reverse order.

Shock Absorbers

Corvette Stingray shock absorbers are the sealed, hydraulic type with no provision for adding fluid or making adjustments. They should be replaced when evidence of faulty operation is discovered.

BOUNCE TEST

Each shock absorber can be tested by bouncing the corner of the vehicle until maximum up and down movement is obtained. Release the car. It should stop bouncing in one or two

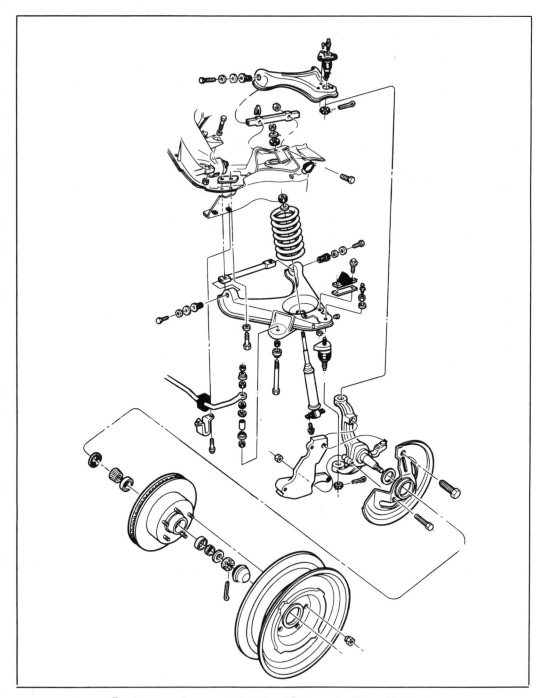

Front suspension—exploded view (© Chevrolet Motor Division)

bounces. Compare both front corners or both rear corners but do not compare the front to the rear. If one corner bounces longer than the other it should be inspected for damage and possibly be replaced.

REMOVAL AND INSTALLATION

1. To remove, raise the vehicle and hold the upper stem of the shock absorber with an open-end wrench. This prevents the stem from turning and allows the removal of the retaining nut, washer, and rubber grommet.

2. Remove the two bolts that fasten the lower pivot point of the shock absorber to the lower control arm and slip the shock absorber free.

3. Reverse the procedure to install the replacement shock absorbers.

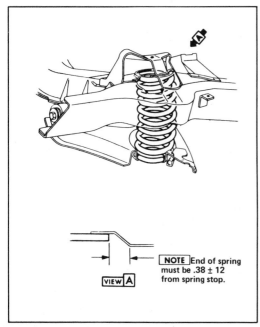

NOTE End of spring must be .38 ± 12 from spring stop.

VIEW A

Coil spring positioning (© Chevrolet Motor Division)

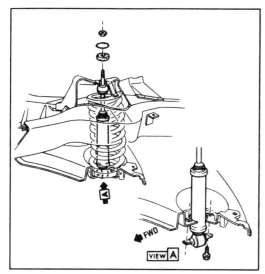

Shock absorber attachments (© Chevrolet Motor Division)

Ball Joints

Erratic front suspension behavior or alignment difficulties suggest possible excessive ball-joint wear. To check, raise the vehicle so that the front suspension hangs freely and remove the wheel and tire assembly. Check the upper ball joint by supporting the lower control arm and by separating the upper ball-joint stud from the steering knuckle. With the steering knuckle and hub hanging freely, install the retaining nut on the ball joint stud

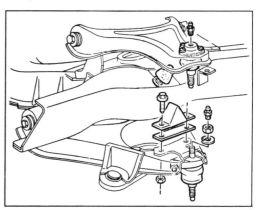

Upper and lower ball joint assemblies (© Chevrolet Motor Division)

and note the torque required to rotate the ball joint with a torque wrench. A ball joint in good condition will require a torque of 2–10 ft lbs. Less than 2 ft lbs torque indicates excessive wear and warrants replacement of the ball joint.

To test the lower, control-arm ball joint, support the lower control arm so that the wheel hub hangs freely. Measure between the tip of the ball joint stud and the tip of the grease fitting found on the top side of the ball joint. Now position the support under the wheel hub and repeat the measurement. A difference in measurement of more than $1/16$ in. dictates replacement of the lower ball joint.

REMOVAL AND INSTALLATION

Replacement of the ball joints may be done without removing the control arms from the vehicle.

1. Raise the vehicle and remove the wheel and tire. Be sure that the lift is positioned so that the front suspension will hang freely.

2. Remove the stabilizer link from the lower control arm, then disconnect the top ball joint from the steering knuckle and let the knuckle and the wheel hub hang unsupported.

3. The ball joint assembly is riveted to the control arm. Use a suitable cold chisel and knock the heads off the rivets and remove the ball joint.

4. Clean the mounting surface on the control arm and check for signs of cracks or other damage.

5. Measure the thread diameter of the kit-supplied mounting bolts and drill out the

control arm rivet holes to the appropriate size.

6. Install the replacement ball joint assembly and torque the new securing bolts to 15–25 ft lbs (1963–67), 50 ft lbs (1968–79).

7. Lift the lower control arm so that the upper ball joint stud can be rejoined to the steering knuckle. Torque the retaining nut to 42–47 (1963–67), 80 ft lbs (1968–79) ft lbs and install a new cotter pin.

8. To replace the lower ball joint, support the lower control arm, disconnect the lower ball joint from the steering knuckle and lift the knuckle and wheel hub out of the way.

NOTE: *Removal of the spring is not necessary so long as the lower control arm is adequately supported.*

9. The lower ball joint assembly is also riveted to the control arm surface. Chisel it free as with the upper ball joint.

10. Replace the joint as previously described, then reconnect the lower ball joint stud to the steering knuckle.

NOTE: *It may be necessary to install grease fittings on the replacement ball joints if none are provided.*

Steering Knuckle
REMOVAL AND INSTALLATION

1. Raise and support the vehicle on the lower control arm.

2. Remove the wheel and tire, brake drum or disc caliper, and hub and bearing assembly.

3. On drum brakes, remove the backing plate from the steering knuckle and wire it to the frame. Do not disconnect the brake hose.

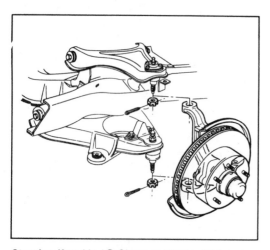

Steering Knuckle (© Chevrolet Motor Division)

4. Remove the upper and lower ball joint stud-retaining nuts and rap the steering knuckle free of the upper and lower control arms.

5. Reverse the procedure to replace the steering knuckle.

6. Torque the upper stud nut to 50 ft lbs, and the lower stud nut to 90 ft lbs.

Upper and Lower Control Arms
SHAFT REMOVAL AND INSTALLATION

1. To remove the lower, control arm shaft, remove the front coil spring as previously described.

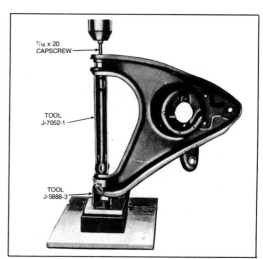

7/16 x 20 CAPSCREW

TOOL J-7052-1

TOOL J-5888-3

Removing the lower control arm shaft (© Chevrolet Motor Division)

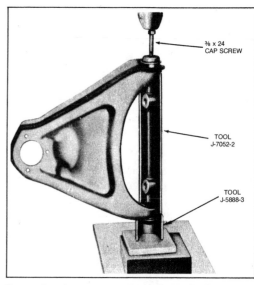

3/8 x 24 CAP SCREW

TOOL J-7052-2

TOOL J-5888-3

Removing the upper control arm shaft (© Chevrolet Motor Division)

2. Count the shims at each end of the cross-shaft, then unbolt it from the frame and remove the control arm.

3. Remove the bolts, washers, and collars from both ends of the shaft, then screw in a $7/16$ in. x 20 capscrew into one end of the shaft.

4. Support the control arm in a press and press on the capscrew until the bushing is forced from the arm.

5. Unscrew the capscrew and repeat the procedure on the other end on the cross-shaft.

6. Position the replacement cross-shaft and/or bushings in the control arm and start the bushings into the arm.

7. Place the assembly in a press, put a spacer over the bushing, and press into place.

8. Repeat the procedure for the other end, then install the collar and lockwasher but loosely thread in the bolts.

9. Reverse the removal procedure to install the spring and lower control arm. After the arm is installed, lower the vehicle to the floor and tighten the cross-shaft bushing bolts to 45–55 ft lbs.

10. The procedure for replacing the upper, control arm shaft is the same as for the lower control arm shaft, except a ⅜ in.–24 capscrew is used to remove the bushings. Torque the bushing bolts to 35–40 ft lbs.

CONTROL ARM REMOVAL AND INSTALLATION

The upper and lower control arms are removed by combining the operations for replacing the upper and lower cross-shafts and the operations for replacing the steering knuckle.

Stabilizer Bar

REMOVAL AND INSTALLATION

The stabilizer bar is rubber-mounted to the frame in two locations and attaches to the lower control arms through two links.

1. Raise the vehicle and disconnect the links from the stabilizer bar.

2. Unbolt the rubber frame attachments and remove the bar from the car.

3. Reverse the procedure to install the stabilizer.

4. Hand-tighten all connections until the bar and links are fully assembled.

5. Tighten all connections, lower the vehicle, and bounce it a few times.

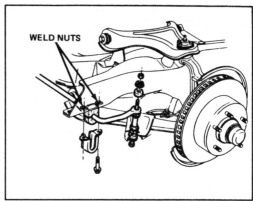

Stabilizer bar mounting (© Chevrolet Motor Division)

6. Raise the car and tighten all connections with a wrench.

Wheel Hub

REMOVAL AND INSTALLATION

1. To remove the wheel hub, snap off the wheel covers and loosen the lug nuts, then raise and secure the vehicle.

2. Remove the lug nuts, wheel and tire, and brake drum or disc brake caliper.

3. Insert a wood spacer between the brake calipers, on disc brake vehicles, and secure the assembly out of the way.

4. Pry off the grease cap and extract the cotter pin from the spindle nut. Back off the spindle nut and washer, and remove the hub—on drum-equipped models—and the hub and disc on all others. Be careful not to drop the bearings as the hub comes off.

Front wheel hub assembly (© Chevrolet Motor Division)

BEARING REPLACEMENT

1. Disassembly of the hub removed the outer roller bearing assembly. The inner roller bearing remains in the hub, held in place by the inner bearing lip seal.

2. Pry out this seal, discard it, and remove the inner roller bearing assembly.

3. Select a suitable brass drift punch and insert it through the inner opening of the bearing hub so that it catches on the notches behind the outer bearing race.

4. Drive the bearing from the hub. Insert the punch through the outer hub opening and repeat the procedure to remove the inner race.

NOTE: *It is good practice to replace bearing roller assemblies when replacing bearing races.*

5. Thoroughly clean the hub assembly then position the replacement inner bearing to its bore and drive it into place.

6. Use a driver for this operation, a suitable socket spacer, or even the old race—positioned over the replacement—and hammer it into its seat. Be sure the race is properly seated, then repeat the operation on the outer race.

7. Lightly coat the inside of the hub and the spindle with grease, then insert the inner roller bearing assembly and install the inner seal.

8. Position the hub or hub and disc assembly over the spindle and slide the outer bearing into its race.

9. Hold the assembly in position to prevent the hub from slipping and forcing out the outer roller bearing, and install the washer and nut, and handtighten.

10. Assemble the backing plate and drum assembly on 1963–1964 models. On 1965 and later models, remove the spacer block from the caliper and position the caliper to the cal-

iper bracket, over the disc. Insert the mounting bolts and torque them to 70 ft lbs.

11. Install the wheel and tire assembly and torque the lug nuts to 75 ft lbs.

12. Rotate the wheel and make the bearing adjustment. Install a new cotter pin, tap on the grease cap and replace the wheel cover.

Front End Alignment
CASTER ADJUSTMENT

Caster is the measured angle between a true vertical line passing through the center of the wheel and a line drawn through the center of the upper and lower ball joints. Adjustments to the caster angle are made by the insertion of shims between the upper control arm

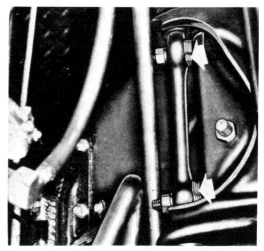

Caster and camber shim location

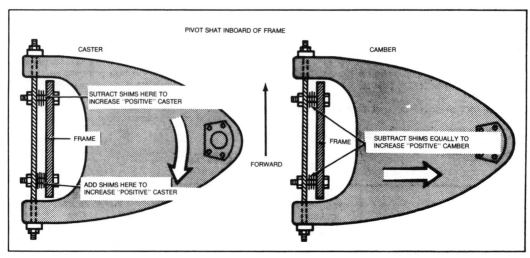

Caster and camber adjustment (© CHEVROLET MOTOR DIVISION)

pivot shaft and the frame bracket. Moving shims front to rear will decrease positive caster. Insertion and removal of a $1/32$ in. shim will effect a $1/4°$ caster change. Adjust caster to specifications.

CAMBER ADJUSTMENT

Camber is the measurement in degrees of the outward or inward tilt of the top of the wheel and tire in relation to the true vertical. Tilting of the top of the tire away from the centerline of the vehicle is called positive camber. Tilting toward the vehicle centerline is negative camber. Camber adjustment is made by adding or removing shims equally at both bolts. Camber and caster adjustment may be made at the same time. A $1/32$ in. shim will effect a $1/6°$ change in camber. Adjust to specifications.

Toe-In

Toe-in is the measurement in inches of the inward departure of the front of the wheels from a line drawn through the horizontal center of the wheel, parallel to the centerline of the vehicle. Toe-in is expressed as the difference in measurement between the extreme front of the wheel pair and the extreme rear of the wheel pair.

Two methods of setting toe-in may be employed. In the first, position the steering gear on high point and mark the 12 o'clock position on the steering shaft, with the wheel in the straight-ahead position. Loosen both tie-rod clamp bolts and adjust each evenly to obtain the total toe-in specified. Secure the

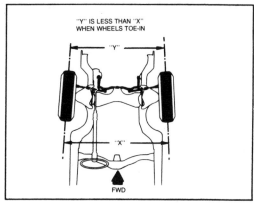

Toe-in adjustment (© Chevrolet Motor Division)

inner tie-rod clamp protrusions forward to 90° down to prevent interference with the stabilizer link bolt.

If a tram gauge is available, position the front wheels straight-ahead. Loosen the tie-rod clamp on one end and adjust the one rod to the total specified toe-in. Loosen the other tie-rod clamp and rotate both rods the same amount in the same direction to put the steering gear on high point and the wheel positioned straightahead. Secure the inner tie-rod clamps with the bolts down and horizontal. Secure the outer bolts vertical and to the rear.

WHEEL BEARING ADJUSTMENT

Raise the front end of the vehicle until the wheels clear the grouund. Pry off the dust cap and extract the cotter pin from the end of the spindle. Slowly rotate the wheel and

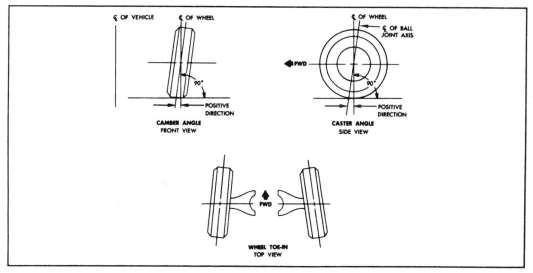

Caster, camber, toe-in (© Chevrolet Motor Division)

Wheel Alignment Specifications

Year	Caster		Camber		Toe-in (in.)	Kingpin Inclination (deg)
	Range (deg)	Pref Setting (deg)	Range (deg)	Pref Setting (deg)		
1963–66	1P to 2P②	1½P	¼P to 1¼P③	¾P	$\frac{7}{32}$ to $\frac{11}{32}$①	6½ to 7½
1967	½P to 1½P	1P	¼P to 1¼P③	¾P	$\frac{3}{16}$ to $\frac{5}{16}$①	6½ to 7½
1968–69	½P to 1½P④	1P	½P to 1¼P⑤	¾P	$\frac{3}{16}$ to $\frac{5}{16}$⑤	6½ to 7½
1970	½P to 1½P④	1P	½P to 1¼P⑤	¾P	$\frac{3}{16}$ to $\frac{5}{16}$⑤	6½ to 7½
1971–73	0 to 2P⑥	1P	0 to 1½P⑤	¾P	$\frac{3}{16}$ to $\frac{5}{16}$⑤	6½ to 7½
1974	½P to 1½P⑥	1P	¼P to 1¼P⑤	¾P	$\frac{3}{32}$ to $\frac{5}{32}$⑤⑦	7¾
1975–76	½P to 1½P④	1P	¼P to 1¼P⑨⑩	¾P	$\frac{1}{32}$ to $\frac{3}{32}$⑦⑧	7¾
1977–78	2P–2½P	2¼P	¼P to 1¼P⑩	¾P	$\frac{3}{16}$ to $\frac{5}{16}$⑧	7¾
1979	2P–2½P	2¼P	¼P to 1P⑫	¾P	.19–.31⑩⑬	7.680

① Rear wheels ¹⁄₁₆–³⁄₁₆
② 1966—½P to 1½P
③ Rear wheels—½° ± ½°
④ W/pwr steering: 1¾P to 2¾P
⑤ Rear wheel alignment: camber ⅞N to ⅛N; toe-in ¹⁄₃₂–³⁄₃₂
⑥ Power steering—1¼P to 3¼P
⑦ 1975 rear wheels toe-in—0 ± ¹⁄₃₂
⑧ 1976–78 rear wheels toe-in—¹⁄₁₆ ± ¹⁄₃₂
⑨ 1975 rear wheels camber—1¹⁄₁₆N ± ¼
⑩ 1976–78 rear wheels camber—⅞N ± ¼
⑪ Degrees
⑫ 1979 rear wheels camber— —.5° ± .5°
⑬ 1979 rear wheels toe-in—.19° ± .06°
N Negative
P Positive

torque the spindle nut to 12 ft lbs. Turn the spindle nut back one flat and install a new cotter pin. If this one-flat turn back does not align a slot and cotter pin hole, continue to turn back no more than ½ flat to achieve the alignment.

Spin the wheel to check for free rolling, then reinstall the dust cap and repeat the adjustment on the other front wheel.

REAR SUSPENSION

The Stingray rear suspension is a three-link independent system. Longitudinal location is provided by control arms which pivot at the front on bolts through the frame step-up. The lower link is a strut rod which also serves as a camber rod with adjustment permitted by an eccentric cam on the inner end. The universal-jointed axle driveshafts double as the upper locating links. Shock absorbers attach to the frame at the top and attach to the spindle/camber rod strut at the bottom. Springing is provided by a 9-leaf (7 on heavy duty, 10 on all 1975–76 models), transverse spring bolted to the rear cover of the differential carrier. 6½ in. rubber-cushioned link bolts locate the spring ends to the control arms.

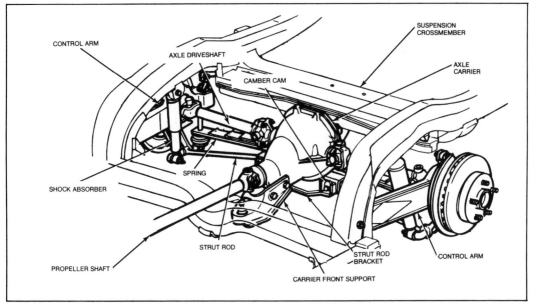

Rear suspension (© Chevrolet Motor Division)

Spring

REMOVAL AND INSTALLATION

1. Jack the rear of the car up high enough to provide working clearance.

2. Position a floor jack under the link bolt on one side. Raise the jack until the spring is compressed tightly, and install a ¼ in., or larger, chain around the suspension cross-member and the spring. Use a C-clamp to hold the chain to the spring.

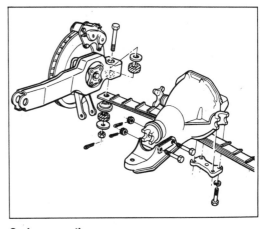

Spring mounting

3. Lower the jack to permit access to the link bolt, and then remove the link bolt nut, cushions, and retainers.

4. Raise the spring again and remove the chain and C-clamp.

5. Slowly lower the spring until all tension is released.

6. Perform the same steps on the other side.

7. Remove the four, spring pad bolts and plate.

8. Withdraw the spring over the exhaust pipes and down from the car.

9. To install, position the spring on the bottom carrier mounting pad with the center bolt aligned with the hole in the mounting pad.

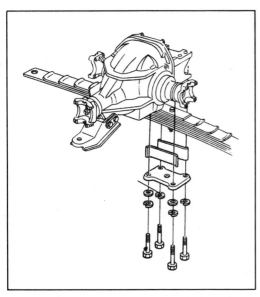

Removing spring clamp plate (© Chevrolet Motor Division)

10. Install the center clamp and the four mounting bolts. Tighten the bolts to 55–75 ft lbs.

11. Jack one end of the spring and secure with chain as in the removal procedure.

12. Lower the jack and position the control arm for the link bolt installation. Install the link bolt, rubber cushions, and retainers. Install the castellated nut on the link bolt and secure with a cotter pin.

13. Raise the spring and remove the C-clamp and chain.

14. Repeat the above operation on the other side.

15. Lower the car.

Shock Absorbers

BOUNCE TEST

Each shock absorber can be tested by bouncing the corner of the vehicle until maximum up and down movement is obtained. Release the car. It should stop bouncing in one or two bounces. Compare both front corners or both rear corners but do not compare the front to the rear. If one corner bounces longer than the other it should be inspected for damage and possibly be replaced.

REMOVAL AND INSTALLATION

1. Remove the upper shock absorber bolt and nut.

2. Remove the lower mounting nut and lockwasher.

3. Slide the upper eye of the shock absorber out of the frame bracket.

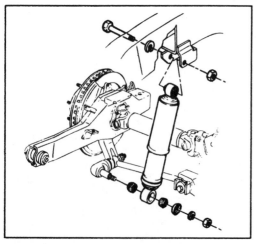

Shock absorber mounting (© Chevrolet Motor Division)

4. Pull the lower eye off the strut rod shaft and remove the rubber grommets.

5. To install, position the upper shock absorber eye in the frame mounting bracket and install the bolt, lockwasher, and nut.

6. Install the inner rubber grommet and then the shock absorber eye on the strut rod shaft. Install the outer grommet, washer, lockwasher, and nut.

7. Torque the upper nut to 40–60 ft lbs and the lower nut to 50–60 ft lbs.

Strut Rod and Bracket

REMOVAL AND INSTALLATION

1. Jack the rear of the car high enough to allow working clearance.

2. Disconnect the lower shock absorber eye from the strut rod shaft.

3. Remove the strut rod shaft cotter pin and nut. Drive the shaft out of the spindle support.

CAUTION: *The strut rod shaft is often very hard to remove; take care not to distort either the shaft or the spindle support in the removal process.*

4. Scribe the camber adjusting cam-to-bracket relationship for correct relocation.

5. Loosen the cam adjusting bolt and nut.

6. Remove the four bracket-to-carrier bolts, and lower the bracket.

7. Remove the cam, bolt, and nut. Remove the strut from the bracket and remove the bushing caps.

8. Inspect the strut rod bushings and replace if necessary.

9. Install the inside bushing caps and slip the strut rod into the bracket.

10. Install the cam and bolt assemblies, and align the previously scribed marks. Hand-tighten the adjustment nut.

11. Raise the bracket assembly and install

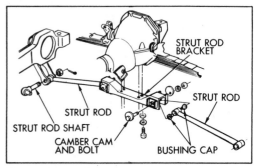

Strut rod mounting

the four bracket-to-carrier bolts. Torque the bolts to 15–22 ft lbs.

12. Raise the outer end of the strut rod into the spindle support. Install the strut rod shaft through the spindle support and strut rod.

NOTE: *The strut rod shaft has a flat side which should line up with the matching flat in the spindle support.*

13. Replace the shock absorber lower eye on the strut rod shaft. Torque the nut to 50–60 ft lbs.

14. Lower the car and then tighten the camber cam nut to 55–77 ft lbs. Tighten the strut rod shaft nut to 80 ft lbs and install a new cotter pin.

Adjustments

CAMBER

The rear wheel camber adjustment is made by rotating the eccentric cam and bolt assembly that connects the strut rod to the differential carrier bracket. Loosen the locknut and turn the eccentric cam bolt until the correct wheel camber angle is obtained. Secure the locknut and torque to 55–77 ft lbs.

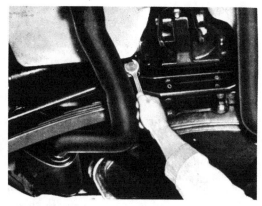

Adjusting camber

TOE-IN

Rear wheel toe-in is adjusted by the placement of shims of different thickness on both sides of the control arm pivot bushings. These shims are available in $1/64$ in., $1/32$ in., $1/8$ in., and $1/4$ in. sizes. To make this adjustment, remove the pivot bolt and position the torque arm so that the correct toe-in specifications are achieved. Insert shims in the gap nearest the car centerline between the bushing and the frame inner wall. Use shims of only the thickness required to bridge the

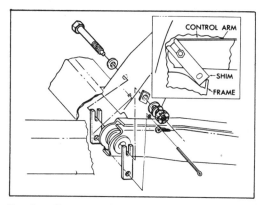

Toe-in adjustment shim location

gap. Do not overshim or force the shims during the adjusting. Insert shims in the outside gap until solidarity is reached between the pivot bushing and the frame walls. Insert the bolt, torque the nut to 50 ft lbs, and install a cotter pin.

Wheel Bearings

ADJUSTMENT

The spindle bearings are of a tapered, roller design and require an end-play of 0.001 in. to 0.008 in. To measure endplay, lift the rear wheels clear of the ground and disconnect the axle driveshaft from the spindle. There is insufficient clearance to drop the axle driveshaft when the rear suspension is correctly adjusted so the strut rod eccentric cam/bolt must be loosened and rotated so that the strut rod forces the trailing arm away from the vehicle centerline and permits the driveshaft to be lowered.

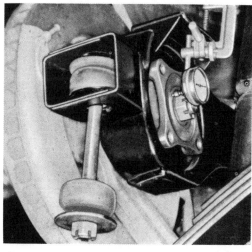

Checking spindle bearing play

1. Mark the eccentric cam and the attaching bracket so that the correct camber adjustment can be returned to.

2. Remove the rear wheels and attach a dial indicator to the torque arm so that its indicator point will contact the end of the spindle.

3. Move the disc in and out and observe the dial indicator reading. If the reading exceeds the 0.001 in. to 0.008 in. tolerances, the bearings must be adjusted.

4. Set the handbrake and remove the drive spindle nut.

5. Release the brake and remove the brake drum or caliper and disc as described in Chapter 9.

6. Remove the spindle flange then reinstall the nut until it is flush with the end of the spindle. Use a puller to withdraw the spindle from its support.

7. Remove the spindle-support dust deflector and pry out the inner seal. Remove the inner bearing race, roller assembly, shim, and bearing spacer from the spindle support.

8. Check the size of the old shim and, if the dial indicator reading exceeded 0.008 in., replace it with one that is thinner by the required amount to bring end-play within allowable tolerances. A dial indicator reading of less than 0.001 in. requires a shim thick enough to move the end-play beyond the 0.001 in. minimum.

NOTE: *Shims are available in 0.003 in. increments and range in thickness from 0.097 in. to 1.48 in.*

9. Insert the spindle bearing and seal in the spindle support and install the bearing spacer and shim.

10. Place the inner race and roller assembly on the spindle and a suitable spacer to aid in pressing the bearing into position.

11. Start the nut onto the spindle and against the press spacer. Tighten the nut and press the bearing in a sufficient amount to permit the installation of the spindle drive flange.

12. Remove the spindle nut and washer and discard the nut. Use a new replacement for assembly.

13. Tap the replacement inner seal in place, install the dust deflector, drive flange, spindle washer, and nut. Torque the nut to 100 ft lbs and install a new cotter pin.

REPLACEMENT

Outer Bearing

1. With the wheel spindle removed, attach a bearing puller around the bearing and secure the tool and spindle in a press, and remove the bearing from the spindle.

2. Remove the outer seal and replace if necessary.

3. Position the replacement seal on the spindle before installing the bearing assembly.

4. Pack the replacement bearing with a high melting point grease and place it on the spindle, large end facing the spindle shoulder.

5. Support the spindle and press the bearing into position. Install the reassembled spindle to the spindle support.

STEERING

The Corvette steering system is a recirculating ball, relay type. A pitman arm connects the steering gear to the relay rod by way of a pivoted joint. The opposite end of this transverse relay rod attaches to a frame-mounted idler arm by way of another pivoting joint.

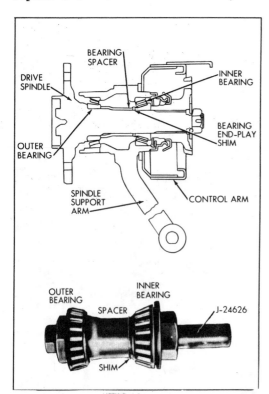

Sectional view of spindle (© Chevrolet Motor Division)

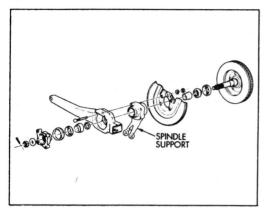

Support arm—exploded view (© Chevrolet Motor Division)

These joints are the adjustable ball and socket type.

Two adjustable tie-rods join each steering arm to the relay rod through self-adjusting ball and socket joints. The steering arms have two tie-rod end holes drilled in them to provide a road steering ratio of: 19.6:1 or 20.2:1 on earlier models; a faster ratio of 17:1 or 17:6.1 on later models. This adjustment is made by disconnecting the tie-rod ends from one steering arm hole and moving to the other. The latest models (1969–1979) have Function Locking Energy Absorbing steering columns. With this design, the mast jacket and steering shaft are designed to collapse during conditions generated by a front end collision.

The collapsible mast jacket has ball bearings embedded in plastic and pressed between the upper and lower jackets. A predetermined load will collapse the assembly. The steering shaft collapses under predetermined loads, shearing the plastic pins. Additionally, these columns contain an anti-theft ignition switch and ignition lock system. This system prevents the removal of the ignition key unless the automatic transmission is in Park or the manual transmission is in Reverse, and the key is in the "Lock" position. In this position, a rod and lock plate mechanism lock the steering wheel and shift lever.

Steering Wheel

REMOVAL AND INSTALLATION

1963–67 Standard Wheel

1. Disconnect the battery ground cable.
2. Pry off the horn cap with a small screwdriver.
3. Remove the steering shaft nut and washer.
4. Install a wheel puller in the two threaded holes provided. Remove the steering wheel.

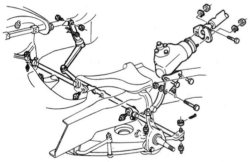

Steering linkage—1963–67 (© Chevrolet Motor Division)

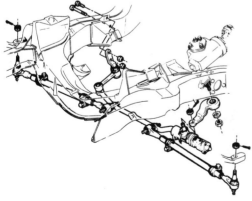

Steering linkage—1978–79 (© Chevrolet Motor Division)

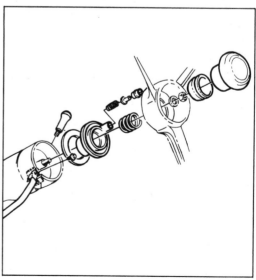

Standard steering wheel—1963–67 (© Chevrolet Motor Division)

5. To install, align the wheel in a straight, up-and-down position.

6. Install the washer and nut on the shaft, and while holding the wheel, tighten the nut to 35–40 ft lbs.

7. Reinstall the contact assembly and horn cap.

1968–76 Standard Wheel

1. Disconnect the battery ground cable.

2. Pry the horn cap off with a small screwdriver and remove the upper horn contact.

3. Remove the six steering wheel retaining screws and remove the wheel.

NOTE: *To remove the wheel for turn signal switch service, follow Steps 3–6 of the "1963–67 Standard Wheel" procedure. Tighten the nut to 30 ft lbs. On 1975–76 models, it is necessary to remove the snapring from the steering shaft first. Don't forget to install the snap-ring after tightening the nut.*

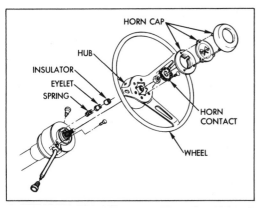

Standard steering wheel—1968–76 (© Chevrolet Motor Division)

4. To install, attach the wheel to the hub with the six screws.

5. Install the upper horn contact and the horn cap.

1965–67 Telescoping Wheel

1. Disconnect the battery ground cable.

2. Pry off the horn cap with a small screwdriver and remove the horn contact assembly.

3. Remove the lock screw-to-lock knob retaining screws, and remove the lock screw, lock knob, and the spacer.

4. Remove the six steering wheel-to-hub screws and remove the wheel.

5. Replace the steering wheel on the hub and install the six retaining screws.

6. Install the spacer on the steering wheel and position the lock knob.

7. The lock screw installs through the lock knob, is turned into the shaft, and adjusted to the lock position.

8. Attach the spacer to the steering wheel. Put the lock knob in lock position and attach it to the lock screw with two screws.

9. Remove the three, spacer retaining screws and install the horn contact to the spacer and the steering wheel with three screws.

10. Install the horn cap.

1968–76 Telescoping Wheel

1. Disconnect the battery ground cable.

2. Remove the horn cap and upper horn contact.

3. Remove the shim, star screw, lock lever, and spacer.

NOTE: *To remove the wheel for turn signal switch service, follow Steps 3–6 of the "1963–67 Standard Wheel" procedure.*

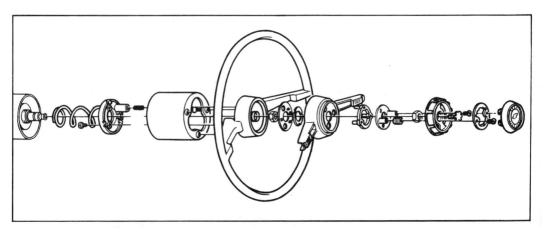

Tilt and telescoping wheel—1965–66 (© Chevrolet Motor Division)

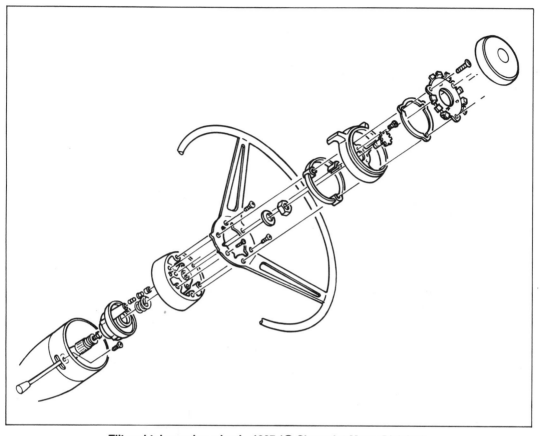

Tilt and telescoping wheel—1967 (© Chevrolet Motor Division)

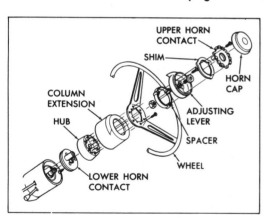

Tilt and telescoping wheel 1968–76 (© Chevrolet Motor Division)

Steering wheel puller—typical (© Chevrolet Motor Division)

Tighten the nut to 30 ft lbs. On 1975–76 models, it is necessary to remove the snapring from the steering shaft first. Don't forget to install the snap-ring after tightening the nut.

4. Remove the six, steering wheel retaining screws and remove the wheel.

5. Replace the steering wheel on the hub and install the six retaining screws.

6. Position the spacer and lock lever on the steering wheel.

7. Install the star screw through the lock lever, turn it into the shaft, and put it into lock position.

8. Install the spacer to the steering wheel

with three screws. Position the lock lever in "Lock."

9. Attach the star screw with two screws and remove the three, spacer retaining screws.

10. Install the shims and the upper horn contact.

11. Install the horn cap.

1977–79 Standard Wheel

1. Disconnect the battery ground cable.

2. Pry off the horn button cap.

3. Remove the snap ring then the steering wheel nut.

4. Install a wheel puller in the threaded holes provided. Butt the center bolt of the tool against the steering shaft and turn clockwise to remove the hub assembly.

5. When installing make sure the turn signal is in the neutral position then install the hub on the steering shaft and secure it with the nut. Torque the nut to 30 ft lbs.

6. Install the snap ring.

7. Attach the steering wheel to the hub assembly with the attaching screws.

8. Install the horn contact and attach with the three screws.

9. Snap the horn button in place.

10. Connect the battery ground cable.

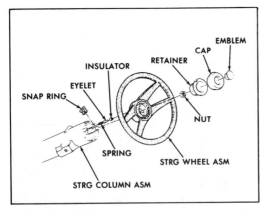

Standard steering wheel—1977–79 (© Chevrolet Motor Division)

1977–79 Tilt Telescoping Wheel

1. Disconnect the battery ground cable.

2. Pry off the horn button cap.

3. Remove the three screws and remove the upper horn contact assembly.

4. If used, remove the shim then remove the screw securing the center star screw. Remove the star screw and lever.

5. Remove the snap ring and nut from

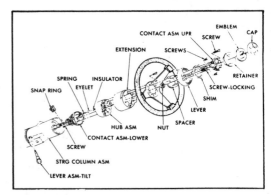

Tilt and telescoping wheel 1977–79 (© Chevrolet Motor Division)

the shaft and remove the steering wheel assembly with a wheel puller.

6. If it is necessary to dissassemble the steering wheel remove the three screws securing the steering wheel and separate then remove the four screws securing the extension to the steering wheel then separate.

7. To assemble the steering wheel position the extension to the steering wheel and install the attaching screws. Torque the screws to 20 in. lbs.

8. Position the spring, eyelet and insulator to the lower contact assembly. Position the assembly to the steering wheel and install the three screws.

9. Position the steering wheel assembly to the steering column and torque the nut to 30 ft lbs.

10. Install the snap ring.

11. Position the lever to the steering column and install the star screw. Install the screws. Remove the switch by pulling it

12. Position the upper contact assembly and shim if used and install the three retaining screws.

13. Install the retainer and horn button cap.

14. Connect the battery ground cable.

Turn Signal Switch

REPLACEMENT

1963

The 1963 turn signal switch is mounted on the lower part of the steering column. The switch is operated by a cable from the signal housing located under the steering wheel.

CAUTION: *It is very important that the specific size screws, bolts, and nuts are used during assembly. Use of over-length screws could prevent a portion of the col-*

umn from compressing under impact on 1969–79 models.

1. Remove the screws holding the switch case to the mast jacket.

2. Remove the control cable from the spring clip at the switch.

3. Loosen the cable-to-switch retaining screw.

4. Disconnect the switch wire.

5. Put the column lever in neutral.

6. Move the switch slide so that it is in the center of the slot on the switch.

7. Install the cable into the spring clip without disturbing the switch slide. Fasten the cable with the screw.

8. Install the switch on the column.

1964–66

1. Remove the steering wheel as previously outlined.

2. Remove the terminal wires from the connector and remove the mast jacket harness cover.

3. Remove the turn signal lever and the three switch retaining screws.

4. Remove the retainer plate, switch housing, and the switch from the mast jacket. Pull each wire separately through the mast jacket slot to prevent damaging the harness.

5. Transfer the wiring harness to the replacement switch and install the components using a reverse of the removal procedure.

1967–68

1. Remove the steering wheel as previously outlined.

2. From under the dash, disconnect the switch harness connector from the chassis harness.

3. Remove the preload spring and the cancelling cam.

4. Remove the turn signal lever. Push the flasher knob in and remove it by unscrewing.

5. Remove the lower trim cover.

6. Remove the retaining ring and the thrust and wave washers from the top of the steering shaft. Cut the wiring above the connector.

7. Unscrew the switch, and slide it, the cover, and the upper bearing housing out of the column. Pull the wire through the column protector and escutcheon.

8. Install the new switch by assembling it and the upper bearing housing into the switch cover, and then working the wire down through the escutcheon and column protector until the switch can be positioned on the mast jacket.

9. Install the switch and remaining components in a reverse order of removal.

Standard Wheel 1969–79

1. Remove the steering wheel as previously outlined.

2. On 1969–75 Models loosen the three cover screws and lift the cover off the shaft. On 1976–79 Models pry the lock plate cover off with a screwdriver blade.

3. Position the special lockplate compressing tool (J-23131 1969–70 or J-23653 1971–75) on the end of the steering shaft and compress the lockplate by turning the shaft nut clockwise. Pry the wire snap-ring out of the shaft groove.

4. Remove the tool and lift the lockplate off the shaft.

5. Slip the cancelling cam, upper bearing pre-load spring, and thrust washer off the shaft.

6. Remove the turn signal lever. Push the flasher knob in and unscrew it.

7. Pull the switch connector out of the mast jacket and tape the upper part to facilitate switch removal. On tilt wheels, place the turn signal and shifter housing in Low position and remove the harness cover.

8. Remove the three switch mounting screws. Remove the switch by pulling it straight up while guiding the wiring harness cover through the column.

9. Install the replacement switch by working the connector and cover down through the housing and under the bracket. On tilt models, the connector is worked down through the housing, under the bracket, and then the cover is installed on the harness.

10. Install the switch mounting screws and the connector on the mast jacket bracket. Install the column-to-dash trim plate.

11. Install the flasher knob and the turn signal lever.

12. With the turn signal lever in neutral and the flasher knob out, slide the thrust washer, upper bearing pre-load spring, and cancelling cam onto the shaft.

13. Position the lockplate on the shaft and press it down until a new snap-ring can be inserted in the shaft groove.

14. Install the cover and the steering wheel.

Tilt-Telescope 1969–79

1. Remove the steering wheel as previously outlined and press off the hub with a puller.

2. Remove the steering column/dash trim cover.

3. Remove the C-ring plastic retainer, if so equipped.

4. Install the special lockplate compressing tool (J-23131 1969–70 or J-23653 1971–75) over the steering shaft. Position a $^5/_{16}$ in. nut under each tool leg and reinstall the star screw to prevent the shaft from moving.

5. Compress the lockplate by turning the shaft nut clockwise until the C-ring can be removed.

6. Remove the tool and lift out the lockplate, horn contact carrier, and the upper bearing preload spring.

NOTE: *1969 Corvette assembly order is: horn control carrier, lockplate, and upper bearing preload spring.*

7. Pull the switch connector out of the mast jacket and tape the upper part to facilitate switch removal.

8. Remove the turn signal lever. Push the flasher in and unscrew it.

9. Position the turn signal and shifter housing in Low position. Remove the switch by pulling it straight up while guiding the wiring harness out of the housing.

10. Install the replacement switch by working the harness connector down through the housing and under the mounting bracket.

11. Install the harness cover and clip the connector to the mast jacket.

12. Install the switch mounting screws, signal lever, and the flasher knob.

13. With the turn signal lever in neutral and the flasher knob out, install the upper bearing pre-load spring, horn contact carrier, and lockplate onto the shaft. Horn contact carrier is last on 1969 models.

14. Position the tool as in Step 4 and compress the plate far enough to allow the C-ring to be installed.

15. Remove the tool. Install the plastic C-ring retainer.

16. Install the column/dash trim cover. Install the steering wheel.

Ignition Switch

REMOVAL AND INSTALLATION

1969–79

See Chapter 5 for "1964–68 Ignition Switch Removal and Installation"

The switch is located inside the channel section of the brake pedal support and is completely inaccessible without first lowering the steering column. The switch is actuated by a rod and rack assembly. A gear on the end of the lock cylinder engages the toothed upper end of the rod.

1. Lower the steering column; be sure to properly support it.

2. Put the switch in "Lock" position on models through 1977 and the "Off-Unlocked" position on 1978 and later models. With the cylinder removed, the rod is in "Lock" or "Off-Unlocked" position when it is in the next to the uppermost detent.

3. Remove the two switch screws and remove the switch assembly.

4. Before installing, place the new switch in "Lock" or "Off-Unlocked" position and make sure the lock cylinder and actuating rod

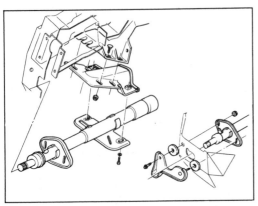

Steering column to dash panel (© Chevrolet Motor Division)

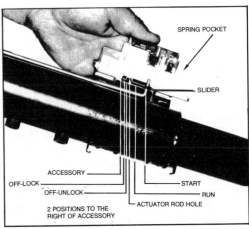

Positioning the ignition switch (© Chevrolet Motor Division)

are in "Lock" or "Off-Unlocked" position (second detent from the top).

5. Install the activating rod into the switch and assemble the switch on the column. Tighten the mounting screws. Use only the specified screws since overlength screws could impair the collapsibility of the column.

6. Reinstall the steering column.

Steering Linkage

The Corvette has two tie-rods. Each rod is a three-piece assembly made up of the rod itself and two tie-rod ends. The ends screw onto the rod and are clamped in place. Right and left-hand threads are used to assist toe-in and centering adjustments. The ends are self-adjusting and, with the exception of periodic lubrication, require no servicing.

ADJUSTMENTS

Relay Arm Ball Joint

1. Remove the cotter pin and adjust the end plug slot clockwise until the inside springs are bottomed.

2. Turn the plug ¾ turn counterclockwise and reinsert the cotter pin.

Steering Ratio

1. Two-position steering arms permit an adjustment for quicker steering. Do not make this adjustment on Corvettes equipped with power steering, as frame interference will result.

2. Disconnect the tie-rod ball joint stud from the steering arm.

3. Insert the stud in the forward hole for a quick steering ratio, or the rear hole for a slower ratio.

4. Install the nut and cotter pin. Repeat this operation on the opposite side.

5. Reset the toe-in after a steering ratio adjustment.

Power Steering Gear

The optional power steering on the Corvette is of the linkage assist type. The steering gear and linkage is identical to that used on manual steering cars. All procedures for the manual gear apply to the power steering gear. A belt-driven pump supplies hydraulic pressure to a sensing valve, and then on demand to a power cylinder on the linkage, which provides the power assist to the linkage.

Steering ratio adjustment

Power Steering Pump

REMOVAL AND INSTALLLATION

1. Remove the hoses at the pump, and tape the ends to prevent dirt from entering.

2. Plug the pump fittings to keep the fluid in the pump.

3. Loosen the bracket retaining nuts and remove the drive belt.

4. Withdraw the bracket-to-pump bolts and remove the pump from the car. On large block Corvettes, the alternator drive belt must be removed first.

5. Place the pump on the bracket and install the attaching pieces hand-tight.

6. Install the hoses and tighten the fittings.

7. Refill the pump reservoir. Turn the pulley backward to bleed the pump.

8. Install the belt over the pulley and tighten to the correct tension.

9. Bleed the hydraulic system.

Brakes

BRAKE SYSTEM

1963–64 Corvettes are equipped with four-wheel drum brakes. These are hydraulically operated, self-adjusting, and feature double-piston wheel cylinders. Three brake options were available with the drum system. Power brakes featured a Moraine vacuum assist master cylinder and were the first power brakes ever offered on the Corvette. The second option was the standard drums (honed to a 20 micro-inch finish and equipped with special heat resistant springs) and metallic linings for more fade resistance. The third option was intended for heavy-duty or competition usage. These cerametallic linings were larger and the drums were finned and scooped.

In 1965, the four-wheel disc brake system was introduced. This system includes a fixed caliper, rotating vented disc, and four-piston pad actuation. A heavy-duty, optional disc brake system is available for special purposes. A different front caliper, brake pad, and brake line pressure regulator are used. Heavy-duty brake calipers are easily recognized by the two, pad retaining pins instead of the standard brake's single pin.

Adjustment
DRUM BRAKES

Rotate the star wheel adjuster until a slight drag is felt between the shoes and drum, then back off 1¼ turns on the adjuster. Backing the car and firmly braking will allow the self-adjustment feature to complete the adjustment.

DISC BRAKES

These brakes are inherently self-adjusting and no adjustment is ever necessary or possible.

HYDRAULIC SYSTEM
Master Cylinder—Drum Brakes
REMOVAL AND INSTALLATION

1. Disconnect the hydraulic lines from the cylinder. Plug the lines to keep dirt out of the lines and master cylinder.

2. Remove the clevis pin and clip from the brake pedal arm.

3. Remove the main cylinder-to-firewall nuts and lockwashers, and remove the master cylinder.

4. Install the master cylinder on the fire-

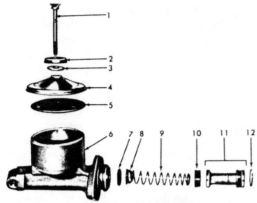

1. Thumbscrew
2. Vent cover
3. Flat washer
4. Reservoir cover
5. Gasket
6. Body
7. Valve seat
8. Valve assembly
9. Spring
10. Primary cup
11. Secondary cup and piston
12. Lockring

Exploded view of 1963–64 master cylinder

wall studs. Install the lockwashers, and tighten the nuts.

5. Insert the clevis pin through the clevis and the brake pedal and secure with a cotter pin.

6. Install the hydraulic lines to the master cylinder.

7. Refill the cylinder with brake fluid and bleed the lines.

8. Adjust the brake pedal as necessary.

OVERHAUL

NOTE: *Overhaul of the main cylinder portion of power brake master cylinders is the same as that for manual master cylinders.*

1. Secure the master cylinder in a vise and remove the push rod assembly and the protective boot. This exposes the lock ring which, when removed, allows extraction of the piston stop, secondary cup, and piston.

2. Remove the cylinder end plug and push out the primary cup, spring, valve assembly, and seat.

3. Wash the component parts with clean alcohol only, and be sure that all traces of gasoline or kerosene are removed. Gasoline will cause premature deterioration of the cylinder's rubber parts.

4. Carefully inspect the washed metal parts and the cylinder bore. A corroded cylinder must be replaced. Discoloration or stains should be removed with crocus cloth. When doing so, wrap the cloth around a finger and rotate the cylinder around the supported cloth. Do not polish the bore lengthwise as this can cause a fluid leak.

5. Check the piston-to-cylinder clearance with a feeler gauge. Clearance should be between 0.001 in. and 0.005 in.

6. To reassemble, moisten the cylinder bore with clean brake fluid and replace the valve seat, valve assembly, and spring.

NOTE: *Be sure that the valve and seat are properly installed before proceeding. An incorrectly assembled check valve will distort and fail to provide a check valve seal, which will result in a reduction of brake pedal travel and a corresponding loss of actual braking.*

7. Moisten the primary cup with clean brake fluid and install it, flat side out, and seated over the spring. The primary cup is distinguished by a brass support ring at its base.

8. Dip the secondary cup in clean brake fluid and slip it over the end of the piston.

9. Insert the completed assembly, with the bleeder brake end of the piston installed first. Secure the parts with the piston stop and the snap-ring, and install the end plug.

10. Attach the rubber boot and push rod, and replace the cylinder on the firewall.

11. Attach the brake pedal clevis and adjust the push rod-to-piston clearance. Correct adjustment calls for a barely perceptible free pedal before piston/push rod contact.

Master Cylinder—Disc Brakes

The early disc brake master cylinder is serviced in the same manner as the drum brake master cylinder. The later master cylinder is the dual reservoir type. This offers a separate brake circuit for the front and rear wheel pairs and prevents total loss of braking should one circuit fail.

This master cylinder is actually two complete master cylinders contained in a single housing, with the front reservoir controlling the front brake pairs and the rear reservoir, the rear brake pairs. The heavy-duty option includes a pressure regulator switch in the rear brake line just below the master cylinder.

Two dual master cylinders have been used on the Corvette and are easily identified by referring to the following chart.

Be absolutely certain that replacement parts are identified as identical to those being replaced when overhauling the dual master cylinder. The displacement capability of the master cylinder is dependent upon the length of the secondary piston.

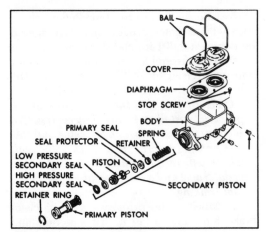

Exploded view of 1967–76 master cylinder (© Chevrolet Motor Division)

OVERHAUL

1. Remove the unit from the vehicle using the same general procedure as described for conventional master cylinders.

2. Remove the mounting gasket and boot, and the main cover; purge the unit of its fluid.

3. Secure the cylinder in a vise and remove the push rod retainer and the secondary piston stop bolt found inside the forward reservoir.

4. Compress the retaining ring and extract it along with the primary piston assembly.

5. Blow compressed air into the piston stop screw hole to force the secondary piston, spring, and its retainer from the bore of the cylinder. An alternate method uses a piece of wire, hooked on one end, to snag and extract the secondary piston.

6. Check the brass tube-fitting inserts and if they are damaged, remove them. Leave undamaged inserts in place.

7. If replacement is necessary, thread a 6–32 x ⅝ in. self-tapping screw into the insert. Hook the head of the screw with a claw hammer and pry the insert free.

8. An alternate way to remove the inserts is to first drill the outlet holes to $^{13}/_{64}$ in. and thread them with a ¼ in.–20 tap. Position a thick washer over the hole to serve as a spacer then thread a ¼ in.–20 x ¾ in. hex head bolt into the insert and tighten the bolt until the insert is freed.

9. Use denatured alcohol and compressed air to clean the component parts. Slight rust may be removed with fine crocus cloth.

10. Replace the brass tube inserts at this time by positioning them in their holes and threading a brake line tube nut into the outlet hole. Turn down the nut until the insert is seated.

11. Check the piston assemblies for correct identification and when satisfied, position the replacement secondary seals in the twin grooves of the secondary piston.

12. The outside seal is correctly placed when its lips face the piston's flat end. The lips of the inner seal face the piston compensating holes.

13. Slip the primary seal and its protector over the end of the secondary piston opposite the secondary seals. The flat side of this seal should face the piston's compensating hole flange.

14. Replace the primary piston assembly with the assembled component found in the overhaul kit.

15. Moisten the cylinder bore and the secondary piston's inner and outer seals with new brake fluid. Assemble the secondary piston spring to its retainer and position them over the end of the piston with the retainer inside the lips of the primary seal.

16. Insert the combined spring and piston assembly into the cylinder and use a small wooden dowel or pencil to seat the spring against the end of the bore.

17. Moisten the primary piston seals with new brake fluid and push it, push rod receptacle end out, into the cylinder.

18. Keep the piston pushed in and snap the retaining ring into place.

19. Relax the pressure on the pistons and allow them to seek their static positions.

20. Replace the secondary piston stop screw and torque it to 25–40 in. lbs.

21. Replace the reservoir diaphragm and cover.

Pressure Regulating Valve (Rear Metering)

1965–68 With H.D. Brakes

The pressure regulating valve is mounted in the rear brake line just below the main cylinder. The valve controls the hydraulic pressure to the front or rear brakes, as applicable, resulting in the correct pressure balance between the front and rear hydraulic systems. The valve guards against premature lock-up of the front or rear wheels when the brakes are applied.

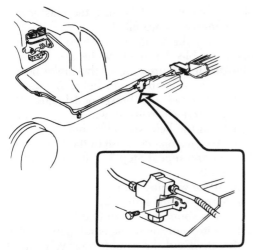

Pressure regulating valve—Typical (© Chevrolet Motor Division)

REMOVAL AND INSTALLATION

1. Place some dry rags under the valve to absorb any fluid spilled during removal.

2. Disconnect the hydraulic brake lines and protect the openings from dirt.

3. Remove the mounting screw and remove the valve.

4. To install position the valve and install the mounting screw.

5. Connect the hydraulic lines and bleed the brake system.

Brake Pressure Indicator and Distribution Switch

1967–76

This switch is connected to the hydraulic lines from the master cylinder and is a pressure differential type, designed to light the brake warning lamp on the instrument panel if either the front or rear hydraulic system fails. The brake warning light will come on

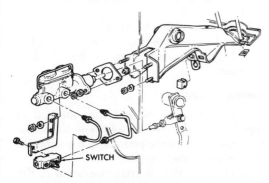

Brake pressure indicator and distribution switch—typical (© Chevrolet Motor Division)

only when the brakes are applied. It will not remain on when the brakes are released. This switch is a non-adjustable and non-serviceable component and must be replaced if found defective.

REMOVAL AND INSTALLATION

1. Disconnect the negative battery cable.

2. Disconnect the electrical lead from the switch assembly.

3. Place dry rags below the switch to absorb any spilled fluid.

4. Clean any dirt from the switch and hydraulic lines and disconnect the hydraulic lines at the switch. Cover the open line ends to protect the system from dirt.

5. Remove the mounting screw and remove the switch.

6. To install reverse the above and bleed the brake system.

TESTING AND CENTERING THE SWITCH

Whenever work on the brake system is done, it is possible that the brake warning light will come on and refuse to go off when the work is finished. In this event, the switch must be centered.

1. Raise and support the vehicle.

2. Attach a bleeder hose to the rear brake bleed screw and immerse the other end of the hose in a jar of clean brake fluid.

3. Be sure that the master cylinder is full.

4. Turn the ignition key ON. Open the bleed screw while an assistant applies heavy pressure on the brake pedal. The warning lamp should light. Close the bleed screw before the helper releases the pedal.

To reset the switch, apply heavy pressure to the pedal. This will apply hydraulic pressure to the switch which will recenter it.

5. Repeat Step 4 for the front bleed screw.

6. Turn the ignition OFF and lower the vehicle.

NOTE: *If the warning lamp does not light during Step 4, the switch is defective and must be replaced.*

Combination Valve

1977–79

The combination valve is mounted on the frame and is connected to the hydraulic lines from the master cylinder. The proportioning section of the combination valve proportions outlet pressure to the rear brakes after a predetermined rear input pressure has been

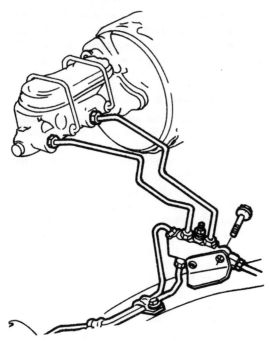

Combination valve mounted below master cylinder (© Chevrolet Motor Division)

reached. This is done to prevent rear wheel lock-up. The valve is designed to have a by-pass feature which assures full system pressure to the rear brakes if the front brake system fails and full system pressure to the front brakes if the rear brake system fails.

The warning switch is designed to constantly compare front and rear brake pressure from the master cylinder and turn on the light on the dash in case of front or rear system failure. The warning light switch portion of the combination valve is not serviceable. If the switch is found defective the combination valve must be replaced.

REMOVAL AND INSTALLATION

1. Disconnect the hydraulic lines at the combination valve. Plug the lines to prevent loss of fluid and to protect the system from dirt.

2. Disconnect the valve switch wire terminal and remove the combination valve.

3. To install reverse the above and bleed the brake system.

TESTING

1. Raise the vehicle on a hoist.

2. Attach a bleeder hose to a rear brake bleed screw and immerse the other end of the hose in a container partially filled with clean brake fluid. Make sure the master cylinder reservoirs are filled.

3. Turn the ignition switch to "On" and open the bleeder screw while a helper applies moderate pressure to the brake pedal. The warning lamp should light. Before the helper releases the brake pedal close the bleeder screw. Press down on the brake pedal and the light should go out.

4. Attach a bleeder hose to the front brake bleeder and repeat Step 3. Turn the ignition switch off.

5. If the warning lamp does not light during Steps 3 and 4 but does light when a jumper is connected to ground, the warning light switch portion of the combination valve is defective and the combination valve must be replaced.

Brake Bleeding

The hydraulic brake system must be bled any time one of the lines is disconnected or air enters the system. This may be done manually or by the pressure method. Correct bleeding sequence is: left rear wheel cylinder, right rear, right front, left front.

Pressure Bleeding

1. Clean the top of the master cylinder, remove the cover, and attach the pressure bleeding adapter.

2. Check the pressure bleeder reservoir for correct pressure and fluid level, then open the release valve.

3. Fasten a bleeder hose to the wheel cylinder bleeder nipple and submerge the free end of the hose in a transparent receptacle. The receptacle should contain enough brake fluid to cover the open end of the hose.

4. Open the wheel cylinder bleeder nipple and allow the fluid to flow until all bubbles disappear and an uncontaminated flow exists.

5. Close the nipple, remove the bleeder hose and repeat the procedure on the other wheel cylinders according to the bleeding sequence.

Manual Bleeding

An alternative to the pressure method of bleeding requires two people to perform: one to depress the brake pedal and the other to open the bleeder nipples.

1. Observe the cleaning operation of the pressure method, then remove the cover and fill the reservoir.

2. Attach a bleeder hose and clear container as before.

3. Have the assistant depress the brake pedal to the floor, and then pause until fluid flow ceases and the bleeder nipple is closed.

4. Allow the pedal to return and repeat the procedure until a steady, bubble-free flow is seen.

5. Secure the nipple and move to the other wheels in the correct sequence.

6. Periodically check the master cylinder for an adequate supply of fluid. If the reservoir runs dry, air will enter the system and bleeding will have to be done again.

DRUM BRAKES (FRONT OR REAR)

Brake Drums

REMOVAL AND INSTALLATION

1. Jack the car so wheels are off the ground.

2. Remove the wheel or wheels where brake drums are to be removed.

3. Pull the brake drum off—it may be necessary to gently tap the rear edges of the drum to start it off the studs.

4. If extreme resistance to removal is encountered, it will be necessary to retract the adjusting screw. Knock out the access hole in the brake drum and turn the adjuster to retract the linings.

5. Install brake drums after adjusting the linings.

6. Install the drums in the same position on the hub or axle shaft as removed.

INSPECTION

When a drum is removed, it should be inspected for cracks, scores, or other imperfections. These must be corrected before the drum is replaced.

CAUTION: *If the drum is found to be cracked, replace it. Do not attempt to service a cracked drum.*

Minor drum score marks can be removed with fine emery cloth. Heavy score marks must be removed by "turning the drum." This is removing the metal from the entire inner surface of the drum in order to level the surface. Automotive machine shops and some large parts stores are equipped to perform this operation.

If the drum is not scored, it should be polished with fine emery cloth before replacement. If the drum is resurfaced, it should not be enlarged past 0.060 in. of the original diameter.

It is advisable, while the drums are off, to check them for out-of-round. An inside micrometer is necessary for an exact measurement, therefore unless this tool is available, the drums should be taken to a machine shop to be checked. Any drum which is more than 0.006 in. out-of-round will result in an inaccurate brake adjustment and other problems, and should be refinished or replaced.

NOTE: *If the micrometer is available, make all measurements at right angles to each other and at the open and closed edges of the drum machined surface.*

Check the drum with a micrometer in the following manner:

1. Position the drum on a level surface.

2. Insert the micrometer with its adapter bars if necessary.

3. Obtain a reading on the micrometer at the point of maximum contact. Record this.

4. Rotate the micrometer 45° and take a similar reading. The two readings must not vary more than 0.006 in.

Brake Shoes

INSPECTION

Remove the drum and inspect the lining thickness on both brake shoes. A front brake lining should be replaced if it is less than ⅛ in. thick at the lowest point on the brake shoe. The limit for rear brake linings is ¹/₁₆.

NOTE: *Brake shoes should always be replaced in axle sets.*

REMOVAL AND INSTALLATION

1. Support the car on jackstands, slacken the parking brake cable and remove the rear wheels, rear brake drums, and front drums and hub assemblies.

2. Free the brake shoe return springs, actuator pull-back spring, hold-down pins and springs, and actuator assembly.

3. On rear wheels, disconnect the adjusting mechanism and spring, and remove the primary shoe.

4. Disconnect the parking brake lever from the secondary shoe and remove the shoe. Front wheel shoes may be removed simultaneously.

5. Clean and inspect all parts. Scored or out-of-round drums should be reconditioned or replaced.

Freeing hold-down pins and springs

6. Check wheel bearings, oil seals, wheel cylinders, and rear axle seals; repacking or replacing as needed.

7. Inspect the replacement shoes for nicks or burrs, lubricate the backing plate contact points, brake cable and levers, and adjusting screws, then reassemble.

8. Be sure that the left and right-hand adjusting screws are not mixed. The star wheel should be nearest the secondary shoe when properly installed.

9. Reverse the procedure for reassembly. When completed, make an initial adjustment as described under adjustments.

Metallic brakes

Maintenance procedures for the metalic lining-only option are the same as those for standard brakes. Do not substitute these linings in standard drums, unless they have been honed to a 20 micro-inch finish and equipped with the special heat resistant springs.

The oversize metallic lining and finned drum option requires attention to the following maintenence deviations: The adjusting screw uses a solid film lubricant, and should not be cleaned with solvent or lubricated. The final brake adjustment also differs for this option in that the self-adjustment feature actuates when firm pedal application is made when the car is moving forward. Maintenance procedures require these linings to be broken in. Make an initial adjustment then use moderate pedal pressure to make six to eight stops from approximately 30 mph. Follow this with six to eight stops from approxi-mately 60 mph; making each stop at a one-mile interval.

Wheel Cylinder
REMOVAL AND INSTALLATION

1. Jack and support the axle.
2. Remove the wheel and drum.
3. Disconnect the wheel cylinder pipe or hose from the fitting at the flange plate.
4. Disconnect the brake shoe retracting spring from the brake shoes.
5. On rear wheels remove the two cap screws which hold the rear wheel cylinder to the flange plate and remove the wheel cylinder.
6. On front wheels remove the anchor pin which holds the front wheel cylinder to the flange plate and remove the wheel cylinder.

OVERHAUL

Wheel cylinder overhaul procedures are similar to those for the master cylinder. Overhaul kits containing the necessary replacements are readily available. When rebuilding and installing the wheel cylinders, avoid introducing contaminants into the system. Piston-to-cylinder clearance should be 0.003 in. to 0.006 in. and is checked in the same manner as for the master cylinder. Cleaning and honing procedures are the same.

To reassemble, moisten the pistons and cups with clean brake fluid and position the spring in the center of the cylinder. Install the rubber cups—flat side out—followed by the pistons—flat side in. Complete the assembly with the push rods and protective boots. The front wheel cylinder housings are secured to the backing plate by a threaded anchor pin. Torque the pin to 65 ft lbs.

Wheel Bearings

Wheel bearing removal and installation and adjustment procedures are covered in Chapter 8.

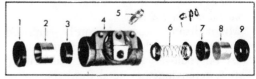

1. Pushrod boot	6. Spring
2. Piston	7. Piston cup
3. Piston cup	8. Piston
4. Housing	9. Pushrod boot
5. Fluid inlet	

Exploded view of wheel cylinder

Parking Brake
ADJUSTMENT

The rear brakes do double duty as both wheel brakes and parking brakes. Such an arrangement makes proper adjustment of the parking brakes dependent upon proper adjustment of the wheel brakes. With the wheel brakes correctly adjusted, remove the idler return spring and loosen the locknut on the convex side of the rear brake cable equalizer. Next, tighten the adjustment nut against the concave side of the equalizer until a 16 lb strand tension is achieved in the forward brake cable. Tighten the locknut and attach the idler return spring.

DISC BRAKES FRONT OR REAR

Brake Pads
INSPECTION

Brake pads should be replaced when the lining is worn to the approximate thickness of the metal part of the shoe.

REPLACEMENT

1. Drain ⅔ of the brake fluid from the master cylinder.

NOTE: *The insertion of the thicker replacement brakes will push the caliper pistons back into their bores and the resulting hydraulic action will cause a full master cylinder to overflow.*

2. Raise and support the car and remove the wheels.

3. Extract and discard the cotter pin found on the inside end of the brake pad retaining

Brake pad replacement

pin(s) (two retaining pins on heavy duty brakes).

4. Withdraw the retaining pin(s) and remove the pads.

5. Force the caliper pistons into their bores and insert the replacement pads.

6. Replace the retaining pins and secure them with new ³/₃₂ in. x ⅝ in. plated cotter pins.

7. Refill the master cylinder and bleed the system if necessary.

Calipers
REMOVAL AND OVERHAUL

1. With the vehicle securely raised and its wheels removed, disconnect the front caliper's brake hose at its support bracket and the rear unit's line from the inside caliper.

2. Tape the open end of each line to prevent dirt from entering.

3. Pull the cotter pins, retaining pins, and brake pads, and unbolt the caliper from its mounting bracket.

4. Remove the two large bolts and split the caliper case.

5. Remove the fluid transfer hole's O-rings.

6. The pistons are retained by ring-like boots. To remove them, fully depress the pistons and, with a screwdriver, lever the boots from their seats. Remove the pistons, springs, and seals.

7. Clean all parts with non-mineral based solvent and compressed air, and replace the rubber parts with those in the brake service kit.

8. Inspect the piston bores for damage or corrosion. Polish corroded bores with crocus cloth and, if this is not enough, replace the caliper.

9. Maintain the proper tolerances by referring to the following chart.

Caliper Piston-to-Bore Clearance

1—³⁄₈ in. bore	0.0035–0.009
1—⁷⁄₈ in. bore	0.0045–0.010

10. Reverse the disassembly procedure to reassemble.

NOTE: *Remember, when positioning the piston seal on the piston, that it goes in the groove nearest the piston's flat end with the lap facing the largest end. If placement is correct, the seal lips will be in the groove and not extend over the groove's step.*

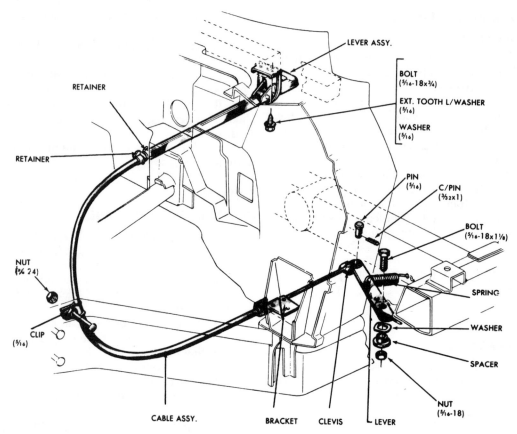

1963–64 parking brake assembly

Disc

REMOVAL AND MAINTENANCE

Braking performance is greatly affected by the disc run-out. Lateral run-out must not exceed 0.005 in. total. Discs should not be refinished to a thickness of less than 1.215 in.

Should it become necessary to replace the disc, the rivets that attach the disc to its hub must be drilled out. The replacement disc does not have to be riveted to the hub as the lug nuts adequately secure both.

Wheel Bearings

Wheel bearing removal and installation and adjustment procedures are covered in Chapter 8.

Parking Brake

ADJUSTMENT

The parking brake is a conventional drum brake located in the rear wheel disc. Adjustments are similar to those for a regular drum brake.

1. Block the front wheels. Jack the rear wheels off the ground and remove the wheels. Release the handbrake.

Checking disc run-out

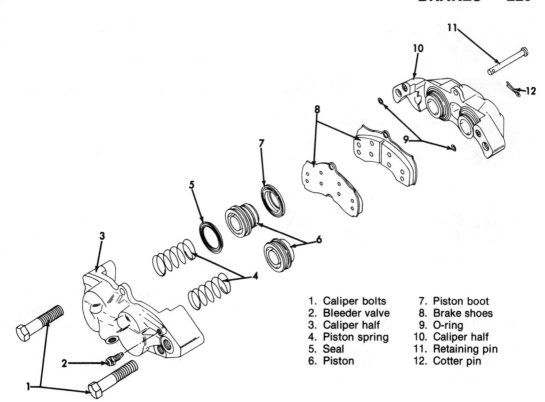

1. Caliper bolts
2. Bleeder valve
3. Caliper half
4. Piston spring
5. Seal
6. Piston
7. Piston boot
8. Brake shoes
9. O-ring
10. Caliper half
11. Retaining pin
12. Cotter pin

Exploded view of caliper

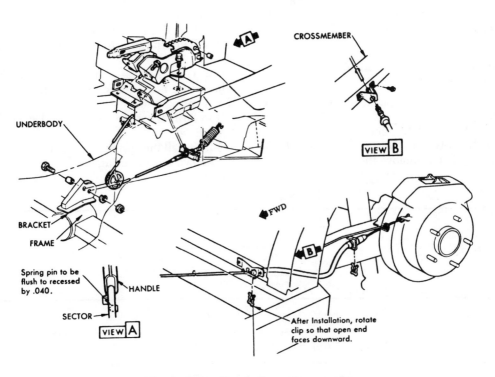

CROSSMEMBER

VIEW B

UNDERBODY

BRACKET

FRAME

Spring pin to be
flush to recessed
by .040.

HANDLE

SECTOR

VIEW A

FWD

B

After Installation, rotate
clip so that open end
faces downward.

Disc brake parking brake cable assembly

Parking brake adjustment on disc brake model

control arm and hang the caliper above the disc with wire.

3. Drill the disc retaining rivets out and remove the disc from the axle hub.

4. Insert a screwdriver into the adjusting hole and turn the screw several times to expand the shoes.

5. Push the brake shoes forward until the front shoe hold-down spring can be seen through the adjusting hole.

6. Insert a pair of needle-nosed pliers through the hole and grasp the hold-down pin. Depress the spring with a screwdriver inserted from the side and turn the pin 90° to free the spring and retainer. remove the spring and retainer.

7. Repeat this operation on the rear brake shoe.

8. Retract the shoes by turning the adjuster screw. Pull the shoes from the adjuster and remove the adjuster and spring.

9. Separate the shoes at the anchor pin and lift the shoes up and out of the housing, while allowing the straight part of the return spring to go between the outer tip of the anchor pin and the axle flange plate.

10. Lightly lubricate the backing plate shoe contact surfaces, anchor pin, and adjusting screw threads.

11. Install the return spring on the replacement shoes and position the shoes on the anchor pin.

12. Install the adjuster spring and adjuster. Turn the adjuster screw to expand the shoes.

13. Turn the axle shaft flange so that the adjustment hole aligns with the front hold-down spring pin.

14. Push the shoe forward and over the hold-down pin.

15. Install the spring and retainer over the hold-down pin and using needle-nosed pliers

2. Rotate the disc until the adjusting screw can be seen through the hole in the disc.

3. Loosen the parking brake cables at the equalizer until they go slack. Insert a screwdriver and adjust with an up-and-down motion.

4. Tighten the adjuster until the disc cannot move, then back off six to eight notches.

5. Apply the parking brake to the fourth notch. Tighten the cables at the equalizer to give a light drag with the wheel mounted.

6. Release the parking brake and check for a no drag condition.

BRAKE SHOE REMOVAL AND REPLACEMENT

1. Jack the car up and remove the wheel and tire.

2. Remove the brake caliper as previously outlined. Do not disconnect the brake line, but remove the line clip from the

Brake Specifications

Year	Brake Cylinder Bore			Drum or Disc Diameter (in.)	
	Master Cylinder (in.)	Wheel Cylinder Diameter (in.)			
		Front	Rear	Front	Rear
1963–64	1.0①	1³⁄₁₆	1.0	11.00	11.00
1965–79	1.0②	1⅞	1⅜	11.75 (Disc)	11.75 (Disc)

① Metallic brakes—⅞   ② 1.125—1977–79

again, and a screwdriver as in Step 6, depress the spring and twist the pin 90°.

16. Repeat the above step on the rear shoe. Another pair of needle-nosed pliers will have to be utilized to hold the pin in position, as head of this pin is not accessible.

17. Turn the adjuster screw to retract the shoes.

18. Install the brake disc onto the studs, making sure that the adjustment holes in the disc and flange align.

19. Install the caliper as previously outlined.

20. Adjust the parking brake as previously described.

21. Install the tire and wheel and lower the car.

22. After installation of new parking brake linings, the shoes should be burnished. At a speed of 50 mph, apply the parking brakes until a slight drag is felt. Keep the brakes on for approximately 50–60 seconds.

Body

10

DOORS

Removal and Installation
1963-67

1. Remove window cranks, armrest (1963–64), and door control knob.
2. Remove the door trim panel by carefully prying it off.
3. Scribe the door hinge position on the body.
4. Remove the hinge bolts, while an assis-

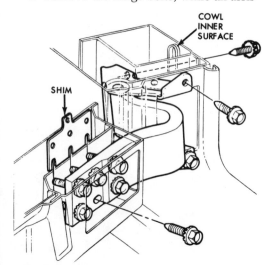

1963-67 door hinge

tant supports the door. On cars with electric windows, disconnect the wiring.
5. Remove the door, noting the position and number of any hinge shims.
6. To install, position the hinges on the previously scribed mark and hand-tighten the bolts. Remember to install any shims under the hinges.
7. Check for proper door closing and adjust the hinge bolt positioning in the slotted holes.
8. The door lock striker position is movable, should further adjustment be necessary.

1968-76

1. Remove the window crank and door lock control.
2. Remove the retaining screws and remove the door panel by carefully prying it off.
3. Remove the door lock handle screw and slide the handle off.
4. Peel the inside plastic cover off the door.
5. Remove the hinge access cover.
6. Remove the door threshold plate, the side kick panel, and the radio speaker.
7. Remove the air intake ducts, lower mast jacket cover, and the instrument panel pad and/or dash panel pad.

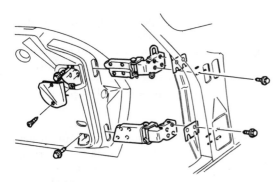

1968–79 door hinge

8. Disconnect and remove the wiring between the hinge pillar and door on cars with electric windows.

9. Scribe the door hinge position and remove the door. An assistant should be used to hold the door during removal. Note the location and number of hinge shims.

10. To install, position the hinges on the previously scribed mark and hand-tighten the bolts. Remember to install any shims under the proper hinges.

11. Check for proper door closing, and if necessary adjust hinge bolt position in the dotted holes.

12. The floor lock strike is movable for further adjustment.

ENGINE HOOD

REMOVAL AND INSTALLATION

1. Scribe the hinge positioning and the prop mounting location on the hood.

2. While an assistant supports the hood, loosen and remove the hinge and prop bracket bolts.

3. Lift hood off the car.

4. To install the hood, position the hinges on the previously scribed lines and screw bolts in hand-tight.

5. Adjust the hinge bolt positioning for correct opening and closing, then tighten the hinge bolts.

6. Install and tighten the prop to the hood.

FIBERGLASS BODY REPAIR

The process of effecting repairs to the Stingray body is one of filling a damaged area with either glass cloth and resin or plastic solder. While this may appear to be an oversimplification, it is interesting to note that the

factory interpretations of body damage are restricted to the two general categories of minor and major. Repair kits, appropriate to the definitions, are made available accordingly.

Minor repairs are made with the Plastic Solder Repair Kit. Proper use of the materials contained in this kit will produce an easy, quick, and lasting repair of small cracks and holes, as well as surface imperfections.

Major repairs are required for large holes, torn panels, and separated joints. Such repairs require the adhesive qualities of the resin and the reinforcing qualities of the glass fibers found in the Resin Repair Kit. This kit contains resin, hardener, thixatrope, fiberglass cloth, mixing utensils, and protective creams.

The cream protects the skin from a noncontagious form of dermatitis known as occupational, or contact dermatitis. Improvements in resin formulas have virtually eliminated this problem but the creams are still included in the kit for those who may be sensitive to the resins or dust. While the creams are not generally required when

Mixing plastic solder

Applying hardener/resin to fiberglass cloth

using the plastic solder kit, their application is recommended whenever the materials in the resin kit are used. To obtain maximum benefit from them, it is necessary to first wash, then dry the hands thoroughly. Next, squeeze about ½ in. of no. 71 cream into the cuticle, between the fingers, and around the wrists, spreading it evenly and lightly until it disappears. Apply a second coat and then set the cream by holding both hands under cold running water. When the cream has set, apply the no. 55 cream over the no. 71 cream in the same manner. Do not rub your hands together when rinsing in water.

In working with fiberglass, remember that the materials being used are potentially harmful to the careless worker. The resin mixture should be removed from the hands as soon as possible and imperatively before the mixture starts to gel. This gel condition may be observed by the action of the material. To ensure complete removal of resin, apply lacquer thinner followed by a careful washing in soap and water. Minor skin irritation from glass and powdered, cured resin can be minimized by washing in cold water. Avoid getting the resin material on clothing.

Minute particles of glass fibers are potentially harmful if inhaled into the lungs, so always use respirators when grinding. It is also advisable to use a belt sander with a vacuum attachment to control dust. As an added safeguard, always work with resin mixtures in well-ventilated areas to reduce the effects of toxic fumes.

An important point to remember when working on the Corvette body, is to always use materials that are comparable to those being repaired. Repair kits, conforming to original equipment specifications, may be ordered from dealers. Keep the work area, materials, and tools clean and dry, as dirt or moisture can adversely affect the chemical reactions in fiberglass repair.

Prior to making repairs, look for hidden damage such as hairline cracks and other breakage. This is best accomplished by applying pressure around the obviously damaged area. Check for minor damage around exhaust pipes, grille, and other points of wear. Detection at this point can prevent additional repairs at a later date.

MINOR REPAIRS

Minor repairs are those necessary to correct surface imperfections. These are best made by using the materials found in the Plastic Solder Kit. To properly utilize this kit, it is necessary to first remove the exterior finish from the damaged area with paint remover or a power sander. After checking for additional damage, mix the Plastic Solder materials according to kit directions and apply the finished mixture with a putty knife or rubber squeegee. Work into the damaged area, building it up to the desired contour. It may be necessary to use several ½ in. layers for deep filing and on vertical surfaces. Complete the repair in the usual manner of grinding, sanding and painting.

MAJOR REPAIRS

The procedure used for making major repairs is basic for repairing any fiberglass panel or component and is made using the Resin Repair Kit.

Check for hidden damage as previously outlined. When the initial inspection has been made, use paint remover to strip the finish from the damaged area and look for additional breakage.

With the second inspection completed, the actual repair work is begun by first grinding the damaged area so that it forms a "V" at the broken or cracked portion. Shape the sides of the "V" to a shallow pitch so that it will provide a maximum bonding surface.

If the rear of the damaged area is accessible, clean behind it to allow the use of resin-saturated glass cloth laminates on both sides of the damage. Cut fiberglass cloth to size, using a minimum of five layers for the average repair.

Mix resin and hardener, one part hardener to four parts resin. Thicken the material if needed, by adding thixatrope. Cleanliness must be observed at all times during the operation. Make certain that all containers are clean and dry and that resin and hardener cans are kept closed when not in use. Also do not use waxed cups for mixing or allow resin to enter hardener can or vice versa.

Prepare the laminates by saturating the layers of fiberglass cloth with the resin mixture. Apply the laiminates to the panel, making certain that all wrinkles are smoothed out and the general contour of the area is followed.

With the laminates in place, use heat lamps to cure the repaired area. Place the lamps no closer than 12 in. away from the repair and allow at least 15–20 minutes curing time. Trim the repair to shape when the gel stage is reached. When the laminates have cured, complete the normal finishing procedures. Small pits or surface irregularities can be covered with plastic solder.

SPECIFIC REPAIR

Scratches, Spot Refinishing

Minor scrapes and scratches will normally require nothing more than a paint refinishing job. For scratches that have gone through to the plastic remove all paint from the area around the scratch with lacquer removing solvent. Next, feather-sand the area, first with no. 220 wet or dry paper. Cutting too deeply into the fiberglass mat during the sanding process will make it necessary to change the repair procedure to that suggested for dents and pits.

Use a surface preparatory solvent or its equivalent for initial clean-up of the repair area, then follow with a tack rag. Use non-staining type masking tape on the body to mask and protect surrounding areas when painting. Complete the refinishing as outlined in the paint refinishing portion of this chapter.

Dents or Pits and Cracked Glaze Coat

A heavy glancing blow to the Corvette body will usually result in a large pit or indentation in the panel. The following repair procedure for this type of damage may also be used to remedy cracks in the glaze or finish coat of the paint, however, it should only be used to effect a plastic build-up when the damaged area is neither extensive nor pierced.

To begin this repair, first use lacquer

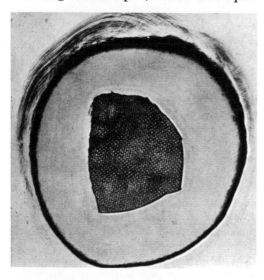

Back-up laminates under damage

thinner or its equivalent to remove the paint. Next provide a good bonding surface by scuffing the area surrounding the damage. Use the preparatory solvent for the initial clean-up of the repair area, then finish with a tack rag.

Fill surface imperfections with plastic solder, then feather-sand the repaired area with no. 220 sandpaper and finish-sand with no. 320. Complete refinishing as outlined in this chapter.

Holes

Due to the strength of reinforced plastic, this type of damage is not common. Grind or file away all cracked or splintered material around the hole and bevel the edges to a 30° angle. Use lacquer solvent to remove the exterior paint. Completely remove all dirt, deadener, and paint from the underside of the damaged panel for a 4 in. area around the hole, then scuff the plastic surface on both sides of the panel, using no. 80-d sandpaper.

Cut two pieces of glass cloth that are large enough to overlap the hole. These pieces will be used for back-up lamination. If the damaged panel is rather thick, an appropriate number of laminates should be tailored to the approximate shape of the hole and used for build-up. The amount of resin needed for the backup inserts will be determined by the size of the damaged area. Use two back-up laminations on the underside of the panel and complete the repair procedure.

Use plastic solder for final filling. Block-sand the plastic fill with no. 80-d sandpaper and finish-sand with no. 220 and no. 320 wet or dry sandpaper. Prepare the area for paint refinishing.

Cracks

It should be noted that the best results will be obtained when the ambient temperature is at least 70° F to 75° F. Begin the repair by removing the broken portion of the panel, cutting along the break line with a hacksaw blade. Use lacquer remover or its equivalent to remove the paint from a distance, 2–3 in. from the fracture on the underside of both portions of the panel. Scuff the area clean.

Grind or file away all cracked and fractured material along the break. Bevel the edges of the fracture at a 30° angle using a file or grinder and scuff the plastic surfaces long the edge of the break. Align the fractured panels with C-clamps, leaving ⅛ in. clearance for alignment.

Cut a strip of fiberglass cloth to a size sufficient to overlap the fracture by 1–2 in. on all sides. Prepare the plastic mixture, according to resin repair kit directions and saturate the glass fiber cloth with the mixture. Squeeze the excess mixture from the cloth. Using excessive amounts of plastic should be avoided since the strength of the patch is directly proportional to the glass fiber content of the patch.

Should a low spot exist, prepare another plastic mixture, mixing resin and hardener throughly. Add short fibers cut from glass cloth to this mixture to give it a putty-like consistency. Using a spatula, liberally apply the plastic mixture to the fracture and the surrounding area, depositing enough material build-up to allow for sanding and filing.

When the patch has hardened, shape it to conform with the general contour of the panel by filing or grinding. Avoid gouging the repair or the surrounding area. Fill any imperfections that appear with plastic solder. When the fill has sufficiently hardened, finish-sand the surface and paint.

Crack at Panel Junction

A minimum of time and effort is required to repair a crack at the junction of two panels. First step is to provide a good bonding strip by cutting all splintered material from the crack and sanding the adjacent area. Fill the crack with plastic solder. When the patch has hardened, sand the area to match the contour of the surrounding panel.

Panel Replacement

In cases of extensive damage it is often advisable to install a replacement panel. Such repair panels are available for this purpose. The complete panel may be installed or sections may be cut from it to accommodate the necessary repair. Proper alignment should be checked prior to plastic application by fitting the panel and installing all attaching parts. When availability of the correct panel has been assured, you may then cut out the damaged section with a hacksaw blade. Remove dirt, deadener, and paint from the underside of the old panel for a distance of 2–3 in. back from the attaching line. Bevel the mating edges at a 30° so that a single "V" butt joint will be formed on the exterior surface when the pieces are joined. Perform any necessary reshaping to assure a close fit of the replacement section.

Cut two back-up pieces of glass fiber cloth of a sufficient size to run the entire length of the joint and overlap the junction line on either side by 2–3 in. Align the replacement section and clamp in place, forming a closed "V" butt joint at the panel junction. In cases where panels cannot be clamped, use $3/16$ in. bolts with large washers on inner and outer panels, or straps and sheet metal screws.

Prepare a sufficient amount of liquid plastic in an un-waxed paper cup, as outlined in resin repair procedures. Saturate the back-up plies of cloth, then use a squeegee to remove any excess plastic from the cloth. Place the saturated plies on the underside of the damaged panels and, if necessary, use paper to hold them in place until the plastic gels. For fill purposes on exterior surfaces, use glass cloth or another plastic mixture of resin, hardener and ½ in. lengths of cut glass fiber mixed to a putty-like consistency. Use the saturated glass cloth or reinforced plastic material to fill the "V" groove; building the area with sufficient material to allow for finish operations. When the patch has hardened, file or sand the patch to the general body contour using no. 80-d. Finish-sand and prepare for painting.

Paint Refinishing

Lacquer preparations and painting procedures for the stingray plastic body are the same as for metal bodies. To facilitate paint matching, it is easier to refinish panels to the nearest break line. Wipe the entire work area with a clean cloth soaked with the preparatory solvent to remove all traces of wax, polish and grease, then wipe surface dry with a second clean cloth. The old paint finish may be removed by sanding with coarse sandpaper or using solvent. Use no. 220 wet or dry sandpaper for initial feather-sanding or paint edges and finish with no. 440 wet or dry papers.

To obtain the best results, always feather-sand from the outside of the paint break toward the center so as to eliminate the possibility of low spots in the paint. This done, surface preparation may be carried out using first, the preparatory solvent and then a tack rag to thoroughly clean the surface. Avoid touching the surface with bare hands from this point on, as skin oil deposited on the surface of the panel may adversely affect the adhesion of the paint to the body.

With surface preparation completed, spray the bare plastic and feathered areas with a mixture of one part primer-surfacer to two parts thinner. Apply two or more medium coats and allow each to flash or dull before applying each succeeding coat. Allow at least one hour between the application of the final coat and the beginning of sanding operations. Best results will be obtained if no. 320 wet or dry sandpaper is used. If dry sanding is preferred, then no. 360 paper is called for.

Should pinpoint imperfections become evident at this time, knife them out with putty and allow ½ hours for drying. Finish-sand when dry. These small pits in the plastic may be filled before the primer-surfacer is applied. Following sanding operations, wipe clean and fill the imperfections with plastic solder. This material is faster than body glazing compounds when they are used on the Corvette, although both are acceptable. In

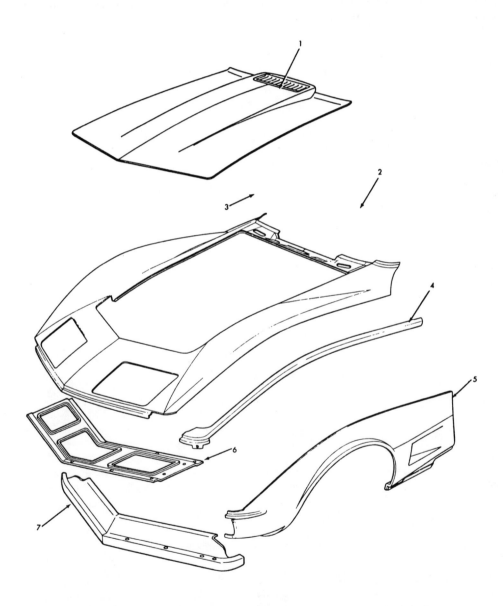

1. Panel—hood
2. Panel—access door
3. Panel—grille
4. Boding strip—front fender upper to lower
5. Panel—front fender lower rear
6. Panel—lower
7. Panel—lower ext.

1973–75 front body panels

fact, most glazing putty failures are due to insufficient drying time for the putty or excessively heavy applications.

When the surface imperfections have been removed, dust the repaired area and spray with one coat of make-ready sealer, reduced one part to one and a half parts thinner. To ensure maximum sealing, allow at least 30 minutes to dry. The surface may be scuffed lightly with no. 440 sandpaper to remove nibs, then dusted and tack-wiped. Spray the primed surface in three or four wet, double-color coats. Let each coat flash before spraying the succeeding coat.

Allow a minimum of four hours for drying, preferably overnight; then handrub with rubbing compound or machine polish using machine compound no. 14. Complete the final finishing by hand or machine polishing with liquid polish or dry-buff with a polishing disc or lamb's wool bonnet. Allow thirty days before waxing to ensure hardening of the lacquer and dispersal of trapped solvents.

Troubleshooting

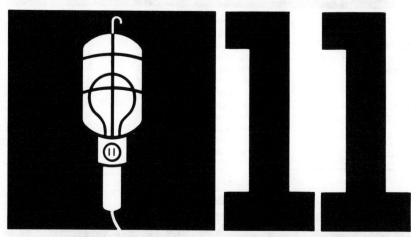

This section is designed to aid in the quick, accurate diagnosis of automotive problems. While automotive repairs can be made by many people, accurate troubleshooting is a rare skill for the amateur and professional alike.

In its simplest state, troubleshooting is an exercise in logic. It is essential to realize that an automobile is really composed of a series of systems. Some of these systems are interrelated; others are not. Automobiles operate within a framework of logical rules and physical laws, and the key to troubleshooting is a good understanding of all the automotive systems.

This section breaks the car or truck down into its component systems, allowing the problem to be isolated. The charts and diagnostic road maps list the most common problems and the most probable causes of trouble. Obviously it would be impossible to list every possible problem that could happen along with every possible cause, but it will locate MOST problems and eliminate a lot of unnecessary guesswork. The systematic format will locate problems within a given system, but, because many automotive systems are interrelated, the solution to your particular problem may be found in a number of systems on the car or truck.

USING THE TROUBLESHOOTING CHARTS

This book contains all of the specific information that the average do-it-yourself mechanic needs to repair and maintain his or her car or truck. The troubleshooting charts are designed to be used in conjunction with the specific procedures and information in the text. For instance, troubleshooting a point-type ignition system is fairly standard for all models, but you may be directed to the text to find procedures for troubleshooting an individual type of electronic ignition. You will also have to refer to the specification charts throughout the book for specifications applicable to your car or truck.

TOOLS AND EQUIPMENT

The tools illustrated in Chapter 1 (plus two more diagnostic pieces) will be adequate to troubleshoot most problems. The two other tools needed are a voltmeter and an ohmmeter. These can be purchased separately or in combination, known as a VOM meter.

In the event that other tools are required, they will be noted in the procedures.

Troubleshooting Engine Problems

See Chapters 2, 3, 4 for more information and service procedures.

Index to Systems

System	To Test	Group
Battery	Engine need not be running	1
Starting system	Engine need not be running	2
Primary electrical system	Engine need not be running	3
Secondary electrical system	Engine need not be running	4
Fuel system	Engine need not be running	5
Engine compression	Engine need not be running	6
Engine vacuum	Engine must be running	7
Secondary electrical system	Engine must be running	8
Valve train	Engine must be running	9
Exhaust system	Engine must be running	10
Cooling system	Engine must be running	11
Engine lubrication	Engine must be running	12

Index to Problems

Problem: Symptom	Begin at Specific Diagnosis, Number ____
Engine Won't Start:	
Starter doesn't turn	1.1, 2.1
Starter turns, engine doesn't	2.1
Starter turns engine very slowly	1.1, 2.4
Starter turns engine normally	3.1, 4.1
Starter turns engine very quickly	6.1
Engine fires intermittently	4.1
Engine fires consistently	5.1, 6.1
Engine Runs Poorly:	
Hard starting	3.1, 4.1, 5.1, 8.1
Rough idle	4.1, 5.1, 8.1
Stalling	3.1, 4.1, 5.1, 8.1
Engine dies at high speeds	4.1, 5.1
Hesitation (on acceleration from standing stop)	5.1, 8.1
Poor pickup	4.1, 5.1, 8.1
Lack of power	3.1, 4.1, 5.1, 8.1
Backfire through the carburetor	4.1, 8.1, 9.1
Backfire through the exhaust	4.1, 8.1, 9.1
Blue exhaust gases	6.1, 7.1
Black exhaust gases	5.1
Running on (after the ignition is shut off)	3.1, 8.1
Susceptible to moisture	4.1
Engine misfires under load	4.1, 7.1, 8.4, 9.1
Engine misfires at speed	4.1, 8.4
Engine misfires at idle	3.1, 4.1, 5.1, 7.1, 8.4

Sample Section

Test and Procedure	Results and Indications	Proceed to
4.1—Check for spark: Hold each spark plug wire approximately ¼″ from ground with gloves or a heavy, dry rag. Crank the engine and observe the spark.	→ If no spark is evident:	→4.2
	→ If spark is good in some cases:	→4.3
	→ If spark is good in all cases:	→4.6

Specific Diagnosis

This section is arranged so that following each test, instructions are given to proceed to another, until a problem is diagnosed.

Section 1—Battery

Test and Procedure	Results and Indications	Proceed to
1.1—Inspect the battery visually for case condition (corrosion, cracks) and water level.	If case is cracked, replace battery:	**1.4**
	If the case is intact, remove corrosion with a solution of baking soda and water (**CAUTION:** *do not get the solution into the battery*), and fill with water:	**1.2**

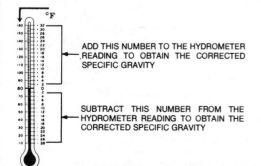

DIRT ON TOP OF BATTERY

CORROSION

PLUGGED VENT

LOOSE CABLE OR POSTS

CRACKS

LOW WATER LEVEL

Inspect the battery case

1.2—Check the battery cable connections: Insert a screwdriver between the battery post and the cable clamp. Turn the headlights on high beam, and observe them as the screwdriver is gently twisted to ensure good metal to metal contact.	If the lights brighten, remove and clean the clamp and post; coat the post with petroleum jelly, install and tighten the clamp:	**1.4**
	If no improvement is noted:	**1.3**

TESTING BATTERY CABLE CONNECTIONS USING A SCREWDRIVER

1.3—Test the state of charge of the battery using an individual cell tester or hydrometer.	If indicated, charge the battery. **NOTE:** *If no obvious reason exists for the low state of charge (i.e., battery age, prolonged storage), proceed to:*	**1.4**

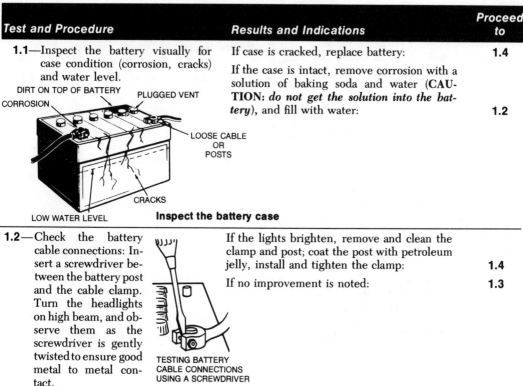

°F

ADD THIS NUMBER TO THE HYDROMETER READING TO OBTAIN THE CORRECTED SPECIFIC GRAVITY

SUBTRACT THIS NUMBER FROM THE HYDROMETER READING TO OBTAIN THE CORRECTED SPECIFIC GRAVITY

Specific Gravity (@ 80° F.)

Minimum		Battery Charge
1.260	....	100% Charged
1.230	....	75% Charged
1.200	....	50% Charged
1.170	....	25% Charged
1.140	....	Very Little Power Left
1.110	....	Completely Discharged

The effects of temperature on battery specific gravity (left) and amount of battery charge in relation to specific gravity (right)

1.4—Visually inspect battery cables for cracking, bad connection to ground, or bad connection to starter.	If necessary, tighten connections or replace the cables:	
		2.1

Section 2—Starting System
See Chapter 3 for service procedures

Test and Procedure	Results and Indications	Proceed to
Note: Tests in Group 2 are performed with coil high tension lead disconnected to prevent accidental starting.		
2.1—Test the starter motor and solenoid: Connect a jumper from the battery post of the solenoid (or relay) to the starter post of the solenoid (or relay).	If starter turns the engine normally:	**2.2**
	If the starter buzzes, or turns the engine very slowly:	**2.4**
	If no response, replace the solenoid (or relay).	**3.1**
	If the starter turns, but the engine doesn't, ensure that the flywheel ring gear is intact. If the gear is undamaged, replace the starter drive.	**3.1**
2.2—Determine whether ignition override switches are functioning properly (clutch start switch, neutral safety switch), by connecting a jumper across the switch(es), and turning the ignition switch to "start".	If starter operates, adjust or replace switch:	**3.1**
	If the starter doesn't operate:	**2.3**
2.3—Check the ignition switch "start" position: Connect a 12V test lamp or voltmeter between the starter post of the solenoid (or relay) and ground. Turn the ignition switch to the "start" position, and jiggle the key.	If the lamp doesn't light or the meter needle doesn't move when the switch is turned, check the ignition switch for loose connections, cracked insulation, or broken wires. Repair or replace as necessary:	**3.1**
	If the lamp flickers or needle moves when the key is jiggled, replace the ignition switch.	**3.3**

Checking the ignition switch "start" position

STARTER RELAY
(IF EQUIPPED)

Test and Procedure	Results and Indications	Proceed to
2.4—Remove and bench test the starter, according to specifications in the engine electrical section.	If the starter does not meet specifications, repair or replace as needed:	**3.1**
	If the starter is operating properly:	**2.5**
2.5—Determine whether the engine can turn freely: Remove the spark plugs, and check for water in the cylinders. Check for water on the dipstick, or oil in the radiator. Attempt to turn the engine using an 18″ flex drive and socket on the crankshaft pulley nut or bolt.	If the engine will turn freely only with the spark plugs out, and hydrostatic lock (water in the cylinders) is ruled out, check valve timing:	**9.2**
	If engine will not turn freely, and it is known that the clutch and transmission are free, the engine must be disassembled for further evaluation:	**Chapter 3**

Section 3—Primary Electrical System

Test and Procedure	Results and Indications	Proceed to
3.1—Check the ignition switch "on" position: Connect a jumper wire between the distributor side of the coil and ground, and a 12V test lamp between the switch side of the coil and ground. Remove the high tension lead from the coil. Turn the ignition switch on and jiggle the key.	If the lamp lights:	**3.2**
	If the lamp flickers when the key is jiggled, replace the ignition switch:	**3.3**
	If the lamp doesn't light, check for loose or open connections. If none are found, remove the ignition switch and check for continuity. If the switch is faulty, replace it:	**3.3**

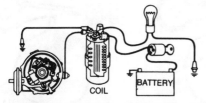

Checking the ignition switch "on" position

3.2—Check the ballast resistor or resistance wire for an open circuit, using an ohmmeter. See Chapter 3 for specific tests.	Replace the resistor or resistance wire if the resistance is zero. **NOTE:** *Some ignition systems have no ballast resistor.*	**3.3**

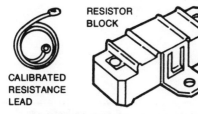

Two types of resistors

3.3—On point-type ignition systems, visually inspect the breaker points for burning, pitting or excessive wear. Gray coloring of the point contact surfaces is normal. Rotate the crankshaft until the contact heel rests on a high point of the distributor cam and adjust the point gap to specifications. On electronic ignition models, remove the distributor cap and visually inspect the armature. Ensure that the armature pin is in place, and that the armature is on tight and rotates when the engine is cranked. Make sure there are no cracks, chips or rounded edges on the armature.	If the breaker points are intact, clean the contact surfaces with fine emery cloth, and adjust the point gap to specifications. If the points are worn, replace them. On electronic systems, replace any parts which appear defective. If condition persists:	**3.4**

Test and Procedure	Results and Indications	Proceed to
3.4—On point-type ignition systems, connect a dwell-meter between the distributor primary lead and ground. Crank the engine and observe the point dwell angle. On electronic ignition systems, conduct a stator (magnetic pickup assembly) test. See Chapter 3.	On point-type systems, adjust the dwell angle if necessary. **NOTE:** *Increasing the point gap decreases the dwell angle and vice-versa.*	**3.6**
	If the dwell meter shows little or no reading;	**3.5**
	On electronic ignition systems, if the stator is bad, replace the stator. If the stator is good, proceed to the other tests in Chapter 3.	

CLOSE OPEN

NORMAL DWELL

WIDE GAP

SMALL DWELL

INSUFFICIENT DWELL

NARROW GAP

LARGE DWELL

EXCESSIVE DWELL

Dwell is a function of point gap

3.5—On the point-type ignition systems, check the condenser for short: connect an ohmeter across the condenser body and the pigtail lead.	If any reading other than infinite is noted, replace the condenser	**3.6**

OHMMETER

Checking the condenser for short

3.6—Test the coil primary resistance: On point-type ignition systems, connect an ohmmeter across the coil primary terminals, and read the resistance on the low scale. Note whether an external ballast resistor or resistance wire is used. On electronic ignition systems, test the coil primary resistance as in Chapter 3.	Point-type ignition coils utilizing ballast resistors or resistance wires should have approximately 1.0 ohms resistance. Coils with internal resistors should have approximately 4.0 ohms resistance. If values far from the above are noted, replace the coil.	**4.1**

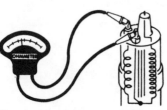

Check the coil primary resistance

Section 4—Secondary Electrical System

See Chapters 2–3 for service procedures

Test and Procedure	Results and Indications	Proceed to
4.1—Check for spark: Hold each spark plug wire approximately ¼" from ground with gloves or a heavy, dry rag. Crank the engine, and observe the spark.	If no spark is evident:	**4.2**
	If spark is good in some cylinders:	**4.3**
	If spark is good in all cylinders:	**4.6**

Check for spark at the plugs

4.2—Check for spark at the coil high tension lead: Remove the coil high tension lead from the distributor and position it approximately ¼" from ground. Crank the engine and observe spark. **CAUTION: *This test should not be performed on engines equipped with electronic ignition.***	If the spark is good and consistent:	**4.3**
	If the spark is good but intermittent, test the primary electrical system starting at 3.3:	**3.3**
	If the spark is weak or non-existent, replace the coil high tension lead, clean and tighten all connections and retest. If no improvement is noted:	**4.4**
4.3—Visually inspect the distributor cap and rotor for burned or corroded contacts, cracks, carbon tracks, or moisture. Also check the fit of the rotor on the distributor shaft (where applicable).	If moisture is present, dry thoroughly, and retest per 4.1:	**4.1**
	If burned or excessively corroded contacts, cracks, or carbon tracks are noted, replace the defective part(s) and retest per 4.1:	**4.1**
	If the rotor and cap appear intact, or are only slightly corroded, clean the contacts thoroughly (including the cap towers and spark plug wire ends) and retest per 4.1:	
	If the spark is good in all cases:	**4.6**
	If the spark is poor in all cases:	**4.5**

Inspect the distributor cap and rotor

Test and Procedure	Results and Indications	Proceed to
4.4—Check the coil secondary resistance: On point-type systems connect an ohmmeter across the distributor side of the coil and the coil tower. Read the resistance on the high scale of the ohmmeter. On electronic ignition systems, see Chapter 3 for specific tests.	The resistance of a satisfactory coil should be between 4,000 and 10,000 ohms. If resistance is considerably higher (i.e., 40,000 ohms) replace the coil and retest per 4.1. **NOTE:** *This does not apply to high performance coils.*	

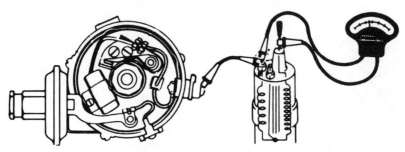

Testing the coil secondary resistance

4.5—Visually inspect the spark plug wires for cracking or brittleness. Ensure that no two wires are positioned so as to cause induction firing (adjacent and parallel). Remove each wire, one by one, and check resistance with an ohmmeter.	Replace any cracked or brittle wires. If any of the wires are defective, replace the entire set. Replace any wires with excessive resistance (over $8000\,\Omega$ per foot for suppression wire), and separate any wires that might cause induction firing.	**4.6**

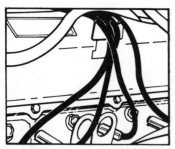

Misfiring can be the result of spark plug leads to adjacent, consecutively firing cylinders running parallel and too close together

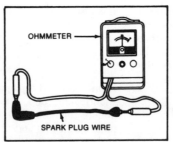

On point-type ignition systems, check the spark plug wires as shown. On electronic ignitions, do not remove the wire from the distributor cap terminal; instead, test through the cap

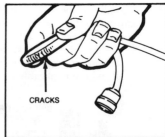

Spark plug wires can be checked visually by bending them in a loop over your finger. This will reveal any cracks, burned or broken insulation. Any wire with cracked insulation should be replaced

4.6—Remove the spark plugs, noting the cylinders from which they were removed, and evaluate according to the color photos in the middle of this book.	See following.	**See following.**

Test and Procedure	Results and Indications	Proceed to
4.7—Examine the location of all the plugs.	The following diagrams illustrate some of the conditions that the location of plugs will reveal.	4.8

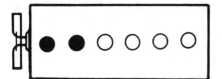

Two adjacent plugs are fouled in a 6-cylinder engine, 4-cylinder engine or either bank of a V-8. This is probably due to a blown head gasket between the two cylinders

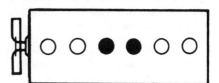

The two center plugs in a 6-cylinder engine are fouled. Raw fuel may be "boiled" out of the carburetor into the intake manifold after the engine is shut-off. Stop-start driving can also foul the center plugs, due to overly rich mixture. Proper float level, a new float needle and seat or use of an insulating spacer may help this problem

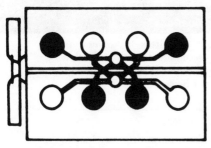

An unbalanced carburetor is indicated. Following the fuel flow on this particular design shows that the cylinders fed by the right-hand barrel are fouled from overly rich mixture, while the cylinders fed by the left-hand barrel are normal

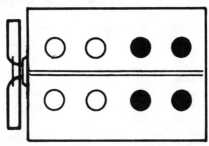

If the four rear plugs are overheated, a cooling system problem is suggested. A thorough cleaning of the cooling system may restore coolant circulation and cure the problem

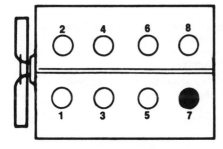

Finding one plug overheated may indicate an intake manifold leak near the affected cylinder. If the overheated plug is the second of two adjacent, consecutively firing plugs, it could be the result of ignition cross-firing. Separating the leads to these two plugs will eliminate cross-fire

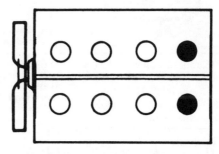

Occasionally, the two rear plugs in large, lightly used V-8's will become oil fouled. High oil consumption and smoky exhaust may also be noticed. It is probably due to plugged oil drain holes in the rear of the cylinder head, causing oil to be sucked in around the valve stems. This usually occurs in the rear cylinders first, because the engine slants that way

Test and Procedure	Results and Indications	Proceed to
4.8—Determine the static ignition timing. Using the crankshaft pulley timing marks as a guide, locate top dead center on the compression stroke of the number one cylinder.	The rotor should be pointing toward the No. 1 tower in the distributor cap, and, on electronic ignitions, the armature spoke for that cylinder should be lined up with the stator.	**4.8**
4.9—Check coil polarity: Connect a voltmeter negative lead to the coil high tension lead, and the positive lead to ground (**NOTE:** *Reverse the hook-up for positive ground systems*). Crank the engine momentarily. Checking coil polarity	If the voltmeter reads up-scale, the polarity is correct: If the voltmeter reads down-scale, reverse the coil polarity (switch the primary leads):	**5.1** **5.1**

Section 5—Fuel System
See Chapter 4 for service procedures

Test and Procedure	Results and Indications	Proceed to
5.1—Determine that the air filter is functioning efficiently: Hold paper elements up to a strong light, and attempt to see light through the filter.	Clean permanent air filters in solvent (or manufacturer's recommendation), and allow to dry. Replace paper elements through which light cannot be seen:	**5.2**
5.2—Determine whether a flooding condition exists: Flooding is identified by a strong gasoline odor, and excessive gasoline present in the throttle bore(s) of the carburetor. If the engine floods repeatedly, check the choke butterfly flap	If flooding is not evident: If flooding is evident, permit the gasoline to dry for a few moments and restart. If flooding doesn't recur: If flooding is persistent:	**5.3** **5.7** **5.5**
5.3—Check that fuel is reaching the carburetor: Detach the fuel line at the carburetor inlet. Hold the end of the line in a cup (not styrofoam), and crank the engine. Check the fuel pump by disconnecting the output line (fuel pump-to-carburetor) at the carburetor and operating the starter briefly	If fuel flows smoothly: If fuel doesn't flow (**NOTE:** *Make sure that there is fuel in the tank*), or flows erratically:	**5.7** **5.4**

Test and Procedure	Results and Indications	Proceed to
5.4—Test the fuel pump: Disconnect all fuel lines from the fuel pump. Hold a finger over the input fitting, crank the engine (with electric pump, turn the ignition or pump on); and feel for suction.	If suction is evident, blow out the fuel line to the tank with low pressure compressed air until bubbling is heard from the fuel filler neck. Also blow out the carburetor fuel line (both ends disconnected):	5.7
	If no suction is evident, replace or repair the fuel pump: **NOTE:** *Repeated oil fouling of the spark plugs, or a no-start condition, could be the result of a ruptured vacuum booster pump diaphragm, through which oil or gasoline is being drawn into the intake manifold (where applicable).*	5.7
5.5—Occasionally, small specks of dirt will clog the small jets and orifices in the carburetor. With the engine cold, hold a flat piece of wood or similar material over the carburetor, where possible, and crank the engine.	If the engine starts, but runs roughly the engine is probably not run enough. If the engine won't start:	5.9
5.6—Check the needle and seat: Tap the carburetor in the area of the needle and seat.	If flooding stops, a gasoline additive (e.g., Gumout) will often cure the problem:	5.7
	If flooding continues, check the fuel pump for excessive pressure at the carburetor (according to specifications). If the pressure is normal, the needle and seat must be removed and checked, and/or the float level adjusted:	5.7
5.7—Test the accelerator pump by looking into the throttle bores while operating the throttle. **Check for gas at the carburetor by looking down the carburetor throat while someone moves the accelerator**	If the accelerator pump appears to be operating normally:	5.8
	If the accelerator pump is not operating, the pump must be reconditioned. Where possible, service the pump with the carburetor(s) installed on the engine. If necessary, remove the carburetor. Prior to removal:	5.8
5.8—Determine whether the carburetor main fuel system is functioning: Spray a commercial starting fluid into the carburetor while attempting to start the engine.	If the engine starts, runs for a few seconds, and dies:	5.9
	If the engine doesn't start:	6.1

Test and Procedure	Results and Indications	Proceed to
5.9—Uncommon fuel system malfunctions: See below:	If the problem is solved:	**6.1**
	If the problem remains, remove and recondition the carburetor.	

Condition	Indication	Test	Prevailing Weather Conditions	Remedy
Vapor lock	Engine will not restart shortly after running.	Cool the components of the fuel system until the engine starts. Vapor lock can be cured faster by draping a wet cloth over a mechanical fuel pump.	Hot to very hot	Ensure that the exhaust manifold heat control valve is operating. Check with the vehicle manufacturer for the recommended solution to vapor lock on the model in question.
Carburetor icing	Engine will not idle, stalls at low speeds.	Visually inspect the throttle plate area of the throttle bores for frost.	High humidity, 32–40° F.	Ensure that the exhaust manifold heat control valve is operating, and that the intake manifold heat riser is not blocked.
Water in the fuel	Engine sputters and stalls; may not start.	Pump a small amount of fuel into a glass jar. Allow to stand, and inspect for droplets or a layer of water.	High humidity, extreme temperature changes.	For droplets, use one or two cans of commercial gas line anti-freeze. For a layer of water, the tank must be drained, and the fuel lines blown out with compressed air.

Section 6—Engine Compression
See Chapter 3 for service procedures

6.1—Test engine compression: Remove all spark plugs. Block the throttle wide open. Insert a compression gauge into a spark plug port, crank the engine to obtain the maximum reading, and record.	If compression is within limits on all cylinders:	**7.1**
	If gauge reading is extremely low on all cylinders:	**6.2**
	If gauge reading is low on one or two cylinders: (If gauge readings are identical and low on two or more adjacent cylinders, the head gasket must be replaced.)	**6.2**

Checking compression

6.2—Test engine compression (wet): Squirt approximately 30 cc. of engine oil into each cylinder, and retest per 6.1.	If the readings improve, worn or cracked rings or broken pistons are indicated:	**See Chapter 3**
	If the readings do not improve, burned or excessively carboned valves or a jumped timing chain are indicated:	**7.1**
	NOTE: *A jumped timing chain is often indicated by difficult cranking.*	

Section 7—Engine Vacuum
See Chapter 3 for service procedures

Test and Procedure	Results and Indications	Proceed to
7.1—Attach a vacuum gauge to the intake manifold beyond the throttle plate. Start the engine, and observe the action of the needle over the range of engine speeds.	See below.	**See below**

INDICATION: normal engine in good condition

Proceed to: 8.1

Normal engine
Gauge reading: steady, from 17–22 in./Hg.

INDICATION: sticking valves or ignition miss

Proceed to: 9.1, 8.3

Sticking valves
Gauge reading: intermittent fluctuation at idle

INDICATION: late ignition or valve timing, low compression, stuck throttle valve, leaking carburetor or manifold gasket

Proceed to: 6.1

Incorrect valve timing
Gauge reading: low (10–15 in./Hg) but steady

INDICATION: improper carburetor adjustment or minor intake leak.

Proceed to: 7.2

Carburetor requires adjustment
Gauge reading: drifting needle

INDICATION: ignition miss, blown cylinder head gasket, leaking valve or weak valve spring

Proceed to: 8.3, 6.1

Blown head gasket
Gauge reading: needle fluctuates as engine speed increases

INDICATION: burnt valve or faulty valve clearance. Needle will fall when defective valve operates

Proceed to: 9.1

Burnt or leaking valves
Gauge reading: steady needle, but drops regularly

INDICATION: choked muffler, excessive back pressure in system

Proceed to: 10.1

Clogged exhaust system
Gauge reading: gradual drop in reading at idle

INDICATION: worn valve guides

Proceed to: 9.1

Worn valve guides
Gauge reading: needle vibrates excessively at idle, but steadies as engine speed increases

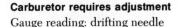

White pointer = steady gauge hand   Black pointer = fluctuating gauge hand

Test and Procedure	Results and Indications	Proceed to
7.2—Attach a vacuum gauge per 7.1, and test for an intake manifold leak. Squirt a small amount of oil around the intake manifold gaskets, carburetor gaskets, plugs and fittings. Observe the action of the vacuum gauge.	If the reading improves, replace the indicated gasket, or seal the indicated fitting or plug:	**8.1**
	If the reading remains low:	**7.3**
7.3—Test all vacuum hoses and accessories for leaks as described in 7.2. Also check the carburetor body (dashpots, automatic choke mechanism, throttle shafts) for leaks in the same manner.	If the reading improves, service or replace the offending part(s):	**8.1**
	If the reading remains low:	**6.1**

Section 8—Secondary Electrical System
See Chapter 2 for service procedures

Test and Procedure	Results and Indications	Proceed to
8.1—Remove the distributor cap and check to make sure that the rotor turns when the engine is cranked. Visually inspect the distributor components.	Clean, tighten or replace any components which appear defective.	**8.2**
8.2—Connect a timing light (per manufacturer's recommendation) and check the dynamic ignition timing. Disconnect and plug the vacuum hose(s) to the distributor if specified, start the engine, and observe the timing marks at the specified engine speed.	If the timing is not correct, adjust to specifications by rotating the distributor in the engine: (Advance timing by rotating distributor opposite normal direction of rotor rotation, retard timing by rotating distributor in same direction as rotor rotation.)	**8.3**
8.3—Check the operation of the distributor advance mechanism(s): To test the mechanical advance, disconnect the vacuum lines from the distributor advance unit and observe the timing marks with a timing light as the engine speed is increased from idle. If the mark moves smoothly, without hesitation, it may be assumed that the mechanical advance is functioning properly. To test vacuum advance and/or retard systems, alternately crimp and release the vacuum line, and observe the timing mark for movement. If movement is noted, the system is operating.	If the systems are functioning:	**8.4**
	If the systems are not functioning, remove the distributor, and test on a distributor tester:	**8.4**
8.4—Locate an ignition miss: With the engine running, remove each spark plug wire, one at a time, until one is found that doesn't cause the engine to roughen and slow down.	When the missing cylinder is identified:	**4.1**

Section 9—Valve Train
See Chapter 3 for service procedures

Test and Procedure	Results and Indications	Proceed to
9.1—Evaluate the valve train: Remove the valve cover, and ensure that the valves are adjusted to specifications. A mechanic's stethoscope may be used to aid in the diagnosis of the valve train. By pushing the probe on or near push rods or rockers, valve noise often can be isolated. A timing light also may be used to diagnose valve problems. Connect the light according to manufacturer's recommendations, and start the engine. Vary the firing moment of the light by increasing the engine speed (and therefore the ignition advance), and moving the trigger from cylinder to cylinder. Observe the movement of each valve.	Sticking valves or erratic valve train motion can be observed with the timing light. The cylinder head must be disassembled for repairs.	**See Chapter 3**
9.2—Check the valve timing: Locate top dead center of the No. 1 piston, and install a degree wheel or tape on the crankshaft pulley or damper with zero corresponding to an index mark on the engine. Rotate the crankshaft in its direction of rotation, and observe the opening of the No. 1 cylinder intake valve. The opening should correspond with the correct mark on the degree wheel according to specifications.	If the timing is not correct, the timing cover must be removed for further investigation.	**See Chapter 3**

Section 10—Exhaust System

Test and Procedure	Results and Indications	Proceed to
10.1—Determine whether the exhaust manifold heat control valve is operating: Operate the valve by hand to determine whether it is free to move. If the valve is free, run the engine to operating temperature and observe the action of the valve, to ensure that it is opening.	If the valve sticks, spray it with a suitable solvent, open and close the valve to free it, and retest. If the valve functions properly: If the valve does not free, or does not operate, replace the valve:	**10.2** **10.2**
10.2—Ensure that there are no exhaust restrictions: Visually inspect the exhaust system for kinks, dents, or crushing. Also note that gases are flowing freely from the tailpipe at all engine speeds, indicating no restriction in the muffler or resonator.	Replace any damaged portion of the system:	**11.1**

Section 11—Cooling System
See Chapter 3 for service procedures

Test and Procedure	Results and Indications	Proceed to
11.1—Visually inspect the fan belt for glazing, cracks, and fraying, and replace if necessary. Tighten the belt so that the longest span has approximately ½″ play at its mid-point under thumb pressure (see Chapter 1).	Replace or tighten the fan belt as necessary:	**11.2**

Checking belt tension

Test and Procedure	Results and Indications	Proceed to
11.2—Check the fluid level of the cooling system.	If full or slightly low, fill as necessary:	**11.5**
	If extremely low:	**11.3**
11.3—Visually inspect the external portions of the cooling system (radiator, radiator hoses, thermostat elbow, water pump seals, heater hoses, etc.) for leaks. If none are found, pressurize the cooling system to 14–15 psi.	If cooling system holds the pressure:	**11.5**
	If cooling system loses pressure rapidly, reinspect external parts of the system for leaks under pressure. If none are found, check dipstick for coolant in crankcase. If no coolant is present, but pressure loss continues:	**11.4**
	If coolant is evident in crankcase, remove cylinder head(s), and check gasket(s). If gaskets are intact, block and cylinder head(s) should be checked for cracks or holes.	
	If the gasket(s) is blown, replace, and purge the crankcase of coolant:	**12.6**
	NOTE: *Occasionally, due to atmospheric and driving conditions, condensation of water can occur in the crankcase. This causes the oil to appear milky white. To remedy, run the engine until hot, and change the oil and oil filter.*	
11.4—Check for combustion leaks into the cooling system: Pressurize the cooling system as above. Start the engine, and observe the pressure gauge. If the needle fluctuates, remove each spark plug wire, one at a time, noting which cylinder(s) reduce or eliminate the fluctuation.	Cylinders which reduce or eliminate the fluctuation, when the spark plug wire is removed, are leaking into the cooling system. Replace the head gasket on the affected cylinder bank(s).	

Pressurizing the cooling system

Test and Procedure	Results and Indications	Proceed to
11.5—Check the radiator pressure cap: Attach a radiator pressure tester to the radiator cap (wet the seal prior to installation). Quickly pump up the pressure, noting the point at which the cap releases.	If the cap releases within ± 1 psi of the specified rating, it is operating properly:	**11.6**
	If the cap releases at more than ± 1 psi of the specified rating, it should be replaced:	**11.6**

Checking radiator pressure cap

Test and Procedure	Results and Indications	Proceed to
11.6—Test the thermostat: Start the engine cold, remove the radiator cap, and insert a thermometer into the radiator. Allow the engine to idle. After a short while, there will be a sudden, rapid increase in coolant temperature. The temperature at which this sharp rise stops is the thermostat opening temperature.	If the thermostat opens at or about the specified temperature:	**11.7**
	If the temperature doesn't increase: (If the temperature increases slowly and gradually, replace the thermostat.)	**11.7**
11.7—Check the water pump: Remove the thermostat elbow and the thermostat, disconnect the coil high tension lead (to prevent starting), and crank the engine momentarily.	If coolant flows, replace the thermostat and retest per 11.6:	**11.6**
	If coolant doesn't flow, reverse flush the cooling system to alleviate any blockage that might exist. If system is not blocked, and coolant will not flow, replace the water pump.	

Section 12—Lubrication
See Chapter 3 for service procedures

Test and Procedure	Results and Indications	Proceed to
12.1—Check the oil pressure gauge or warning light: If the gauge shows low pressure, or the light is on for no obvious reason, remove the oil pressure sender. Install an accurate oil pressure gauge and run the engine momentarily.	If oil pressure builds normally, run engine for a few moments to determine that it is functioning normally, and replace the sender.	—
	If the pressure remains low:	**12.2**
	If the pressure surges:	**12.3**
	If the oil pressure is zero:	**12.3**
12.2—Visually inspect the oil: If the oil is watery or very thin, milky, or foamy, replace the oil and oil filter.	If the oil is normal:	**12.3**
	If after replacing oil the pressure remains low:	**12.3**
	If after replacing oil the pressure becomes normal:	—

Test and Procedure	Results and Indications	Proceed to
12.3—Inspect the oil pressure relief valve and spring, to ensure that it is not sticking or stuck. Remove and thoroughly clean the valve, spring, and the valve body.	If the oil pressure improves: If no improvement is noted:	— **12.4**
12.4—Check to ensure that the oil pump is not cavitating (sucking air instead of oil): See that the crankcase is neither over nor underfull, and that the pickup in the sump is in the proper position and free from sludge.	Fill or drain the crankcase to the proper capacity, and clean the pickup screen in solvent if necessary. If no improvement is noted:	**12.5**
12.5—Inspect the oil pump drive and the oil pump:	If the pump drive or the oil pump appear to be defective, service as necessary and retest per 12.1: If the pump drive and pump appear to be operating normally, the engine should be disassembled to determine where blockage exists:	**12.1** **See Chapter 3**
12.6—Purge the engine of ethylene glycol coolant: Completely drain the crankcase and the oil filter. Obtain a commercial butyl cellosolve base solvent, designated for this purpose, and follow the instructions precisely. Following this, install a new oil filter and refill the crankcase with the proper weight oil. The next oil and filter change should follow shortly thereafter (1000 miles).		

TROUBLESHOOTING EMISSION CONTROL SYSTEMS

See Chapter 4 for procedures applicable to individual emission control systems used on specific combinations of engine/transmission/model.

TROUBLESHOOTING THE CARBURETOR
See Chapter 4 for service procedures

Carburetor problems cannot be effectively isolated unless all other engine systems (particularly ignition and emission) are functioning properly and the engine is properly tuned.

Condition	Possible Cause
Engine cranks, but does not start	1. Improper starting procedure 2. No fuel in tank 3. Clogged fuel line or filter 4. Defective fuel pump 5. Choke valve not closing properly 6. Engine flooded 7. Choke valve not unloading 8. Throttle linkage not making full travel 9. Stuck needle or float 10. Leaking float needle or seat 11. Improper float adjustment
Engine stalls	1. Improperly adjusted idle speed or mixture **Engine hot** 2. Improperly adjusted dashpot 3. Defective or improperly adjusted solenoid 4. Incorrect fuel level in fuel bowl 5. Fuel pump pressure too high 6. Leaking float needle seat 7. Secondary throttle valve stuck open 8. Air or fuel leaks 9. Idle air bleeds plugged or missing 10. Idle passages plugged **Engine Cold** 11. Incorrectly adjusted choke 12. Improperly adjusted fast idle speed 13. Air leaks 14. Plugged idle or idle air passages 15. Stuck choke valve or binding linkage 16. Stuck secondary throttle valves 17. Engine flooding—high fuel level 18. Leaking or misaligned float
Engine hesitates on acceleration	1. Clogged fuel filter 2. Leaking fuel pump diaphragm 3. Low fuel pump pressure 4. Secondary throttle valves stuck, bent or misadjusted 5. Sticking or binding air valve 6. Defective accelerator pump 7. Vacuum leaks 8. Clogged air filter 9. Incorrect choke adjustment (engine cold)
Engine feels sluggish or flat on acceleration	1. Improperly adjusted idle speed or mixture 2. Clogged fuel filter 3. Defective accelerator pump 4. Dirty, plugged or incorrect main metering jets 5. Bent or sticking main metering rods 6. Sticking throttle valves 7. Stuck heat riser 8. Binding or stuck air valve 9. Dirty, plugged or incorrect secondary jets 10. Bent or sticking secondary metering rods. 11. Throttle body or manifold heat passages plugged 12. Improperly adjusted choke or choke vacuum break.
Carburetor floods	1. Defective fuel pump. Pressure too high. 2. Stuck choke valve 3. Dirty, worn or damaged float or needle valve/seat 4. Incorrect float/fuel level 5. Leaking float bowl

Condition	Possible Cause
Engine idles roughly and stalls	1. Incorrect idle speed 2. Clogged fuel filter 3. Dirt in fuel system or carburetor 4. Loose carburetor screws or attaching bolts 5. Broken carburetor gaskets 6. Air leaks 7. Dirty carburetor 8. Worn idle mixture needles 9. Throttle valves stuck open 10. Incorrectly adjusted float or fuel level 11. Clogged air filter
Engine runs unevenly or surges	1. Defective fuel pump 2. Dirty or clogged fuel filter 3. Plugged, loose or incorrect main metering jets or rods 4. Air leaks 5. Bent or sticking main metering rods 6. Stuck power piston 7. Incorrect float adjustment 8. Incorrect idle speed or mixture 9. Dirty or plugged idle system passages 10. Hard, brittle or broken gaskets 11. Loose attaching or mounting screws 12. Stuck or misaligned secondary throttle valves
Poor fuel economy	1. Poor driving habits 2. Stuck choke valve 3. Binding choke linkage 4. Stuck heat riser 5. Incorrect idle mixture 6. Defective accelerator pump 7. Air leaks 8. Plugged, loose or incorrect main metering jets 9. Improperly adjusted float or fuel level 10. Bent, misaligned or fuel-clogged float 11. Leaking float needle seat 12. Fuel leak 13. Accelerator pump discharge ball not seating properly 14. Incorrect main jets
Engine lacks high speed performance or power	1. Incorrect throttle linkage adjustment 2. Stuck or binding power piston 3. Defective accelerator pump 4. Air leaks 5. Incorrect float setting or fuel level 6. Dirty, plugged, worn or incorrect main metering jets or rods 7. Binding or sticking air valve 8. Brittle or cracked gaskets 9. Bent, incorrect or improperly adjusted secondary metering rods 10. Clogged fuel filter 11. Clogged air filter 12. Defective fuel pump

TROUBLESHOOTING FUEL INJECTION PROBLEMS

Each fuel injection system has its own unique components and test procedures, for which it is impossible to generalize. Refer to Chapter 4 of this Repair & Tune-Up Guide for specific test and repair procedures, if the vehicle is equipped with fuel injection.

TROUBLESHOOTING ELECTRICAL PROBLEMS

See Chapter 5 for service procedures

For any electrical system to operate, it must make a complete circuit. This simply means that the power flow from the battery must make a complete circle. When an electrical component is operating, power flows from the battery to the component, passes through the component causing it to perform its function (lighting a light bulb), and then returns to the battery through the ground of the circuit. This ground is usually (but not always) the metal part of the car or truck on which the electrical component is mounted.

Perhaps the easiest way to visualize this is to think of connecting a light bulb with two wires attached to it to the battery. If one of the two wires attached to the light bulb were attached to the negative post of the battery and the other were attached to the positive post of the battery, you would have a complete circuit. Current from the battery would flow to the light bulb, causing it to light, and return to the negative post of the battery.

The normal automotive circuit differs from this simple example in two ways. First, instead of having a return wire from the bulb to the battery, the light bulb returns the current to the battery through the chassis of the vehicle. Since the negative battery cable is attached to the chassis and the chassis is made of electrically conductive metal, the chassis of the vehicle can serve as a ground wire to complete the circuit. Secondly, most automotive circuits contain switches to turn components on and off as required.

Every complete circuit from a power source must include a component which is using the power from the power source. If you were to disconnect the light bulb from the wires and touch the two wires together (don't do this) the power supply wire to the component would be grounded before the normal ground connection for the circuit.

Because grounding a wire from a power source makes a complete circuit—less the required component to use the power—this phenomenon is called a short circuit. Common causes are: broken insulation (exposing the metal wire to a metal part of the car or truck), or a shorted switch.

Some electrical components which require a large amount of current to operate also have a relay in their circuit. Since these circuits carry a large amount of current, the thickness of the wire in the circuit (gauge size) is also greater. If this large wire were connected from the component to the control switch on the instrument panel, and then back to the component, a voltage drop would occur in the circuit. To prevent this potential drop in voltage, an electromagnetic switch (relay) is used. The large wires in the circuit are connected from the battery to one side of the relay, and from the opposite side of the relay to the component. The relay is normally open, preventing current from passing through the circuit. An additional, smaller, wire is connected from the relay to the control switch for the circuit. When the control switch is turned on, it grounds the smaller wire from the relay and completes the circuit. This closes the relay and allows current to flow from the battery to the component. The horn, headlight, and starter circuits are three which use relays.

It is possible for larger surges of current to pass through the electrical system of your car or truck. If this surge of current were to reach an electrical component, it could burn it out. To prevent this, fuses, circuit breakers or fusible links are connected into the current supply wires of most of the major electrical systems. When an electrical current of excessive power passes through the component's fuse, the fuse blows out and breaks the circuit, saving the component from destruction.

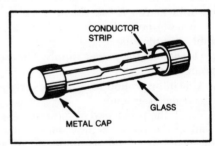

Typical automotive fuse

A circuit breaker is basically a self-repairing fuse. The circuit breaker opens the circuit the same way a fuse does. However, when either the short is removed from the circuit or the surge subsides, the circuit breaker resets itself and does not have to be replaced as a fuse does.

A fuse link is a wire that acts as a fuse. It is normally connected between the starter relay and the main wiring harness. This connection is usually under the hood. The fuse link (if installed) protects all the

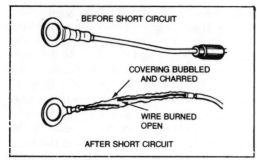

Most fusible links show a charred, melted insulation when they burn out

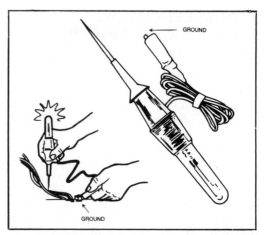

The test light will show the presence of current when touched to a hot wire and grounded at the other end

chassis electrical components, and is the probable cause of trouble when none of the electrical components function, unless the battery is disconnected or dead.

Electrical problems generally fall into one of three areas:

1. The component that is not functioning is not receiving current.

2. The component itself is not functioning.

3. The component is not properly grounded.

The electrical system can be checked with a test light and a jumper wire. A test light is a device that looks like a pointed screwdriver with a wire attached to it and has a light bulb in its handle. A jumper wire is a piece of insulated wire with an alligator clip attached to each end.

If a component is not working, you must follow a systematic plan to determine which of the three causes is the villain.

1. Turn on the switch that controls the inoperable component.

2. Disconnect the power supply wire from the component.

3. Attach the ground wire on the test light to a good metal ground.

4. Touch the probe end of the test light to the end of the power supply wire that was disconnected from the component. If the component is receiving current, the test light will go on.

NOTE: *Some components work only when the ignition switch is turned on.*

If the test light does not go on, then the problem is in the circuit between the battery and the component. This includes all the switches, fuses, and relays in the system. Follow the wire that runs back to the battery. The problem is an open circuit between the

battery and the component. If the fuse is blown and, when replaced, immediately blows again, there is a short circuit in the system which must be located and repaired. If there is a switch in the system, bypass it with a jumper wire. This is done by connecting one end of the jumper wire to the power supply wire into the switch and the other end of the jumper wire to the wire coming out of the switch. If the test light lights with the jumper wire installed, the switch or whatever was bypassed is defective.

NOTE: *Never substitute the jumper wire for the component, since it is required to use the power from the power source.*

5. If the bulb in the test light goes on, then the current is getting to the component that is not working. This eliminates the first of the three possible causes. Connect the power supply wire and connect a jumper wire from the component to a good metal ground. Do this with the switch which controls the component turned on, and also the ignition switch turned on if it is required for the component to work. If the component works with the jumper wire installed, then it has a bad ground. This is usually caused by the metal area on which the component mounts to the chassis being coated with some type of foreign matter.

6. If neither test located the source of the trouble, then the component itself is defective. Remember that for any electrical system to work, all connections must be clean and tight.

Troubleshooting Basic Turn Signal and Flasher Problems

See Chapter 5 for service procedures

Most problems in the turn signals or flasher system can be reduced to defective flashers or bulbs, which are easily replaced. Occasionally, the turn signal switch will prove defective.

F = Front   R = Rear   ● = Lights off   ○ = Lights on

Condition		Possible Cause
Turn signals light, but do not flash	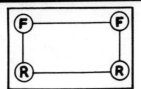	Defective flasher
No turn signals light on either side	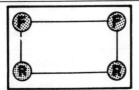	Blown fuse. Replace if defective. Defective flasher. Check by substitution. Open circuit, short circuit or poor ground.
Both turn signals on one side don't work	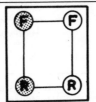	Bad bulbs. Bad ground in both (or either) housings.
One turn signal light on one side doesn't work	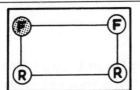	Defective bulb. Corrosion in socket. Clean contacts. Poor ground at socket.
Turn signal flashes too fast or too slowly	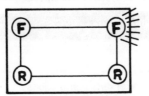	Check any bulb on the side flashing too fast. A heavy-duty bulb is probably installed in place of a regular bulb. Check the bulb flashing too slowly. A standard bulb was probably installed in place of a heavy-duty bulb. Loose connections or corrosion at the bulb socket.
Indicator lights don't work in either direction		Check if the turn signals are working. Check the dash indicator lights. Check the flasher by substitution.
One indicator light doesn't light		On systems with one dash indicator: See if the lights work on the same side. Often the filaments have been reversed in systems combining stoplights with tail-lights and turn signals. Check the flasher by substitution. On systems with two indicators: Check the bulbs on the same side. Check the indicator light bulb. Check the flasher by substitution.

Troubleshooting Lighting Problems
See Chapter 5 for service procedures

Condition	Possible Cause
One or more lights don't work, but others do	1. Defective bulb(s) 2. Blown fuse(s) 3. Dirty fuse clips or light sockets 4. Poor ground circuit
Lights burn out quickly	1. Incorrect voltage regulator setting or defective regulator 2. Poor battery/alternator connections
Lights go dim	1. Low/discharged battery 2. Alternator not charging 3. Corroded sockets or connections 4. Low voltage output
Lights flicker	1. Loose connection 2. Poor ground. (Run ground wire from light housing to frame) 3. Circuit breaker operating (short circuit)
Lights "flare"—Some flare is normal on acceleration—If excessive, see "Lights Burn Out Quickly"	High voltage setting
Lights glare—approaching drivers are blinded	1. Lights adjusted too high 2. Rear springs or shocks sagging 3. Rear tires soft

Troubleshooting Dash Gauge Problems
Most problems can be traced to a defective sending unit or faulty wiring. Occasionally, the gauge itself is at fault. See Chapter 5 for service procedures.

Condition	Possible Cause

COOLANT TEMPERATURE GAUGE

Gauge reads erratically or not at all	1. Loose or dirty connections 2. Defective sending unit. 3. Defective gauge. To test a bi-metal gauge, remove the wire from the sending unit. Ground the wire for an instant. If the gauge registers, replace the sending unit. To test a magnetic gauge, disconnect the wire at the sending unit. With ignition ON gauge should register COLD. Ground the wire; gauge should register HOT.

AMMETER GAUGE—TURN HEADLIGHTS ON (DO NOT START ENGINE). NOTE REACTION

Ammeter shows charge Ammeter shows discharge Ammeter does not move	1. Connections reversed on gauge 2. Ammeter is OK 3. Loose connections or faulty wiring 4. Defective gauge

Condition	Possible Cause

OIL PRESSURE GAUGE

Condition	Possible Cause
Gauge does not register or is inaccurate	1. On mechanical gauge, Bourdon tube may be bent or kinked. 2. Low oil pressure. Remove sending unit. Idle the engine briefly. If no oil flows from sending unit hole, problem is in engine. 3. Defective gauge. Remove the wire from the sending unit and ground it for an instant with the ignition ON. A good gauge will go to the top of the scale. 4. Defective wiring. Check the wiring to the gauge. If it's OK and the gauge doesn't register when grounded, replace the gauge. 5. Defective sending unit.

ALL GAUGES

Condition	Possible Cause
All gauges do not operate All gauges read low or erratically All gauges pegged	1. Blown fuse 2. Defective instrument regulator 3. Defective or dirty instrument voltage regulator 4. Loss of ground between instrument voltage regulator and frame 5. Defective instrument regulator

WARNING LIGHTS

Condition	Possible Cause
Light(s) do not come on when ignition is ON, but engine is not started Light comes on with engine running	1. Defective bulb 2. Defective wire 3. Defective sending unit. Disconnect the wire from the sending unit and ground it. Replace the sending unit if the light comes on with the ignition ON. 4. Problem in individual system 5. Defective sending unit

Troubleshooting Clutch Problems

It is false economy to replace individual clutch components. The pressure plate, clutch plate and throwout bearing should be replaced as a set, and the flywheel face inspected, whenever the clutch is overhauled. See Chapter 6 for service procedures.

Condition	Possible Cause
Clutch chatter	1. Grease on driven plate (disc) facing 2. Binding clutch linkage or cable 3. Loose, damaged facings on driven plate (disc) 4. Engine mounts loose 5. Incorrect height adjustment of pressure plate release levers 6. Clutch housing or housing to transmission adapter misalignment 7. Loose driven plate hub
Clutch grabbing	1. Oil, grease on driven plate (disc) facing 2. Broken pressure plate 3. Warped or binding driven plate. Driven plate binding on clutch shaft
Clutch slips	1. Lack of lubrication in clutch linkage or cable (linkage or cable binds, causes incomplete engagement) 2. Incorrect pedal, or linkage adjustment 3. Broken pressure plate springs 4. Weak pressure plate springs 5. Grease on driven plate facings (disc)

Troubleshooting Clutch Problems (cont.)

Condition	Possible Cause
Incomplete clutch release	1. Incorrect pedal or linkage adjustment or linkage or cable binding 2. Incorrect height adjustment on pressure plate release levers 3. Loose, broken facings on driven plate (disc) 4. Bent, dished, warped driven plate caused by overheating
Grinding, whirring grating noise when pedal is depressed	1. Worn or defective throwout bearing 2. Starter drive teeth contacting flywheel ring gear teeth. Look for milled or polished teeth on ring gear.
Squeal, howl, trumpeting noise when pedal is being released (occurs during first inch to inch and one-half of pedal travel)	Pilot bushing worn or lack of lubricant. If bushing appears OK, polish bushing with emery cloth, soak lube wick in oil, lube bushing with oil, apply film of chassis grease to clutch shaft pilot hub, reassemble. NOTE: Bushing wear may be due to misalignment of clutch housing or housing to transmission adapter
Vibration or clutch pedal pulsation with clutch disengaged (pedal fully depressed)	1. Worn or defective engine transmission mounts 2. Flywheel run out. (Flywheel run out at face not to exceed 0.005") 3. Damaged or defective clutch components

Troubleshooting Manual Transmission Problems
See Chapter 6 for service procedures

Condition	Possible Cause
Transmission jumps out of gear	1. Misalignment of transmission case or clutch housing. 2. Worn pilot bearing in crankshaft. 3. Bent transmission shaft. 4. Worn high speed sliding gear. 5. Worn teeth or end-play in clutch shaft. 6. Insufficient spring tension on shifter rail plunger. 7. Bent or loose shifter fork. 8. Gears not engaging completely. 9. Loose or worn bearings on clutch shaft or mainshaft. 10. Worn gear teeth. 11. Worn or damaged detent balls.
Transmission sticks in gear	1. Clutch not releasing fully. 2. Burred or battered teeth on clutch shaft, or sliding sleeve. 3. Burred or battered transmission mainshaft. 4. Frozen synchronizing clutch. 5. Stuck shifter rail plunger. 6. Gearshift lever twisting and binding shifter rail. 7. Battered teeth on high speed sliding gear or on sleeve. 8. Improper lubrication, or lack of lubrication. 9. Corroded transmission parts. 10. Defective mainshaft pilot bearing. 11. Locked gear bearings will give same effect as stuck in gear.
Transmission gears will not synchronize	1. Binding pilot bearing on mainshaft, will synchronize in high gear only. 2. Clutch not releasing fully. 3. Detent spring weak or broken. 4. Weak or broken springs under balls in sliding gear sleeve. 5. Binding bearing on clutch shaft, or binding countershaft. 6. Binding pilot bearing in crankshaft. 7. Badly worn gear teeth. 8. Improper lubrication. 9. Constant mesh gear not turning freely on transmission mainshaft. Will synchronize in that gear only.

Condition	Possible Cause
Gears spinning when shifting into gear from neutral	1. Clutch not releasing fully. 2. In some cases an extremely light lubricant in transmission will cause gears to continue to spin for a short time after clutch is released. 3. Binding pilot bearing in crankshaft.
Transmission noisy in all gears	1. Insufficient lubricant, or improper lubricant. 2. Worn countergear bearings. 3. Worn or damaged main drive gear or countergear. 4. Damaged main drive gear or mainshaft bearings. 5. Worn or damaged countergear anti-lash plate.
Transmission noisy in neutral only	1. Damaged main drive gear bearing. 2. Damaged or loose mainshaft pilot bearing. 3. Worn or damaged countergear anti-lash plate. 4. Worn countergear bearings.
Transmission noisy in one gear only	1. Damaged or worn constant mesh gears. 2. Worn or damaged countergear bearings. 3. Damaged or worn synchronizer.
Transmission noisy in reverse only	1. Worn or damaged reverse idler gear or idler bushing. 2. Worn or damaged mainshaft reverse gear. 3. Worn or damaged reverse countergear. 4. Damaged shift mechanism.

TROUBLESHOOTING AUTOMATIC TRANSMISSION PROBLEMS

Keeping alert to changes in the operating characteristics of the transmission (changing shift points, noises, etc.) can prevent small problems from becoming large ones. If the problem cannot be traced to loose bolts, fluid level, misadjusted linkage, clogged filters or similar problems, you should probably seek professional service.

Transmission Fluid Indications

The appearance and odor of the transmission fluid can give valuable clues to the overall condition of the transmission. Always note the appearance of the fluid when you check the fluid level or change the fluid. Rub a small amount of fluid between your fingers to feel for grit and smell the fluid on the dipstick.

If the fluid appears:	It indicates:
Clear and red colored	Normal operation
Discolored (extremely dark red or brownish) or smells burned	Band or clutch pack failure, usually caused by an overheated transmission. Hauling very heavy loads with insufficient power or failure to change the fluid often result in overheating. Do not confuse this appearance with newer fluids that have a darker red color and a strong odor (though not a burned odor).
Foamy or aerated (light in color and full of bubbles)	1. The level is too high (gear train is churning oil) 2. An internal air leak (air is mixing with the fluid). Have the transmission checked professionally.
Solid residue in the fluid	Defective bands, clutch pack or bearings. Bits of band material or metal abrasives are clinging to the dipstick. Have the transmission checked professionally.
Varnish coating on the dipstick	The transmission fluid is overheating

TROUBLESHOOTING DRIVE AXLE PROBLEMS

First, determine when the noise is most noticeable.

Drive Noise: Produced under vehicle acceleration.

Coast Noise: Produced while coasting with a closed throttle.

Float Noise: Occurs while maintaining constant speed (just enough to keep speed constant) on a level road.

External Noise Elimination

It is advisable to make a thorough road test to determine whether the noise originates in the rear axle or whether it originates from the tires, engine, transmission, wheel bearings or road surface. Noise originating from other places cannot be corrected by servicing the rear axle.

ROAD NOISE

Brick or rough surfaced concrete roads produce noises that seem to come from the rear axle. Road noise is usually identical in Drive or Coast and driving on a different type of road will tell whether the road is the problem.

TIRE NOISE

Tire noise can be mistaken as rear axle noise, even though the tires on the front are at fault. Snow tread and mud tread tires or tires worn unevenly will frequently cause vibrations which seem to originate elsewhere; *temporarily, and for test purposes only,* inflate the tires to 40–50 lbs. This will significantly alter the noise produced by the tires,

but will not alter noise from the rear axle. Noises from the rear axle will normally cease at speeds below 30 mph on coast, while tire noise will continue at lower tone as speed is decreased. The rear axle noise will usually change from drive conditions to coast conditions, while tire noise will not. Do not forget to lower the tire pressure to normal after the test is complete.

ENGINE/TRANSMISSION NOISE

Determine at what speed the noise is most pronounced, then stop in a quiet place. With the transmission in Neutral, run the engine through speeds corresponding to road speeds where the noise was noticed. Noises produced with the vehicle standing still are coming from the engine or transmission.

FRONT WHEEL BEARINGS

Front wheel bearing noises, sometimes confused with rear axle noises, will not change when comparing drive and coast conditions. While holding the speed steady, lightly apply the footbrake. This will often cause wheel bearing noise to lessen, as some of the weight is taken off the bearing. Front wheel bearings are easily checked by jacking up the wheels and spinning the wheels. Shaking the wheels will also determine if the wheel bearings are excessively loose.

REAR AXLE NOISES

Eliminating other possible sources can narrow the cause to the rear axle, which normally produces noise from worn gears or bearings. Gear noises tend to peak in a narrow speed range, while bearing noises will usually vary in pitch with engine speeds.

Noise Diagnosis

The Noise Is:	Most Probably Produced By:
1. Identical under Drive or Coast	Road surface, tires or front wheel bearings
2. Different depending on road surface	Road surface or tires
3. Lower as speed is lowered	Tires
4. Similar when standing or moving	Engine or transmission
5. A vibration	Unbalanced tires, rear wheel bearing, unbalanced driveshaft or worn U-joint
6. A knock or click about every two tire revolutions	Rear wheel bearing
7. Most pronounced on turns	Damaged differential gears
8. A steady low-pitched whirring or scraping, starting at low speeds	Damaged or worn pinion bearing
9. A chattering vibration on turns	Wrong differential lubricant or worn clutch plates (limited slip rear axle)
10. Noticed only in Drive, Coast or Float conditions	Worn ring gear and/or pinion gear

Troubleshooting Steering & Suspension Problems

Condition	Possible Cause
Hard steering (wheel is hard to turn)	1. Improper tire pressure 2. Loose or glazed pump drive belt 3. Low or incorrect fluid 4. Loose, bent or poorly lubricated front end parts 5. Improper front end alignment (excessive caster) 6. Bind in steering column or linkage 7. Kinked hydraulic hose 8. Air in hydraulic system 9. Low pump output or leaks in system 10. Obstruction in lines 11. Pump valves sticking or out of adjustment 12. Incorrect wheel alignment
Loose steering (too much play in steering wheel)	1. Loose wheel bearings 2. Faulty shocks 3. Worn linkage or suspension components 4. Loose steering gear mounting or linkage points 5. Steering mechanism worn or improperly adjusted 6. Valve spool improperly adjusted 7. Worn ball joints, tie-rod ends, etc.
Veers or wanders (pulls to one side with hands off steering wheel)	1. Improper tire pressure 2. Improper front end alignment 3. Dragging or improperly adjusted brakes 4. Bent frame 5. Improper rear end alignment 6. Faulty shocks or springs 7. Loose or bent front end components 8. Play in Pitman arm 9. Steering gear mountings loose 10. Loose wheel bearings 11. Binding Pitman arm 12. Spool valve sticking or improperly adjusted 13. Worn ball joints
Wheel oscillation or vibration transmitted through steering wheel	1. Low or uneven tire pressure 2. Loose wheel bearings 3. Improper front end alignment 4. Bent spindle 5. Worn, bent or broken front end components 6. Tires out of round or out of balance 7. Excessive lateral runout in disc brake rotor 8. Loose or bent shock absorber or strut
Noises (see also "Troubleshooting Drive Axle Problems")	1. Loose belts 2. Low fluid, air in system 3. Foreign matter in system 4. Improper lubrication 5. Interference or chafing in linkage 6. Steering gear mountings loose 7. Incorrect adjustment or wear in gear box 8. Faulty valves or wear in pump 9. Kinked hydraulic lines 10. Worn wheel bearings
Poor return of steering	1. Over-inflated tires 2. Improperly aligned front end (excessive caster) 3. Binding in steering column 4. No lubrication in front end 5. Steering gear adjusted too tight
Uneven tire wear (see "How To Read Tire Wear")	1. Incorrect tire pressure 2. Improperly aligned front end 3. Tires out-of-balance 4. Bent or worn suspension parts

HOW TO READ TIRE WEAR

The way your tires wear is a good indicator of other parts of the suspension. Abnormal wear patterns are often caused by the need for simple tire maintenance, or for front end alignment.

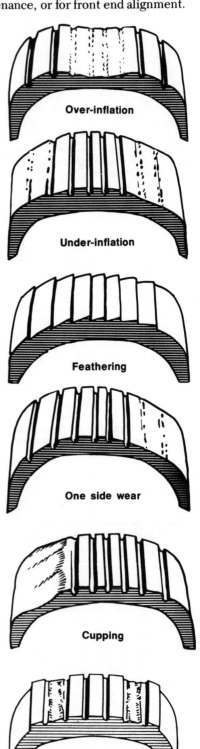

Excessive wear at the center of the tread indicates that the air pressure in the tire is consistently too high. The tire is riding on the center of the tread and wearing it prematurely. Occasionally, this wear pattern can result from outrageously wide tires on narrow rims. The cure for this is to replace either the tires or the wheels.

Over-inflation

This type of wear usually results from consistent under-inflation. When a tire is under-inflated, there is too much contact with the road by the outer treads, which wear prematurely. When this type of wear occurs, and the tire pressure is known to be consistently correct, a bent or worn steering component or the need for wheel alignment could be indicated.

Under-inflation

Feathering is a condition when the edge of each tread rib develops a slightly rounded edge on one side and a sharp edge on the other. By running your hand over the tire, you can usually feel the sharper edges before you'll be able to see them. The most common causes of feathering are incorrect toe-in setting or deteriorated bushings in the front suspension.

Feathering

When an inner or outer rib wears faster than the rest of the tire, the need for wheel alignment is indicated. There is excessive camber in the front suspension, causing the wheel to lean too much putting excessive load on one side of the tire. Misalignment could also be due to sagging springs, worn ball joints, or worn control arm bushings. Be sure the vehicle is loaded the way it's normally driven when you have the wheels aligned.

One side wear

Cups or scalloped dips appearing around the edge of the tread almost always indicate worn (sometimes bent) suspension parts. Adjustment of wheel alignment alone will seldom cure the problem. Any worn component that connects the wheel to the suspension can cause this type of wear. Occasionally, wheels that are out of balance will wear like this, but wheel imbalance usually shows up as bald spots between the outside edges and center of the tread.

Cupping

Second-rib wear is usually found only in radial tires, and appears where the steel belts end in relation to the tread. It can be kept to a minimum by paying careful attention to tire pressure and frequently rotating the tires. This is often considered normal wear but excessive amounts indicate that the tires are too wide for the wheels.

Second-rib wear

Troubleshooting Disc Brake Problems

Condition	Possible Cause
Noise—groan—brake noise emanating when slowly releasing brakes (creep-groan)	Not detrimental to function of disc brakes—no corrective action required. (This noise may be eliminated by slightly increasing or decreasing brake pedal efforts.)
Rattle—brake noise or rattle emanating at low speeds on rough roads, (front wheels only).	1. Shoe anti-rattle spring missing or not properly positioned. 2. Excessive clearance between shoe and caliper. 3. Soft or broken caliper seals. 4. Deformed or misaligned disc. 5. Loose caliper.
Scraping	1. Mounting bolts too long. 2. Loose wheel bearings. 3. Bent, loose, or misaligned splash shield.
Front brakes heat up during driving and fail to release	1. Operator riding brake pedal. 2. Stop light switch improperly adjusted. 3. Sticking pedal linkage. 4. Frozen or seized piston. 5. Residual pressure valve in master cylinder. 6. Power brake malfunction. 7. Proportioning valve malfunction.
Leaky brake caliper	1. Damaged or worn caliper piston seal. 2. Scores or corrosion on surface of cylinder bore.
Grabbing or uneven brake action— Brakes pull to one side	1. Causes listed under "Brakes Pull". 2. Power brake malfunction. 3. Low fluid level in master cylinder. 4. Air in hydraulic system. 5. Brake fluid, oil or grease on linings. 6. Unmatched linings. 7. Distorted brake pads. 8. Frozen or seized pistons. 9. Incorrect tire pressure. 10. Front end out of alignment. 11. Broken rear spring. 12. Brake caliper pistons sticking. 13. Restricted hose or line. 14. Caliper not in proper alignment to braking disc. 15. Stuck or malfunctioning metering valve. 16. Soft or broken caliper seals. 17. Loose caliper.
Brake pedal can be depressed without braking effect	1. Air in hydraulic system or improper bleeding procedure. 2. Leak past primary cup in master cylinder. 3. Leak in system. 4. Rear brakes out of adjustment. 5. Bleeder screw open.
Excessive pedal travel	1. Air, leak, or insufficient fluid in system or caliper. 2. Warped or excessively tapered shoe and lining assembly. 3. Excessive disc runout. 4. Rear brake adjustment required. 5. Loose wheel bearing adjustment. 6. Damaged caliper piston seal. 7. Improper brake fluid (boil). 8. Power brake malfunction. 9. Weak or soft hoses.

Troubleshooting Disc Brake Problems (cont.)

Condition	Possible Cause
Brake roughness or chatter (pedal pumping)	1. Excessive thickness variation of braking disc. 2. Excessive lateral runout of braking disc. 3. Rear brake drums out-of-round. 4. Excessive front bearing clearance.
Excessive pedal effort	1. Brake fluid, oil or grease on linings. 2. Incorrect lining. 3. Frozen or seized pistons. 4. Power brake malfunction. 5. Kinked or collapsed hose or line. 6. Stuck metering valve. 7. Scored caliper or master cylinder bore. 8. Seized caliper pistons.
Brake pedal fades (pedal travel increases with foot on brake)	1. Rough master cylinder or caliper bore. 2. Loose or broken hydraulic lines/connections. 3. Air in hydraulic system. 4. Fluid level low. 5. Weak or soft hoses. 6. Inferior quality brake shoes or fluid. 7. Worn master cylinder piston cups or seals.

Troubleshooting Drum Brakes

Condition	Possible Cause
Pedal goes to floor	1. Fluid low in reservoir. 2. Air in hydraulic system. 3. Improperly adjusted brake. 4. Leaking wheel cylinders. 5. Loose or broken brake lines. 6. Leaking or worn master cylinder. 7. Excessively worn brake lining.
Spongy brake pedal	1. Air in hydraulic system. 2. Improper brake fluid (low boiling point). 3. Excessively worn or cracked brake drums. 4. Broken pedal pivot bushing.
Brakes pulling	1. Contaminated lining. 2. Front end out of alignment. 3. Incorrect brake adjustment. 4. Unmatched brake lining. 5. Brake drums out of round. 6. Brake shoes distorted. 7. Restricted brake hose or line. 8. Broken rear spring. 9. Worn brake linings. 10. Uneven lining wear. 11. Glazed brake lining. 12. Excessive brake lining dust. 13. Heat spotted brake drums. 14. Weak brake return springs. 15. Faulty automatic adjusters. 16. Low or incorrect tire pressure.

Condition	Possible Cause
Squealing brakes	1. Glazed brake lining. 2. Saturated brake lining. 3. Weak or broken brake shoe retaining spring. 4. Broken or weak brake shoe return spring. 5. Incorrect brake lining. 6. Distorted brake shoes. 7. Bent support plate. 8. Dust in brakes or scored brake drums. 9. Linings worn below limit. 10. Uneven brake lining wear. 11. Heat spotted brake drums.
Chirping brakes	1. Out of round drum or eccentric axle flange pilot.
Dragging brakes	1. Incorrect wheel or parking brake adjustment. 2. Parking brakes engaged or improperly adjusted. 3. Weak or broken brake shoe return spring. 4. Brake pedal binding. 5. Master cylinder cup sticking. 6. Obstructed master cylinder relief port. 7. Saturated brake lining. 8. Bent or out of round brake drum. 9. Contaminated or improper brake fluid. 10. Sticking wheel cylinder pistons. 11. Driver riding brake pedal. 12. Defective proportioning valve. 13. Insufficient brake shoe lubricant.
Hard pedal	1. Brake booster inoperative. 2. Incorrect brake lining. 3. Restricted brake line or hose. 4. Frozen brake pedal linkage. 5. Stuck wheel cylinder. 6. Binding pedal linkage. 7. Faulty proportioning valve.
Wheel locks	1. Contaminated brake lining. 2. Loose or torn brake lining. 3. Wheel cylinder cups sticking. 4. Incorrect wheel bearing adjustment. 5. Faulty proportioning valve.
Brakes fade (high speed)	1. Incorrect lining. 2. Overheated brake drums. 3. Incorrect brake fluid (low boiling temperature). 4. Saturated brake lining. 5. Leak in hydraulic system. 6. Faulty automatic adjusters.
Pedal pulsates	1. Bent or out of round brake drum.
Brake chatter and shoe knock	1. Out of round brake drum. 2. Loose support plate. 3. Bent support plate. 4. Distorted brake shoes. 5. Machine grooves in contact face of brake drum (Shoe Knock). 6. Contaminated brake lining. 7. Missing or loose components. 8. Incorrect lining material. 9. Out-of-round brake drums. 10. Heat spotted or scored brake drums. 11. Out-of-balance wheels.

Troubleshooting Drum Brakes (cont.)

Condition	Possible Cause
Brakes do not self adjust	1. Adjuster screw frozen in thread. 2. Adjuster screw corroded at thrust washer. 3. Adjuster lever does not engage star wheel. 4. Adjuster installed on wrong wheel.
Brake light glows	1. Leak in the hydraulic system. 2. Air in the system. 3. Improperly adjusted master cylinder pushrod. 4. Uneven lining wear. 5. Failure to center combination valve or proportioning valve.

Appendix

General Conversion Table

Multiply by	To convert	To	
2.54	Inches	Centimeters	.3937
30.48	Feet	Centimeters	.0328
.914	Yards	Meters	1.094
1.609	Miles	Kilometers	.621
6.45	Square inches	Square cm.	.155
.836	Square yards	Square meters	1.196
16.39	Cubic inches	Cubic cm.	.061
28.3	Cubic feet	Liters	.0353
.4536	Pounds	Kilograms	2.2045
3.785	Gallons	Liters	.264
.068	Lbs./sq. in. (psi)	Atmospheres	14.7
.138	Foot pounds	Kg. m.	7.23
1.014	H.P. (DIN)	H.P. (SAE)	.9861
—	To obtain	From	Multiply by

Note: 1 cm. equals 10 mm.; 1 mm. equals .0394″.

Conversion—Common Fractions to Decimals and Millimeters

Common Fractions	Decimal Fractions	Millimeters (approx.)	Common Fractions	Decimal Fractions	Millimeters (approx.)	Common Fractions	Decimal Fractions	Millimeters (approx.)
1/128	.008	0.20	11/32	.344	8.73	43/64	.672	17.07
1/64	.016	0.40	23/64	.359	9.13	11/16	.688	17.46
1/32	.031	0.79	3/8	.375	9.53	45/64	.703	17.86
3/64	.047	1.19	25/64	.391	9.92	23/32	.719	18.26
1/16	.063	1.59	13/32	.406	10.32	47/64	.734	18.65
5/64	.078	1.98	27/64	.422	10.72	3/4	.750	19.05
3/32	.094	2.38	7/16	.438	11.11	49/64	.766	19.45
7/64	.109	2.78	29/64	.453	11.51	25/32	.781	19.84
1/8	.125	3.18	15/32	.469	11.91	51/64	.797	20.24
9/64	.141	3.57	31/64	.484	12.30	13/16	.813	20.64
5/32	.156	3.97	1/2	.500	12.70	53/64	.828	21.03
11/64	.172	4.37	33/64	.516	13.10	27/32	.844	21.43
3/16	.188	4.76	17/32	.531	13.49	55/64	.859	21.83
13/64	.203	5.16	35/64	.547	13.89	7/8	.875	22.23
7/32	.219	5.56	9/16	.563	14.29	57/64	.891	22.62
15/64	.234	5.95	37/64	.578	14.68	29/32	.906	23.02
1/4	.250	6.35	19/32	.594	15.08	59/64	.922	23.42
17/64	.266	6.75	39/64	.609	15.48	15/16	.938	23.81
9/32	.281	7.14	5/8	.625	15.88	61/64	.953	24.21
19/64	.297	7.54	41/64	.641	16.27	31/32	.969	24.61
5/16	.313	7.94	21/32	.656	16.67	63/64	.984	25.00
21/64	.328	8.33						

Conversion—Millimeters to Decimal Inches

mm	inches	mm	inches	mm	inches	mm	inches	mm	inches
1	.039 370	31	1.220 470	61	2.401 570	91	3.582 670	210	8.267 700
2	.078 740	32	1.259 840	62	2.440 940	92	3.622 040	220	8.661 400
3	.118 110	33	1.299 210	63	2.480 310	93	3.661 410	230	9.055 100
4	.157 480	34	1.338 580	64	2.519 680	94	3.700 780	240	9.448 800
5	.196 850	35	1.377 949	65	2.559 050	95	3.740 150	250	9.842 500
6	.236 220	36	1.417 319	66	2.598 420	96	3.779 520	260	10.236 200
7	.275 590	37	1.456 689	67	2.637 790	97	3.818 890	270	10.629 900
8	.314 960	38	1.496 050	68	2.677 160	98	3.858 260	280	11.032 600
9	.354 330	39	1.535 430	69	2.716 530	99	3.897 630	290	11.417 300
10	.393 700	40	1.574 800	70	2.755 900	100	3.937 000	300	11.811 000
11	.433 070	41	1.614 170	71	2.795 270	105	4.133 848	310	12.204 700
12	.472 440	42	1.653 540	72	2.834 640	110	4.330 700	320	12.598 400
13	.511 810	43	1.692 910	73	2.874 010	115	4.527 550	330	12.992 100
14	.551 180	44	1.732 280	74	2.913 380	120	4.724 400	340	13.385 800
15	.590 550	45	1.771 650	75	2.952 750	125	4.921 250	350	13.779 500
16	.629 920	46	1.811 020	76	2.992 120	130	5.118 100	360	14.173 200
17	.669 290	47	1.850 390	77	3.031 490	135	5.314 950	370	14.566 900
18	.708 660	48	1.889 760	78	3.070 860	140	5.511 800	380	14.960 600
19	.748 030	49	1.929 130	79	3.110 230	145	5.708 650	390	15.354 300
20	.787 400	50	1.968 500	80	3.149 600	150	5.905 500	400	15.748 000
21	.826 770	51	2.007 870	81	3.188 970	155	6.102 350	500	19.685 000
22	.866 140	52	2.047 240	82	3.228 340	160	6.299 200	600	23.622 000
23	.905 510	53	2.086 610	83	3.267 710	165	6.496 050	700	27.559 000
24	.944 880	54	2.125 980	84	3.307 080	170	6.692 900	800	31.496 000
25	.984 250	55	2.165 350	85	3.346 450	175	6.889 750	900	35.433 000
26	1.023 620	56	2.204 720	86	3.385 820	180	7.086 600	1000	39.370 000
27	1.062 990	57	2.244 090	87	3.425 190	185	7.283 450	2000	78.740 000
28	1.102 360	58	2.283 460	88	3.464 560	190	7.480 300	3000	118.110 000
29	1.141 730	59	2.322 830	89	3.503 903	195	7.677 150	4000	157.480 000
30	1.181 100	60	2.362 200	90	3.543 300	200	7.874 000	5000	196.850 000

To change decimal millimeters to decimal inches, position the decimal point where desired on either side of the millimeter measurement shown and reset the inches decimal by the same number of digits in the same direction. For example, to convert 0.001 mm to decimal inches, reset the decimal behind the 1 mm (shown on the chart) to 0.001; change the decimal inch equivalent (0.039″ shown) to 0.000039″.

Tap Drill Sizes

Screw & Tap Size	National Fine or S.A.E. Threads Per Inch	Use Drill Number
No. 5	44	37
No. 6	40	33
No. 8	36	29
No. 10	32	21
No. 12	28	15
1/4	28	3
5/16	24	1
3/8	24	Q
7/16	20	W
1/2	20	29/64
9/16	18	33/64
5/8	18	37/64
3/4	16	11/16
7/8	14	13/16
1 1/8	12	1 3/64
1 1/4	12	1 11/64
1 1/2	12	1 27/64

Tap Drill Sizes

Screw & Tap Size	National Coarse or U.S.S. Threads Per Inch	Use Drill Number
No. 5	40	39
No. 6	32	36
No. 8	32	29
No. 10	24	25
No. 12	24	17
1/4	20	8
5/16	18	F
3/8	16	5/16
7/16	14	U
1/2	13	27/64
9/16	12	31/64
5/8	11	17/32
3/4	10	21/32
7/8	9	49/64
1	8	7/8
1 1/8	7	63/64
1 1/4	7	1 7/64
1 1/2	6	1 11/32

Decimal Equivalent Size of the Number Drills

Drill No.	Decimal Equivalent	Drill No.	Decimal Equivalent	Drill No.	Decimal Equivalent
80	.0135	53	.0595	26	.1470
79	.0145	52	.0635	25	.1495
78	.0160	51	.0670	24	.1520
77	.0180	50	.0700	23	.1540
76	.0200	49	.0730	22	.1570
75	.0210	48	.0760	21	.1590
74	.0225	47	.0785	20	.1610
73	.0240	46	.0810	19	.1660
72	.0250	45	.0820	18	.1695
71	.0260	44	.0860	17	.1730
70	.0280	43	.0890	16	.1770
69	.0292	42	.0935	15	.1800
68	.0310	41	.0960	14	.1820
67	.0320	40	.0980	13	.1850
66	.0330	39	.0995	12	.1890
65	.0350	38	.1015	11	.1910
64	.0360	37	.1040	10	.1935
63	.0370	36	.1065	9	.1960
62	.0380	35	.1100	8	.1990
61	.0390	34	.1110	7	.2010
60	.0400	33	.1130	6	.2040
59	.0410	32	.1160	5	.2055
58	.0420	31	.1200	4	.2090
57	.0430	30	.1285	3	.2130
56	.0465	29	.1360	2	.2210
55	.0520	28	.1405	1	.2280
54	.0550	27	.1440		

Decimal Equivalent Size of the Letter Drills

Letter Drill	Decimal Equivalent	Letter Drill	Decimal Equivalent	Letter Drill	Decimal Equivalent
A	.234	J	.277	S	.348
B	.238	K	.281	T	.358
C	.242	L	.290	U	.368
D	.246	M	.295	V	.377
E	.250	N	.302	W	.386
F	.257	O	.316	X	.397
G	.261	P	.323	Y	.404
H	.266	Q	.332	Z	.413
I	.272	R	.339		

Anti-Freeze Chart

Temperatures Shown in Degrees Fahrenheit +32 is Freezing

Cooling System Capacity Quarts	*Quarts of ETHYLENE GLYCOL Needed for Protection to Temperatures Shown Below* 1	2	3	4	5	6	7	8	9	10	11	12	13	14
10	+24°	+16°	+ 4°	−12°	−34°	−62°								
11	+25	+18	+ 8	− 6	−23	−47								
12	+26	+19	+10	0	−15	−34	−57°							
13	+27	+21	+13	+ 3	− 9	−25	−45							
14			+15	+ 6	− 5	−18	−34							
15			+16	+ 8	0	−12	−26							
16			+17	+10	+ 2	− 8	−19	−34	−52°					
17			+18	+12	+ 5	− 4	−14	−27	−42					
18			+19	+14	+ 7	0	−10	−21	−34	−50°				
19			+20	+15	+ 9	+ 2	− 7	−16	−28	−42				
20				+16	+10	+ 4	− 3	−12	−22	−34	−48°			
21				+17	+12	+ 6	0	− 9	−17	−28	−41			
22				+18	+13	+ 8	+ 2	− 6	−14	−23	−34	−47°		
23				+19	+14	+ 9	+ 4	− 3	−10	−19	−29	−40		
24				+19	+15	+10	+ 5	0	− 8	−15	−23	−34	−46°	
25				+20	+16	+12	+ 7	+ 1	− 5	−12	−20	−29	−40	−50°
26					+17	+13	+ 8	+ 3	− 3	− 9	−16	−25	−34	−44
27					+18	+14	+ 9	+ 5	− 1	− 7	−13	−21	−29	−39
28					+18	+15	+10	+ 6	+ 1	− 5	−11	−18	−25	−34
29					+19	+16	+12	+ 7	+ 2	− 3	− 8	−15	−22	−29
30					+20	+17	+13	+ 8	+ 4	− 1	− 6	−12	−18	−25

For capacities over 30 quarts divide true capacity by 3. Find quarts Anti-Freeze for the ⅓ and multiply by 3 for quarts to add.

For capacities under 10 quarts multiply true capacity by 3. Find quarts Anti-Freeze for the tripled volume and divide by 3 for quarts to add.

To Increase the Freezing Protection of Anti-Freeze Solutions Already Installed

Cooling System Capacity Quarts	*Number of Quarts of ETHYLENE GLYCOL Anti-Freeze Required to Increase Protection*													
	From +20° F. to					*From +10° F. to*					*From 0° F. to*			
	0°	*−10°*	*−20°*	*−30°*	*−40°*	*0°*	*−10°*	*−20°*	*−30°*	*−40°*	*−10°*	*−20°*	*−30°*	*−40°*
10	1¾	2¼	3	3½	3¾	¾	1½	2¼	2¾	3¼	¾	1½	2	2½
12	2	2¾	3½	4	4½	1	1¾	2½	3¼	3¾	1	1¾	2½	3¼
14	2¼	3¼	4	4¾	5½	1¼	2	3	3¾	4½	1	2	3	3½
16	2½	3½	4½	5¼	6	1¼	2½	3½	4¼	5¼	1¼	2¼	3¼	4
18	3	4	5	6	7	1½	2¾	4	5	5¾	1½	2½	3¾	4¾
20	3¼	4½	5¾	6¾	7½	1¾	3	4¼	5½	6½	1½	2¾	4¼	5¼
22	3½	5	6¼	7¼	8¼	1¾	3¼	4¾	6	7¼	1¾	3¼	4½	5½
24	4	5½	7	8	9	2	3½	5	6½	7½	1¾	3½	5	6
26	4¼	6	7½	8¾	10	2	4	5½	7	8¼	2	3¾	5½	6¾
28	4½	6¼	8	9½	10½	2¼	4¼	6	7½	9	2	4	5¾	7¼
30	5	6¾	8½	10	11½	2½	4½	6½	8	9½	2¼	4¼	6¼	7¾

Test radiator solution with proper hydrometer. Determine from the table the number of quarts of solution to be drawn off from a full cooling system and replace with undiluted anti-freeze, to give the desired increased protection. For example, to increase protection of a 22-quart cooling system containing Ethylene Glycol (permanent type) anti-freeze, from +20° F. to −20° F. will require the replacement of 6¼ quarts of solution with undiluted anti-freeze.

Index